NAVY
AND
EMPIRE

NAVY
AND
EMPIRE

JAMES L. STOKESBURY

ROBERT HALE · LONDON

Copyright © 1983 by James L. Stokesbury
First published in Great Britain 1984

ISBN 0 7090 1787 1

Robert Hale Limited
Clerkenwell House
Clerkenwell Green
London EC1R 0HT

Printed in Great Britain by
St Edmundsbury Press, Bury St Edmunds, Suffolk
and bound by Woolnough Bookbinding Limited

CONTENTS

PART FOUR: THE TWILIGHT OF EMPIRE

ACKNOWLEDGMENTS

Many people have assisted, directly or indirectly, in the preparation of this work. In New York, Ann Elmo has supported and encouraged me for many years; Robert Bender suggested the theme and was instrumental in its development, and Howard Cady saw it through to completion. At Acadia University, the staff of the Vaughan Library have always been most helpful, and my colleagues in the Department of History have provided me with that rarest of academic atmospheres, a happy department in which to work. I have taught courses on European expansion and military history for nearly twenty years now, and I can thank my students during all that period for keeping me awake and alert; I wish they could all say I had done the same for them. Three departmental secretaries shared the typing of the manuscript, and thanks are due to Debbie Bradley, Heather Harvie, and Carolyn Bowlby for their unfailing patience and diligence. I must add the cautionary note that errors of fact or interpretation are my own. My final thanks, as always, go to Liz.

PART ONE

THE DAWN OF EMPIRE

1

Singeing the King of
Spain's Beard

Keep the sea which is the wall of England,
And then is England kept by God's hand.
—from *The Libel of English Policy,* 1436

Storm-battered, with the pumps working every watch, the little squadron fled westward before the contrary winds. Captain John Hawkins, the most famous sailor and adventurer in England, had hoped for fair sailing out of the Caribbean and home at the conclusion of this, his third voyage slaving and trading to the Spanish Main. But the weather had played him false, and now with the Queen's own ship, *Jesus of Lubeck,* threatening to sink under him, he chose to run for the coast of Mexico.

After the storm at last abated, the English reached San Juan de Ulua on September 15, 1568. The harbor, though it was the main port of entry for the route to Mexico City, was little more than a narrow sandbar with a battery on it, behind which ships might lie at rest. Hawkins' position was precarious; he was an interloper in territory the Spanish considered entirely theirs, and though he had traded successfully with them, he was aware that legally they might choose to regard him as a pirate. He also knew that at the end of the month the seasonal flotilla was due in from Spain, guarded by warships and carrying high officials who might not be so willing to turn a blind eye to his presence. His ships in line, he sailed boldly in, and overawing the small Spanish garrison, he seized the island battery for his own security, giving guarantees of good behavior and promising no hostilities in return for a chance to make his repairs and leave unmolested. He tied up his ships in a line, with their bows secured to moorings on the battery, and their sterns out in the water, held there by anchors warped out into the channel. He needed ten days.

Unfortunately for the English, the same winds that had been foul for them had been fair for the Spanish. The next morning their fleet was in sight, two weeks early. Hawkins was caught in a dilemma. If he let the Spanish in, he would be caught in a virtual trap. If he kept them out, he would be committing an act of war; since he had Elizabeth's commission, he would be doing so under her name. He decided to let them enter. They had aboard the Viceroy of New Spain, Don Martin Enriquez, and he gave his word that the English would be unmolested. The two sides exchanged hostages and pleasantries, and the Spanish moored along the bar, to the north or left of the English.

Sixteenth-century notions of honor were slightly peculiar, and His Excellency the Viceroy did not consider that he need abide by any promise given to a heretic Englishman. Over the next several days, the Spanish made preparations for seizing the battery from Hawkins' men and for warping their ships alongside the English and taking them. The attack was set for noon on the twenty-third.

By early morning the Spanish moves were so obvious that the English were thoroughly alarmed. After one of the Spanish hostages, invited to an early dinner with Hawkins, was found with a dagger up his sleeve, the English leader ran up on deck of the *Jesus,* hailed the Spanish admiral on the next ship, and accused him of treachery. Hawkins' Spanish was not up to cursing at long range, so he made his feelings known by grabbing a crossbow and firing a bolt at the Spaniard. He missed, but one of his men fired an arquebus and brought down a man next to the admiral, whereupon the Spaniards sounded their trumpets and launched their attack.

Though it went off prematurely, it still succeeded for the most part. The English on the battery, intermingled as they were with greater numbers of enemies, soon were overpowered. That decided the day; with those guns gone, Hawkins' position was untenable. His ships fared better but still could hope only to escape. The Spanish tried to board the *Jesus* and were driven off while she was warped away from the sandbar. She was still unseaworthy, though, and through a long day of desultory firing—guns still were not very effective at long range at that time—Hawkins transferred what he could of men and stores to his second-best ship, the *Minion*. As a stormy evening came on, only the *Minion* and the smallest of the English vessels, the little *Judith,* commanded by Hawkins' kinsman, Francis Drake, were left. Both anchored to the south of the sandbar. They were in no immediate condition to sail, and the Spanish were sufficiently battered that there was no danger of pursuit.

The *Judith* was gone at daybreak, no one knew where. In the overcrowded *Minion* Hawkins soon got under way. Fate continued to play him false, however. The wind stayed against him, and he eventually reached the coast farther north. He gave his men a choice of trusting the mercies of the Spanish or trying to make home before they starved. About half of them went ashore, the rest stayed with the ship, and she made sail and headed eastward. Those who stayed in Mexico were robbed by Indians and then captured by the Spanish. Eventually they were handed over to the Inquisition. Some were burned at the stake, either in Mexico City or in a few cases in Spain itself; in New Spain at least the authorities strangled them before burning; in Old Spain they were less tender. Those who escaped burning got several hundred lashes or six to twelve years as galley slaves. Few came home again.

The sea was no kinder. All across the Atlantic Hawkins' men starved; they ate rats, cats, parrots, and finally the oxhides that were part of their cargo. Then they died. On January 25, 1569, the *Minion* reached Mount's Bay in Cornwall, with perhaps fifteen men left of the hundred who had sailed from Mexico. The *Judith* had cast anchor in Plymouth five days earlier. Three generations after it had begun, it looked as if English seafaring enterprise was over, with nothing but death and humiliation to show for it.

In those three generations, while English exploration had been only sporadic and ill directed, Portugal and Spain had achieved heights of wealth and power not seen in Europe since the days of imperial Rome. But the Iberian states, especially Portugal, possessed advantages that the northern European countries lacked. The Portuguese were united two hundred years before England, and they initiated the first tentative moves down the African coast as Henry V was trumpeting the fading glories of chivalry at Agincourt. All through the Wars of the Roses daring Portuguese sailors were reaching southward, and Bartholomew Diaz finally rounded the Cape of Good Hope in 1487, a mere two years after Henry Tudor picked his crown off the bush at

Bosworth Field. In 1492 Columbus, a by-product of this development, bumped into America on his way to Cathay, and in 1498 Vasco da Gama at last reached India. The European center of gravity moved suddenly from Germany and Italy to the Atlantic seaboard. Venice declined from a European power to a tourist attraction. In the next generation Cortes conquered Mexico, Pizarro raped the Inca Empire, Magellan's *Victoria* circled the globe, and the Portuguese hacked their way to an Indian Ocean empire that poured the riches of the East into Lisbon.

England missed most of this. Pursuing the dream of domination over France, preoccupied with internal squabbles, or wrapped up in the questions of the English Reformation, her occasional attempts at exploration led only to heroic failure. There may have been shadowy voyages westward as early as the 1480s; the first of which there is definitive knowledge was that of John Cabot, a Venetian resident in Bristol. Cabot has received more credit from posterity than he did from his contemporaries, for the chronicler who wrote of his first voyage— and got the date wrong—said, "On the 24th of June 1496 was new-foundland fowend by Bristol men in a ship called the *Matthew*." It was actually 1497, and when Cabot came home Henry VII granted him ten pounds for his pains. Cabot did not return from a second voyage.

By Cabot's day the Pope had already divided up the world between Spain and Portugal. This was in the Treaty of Tordesillas in 1494, and it granted Spain dominion over the waters and lands west of a line that ran in the mid-Atlantic, and Portugal dominion over everything east of that line. Both states vigorously enforced a policy known as the "closed sea" or *mare clausam*, which meant that any unlicensed vessels found in their waters were liable to treatment as pirates. If the pirates happened to be heretics as well, their fate was likely to be unpleasant, as witnessed by Hawkins' unfortunates.

This forced the English and other northern adventurers to seek a different route to the riches of the East. With the South Atlantic closed to them, they must either go through some as-yet-undiscovered northwest passage, or by a northeast passage, or by land across Europe and Asia. The only thing that encouraged them to try was their total ignorance of the distances and difficulties involved.

Nonetheless, try they did, with a bravery and perseverance worthy of a better reward than most of them got. Cabot having failed to find his way to the northwest, the English finally turned to the northeast. Sir Hugh Willoughby and Richard Chancellor sailed with three ships in 1553. Willoughby and two of his crews died wintering in the ice, possibly as far as Novaya Zemlya. Chancellor with the last ship got to Archangel, and he then traveled overland to Moscow, where he met Ivan the Terrible. He was home next year with a letter from the Tsar to Queen Mary, in which Ivan offered to marry one of the Queen's ladies-in-waiting, along with his other wives, to cement the friendship of the two countries. There were no takers, but the episode led to the foundation of the Muscovy Company to further trade and exploration with the East; one of its servants, Anthony Jenkinson, eventually reached Persia and negotiated a treaty with the Shah there. At last, though, when the English in central Asia found they had farther to go to China than they had already come, they gave it up.

Back in the West, Martin Frobisher reached Baffin Island and a body of water that would lead to Hudson Bay. He brought home what he thought was gold, but it turned out to be pyrites. Other men, John Davis and Humphrey Gilbert, left their names on the map of the Arctic but did not find the magic route to China. For the most part they found a miserable death, though Gilbert's last recorded words before he disappeared in a storm, "I trust we are as near to Heaven by sea as by land," testified the sublimity of their faith as well as their courage.

Gilbert and Davis explored in the 1580s. By then other men already had decided it was better to risk the wrath of Spain than of the Arctic elements. Actually, in the earlier years of the century, England and Spain had been allied; Philip II of Spain was married to Mary Tudor, and there was for a while, before Protestantism and the Inquisition met head-on, a thriving trade between England and the Iberian Peninsula, though not on into the Iberian empires. The first man to move out of the peninsular trade and break into the imperial one was John Hawkins of Plymouth, and he made his first voyage slaving to Africa, and across to Spanish America, in 1562. In all he undertook three voyages, and it was said that the first made him the richest man in Plymouth, and the second the richest man in England. The third brought him to San Juan de Ulua.

So by 1568 the English could not get around the Iberian monopoly of overseas trade, and after Hawkins came home they knew they no longer could participate in it on peaceful terms. The Spanish were faced that very year with a Protestant revolt in the Netherlands, they believed that Queen Elizabeth, whom their militant Church considered a bastard, was fostering that revolt, and they were concluding, as one of the Kings of France once said, that the best way to argue with a heretic is with a sword. Unfortunately for them, one of the survivors of

Hawkins' expedition agreed with them. That was the man over whom some shadow of desertion now lay, the erstwhile master of the *Judith*, Francis Drake.

Francis Drake was in his late twenties when he cast anchor in Plymouth after Hawkins' third voyage. Drake had already had a colorful history, having been at sea since he was a very small boy, when he had been apprenticed to a sailing master. His return home in the *Judith* had been slow and painful but apparently uneventful, for nothing has ever been discovered about it. Hawkins once spoke of his betrayal by Drake, but Hawkins always acted as if there were nothing between them, so probably he accepted whatever explanation Drake offered him, if indeed the latter explained at all, for he was a proud man, determined to go his own way.

Whether from anger at Spanish treachery or from some inner need to redeem himself, Drake now saw his way leading into a personal war against the Spanish Empire. In 1570 and 1571 he was back in the Indies, trying to make good his earlier losses. The next year he sailed with two small ships, and in July, leading a vast array of seventy-three men, he tried unsuccessfully to capture the annual Peruvian treasure at Nombre de Dios; he burned Porto Bello, a minor outpost a few miles up the coast, and crossed the Isthmus of Panama far enough to catch a glimpse of the Pacific. Until then the great ocean had been a Spanish preserve, so much so that their ships sailed along the western coast of Central America and South America virtually unarmed. Drake decided to change that, and when he returned to England in 1573 his exploits and their popularity gave him the opportunity to do so.

Late in 1577, with a small squadron of five vessels, Drake sailed from Plymouth for the Pacific. He burned or broke up two of the smaller storeships, and by the time he had gone through the Straits of Magellan, he was alone in his own *Pelican,* which he renamed the *Golden Hind.* From Valparaiso on up the coast he raided, burned, took ransom, and plundered Spanish shipping, all the time displaying that strange blend of ferocity and extravagant courtesy that was a hallmark of the period. The height of his cruise so far came with the capture of a Spanish treasure galleon, *Nuestra Senora de la Concepcion.* There were far more such galleons captured in fiction than ever in fact, but this one was the real article, and it made Drake and all his men rich in one swoop. All they had to do now was get home again.

Drake turned out to sea and made his way northward; partly he was seeking the exit from the still unfound Northwest Passage, and partly he was filling in time until the weather should be right to cross the Pacific. He eventually struck land somewhere around present-day northern California or Oregon, then coasted south to the latitude of San Francisco Bay. He missed the Golden Gate itself—it is not easy to see, especially in the frequent fogs of the area—but careened his ship somewhere nearby and gathered provisions before sailing off into the vast ocean.

The English were far better off than Magellan had been. By now Spanish ships had regularly sailed the Pacific for nearly fifty years, from their holdings in the Philippines to New Spain, and there was some generalized knowledge available of winds and seasons, most of which Drake had gleaned from his captures along the coast.

Nonetheless, they were sixty-six days out of sight of land before they finally reached what was probably the Carolines. Met by hostile natives—the Spanish called all these island groups the "Ladrones" or "Isles of Thieves"—they sailed on until they finally dropped anchor in the Philippines. From there Drake painfully worked his way south, stopping at Ternate. By now he had passed from Spanish territory to that claimed by Portugal, and as the Sultan of Ternate was hostile to the Portuguese, he was friendly to Drake. Repaired and replenished, the English finally sailed, this time for home. They ran on a reef off Celebes, they stopped at Java, they nearly died of thirst making their way up the west coast of Africa. It was, in other words, a normal voyage home. On the twenty-sixth of September 1580, the *Golden Hind,* her holds full of Spanish treasure, sailed serenely into Plymouth Sound.

The English court and government were placed in a considerable dilemma by Drake's return. Their position vis-à-vis Spain was delicate. The Dutch revolt was temporarily going badly, and Spanish affairs seemed definitely in the ascendant. The Spanish ambassador naturally demanded that Drake be disavowed as a pirate and his stolen treasures returned to Spain. It took the crafty Elizabeth four months to make up her mind, and as usual with all the Tudors, she kept her own counsel while she did it. Not until early April 1581 did she at last visit Drake's ship at Deptford, and not until she commanded him to kneel on his own deck and, having his shoulders touched with a sword, said, "Rise, Sir Francis Drake," did he know he was home safe at last. Spanish protests were not worth the loss of Spanish treasure.

Drake was of course not the only man to think in this vein, and the lure of robbing Spain combined with other motives to make Englishmen think seriously of overseas colonization. There was in the later sixteenth century considerable shifting of the population of England, as well as profound change in agricultural methods. The result was to produce an apparent surplus of people, and some men of affairs, especially Sir Humphrey Gilbert, and then Richard Hakluyt and Sir Walter Raleigh, saw in colonization the answer to a whole series of problems. Sending Englishmen out to settle in America would skim off the excess of newly landless people, it would promote foreign trade, it would spread the gospel—and it would provide bases on the flank of Spanish routes to and from their empire. Gilbert tried to colonize Newfoundland on the voyage on which he died, in 1583.

His half brother Walter Raleigh took up the work, and the next year he sent out an expedition that coasted along the Carolina and Virginia shores, naming the latter after the Queen. A small colony went out and settled at Roanoke in 1585 but did not fare well. The colonists were more interested in finding the gold and jewels they supposed to be lying around waiting for the taking than in doing any work. When Francis Drake appeared with a fleet, they were happy to return home after a bad year.

Raleigh tried yet again, and in 1587 a second colony was set up on the same site. Not for three years did supply and relief expeditions return to Roanoke, and when they did, the entire colony had disappeared, providing one of the longest-lasting mysteries of American history. That was practically the last Elizabethan attempt to found colonies overseas. Englishmen turned back to the more congenial and more profitable business of taking wealth away from Spain rather than producing it in colonies of their own.

Drake's personal war gradually grew and eventually merged into a general English war with the greatest power in Europe. His expedition to the West Indies in 1585–86 illustrates the process. He had twenty-nine vessels, only two of them belonging to Elizabeth's navy and the rest supplied by private investors; the Queen was one of the principal backers, providing about one sixth of the initial funds, and Drake held a royal commission for the adventure. Yet England did not declare war on Spain, and Elizabeth remained free to disclaim any responsibility or share in what her officer might do. In form the expedition was actually a joint-stock venture, the same as any trading expedition of the day might be.

It was only mildly successful. The English took Santo Domingo on the island of Hispaniola, and then they took Cartagena on the coast of South America, both in neat little actions. They ransacked both cities and held them for ransom, but they missed any great treasure, either ashore or afloat, and they lost several hundred men to fever. They brought back Raleigh's Virginia colonists, arriving home in mid-summer of 1586. The truth was, though no one in England fully realized it, there were natural limits to private enterprise, however well it might be organized or however bold and daring its leaders. If the English were to continue their war with Spain, it was going to have to stop being a private one.

For their part, the Spanish too were ready to intensify the struggle. King Philip II was a man of considerable if narrow vision; he was determined to put down the revolt of his Dutch subjects, which had now been draining Spanish resources and energies for nearly twenty years. He and his advisers were still convinced that the English were doing everything in their power to encourage the rebels. That was not entirely true: Elizabeth was happy to see Spain distracted, but though she offered plenty of encouragement, she offered little practical help. Nonetheless, what was important was that Spain *thought* the English were a major factor, and the Spanish finally decided to deal with the problem directly.

One means to do so was by diplomatic intrigue. To that end the Spanish encouraged plots against Elizabeth's life, for if she were to die, the throne would go to poor foolish Catholic Mary of Scotland, an exile and prisoner in England ever since 1568. Mary, one of the most overrated heroines in all of history, lent herself to the plots, and the result was that Elizabeth finally lost patience with her. Early in 1587 the Queen of Scots was executed for treason, and Philip no longer had a close Catholic claimant to the English throne. He therefore turned to his other recourse, direct military intervention, already long urged on him by such leading men of action as the Marquis de Santa Cruz, Spain's foremost sailor.

A year before Mary's execution, Philip ordered preparations for a joint military and naval expedition to invade England. Santa Cruz began the collection of ships and supplies, while the Spanish commander in the Low Countries, the Duke of Parma, was instructed to get his army ready to serve as an expeditionary corps. Slowly the ships were repaired, manned, and supplied; war vessels were hired from the Venetians, armories were built up, and the "enterprise of England" began to take shape. Mary's death gave it new urgency, and Spanish ports began to hum with activity.

The English were well aware of what was going on, for there could be little secrecy to great events in the sixteenth century. The control the state exercised over its subjects, or even the subjects of its enemies, was far less rigid than it is now. There was, and remained, a considerable English merchant community in Spain throughout the Anglo-Spanish wars, and, subject to some harassment and occasional seizure, trade and exchange of information between private persons continued in spite of official hostilities. The proposed invasion was therefore common knowledge among the commercial and seagoing community.

Knowing what the threat was, the English problem was how to meet it, for the resources of the country looked puny in the face of Spanish power. Henry VIII, who had had some concern for the sea and the Navy, had left a royal force of nearly eighty ships when he died. But the Navy had not done well during the reigns of Edward and Mary, and there were just twenty-two of these "royal" ships left when Elizabeth came to the throne in 1558. All her wars notwithstanding, the Navy seldom rose above thirty regular ships before her death. There were, however, significant developments initiated in this period. In 1583, under the threat of war, a naval affairs committee was established, and the direction of the Navy was given into the hands of John Hawkins. He proved not only a capable administrator but also a man who had quite marked ideas on warship design and construction, which made a great difference to the subsequent course of events.

Naval technology just at this time was on the verge of the most significant change in centuries. Throughout the entire Middle Ages ships had been largely single-masted vessels, but then about the thirteenth century a remarkable evolution had begun, so that within a few generations the ship had been transformed from a generally unwieldy, bulky affair into a multimasted, multidecked creation capable of many maneuvers that had been impossible before then. Even more revolutionary than the development of the ship as a vehicle, however, was its transformation into a weapon. Long after the advent of gunpowder and cannon, the ship still remained essentially a platform on which men fought battles as if they were ashore—with, of course, the added hazards of falling overboard encased in armor. Slowly, however, as guns gained in power, the idea developed of using the ship not merely as fighting platform but as a weapon itself. When sides were pierced with gunports, it became possible to carry the weight of guns lower down in the ship, and that made it feasible to carry heavier, more powerful pieces. The 1560s and 1570s saw the peak of this transitional period. At San Juan de Ulua the Spanish still were thinking in terms of hauling their ships alongside the English and boarding them; the gun-power of the ships themselves, and even of the shore batteries, was incidental. At Lepanto in 1571, the greatest naval action of the century was still a galley action, with oared fighting vessels crashing into each other, and men at arms boarding and fighting it out. The Spanish tradition was thus to fight land battles on the water.

But Hawkins was not of this tradition, and neither were the English. In Spain nobles became soldiers, and when they went to sea they exercised the command their rank entitled them to; sailors were lesser persons, and their only function was to carry the soldiers where they wanted to go, and into battle when it suited their betters. Not so in England. Her sailors were free men, and even gentlemen, and they had learned their business in the catch-as-catch-can life of privateering. They did not approach their problems with any built-in preconceptions about military tactics or chivalry. They wanted fast, handy ships, and they wanted gunpower; only half consciously they were developing the ship as a weapon in its own right. Thus the ships that Hawkins built or took into Elizabeth's navy were lower, leaner, and more maneuverable than Spanish ships, with proportionately higher gunpower. As the test would show, they were a long way from perfection yet, but they were on the right track.

Drake's latest expedition provided a further spur to Spanish plans. Even though the losses had not been in themselves unsustainable, the disruption of trade was an embarrassment, and the Spanish could not afford to look weak. All Europe was talking about the way little England romped at will through Spain's empire, and so the preparations were put forward with increasing vigor. As 1587 opened, the English decided they must retain the offensive; something must be done to slow down the enemy.

Their answer was another expedition, directed this time not at the Spanish Empire but at Spain itself. Yet it was still a joint-stock expedition, not one of a truly national force. Of the thirty-odd ships Drake commanded, only a few were royal; other ships were subscribed by the Lord High Admiral, by London merchants, or by the Turkey Company. Drake's instructions were to harass the Spaniards, even in their own ports, and he left England quickly, before the Queen could change her mind—which she did as usual, though too late.

The main Spanish rendezvous was Lisbon, Portugal, at this time being temporarily under the Spanish crown, but after a good passage Drake heard of a Spanish concentration in Cadiz and decided to try his luck there. He arrived off the port on April 19, with his slower ships straggling behind. That afternoon the English swept in like a wolf on the fold. There were a good eighty Spanish vessels in the harbor, in all different states of repair and readiness. The only ones really ready to fight were a dozen galleys, and they came out boldly to meet the English at the harbor entrance. But oared galleys, formidable as they might be to ships becalmed, were no match for the new English warships. As they swept by, their broadsides quickly reduced the galleys to broken wrecks. All afternoon the English ranged about the harbor, seizing ships that were ready for sea and sailing them out under prize crews, stripping gear off those that were not fully rigged, and taking whatever else they could get their hands on. The next morning Drake sent small boats into the shallow inner harbor, where they burned everything they could find, including Santa Cruz's great flagship, helpless because her guns were not yet mounted.

Finally it was time to go; the Spanish were bringing up batteries on the shore, and trying to send fireships among the English. Drake prepared to withdraw—and the wind failed. All that afternoon and night the attackers lay under a flat calm and, fortunately, a pall of smoke. A breeze came with the dawn, and they sailed triumphantly out of Cadiz, having, in Drake's phrase, well and truly "singed the King of Spain's beard." They then rollicked home, picking off a couple of other ports on their way. Philip was furious; his enterprise of England was delayed for a year, and, worst of all, the European bankers, always sensitive to other people's misfortunes, raised the interest on his loans. But being Philip of Spain, he was not to be deterred. He ordered preparations to continue.

Philip now hoped to launch his invasion in the fall. Unfortunately, perhaps, for him, the Marquis de Santa Cruz dragged his feet, then died, to be replaced by the Duke of Medina Sidonia, a man largely ignorant of the sea but all too conscious of his own deficiencies. The English also experienced difficulties. The success of the Cadiz raid was so blatant that, rather than press her advantages, Elizabeth decided to revert to the waiting game and to diplomatic stalling. So the fall and winter passed, with Philip chivying on his commanders and Elizabeth trying to restrain hers. As late as the spring she still hoped for a mediated peace, but there was none; the King of Spain was determined to be finished with England once and for all.

While waiting, the English fought among themselves. Drake the

privateer was disliked by the professional navy men, and as the preparations for war advanced, he was given the lesser command of the
western squadron at the end of the Channel. Lord Howard of Ef-
fingham was Lord High Admiral, the equivalent of a later age's First
Sea Lord; he lacked Drake's actual sea experience but was a good, capable administrator, and more important in the long run, a person able
to handle the prickly characters who served under him. When Drake
suggested a redisposition of the fleet that would have effectively given
himself all of it and left Howard with a corporal's guard in the Channel, the Lord High Admiral responded by agreeing with the plan, then
taking virtually all of his fleet westward and assuming command over
it and Drake's squadron. But he did so with such grace that Drake
swallowed his independence and served willingly under him. In this
way one of the gravest perils of early modern military operations—the
insubordination of subordinate commanders—was avoided, and a
united English fleet stood ready to meet the Invincible Armada as it
slowly approached the Channel. In mid-July scouts brought in the
word that the Spanish were but a few hours behind them.

The Armada was a formidable foe. Medina Sidonia had faithfully
carried out his orders, and he had finally sailed with about 130 ships, of
which some 50 were major warships, the rest supply and transport vessels. The English actually outnumbered them in terms of ships, as they
had nearly 200, though only about 30 were Crown vessels, the others
being privately subscribed. The Spanish had by far the greater tonnage
and nearly as many guns as the English, though the English weight of
gunnery was far higher than their enemies'. Other figures show interesting comparisons between the two fleets; there were perhaps 16,000
sailors on the English vessels, as against only about 8,000 on the Spanish. But the Spanish had some 17,000 soldiers with them, and their soldiers worked the ships' guns, while the English had virtually no
soldiers aboard at all. In effect, then, the Spanish Armada was really a
seaborne army, on transports and naval vessels, while the English were
a navy.

In spite of the outdated nature of his force, Medina Sidonia might
have won his battle at the first meeting, for as he approached Plymouth, the English were trying desperately to beat out of Plymouth
Sound against unfavorable winds. The Spanish naval officers advised
sweeping right in and catching the English against their own lee shore,
but the Duke had been ordered by Philip not to be distracted by the
English fleet: His primary mission was to reach the Netherlands ports,

pick up Parma's expeditionary force, and transport it across to England. It had not occurred to Philip, and it did not to Medina Sidonia, that if he destroyed the enemy fleet, he might then invade as he pleased. Neither should be criticized too harshly for that; naval tactics and strategy were then in their very infancy, and this initial mistake was to be repeated steadily for three and a half centuries by England's enemies.

So the might of Spain sailed serenely up the Channel while the English captains cursed their ships out of Plymouth against the wind. As the battle developed over the next week, the Spanish gradually drew into a formation that resembled a crescent moon, with their warships in the van and on the exposed horns, and the weaker supply vessels herded along in the center and rear. The English could think of no way to break this, and they trailed along on the windward flank, more or less in line ahead, each ship in succession closing up to the Spanish flank vessels, letting off a broadside, then hauling off out of range to reload while another ship took its place. For their part the Spanish galleons on the flank fired their guns in turn, and took their punishment, until partially disabled or more usually out of ammunition, and then fell off to be replaced by another ship. So it went on for a week. There was no boarding, and the Spanish officers in their breastplates and helmets confined themselves to waving their swords and cheering on their gunners. Two Spanish ships were taken, one because she was disabled by a collision and the other because she had an explosion on board that forced her out of position and left her vulnerable. Both sides began to run perilously low on ammunition, and the more active among the English ships were forced into the various Channel ports in a desperate attempt to get new supplies.

Finally the Armada anchored in the French port of Calais. Medina Sidonia had hardly been hurt at all, but he was nearly out of ammunition and could get no more. He sent for help to Parma, but the Spanish commander in the Netherlands was closely blockaded by the Dutch and had nothing to offer anyway. Not really knowing what to do next, the Spanish had their minds made up for them by the English, who launched a fireship attack at night against them. In terrible haste and confusion, the unwieldy mass got under way and stood up the coast toward Gravelines and Parma's army.

Now the English attacked in earnest. The Spanish were virtually out of ammunition for their big guns, so the English closed the range where their weapons began to tell heavily but where the Spanish soldiers with their muskets and arquebuses could not reach them. A small

Dutch squadron still held off Gravelines, and now the Spanish found their heavy warships had too deep a draft to risk the shallows of the Dutch coast. Two ships went down, two were driven aground in the shallows and taken by the Dutch. There were now fairly heavy casualties, and caught with no recourse, Medina Sidonia reluctantly ordered the fleet to bear away into the North Sea. The few English who still had ammunition left followed to speed them along. Lord Howard shadowed the Armada as far north as Newcastle, though in fact his shot lockers were empty. Not knowing this, and considering the few options he saw left open to him, Medina Sidonia decided to return to Spain north around the British Isles. It was a tragic decision.

They were still a coherent fleet when they came out of the North Sea past the Orkneys, but as they sailed west into the Atlantic, storms took up the work the English had been unable to complete. The Armada's morale was low, they were shorthanded of sailors to work the ships, and provisions were running out. As they staggered south past Ireland, the ships began to go down in the mountainous seas. Perhaps forty foundered with all hands, and twenty or more crashed against Ireland and the rockbound western coast of Scotland. The survivors who crawled ashore were robbed by the Irish and, when caught, massacred by the English garrisons. No more than half of the Armada limped home to Spain, a shattered remnant of "invincibility." Behind them the English fleet, almost as exhausted by victory as the Spanish were by defeat, lay writhing under the plague. Few fleets of the time were free of disease, which made no distinction between winners and losers. Verminous and wounded sailors were soon dying in all the South and East Coast ports of England.

Great triumph though it was, the defeat of the Spanish Armada was not as definitive to contemporaries as it has appeared to subsequent generations. Philip of Spain, persistent as always, planned to try again, and did, though he never launched another great Armada. But though the Spanish might not invade England, they still believed they ruled the seas, and they acted as if it were true. Their domination of the European scene actually lasted for another half century, until a twenty-two-year-old French general, the Great Condé, wiped out a Spanish army in 1643 at Rocroi. With the magnificent Spanish infantry lying in slaughtered windrows, everyone could recognize the passing of the old order.

For a while after the Armada, then, things went on as before. Culturally, the great effort had the same effect on England as the Per-

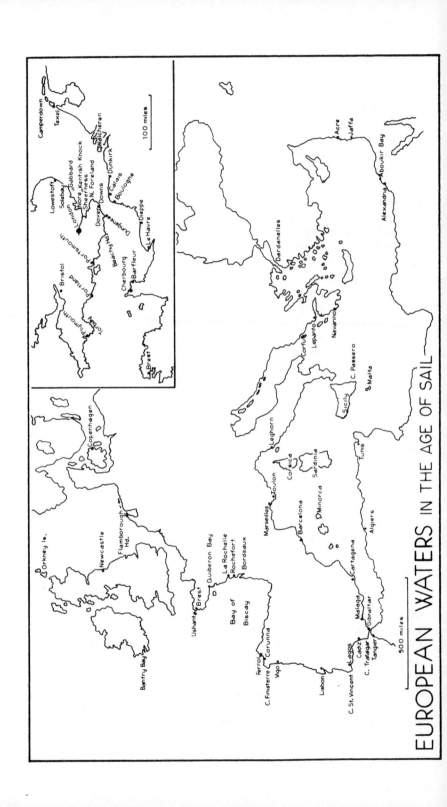

EUROPEAN WATERS IN THE AGE OF SAIL

sian wars had had on Greece, and the Elizabethan Age reached its height in drama and poetry, music and art.

But not in war. The governments of the Tudors were always short of cash, and the English were no more fully aware of the incipient weapon they had stumbled upon—national sea power—than the Spanish. Elizabeth was busy with state and court affairs. There was dissent among the leaders: Drake wanted to raid Spain, Hawkins wanted to blockade the Azores and cut the imperial lifelines; others advocated more military aid to the Dutch, or campaigns in Ireland, where the illusion of glory tempted them. They finally decided upon another joint-stock expedition to the Iberian Peninsula. Drake was to command the ships, Sir John Norris the soldiers, and they took with them the claimant to the Portuguese throne, Don Antonio, who was sure, as exiles always are, that his people were pining to have him back and would rise the moment he set foot ashore. In April 1589 they sailed, 15,000 men in 130 ships, of which only 8 belonged to the Navy.

Everything went wrong. Besieging Corunna, the expedition did some damage but caught the plague. Then they sailed down the coast to Portugal, carrying disease with them. Norris landed his weakened men, but the Portuguese stared sullenly at Don Antonio and failed to respond to his call to arms, while Lisbon's Spanish garrison held on with an iron grip. Norris reembarked his wasted remnants and blamed Drake for not supporting him; Drake countered that the soldiers had nothing to support. So the expedition with its dying crews sailed home again. They had done better than the Spanish the year before, but in terms of the great expectations with which they had set forth, the affair was a dismal failure. Drake passed into temporary retirement and other men came to the fore.

Next, the English halfheartedly tried Hawkins' idea of cutting the Spanish treasure lanes by blockading the Azores. For two years the treasure fleets got through and Philip was able to consider, if not realize, the idea of another armada. In 1591 Lord Thomas Howard with a small squadron was caught at Flores in the Azores when the Spanish fleet arrived to escort the treasure ships in. Howard got away; Sir Richard Grenville stayed to fight, and his *Revenge* fought its famous battle alone against the entire Spanish squadron, sinking four ships before she went down herself after fifteen hours of furious combat.

Such episodes were a source of pride, but they did not win wars, and they did not pay for them. The English, even to the Queen herself, could not decide if they were serious contenders for European power or if they were privateers out to get rich as quickly as possible. In 1595 they decided they had a chance to do both, when news came of a crippled Spanish treasure galleon that had limped into San Juan, Puerto Rico. Hastily Drake and Hawkins were sent off, with a joint command, to scoop up the riches.

Again they failed. Short of supplies, Drake insisted on attacking the Canaries first. Not only were they beaten off, but they also lost some prisoners, who told where they were really headed. Forewarned, the Spanish strengthened Puerto Rico while the English bickered their way across the Atlantic. Hawkins, old and worn out, died as they neared the island. Drake planned the attack, and the Spanish drove it off with heavy losses. The old freebooter then tried his hand at the Isthmus of Panama, and the Spanish defeated him again. There was more dissension, and now plague as well, and Drake died off Porto Bello, leaving his fleet to limp home without him. It was a sad end to a glorious career, and it typified the way things were going for England in the 1590s.

In the year of Drake's death, 1596, new men tried the old game. Sir Walter Raleigh and the Queen's favorite, the Earl of Essex, sailed into Cadiz and burned the city and fifty ships along with it, giving English fortunes a mighty boost. It did not last; they failed miserably in the Azores the next year.

Philip died in 1598, which must have been a great relief to his tired subjects, but his successor, Philip III, swore to continue his father's policy. When the Irish rose up again, under Hugh O'Neill, the Earl of Tyrone, Philip landed a Spanish army to help them out, thinking that two could play the game of Dutch revolt. Essex failed to put down O'Neill and returned to London to the more congenial business of backstairs intrigue, for which he paid with his head. But the Irish rebellion went nowhere; even such astute plotters as the Spanish were lost in the labyrinth of Irish politics, and their army surrendered at Kinsale to the English forces.

Elizabeth did not long outlast these last minor victories. Hawkins was dead, Drake was dead, Grenville and Gilbert gone; all the old names were passing from the scene. They had done much, but no one could say whether it might have any lasting effect. There were to be no more Spanish armadas, but there were also no English colonies overseas as yet. On Elizabeth's death, the Tudor Navy was as weak as it had been fifty years earlier, and the Empire still did not extend beyond the shores of the British Isles.

2

The Route to India

... if you will profit seek, seek it at sea and in quiet trade.
—Sir Thomas Smythe, governor of the
East India Company

A sovereign, especially one as important and as long-lived as Elizabeth I, is hardly allowed even to die in peace. As the great Queen's reign neared its inevitable end early in the new century, the problem of the succession preoccupied men of affairs. Elizabeth kept her own counsel, and her statesmen did not like to remind her of mortality by questioning her about a successor. On her death-bed, however, the matter could be avoided no longer, and she had to be asked for a decision at last. Who should rule? She murmured, "Who but our cousin in Scotland?" And so, in March 1603, she died at last, and with her the Tudor dynasty, that incredible family of rapacious Welshmen who had carried England to new heights of prestige and power.

The Stuarts, who succeeded them and who lasted just over a century, provided a cast of characters that would have challenged the imagination of a romantic novelist. They made virtually every mistake monarchs can make, and the more they made, the more beloved they have been to posterity. They started out on the wrong foot, and they remained out of step with their subjects for most of their dynasty. Yet almost in spite of this, the natural and national energies of Britain burst forth in commerce, war, and the arts, until, a century after Elizabeth's death, Great Britain was one of the two or three major powers of Europe and the world.

James VI of Scotland, when the news arrived that he was now James I of England, was a thoroughly happy man. The truth was, being King of Scotland was not a congenial task. The Scots were an obstreperous lot; they had driven out his mother and put him in the care of a group of Presbyterian divines who knew everything about the Scriptures and nothing about small boys. He developed a prodigious store of learning and an uncanny knack for picking the wrong men to surround him, men who knew how to curry favor by sychophantism and to take every advantage of that favor to enrich themselves. In his late thirties, when he acceded to the throne of England, he was widely known as "the wisest fool in Christendom."

James had long watched the affairs of England with a covetous eye. To the ruler of a poor and often rebellious land, England looked to be a marvel of peace and wealth. James—and his favorites—could hardly wait to make the move south. He did not realize that there were major currents of change at work in English society and that for several years they had been held in check only by the veneration with which Englishmen regarded a queen who had been on the throne longer than most of them had been alive. Faced with new demands for power by Parliament, Elizabeth had turned it all aside by grandly announcing, "This I count the glory of my crown—that I have reigned with your loves." James could make no such claim and must therefore find some other way to meet the changing times.

Yet if Parliament was raising its sights and Puritanism rearing what James regarded as its ugly head, England was still a land of great wealth and of comparative peace, and James was fortunate in that much of the spadework done by the Elizabethans at last reached fruition in the next reign; for partly as a result of what had gone before, and partly, ironically, driven by dissatisfaction with the new royal policies, Englishmen took the first lasting steps to overseas colonization and to empire. In James's reign, and under his son Charles I, the American colonies were firmly planted, and the English finally reached the riches of the East.

It was not, in fact, the East that they had intended to reach. They wanted the Indies and the Spice Islands. Instead, they had to settle for second best: They got India as a consolation prize.

Elizabethan voyages to the Indian Ocean had been sporadic and for the most part unsuccessful. The trip was long, and the risks of Portuguese domination had to be added to all the natural hazards. Actually, what profits these early voyages showed came more from robbing the Portuguese than from doing any real business with the natives. Yet in the 1590s a Dutchman, Van Linschouten, wrote his *Voyages into the East and West Indies;* in 1598 it was translated into English, and it opened up a world of possibilities. Here was a great Portuguese seaborne empire, its tentacles spread across the Indian Ocean. Van Linschouten's book was a virtual invitation to infringe upon that empire, and both the English and the Dutch accepted it. With visions of profit dancing before their eyes, a group of London merchants petitioned Queen Elizabeth for a charter, and on the last day of the old century, December 31, 1600, she granted a royal patent to the "Governor and Company of Merchants of London, trading to the East Indies." Thus was born the Honorable East India Company, one of the greatest commercial and ultimately imperial enterprises in the history of the world.

For an age that had no refrigeration and few ways of preserving meat, spices were practically worth their weight in gold. The first eastern voyages therefore headed for Java, Sumatra, and the Moluccas. Though it took Sir James Lancaster two years to make the round trip, he brought home a million pounds of pepper, and this first voyage showed a 95 percent profit. Subsequent voyages either did as well or failed miserably, depending upon circumstance. Since members of the company subscribed at this time to individual voyages as they chose, they might get rich, or they might lose disastrously; it was only later that the idea of holding general shares in the company developed.

The problem was that trade with Southeast Asia was just about as much as the technology and business organization of the period could handle. The voyage was long and incredibly risky in itself. A crew might die or a ship be lost in any one of a dozen ways, through storm, uncharted rock, scurvy, pirates, starvation, enemy warships, and so on. If the voyage itself were successful, political or business conditions at the farther end might negate it; when Lancaster reached Sumatra he found that the local pepper crop had failed, and he had to go elsewhere to fill his holds. Even the arrival home could be risky; the plague was raging in London when the first voyage returned home, and for one reason or another, the money from the trip was not distributed and claims settled for many years. So if the rewards were potentially great, the risks were equally high.

One thing did change, though: the enemy. James was determined to have peace with Spain. Many of his subjects were now so used to the Spanish war that they regarded it as a normal fact of life, but he himself was a man of peace. He was also anxious to be friends with the power he considered the greatest in Europe. It was long after his day that Britain discovered the possibilities of supporting the second-rate powers of Europe against the first. James was quite happy to be the tail on what he still perceived as the great Spanish kite, so he diligently sought, and got in 1604, a peace with the ancient enemy. Though residual gleams of Spanish gold would still occasionally fill England's thoughts, Spain was never again to be her primary foe. That place was usurped first by the Dutch and then by the French.

Just as the war against Spain had unleashed the dormant energies of Englishmen, so the great revolt had turned the Netherlands into a contender for world power. Philip II of Spain had inherited these territories from his father, Charles V, the last great medieval man. Whereas Charles had been born in the Low Countries and thus was able to hold their loyalty, Philip was a pure Spaniard. His fiscal policies combined with his rigid Catholicism finally drove the Netherlands into revolt in the 1560s. Year after year the war limped along, with now one side, now the other in the ascendant. What finally gave the Dutch an edge was seapower, for they could not hope to defeat the magnificent Spanish armies on land. However, the Dutch could and did dominate their own shallow coastal waters, and slowly they began to make progress, capturing seaport towns as bases and through their commerce financing their unending war.

They were ideally located for commercial purposes. The major rivers of northwestern Europe flowed through their territory, and they had long been the northern nexus of the Mediterranean-Atlantic-Baltic trade. Even during the revolt their prosperity was encouraged by Philip himself, for the Spanish Empire could hardly function without the manufactures, occasional taxes, and shipping of the Low Countries. It was not until the 1590s that Philip finally closed Iberian ports, and thus access to the empire, to his rebellious subjects.

The result was disastrous for Spain, for the Dutch, prompted by works such as Van Linschoten's, simply moved in on the empire itself. Portugal had been part of the Spanish Empire since 1580, when its own direct line of rulers had died off, and the Dutch therefore decided to compete directly in the East. As the English made their first tentative moves toward the Indian Ocean, the Dutch did the same thing.

The Portuguese Empire of the Indian Ocean had been pure maritime supremacy, unlike that of the Spanish in the New World. Spaniards had gone out to conquer and then to settle, and they had made America thoroughly Spanish in culture and character. But the Portuguese had encountered around the Indian Ocean well-developed civilizations older and in many ways superior to their own. They were never strong enough to take these over completely. Their empire, therefore, consisted of a stranglehold on the main bases and axes of the Indian Ocean, and not much more. They had forts at key points—Aden, Ormuz, Diu, Goa, Malacca, and in the Spice Islands—so if an interloper tried to break into or out of their ocean, he had to get past one of their bases. For nearly a hundred years they made good their claims and made themselves rich. By the end of the sixteenth century, however, they had passed their prime. The riches of India had gone into churches and palaces, the men who hacked out an empire went off now to Brazil, or stayed home to play the wastrel. Their last real king, Sebastian I, was a fool who dreamed only of a crusade against the Moors. He finally got it, and he was killed at Alcazar-Quivir in 1578. Two years later, Philip II of Spain sat on the throne of Portugal. So when the Dutch and English began to seep into the Indian Ocean at the turn of the century, the once-great empire was ripe for the plucking.

Unfortunately for the English, they did not initially realize they were involved in a race. The London merchants who founded the East India Company intended to be no more than peaceful traders. Sir Thomas Smythe, one of the first governors of the company, believed that what had ruined Portugal was not some inherent weakness, but rather the expenses incurred in garrisoning the bases in the East. He saw no need for soldiers or any kind of land establishment to support the English trading venture. The English would simply make treaties with the local rulers, and all would be well.

The Dutch had other ideas, both more rapacious and, in view of conditions in the East, more realistic. They moved to gain control of the entire spice trade with a single-minded vision that soon left the English far behind.

Part of the problem was governmental. The Dutch system of government, with authority divided among several different groups, looked as if it was designed not to work. In fact, it was a neat little oligarchy, with power concentrated in a few dozen men who sat on different governing boards and carefully excluded anyone else from a share of the benefits. As soon as the Dutch traders discovered that competition among themselves was raising prices in the East and lowering them in the Netherlands, they moved to form a monopoly in the famous Dutch East India Company. They then exerted their power through the national government so that this company received full support from the state; at times it was difficult to tell if the company served the state's interests, or the state the company's. In fact, both bodies were run by the same men, serving the same people—themselves. The Dutch East India Company therefore had the full backing of its government, and when necessary, of its naval and diplomatic power.

The English, by contrast, were not only left to their own devices, they were even undercut by their government, for James was not a man to let previous charters of monopoly stand in the way of grants to his favorites. In 1604, he granted a license to Sir Edward Michelborne to make a private voyage east, and Michelborne spent two years in the islands, not so much trading as robbing Dutch ships and Chinese merchants. The Dutch were not disposed to distinguish between this private pirate and the English monopoly company; they may have been glad of an excuse to open undeclared hostilities against their rivals. They were careful, however, not to go too far too fast, for they were still engaged in their war with Spain and still wanted at least tacit English support.

In 1609, however, Spain finally agreed to a truce with the Netherlands. Freed now from the burden of Iberian hostility, the Dutch moved in force into the East, with the result that the English were going to have to fight or get out.

Given their different perceptions of what they were doing in the islands, the English never really had a chance against the Dutch. For several years the English tried to dispute the trade, but they were at a perpetual disadvantage: The Dutch were quite willing to fight, while the English passionately wanted to avoid the expense of war. For years the East India Company kept ambassadors at Amsterdam and The Hague, subject to periodic humiliation by the Dutch. Time after time they swallowed their pride, remembered their profits, and tried to negotiate. The Dutch would have none of it. From 1609 they claimed sovereignty over the Spice Islands, and their governors, Pieter Both and then the greatest of their empire builders, Jan Pieterzoon Coen, made life progressively more difficult for the English traders.

In 1619 the British company finally lost patience and sent out a squadron under Sir Thomas Dale to assert their rights. Dale burned several Dutch posts and fought a pitched naval battle with the Dutch ships. This made them agree to negotiate, but the English were not backed by James I, while the Dutch were supported by their government. The resulting treaty, signed at James's insistence, made the English help pay for and maintain bases that were to be controlled by the Dutch.

The end of the unequal struggle came in 1623. At the joint station of Amboina, about twenty Englishmen were in residence with some two hundred Dutch and several hundred native troops under Dutch control. The local governor charged the English with plotting to seize the station. The English factors were arrested and severely tortured, most of them confessing that they had indeed been plotting, while being branded with irons or torn with red-hot tongs. As soon as the tortures stopped they recanted their confessions, and in the midst of the affair instructions arrived, on a Dutch vessel, recalling them to England. Instead of being sent home, most of the English were brutally and publicly executed.

The news did not reach England until 1624, and when it did, there was an enormous public fury. Little was done, however. James made a great show of his grief, which was genuine enough, but he did not allow the distant death of a dozen of his subjects to interfere with the convoluted diplomatic games he was still playing. He died just a few months later. His son Charles I made a few ineffectual protests, while the London mob more characteristically showed the national mood by beating up Dutchmen in the streets. Nothing of substance was done, and the Amboina Massacre was tucked away in the national memory, not to be brought out again for a generation.

That finished the East India Company in the islands. The governors could not ask or find men to go out and risk what looked like certain death at the hands of the Dutch for uncertain profits. They gave up the struggle and moved against a likelier target, the Portuguese trade with India.

The history of empire is full of ironies, and one of the greatest of them is that the English originally prospered in India, as they had failed in the Indies, because they were weak. The Dutch were there before them, again, but they had not fared well. At this time the Mogul Empire, founded by Babar on the bloody field of Panipat in 1526, was at its height. Portuguese power had waned, and the Moguls had no desire to see it replaced by Dutch. They were therefore inhospitable, and the Netherlanders, with their eyes fixed on the spice trade, soon settled for a minor role in India. The subcontinent was always secondary for them, and they had wanted trade there only as a means of picking up goods for use in the Indies, to avoid the normal drain of specie from the Netherlands itself. No one at that time saw the entire Indian subcontinent as a potential area for conquest.

Least of all the English. They came as supplicants, and because their power was laughable, they were allowed in on sufferance. Emperor Jahangir granted the first representative of the company, William Hawkins, permission to trade at Surat in 1607. Naturally, the Portuguese resented this and worked actively to prevent anyone undercutting their own position. In 1611, when several ships of the company's sixth voyage to the East tried to trade, they were driven off by Portuguese warships. They had to be content with some humiliating barter with native fishing boats before sailing on to the Indies.

The next year, however, the English were back again. This time Captain Thomas Best arrived with two ships and tried to anchor and offload cargo at the mouth of the Tapti River, which led up to Surat, a place called Swally Roads. Four Portuguese warships and several galleys came out to drive off the interlopers, but Best made a fight of it. For an entire month he and the Portuguese annoyed each other, to the considerable amusement of the Indians, but in the end, Best made good his claim by force of arms. The Indian view was that anyone who could beat the Portuguese was a friend of theirs, while anyone who took a whole month to do it was no threat. They confirmed the right of the English to trade in Surat, and Thomas Aldworth stayed there to organize the first permanent English factory.

An early crisis came three years later, in 1615. The company sent out four ships under Nicholas Downton. On his first arrival at Surat he discovered that the local Mogul governor had declared war against the Portuguese, and the Indian asked Downton to help him, the Moguls not having any naval power. Downton refused; King James, whose motto was *Beati pacifici,* had issued strict instructions that the company's ships were to fight only if directly attacked. Happily for English-Mogul relations, the Portuguese decided it was time to nip the new threat before it grew, and they sent from Goa their entire disposable force, nine sailing men-of-war and about sixty gunboats. Downton was outnumbered three to one in guns, and six to one in men, and his crews and ships were both worn from the long voyage. Nonetheless, he had no choice; he threw his lot in with the Indians and went to work.

The little campaign lasted for a month, both sides maneuvering around each other, and keeping an eye on the Indians for some hidden advantage, diplomatic or military. There was hard fighting, and Downton's only son was killed in battle, but finally the Portuguese crept back to Goa, shattered, and the English factory at Surat was secure from then on. Not only that, but King James sent out the first royal emissary, Sir Thomas Roe, to the court of Jahangir himself. Roe was not just a trader, but the representative of a foreign power, and therefore he commanded much more respect than did the company's spokesmen. He did not get all he asked, but he behaved himself very well, and the result was a general feeling of goodwill toward the English. As the 1620s opened, it was obvious that their star was rising and the Portuguese star was sinking. That fact could no longer be disguised after 1622, when a joint expedition of company ships and Persian troops took the major base at Ormuz, the bottleneck at the mouth of the Persian Gulf, and destroyed Portuguese power in the area.

The Dutch continued to meddle, however, and it was not until the late 1620s and 1630s that the English position on the western coast of India was more or less secure. Occasionally their factors were imprisoned by the Indians as a result of the piracies of the Dutch, and eventually the company found itself policing the trade routes of the Arabian Sea just so it could maintain its credibility with the Moguls.

The British also made their way into eastern India, operating in the Bay of Bengal. Early settlements were unhealthy, because of climate or politics or both, and it was not until 1639, after peace had been made with a declining Portugal, that the company got a permanent base. Francis Day entered into an agreement with the rulers of the Coromandel Coast and was allowed to claim sovereignty over a small strip of land at Madras. Here he built a fortified factory, which he named Fort St. George, thus giving the English a secure footing on the eastern coast. This was to become the foundation of British power in that part of India, but neither Day's foresight nor his appreciation of local conditions were matched by the directors of the company back in London. To them building a fort seemed like a useless diversion of funds, entirely contrary to their policy of pure trade, and they reprimanded him severely for the waste. They did not, however, give up the fort.

By the 1640s, then, the British were the chief European traders in India, and they were there to stay. They were, in fact, better off in the East than at home, for back in England the company was even more harassed by Charles I than it had been by his father. Its monopoly had been challenged, and its charters infringed, by the King and his favorites. The directors must have sighed with relief as the Crown became increasingly preoccupied with constitutional and religious problems and gradually left them alone to pursue their profits.

Such problems were largely responsible, though not in the first instance, for the founding of the western British Empire at the same time as the eastern. The later years of Elizabeth had seen a few more abortive attempts to colonize the New World, but nothing much had come of them. In 1595 Sir Walter Raleigh turned his attention to American affairs once more, but not to Virginia. Instead he sailed over to Guiana and explored the Orinoco River, looking for the city of gold. Failing to find it, he lost interest in colonization for twenty years. It was not, therefore, until the new century and the new dynasty that the idea was revived, yet in the space of an astonishing forty years, Englishmen established footholds along the fringes of America from the St. Lawrence to the Amazon. The price, in hardship and death, was enormous; the potential rewards were inconceivable even to the heightened imaginations of the day.

Interest in Virginia had waned a bit as the Spanish Wars declined, but the interest had never entirely disappeared. Prompted and promoted by such men as Richard Hakluyt, whose collection of *Principal Navigations, Voyages, and Discoveries of the English Nation* kept the deeds of contemporary explorers in the public eye, a current of colonial ambition surfaced once more soon after James's accession. In 1604–5 Captain George Weymouth coasted the North American shore from the Carolina capes to New England and brought home favorable reports of the prospects. The London Company was chartered in 1606 to settle the lands between thirty-four and forty-one degrees (roughly from modern-day North Carolina to New York), and then the Plymouth Company to settle between thirty-eight and forty-five degrees (Washington, D.C., to the Bay of Fundy). The limits on the territory reflect the fact that it was possible at that time to determine fairly accurately one's latitude by reference to the height of the sun, but it was still virtually impossible to find reliable longitude. As they overlapped by three degrees, they also reflected the devious quality of the royal mind. The Plymouth Company tried in 1607 to settle the mouth of the Kennebec, but after one winter they gave it up as a bad job, and their company was moribund from that time on.

But the London Company tried harder, and late in 1606 they sent out a small squadron under Christopher Newport, which landed about

120 colonists on Chesapeake Bay, at the mouth of the James River, in May 1607. Their instructions were to build a fort and to search for gold and jewels and the passage to the South Sea. The chimera of easy money and the longed-for passage through to the Pacific still hung in men's minds. They were at Jamestown in roughly the same latitude as Drake had been near San Francisco, some fifty degrees of longitude west of them, and yet the will to believe in a passage remained so strong that it overcame any sensible conclusion that it might not exist.

Nor was their choice of site for the fort any more determined by common sense; the only good thing about it was that there was deep water right offshore for ships to lie in. Aside from that, the spot was swampy, turning out to be malarial, and short of fresh water. Since many of the colonists apparently expected to stuff their pockets with jewels and go home again, these deficiencies did not appear insurmountable.

However, at the end of the first year, half the colonists were dead, and the remainder were ready to give up, having been held together largely by the will of John Smith, the toughest—as well as the most argumentative—of their leaders. Through 1608 the colony continued to dwindle away, and small reinforcements were hardly enough to make up for the increasing number of deaths. There was no treasure, there was no passage to the Pacific, there were no Spanish galleons drifting ashore to be plundered; there was only debilitating sickness, near-despair, and unending work, to which most of the colonists had a wholesome aversion. What had seemed like a rich man's game in London taverns now looked like long drudgery and a shallow grave in America at the end of it.

In 1609 the parent organization got a new charter and became the Virginia Company. The next year four hundred more settlers made the crossing; they died even more quickly than their predecessors. In May 1610 there were only sixty still alive, and they actually abandoned the settlement and were aboard ship, hoping to make it to Newfoundland and get home with the fishing fleet, when yet another relief expedition arrived, bringing still more candidates for the little town with the large cemetery.

A turning point was at hand, however. Sir Thomas Dale, who later fought the Dutch in the Indies, took over command in 1611 and introduced an element of discipline that even John Smith had not been able to enforce. His rule was simple: no work, no food. Dale was a veteran of the Dutch wars and stood little nonsense; slowly, under military control and grinding hard work, the colony turned the corner to survival. Better still, in 1612 the colonists finally learned how to cultivate tobacco and at last had a cash crop that could be sent home to England to help defray expenses. Seven years later two more landmarks occurred. A new governor brought over instructions for the election of members to a house of assembly, so that for the first time English institutions of representative government were introduced into the New World. And that same year a Dutch ship cast anchor off Jamestown, bringing the first twenty Negro slaves from Africa. They were welcomed as cheap labor, of which the colony stood in desperate need. So, ironically, one of North America's greatest problems, and the institutional means for resolving it, were both initiated in the same year.

From then on, after more than a decade of living on the edge of extinction, Virginia slowly grew and prospered. King James at home disapproved both of tobacco—which he characterized as "a custom loathsome to the eye, hateful to the nose, harmful to the brain, dangerous to the lungs"—and of popular assemblies, and in 1624 he revoked the charter of the Virginia Company and turned the settlement into a royal colony, giving it an appointed royal governor and council. To the private gentlemen of the old London Company, this appeared the norm; the government let them take all the financial risks and suffer the losses of the early days, and then when the colony got on its feet and looked as if it might become a paying proposition, the Crown moved in and took over. The Stuarts were very good at that.

The stirring of great events in England was responsible for the planting of the second permanent American colony. In the later years of Elizabeth's reign a new form of Protestantism called Puritanism, far more austere and forbidding than the Church of England type of Protestantism, began to gain hold in Britain. In Scotland it took the form of extreme Presbyterianism—though the terms are by no means synonymous—and became the bane of James VI's existence. In England it took both the Presbyterian forms and also shaded off into those more radical ideas that can be loosely grouped under the term "Independency." King James himself was a firm believer in the utility of the Anglican form of religion, and his responses to the Presbyterians or Puritans were firm: "No bishop, no king," and, "They will conform or I shall harry them out of the land." In fact, he did not quite harry them out of the land, for it was one of James's failings that he usually spoke first, and then thought about it afterward, but he did make life mildly unpleasant, and some groups did leave.

The most famous of them was a small group from the little village of Scrooby, near Nottingham. In 1608, harassed by the local authorities, they packed up and moved over to the Netherlands, where their religious ideas were tolerated, if they themselves were not exactly welcomed. After several years they decided Holland was not for them; they were poor people, barely able to make a living, and they recognized that if they stayed there much longer, they would lose their English character and simply disappear in the Dutch population. After agonizing discussion, they decided to go to America.

They thought first of Guiana but eventually made a deal with the Virginia Company whereby they would go to the northern part of its grant and, in effect, work off their passage by turning all profit over to the directors. So they returned to England, and, one eye over their shoulder all the time for fear of royal displeasure, they departed from Plymouth in September 1620 aboard a small ship called the *Mayflower*. The crossing took them over two months; it was not the best season for a western crossing of the North Atlantic, and the *Mayflower* was not much of a ship. Such a voyage is best left to the imagination. The small crew stood watch and were presumably busy enough, and sufficiently inured to the sea, not to notice their misery. But the Pilgrims, just over a hundred of them, spent a great part of the trip battened down belowdecks; the *Mayflower* was about ninety feet long overall, which meant the Pilgrims lived over two months in a space roughly sixty-five by twenty feet, seasick, wet, cold, and thoroughly miserable. It was no wonder that when they sighted land, Cape Cod, four hundred miles north of where they were supposed to be, the passengers had had enough and were more than willing to disembark at the nearest decent spot, Plymouth, on the inner shore of Cape Cod Bay.

Before they landed, the leaders of the group had drawn up an agreement that became known as the *Mayflower* Compact, in effect a social contract as to how they would live and govern themselves. The problems of government, however, were soon superseded by the simple matter of staying alive. It was late December before they were settled and, though they managed to build little huts, they got no more than that done. Like other early settlers elsewhere, they soon took sick and began to die. By spring less than half of them were left.

Still, the survivors had a strong motive for perseverance, and slowly the colony climbed to its feet. The original intention of establishing a fishing and trading station did not work too well, and the Pilgrims were forced to turn to subsistence farming. Their charter had required them to hold lands in common, returning all profits to London. But holding land in common meant, here as elsewhere, that there were no profits, and soon the Pilgrims divided up the land so that each man might work for himself. Their arrangements with the people back in England were renegotiated, and within ten years, though its growth was slow, the Plymouth colony was firmly planted.

In that decade matters had changed for the worse in England. Puritanism was gaining strength, and its new adherents were no longer of the lower and lower-middle classes, such as the Pilgrims had been. Newer, more wealthy and prominent people, seeing little future in the Stuart policies, began to look westward too. In 1629 the Massachusetts Bay Company was formed, and this time the potential colonists intended to do things right. There was already a small, independent settlement at Salem, founded in 1628. This was absorbed by the advance parties of the new company, which came over, directors and all, some nine hundred strong, in 1630. Though half of the originals died or went back home, these were still people of money and means, and they prospered accordingly. Massachusetts became a Puritan haven, and soon there was a steady stream of vessels making the western crossing. By 1634 there were four thousand settlers, and by the time the Civil War broke out in England, there were perhaps sixteen thousand, in pockets from Boston up the coast past the original Salem to Newburyport and across the Merrimac.

The fact that these people came seeking religious liberty for themselves did not mean they intended to extend that freedom to others. They were in fact even stricter in their insistence on conformity to accepted views than were the people from whom they had fled. Having exercised their own judgment and arrived at what they regarded as religious truth, they wanted the process to stop with them. The colonies around Massachusetts Bay therefore soon began to throw out shoots as men of independent views fell foul of orthodoxy, packed their goods, and left.

One of the first to go was a young Welsh preacher named Roger Williams, but instead of returning to England, as some malcontents did, he moved south, past Plymouth, and founded his own settlement near Providence, where everyone lived in complete religious freedom, with minimal control over anything. He was soon followed by one of the few female religious leaders of the period, Anne Hutchinson, and she settled on an island she called Rhode Island. She later moved to Long Island, where she and her followers were killed by Indians in 1643. On hearing of this, the governor of Massachusetts, John Winthrop, who had initially expelled her, remarked, "God's hand is apparently seen therein."

Meanwhile, Thomas Hooker and others, without quarreling with the Massachusetts leadership, led parties overland to the beautiful valley of the Connecticut River and started settlements around Hartford. The Dutch, coming up from New Amsterdam, put a fort at the mouth of the river, but the English were thicker on the ground, and soon there were settlements at Saybrook, and an independent one at New Haven as well.

Though all these colonies were autonomous, the need for occasional common action, as against the Pequot Indians, caused the main ones to consider union, and in 1643 Massachusetts, Plymouth, Connecticut, and New Haven formed the New England Confederation, pledging mutual support and consultation. Rhode Island and the scattered settlements along the Maine coast petitioned to join, but Maine had harbored dissidents from Massachusetts, and everyone knew the Rhode Islanders were an ungodly lot, so the confederation was confined to the original members. By the time news of the Civil War in England arrived, New England was well on its way to permanency and prosperity and had already developed the distinctive character it has preserved for three centuries.

New England was not the only colony of religious refuge set up at this time, for just as the more radical sects were being driven out of England, so the more conservative ones felt increasingly threatened. It was even more difficult to be an English Catholic in the early seventeenth century than it was to be a Puritan. George Calvert, an active promoter of the Stuarts' Spanish policy, converted to Catholicism in the 1620s and was granted the Irish title of Lord Baltimore. He tried unsuccessfully to found a colony on the Avalon Peninsula of Newfoundland, but eventually he received a charter to establish a plantation north of Virginia, in what was named Maryland. Though the Church of England was officially established and no mention was made of toleration, it was clear from the first that this was to be a colony where Catholics were safe, and it was always regarded as that.

While these settlements were growing in what was to be the heart of the New World, efforts continued to found English colonies along the flanks. By now the Newfoundland fisheries were well developed, with French and English fishermen both working off the island. The English generally based themselves for the season in the southeastern part, and the French in the southwestern part. There were no permanent settlements, though it is possible some fishermen occasionally wintered over. From 1610 to 1628 settlers from the West Country of England tried to make a home on the Avalon Peninsula, but the soil was poor and the climate not conducive to growing too much. Finally they gave it up. Various other attempts failed in the next twenty years. In 1628 Sir David Kirke went out as governor, and he stayed for nearly fifteen years of intermittent attempts to build a colony. But though Newfoundland remained absolutely essential to the development of the fishery, and therefore to the growth of a merchant marine and naval manpower pool, it was never more than marginal as a colonial possibility.

Halfway between New England and Newfoundland lay Nova Scotia, or Acadia, as the French called it. In 1621 James I granted a patent to settle the area to Sir William Alexander and a Scottish syndicate, but few could be induced to go there. James was finally constrained to decree that a spot outside Edinburgh Castle was "Nova Scotia," and those men he designated baronets of Nova Scotia knelt on it to take their oath and receive their title, thus fulfilling the requirement that they visit their holdings to receive possession of them. In 1632, Charles I resigned the area to the French, and Scottish efforts, feeble though they had been, lapsed entirely.

The English tried again in the South as well. There were several unsuccessful attempts to settle Guiana. The most important of them was led by Sir Walter Raleigh, in this age of settlement now a relic of the earlier era of exploration. In granting him a charter, King James specifically enjoined that there be no hostilities with the Spaniards. This was manifestly impossible, since the Spanish claimed the whole area and were willing to fight to make it good. In 1617 Raleigh tried to plant a colony, entered into some minor hostilities with local Spanish troops, and when he came home next year, James sacrificed him to Spanish protests by precipitously cutting off his head. Assorted enterprisers then tried to take hold of the Amazon delta, but once again, the government refused to back them, and they quickly fell to Spanish, Portuguese, Indians, fever, or some combination thereof.

Island settling was generally a better proposition than trying to hack out something on the mainland. One of the early Virginia expeditions under Sir George Somers had been shipwrecked in the Bermudas, and from 1615 to 1684 the area prospered. Its location was ideal, and so was its climate. Tobacco was grown both by slave and by indentured white labor, and soon there were fifteen thousand people in the islands. After 1684 the founding company's charter was revoked, and Bermuda became a crown colony.

The Spanish continued to insist that the Caribbean was theirs alone, but as the seventeenth century neared its second quarter, they were hard put to make good their claims. Though they firmly held most of the greater islands, they left the Lesser Antilles almost completely alone, and here the newcomers finally got a foothold. In 1624 Englishmen from Guiana settled on St. Kitts; the Spanish drove them off in 1629, but soon they were back again, and there to stay, and soon pushed on to Nevis, Montserrat, and Antigua. A settlement was planted on Barbados in 1627. Possession of such potential bases would someday give the Royal Navy a stranglehold on the Caribbean.

An even more direct threat to Spain came with the settling of Providence Island, off the coast of Nicaragua, and settlers landed here in the early 1630s. They were, and recognized themselves as, little more than pirates, planning to make their living off the Spanish, and in 1641 the Spanish reacted firmly and drove them off. Nonetheless, English freebooters got a foothold in Honduras, and in the Bahamas as well. The old dream of wealth through Spanish plunder died hard.

The founding of the old British Empire, in both the East and the West, was thus a matter of private initiative, carried out independent of, and sometimes even in spite of, the Crown. The early Stuarts confined themselves to the granting of charters, and indeed, the infringing of or even revoking of them, when it seemed opportune to do so. What, then, of the Navy during these crucial years when the foundation of empire was laid?

The sad truth was that the Navy had fallen on hard times. In 1607 the Venetian ambassador reported home that Britain had thirty-seven ships, "old and rotten and barely fit for service." A decade later they were down to twenty-seven. The Treasurer of the Navy, Sir Robert Mansell, was a villain pure and simple, who made a fine art and a fortune of corruption and got away with it. At that time governments did not differentiate between public and private accounts, so moneys voted for the Navy were handed over to Mansell to administer along with his own funds. Under this system the Navy came out very much on the

short end. Supplies were scrimped, wages went unpaid, ships were left
in poor repair, and morale plummeted to the bottom of the sea. Good
sailors left the service and went fishing or sailed on merchant ships,
and officers who did not possess family interest or the wealth for brib-
ery followed them. Those who remained often served ashore, appointing deputies to do their work at sea. Even if the British government
had been disposed to resent the Amboina Massacre, there was little the
Navy could do about it.

A further problem of James I's reign was that this was the high
point of the era of piracy; the Moorish pirates in particular, raiding out
of ports along the North African shore, virtually ruled the seas. Thousands of sailors were enslaved, and there was a waste of about seventy
English merchant ships a year to pirates. In some cases they were so
bold that they even raided along the southern English coasts, seizing
peasants, whom they carried off to slave markets. Not since the days of
the Norsemen had there been such a scourge at sea. One Algerian pirate, for example, was taken in the Thames estuary; by and large the
Jacobean Navy was impotent in the face of such problems.

Eventually a commission of inquiry was set up under a prosperous
London merchant, Sir Lionel Cranfield. The startling abuses it revealed publicly were solved by the simple expedient of buying out the
perpetrators, and both the Lord High Admiral, the Earl of Nottingham, and Mansell were pensioned off. The new admiral, the Duke
of Buckingham, was the King's current favorite, and though something
of a fop, he set about with fair vigor to restore the Navy.

This was just in time, for Europe was embarking on the great
struggle known as the Thirty Years' War, and eventually all the powers
of the Continent were involved in it. James began by siding with
Spain, in pursuit of his lifelong policy, but when Charles I acceded to
the throne in 1625 he reversed this and went to war with Spain instead.
That year England launched a great expedition against Cadiz, but it
turned out to be a dismal affair. Failing to destroy the Spanish shipping, Lord Wimbledon decided to take the city instead. He landed his
troops, who unfortunately but happily found the storage center for all
the wine bound to the Indies. The troops immediately drank themselves into a blind stupor, and they were with great difficulty gotten
back aboard ship before the Spanish could round them up.

After this unfortunate beginning Charles, under the influence of
Buckingham, reversed his policy yet again and decided to quarrel with
France rather than Spain. This was a mistake, for France, under the

inspired if devious guidance of Cardinal Richelieu, was pulling together and becoming a formidable power. At this time the cardinal was
in the process of reducing the political power of the Huguenots and
was besieging their fortress of La Rochelle on the northern coast of the
Bay of Biscay. Buckingham decided to go to the rescue of his coreli-
gionists and led a fleet over to take the Isle of Rhé, which controlled
the seaward approaches to the port. Again there was a fiasco; the landing parties took the island, but not the citadel on it; the French landed
troops in their turn and besieged the English, who were driven into the
sea after a bitter rear-guard battle. The survivors sailed disconsolately
away. Again Buckingham tried to relieve La Rochelle and failed;
English efforts were cut short, and the bankruptcy of their policy was
illustrated, when a fanatical lieutenant named Felton, disappointed at
not receiving a promotion, assassinated Buckingham in the High Street
of Portsmouth.

From 1629 on, when Charles ruled without a parliament, something was done to revitalize the Navy, and taxes were collected (illegally, according to parliamentarians) for "ship money" from the
country. In 1637 an expedition was sent against the pirate port of
Salee, on the northwestern coast of Africa, and returned home successfully after destroying that base. But events two years later capped
the humiliation of English naval power.

In that year, 1639, a formidable Spanish fleet under Admiral
Oquendo sailed up to attack the Dutch. The Thirty Years' War was
still going on, if not exactly raging, and as part of that war the Spanish
hoped to reclaim their control over the Netherlands, whose independence they had never formally acknowledged. In some disarray the
Spanish took refuge in an anchorage off the southern coast of England
known as the Downs. Here the Dutch Admiral Tromp found them,
and completely disregarding that he was in English territorial waters,
sailed in and thoroughly beat them. The Downs, coupled with Rocroi
four years later, really marked the end of Spanish power and the ascendancy of the Netherlands at sea and of France on land. The English
stood by impotently and watched it happen.

By this time, King Charles hardly had a foreign policy, and even if
he did have one, the Navy was barely a fit instrument to advance it.
The fact was that Englishmen, from the King to his sailors, were too
busy with domestic matters to worry overly much about what went on
beyond the shores of Britain. They were about to embark on the Civil
War.

3

Less Than Royal Navy

*The poorest he that is in England hath as much a life to
live as the greatest he.*
                    —Colonel Thomas Rainborough, 1647

The constitutional crisis that burst over England in midcentury had
long been maturing. It was compounded of many factors: the price revolution, which made government more expensive and less effective, the
growing disagreement over the character of a state church; the divergent views of monarchical power and sovereignty held by the King and
his subjects; and the breakdown of the old hallowed Tudor compromises. The first of the Stuarts, old King James, had blustered and
grumbled but had never pushed his conception of his power to the
breaking point. His son Charles, though he was personally a more attractive character than his father had been, was more determined.
Where James was stubborn in theory, Charles was stubborn in fact.
His refusal to recognize changing attitudes, and his determination to
preserve his position against ideas that were really revolutionary, cost
England dearly. The country paid with a generation of strife; Charles
paid with his head.

To posterity, it is obvious that England was moving toward an
armed conflict, and all the events of Charles's reign seem to fore-
shadow the war that was coming. This was, of course, not the case at
the time, and when he succeeded his father in 1625, there was no immediate reason to anticipate trouble. However, it was not long in com-

ing. Charles's first Parliament met in June of that year, just a month after his marriage to Henrietta Maria of France. It granted him money for the Spanish war, but when it turned to the traditional revenues that the King had long received, it voted that they be collected for one year only, rather than for the life of the monarch, as was hitherto customary.

This was an unprecedented step, and Charles, hurt in both his pride and his pocketbook, soon dissolved Parliament. When next he called for an election, he decided to play politics himself, and he appointed as sheriffs several of the more outspoken parliamentary leaders. This had the effect of making them ineligible for election. His hopes for a more friendly hearing were once again disappointed, however, for new leaders arose, and they were even more radical than those they supplanted. They voted impeachment of his favorite courtier, the Duke of Buckingham, whereupon the King imprisoned some of their leaders. They then refused to conduct any business until their members were freed, and so it went. Once again Charles dissolved Parliament, and in 1627 the only way he could get enough money to send his expedition to La Rochelle was to levy a forced loan.

The fight continued for two more years. Like all the Stuarts, Charles was constantly in need of funds, and he preferred to get them by vote of Parliament if possible. However, they refused to grant money until what they perceived as their grievances were answered and satisfied. In May 1628 they passed the Petition of Right, setting forth their complaints and asking that the King and his government behave itself in the future. Desperate for money, Charles agreed to it and was accordingly voted funds by a momentarily satisfied House of Commons.

In 1629 they were back again, however. In spite of the one-year-only vote of traditional revenues, Charles had simply continued to collect them, especially those customs duties known as "tunnage and poundage." Now Parliament protested against this, taking up the case of one of their members, a London merchant, who had been imprisoned for nonpayment of what he called an illegal tax. Feelings ran very high, and at one point several members of Parliament forcibly held the Speaker of the House in his chair while they passed a series of resolutions against tunnage and poundage, and significantly, against what they called innovations in religion. Charles responded by throwing eight members into the Tower of London, and in March he dissolved Parliament altogether.

Charles did have, and he now played, his one trump card: Only the King might summon Parliament to meet. Dissolved, there was nothing the individual members could do about it. As long as Charles could get along on his customary revenues, and therefore did not need to call Parliament into session, he was safe. And by careful management and the collection of a wide variety of ancient and all-but-forgotten taxes, he managed to get along for eleven years, a period known as the "Eleven Years' Tyranny."

The matter was now at a standoff. Life went on, of course, and the great constitutional question remained in abeyance. The government continued to function, though parliamentarians might fume that it was doing so illegally. And there was nothing the opposition could do about it. Charles made peace with France and with Spain, kept his own house in order, and went about his affairs, and it looked as if he might do so forever.

In the end, religion ruined him. Puritanism and Presbyterianism were gaining ground in Britain, and Charles and his advisers, firm Anglicans all, thoroughly disliked the idea. The Archbishop of Canterbury, William Laud, and Charles's most astute adviser, Peter Wentworth, the Earl of Strafford and Lord Lieutenant of Ireland, both thought that only High Church Anglicanism could preserve the peace of the realm. This was, after all, a period very close to the Religious Wars in France, and the Thirty Years' War in Germany had started over religion; it was a time when men killed each other over their views on transubstantiation, and religious uniformity was still thought essential to order in a country.

Under the pressure of this view, the government decided to impose Anglican usages on the Scots, and a new prayer book was decreed for Scottish churches in 1637. The result was bad; there were riots at Edinburgh, the Scots rose up behind their clergy, and a year later they signed the Solemn League and Covenant, vowing to defend their own religion against the English. Many of the signers wrote their names in blood. The next year they seized Edinburgh Castle, raised an army, and marched for the border, with Presbyterian hymns in their mouths and the gleam of loot in their eyes.

Though there was a certain amount of negotiating, and all this took time, Charles was now caught. His normal revenues were not up to the expenses of war, even a low-level one with his own subjects. At last, in 1640, he summoned Parliament. In doing so, he took the advice of Strafford, whose view was, "Call Parliament; they hate the Scots more than they hate you."

But Strafford was wrong. Long in Ireland, he was thoroughly out of touch with English opinion. Parliament did not hate the Scots more than they did Charles, and they were determined that now it was their turn. They met on April 13, listened sullenly to the government's demands for money, and then immediately turned to their grievances. If Charles thought the last decade could be forgotten, he was sadly mistaken. After a mere twenty-three days, he dissolved Parliament again, having gotten absolutely nothing from them.

There was no escape. The Scottish Army was still there; worse, it now lurched into action, beat the King's forces in August, and forced on Charles a treaty in October, in which he agreed to pay its subsistence to the tune of £850 a day. The Scots were not only in arms against their own King, but they also were going to make him pay the upkeep. With no choice now—he did not have the money—Charles went to Parliament once more. The previous one had been called the "Short Parliament"; this one was to be the "Long Parliament"—in one guise or another, it sat until 1660.

For two years Parliament had its innings, and it swept away all the prerogatives and privileges that had enabled Charles to rule without it. On constitutional issues the members were pretty well united, and they denied the King the right to collect taxes without their consent. They passed a bill saying they should meet every three years whether called by the King or not. They tried Strafford and executed him by an act of attainder—a bill that said, in effect, "We cannot find you guilty of anything, but we are determined to be rid of you, so off with your head!" They made a deal with the Scots whereby they agreed to pay the latter to keep an army in the field, putting pressure on the King, who therefore had to keep Parliament sitting. It was a vicious circle, and Charles was fairly trapped in it.

But Commons finally split. United on politics, they could not agree on religion. When the radical Presbyterians introduced the Root and Branch petition for the abolition of episcopacy, they alienated the moderate Puritans. The Root and Branch was the great watershed of the day; everyone who voted for it eventually sided with Parliament in the Civil War, and every man who voted against it went with the King. Charles thus was finally given some opportunity to build a party of his own. Early in 1642, when the radicals moved to take control of the King's Army, Charles refused to sign the bill. He withdrew from London, and on August 22 he raised the royal standard at Nottingham and called on all true subjects to rally to his side. Englishmen were done with talking.

*   *   *

The turmoil of the years after Charles's accession did much for the Empire, as ship after ship headed westward, full of men and women whose religion would not accept England's dictates, or who had had enough of the political squabbling that seemed to go on without end. These years at last saw the American colonies on a solid footing as the New Englanders moved like a tide up the river valleys and into the western hills, and the coastline around Chesapeake Bay was brought under increasing cultivation. But during the Civil War itself the movement slowed as Puritans stayed home to fight, and the colonies remained spectators, by and large, to the great events happening at home.

For the Navy the opposite was true. It had been relatively uninfluenced by the disagreements between King and Parliament, but when war came, its role was vital. The fact that the Navy sided with Parliament against the Crown was one of the decisive elements of the war.

England in 1642, when war began, was not a military nation. The Navy was weak, and the standing armed forces of the Crown were small, ill-trained, and poorly organized. Few Englishmen had seen military service, except for those who had fought in Ireland against the perpetual rebellion there, or the survivors of troops rented out to the Dutch. Some English or Scottish gentlemen had made a profession of arms and had fought in Dutch service or in the German wars. But on the whole, the Civil War was fought by amateurs.

It therefore took both sides a long time to organize, train, and officer their forces. It was a slow process to impose effective discipline on the men and an even slower one to get officers to obey orders. For three years Royalists and "Roundheads," as the Parliamentarians were called because of their close haircuts, fought occasionally bloody and usually indecisive battles. In 1645 the foremost military leader of the rebels, Oliver Cromwell, organized what was known as the New Model Army, a professional, mobile force, firmly disciplined and prepared to fight to the finish. Slowly the Parliamentarians gained ground, and in 1646, after he had surrendered to the Scots, Charles was handed over to Parliament.

On the winning side there was a gradual split between the Army and its political masters. Charles took advantage of this to escape and begin the war again. This time the Army, under Cromwell's firm leadership, rode over everyone. Charles was defeated and captured again, and early in 1649 he was executed. When Scots, Irish, and even Parliament disputed the Army's position, it turned on all in succession, with the result that by 1650 Oliver Cromwell, backed by armed force and a group of able men proved in battle, was supreme master of England.

On the outbreak of the war, Queen Henrietta Maria had fled home to France, entrusted by Charles with the task of raising loans and supplies for his forces. The monarchs of Europe tended to regard a threat to one as a threat to all, so that even if it was politically opportune to have England distracted by internal troubles, it was potentially dangerous to see subjects in revolt against their sovereign. The role of the Navy therefore became of real importance; if it sided with the King, he would have access to foreign aid; if it sided with Parliament, he must fight alone. Since London, and most of the South and East of England, and the commercial classes, went for Parliament, it was perhaps inevitable that the Navy, which had closer ties with these areas or groups than with the Royalists, should go with the rebels as well. Though its role was less dramatic than that of the Army, it was nonetheless crucial. The hopes of the Scottish Royalists were several times wrecked by their inability to get aid from abroad, and at the end of the war, when a triumphant Cromwell began to put his house in order, he looked to the Navy with a friendly eye.

War tends to strip the fat from a system. In its search for military victory the Army had reformed itself; in its search for a political settlement it had then reformed—a euphemism for "purged"—Parliament. In 1649 Cromwell turned his attention to the Navy. The immediate spur was the fact that the King's nephew and leading cavalryman, Prince Rupert of the Rhine, had gotten away overseas and raised a small naval squadron with which he harassed English shipping. To suppress him, to capture various offshore islands that adhered to the Royalist cause, and to further English trade all became prime objectives of the new leaders of the Commonwealth.

When asked to describe his policy, Cromwell once replied, "Thorough." Applying this to the Navy, he replaced the office of Lord High Admiral with a committee of senior parliamentary naval officers, placing the office "in commission," in the phrase of the day. Though the Lord High Admiral was resurrected after the Restoration, the benefits of having professionals in positions of authority were too obvious to be disregarded. Gradually the Lords Commissioners of the Admiralty became a permanent body, though it was not until 1832 that it merged with the Navy Board, the group responsible for the civil administration of the shore establishment. The Admiralty took over matters of personnel, ship design, tactics as these were developed, and actual naval strategy. In effect, Cromwell did to the Navy what he had already done to the Army, improving its efficiency at the same time as he guaranteed its loyalty. Under the direction of Sir Harry Vane, a close associate of Cromwell, a high-minded administrator and a religious fanatic, the Admiralty Board improved the sailors' food rations and wages and set up the practice of offering prize money for the taking of enemy vessels, an incentive system that over the years made a great many officers rich. In its first two years the committee added forty ships to the Navy, doubling it in size, and over the next decade it added two hundred more, an immense expenditure of treasure and effort, two of whose by-products were the depletion of England's oak reserves and the gift to the world of masterpieces of the modeler's art, the famous "admiralty models."

The committee firmed its control over the existing Navy. It produced the original Articles of War, setting forth the regulations by which the Navy would henceforth live and die, and finally, to ensure its control, it transformed three of the Army's victorious colonels into "generals at sea"—Edward Popham, Richard Deane, and the greatest of them all, Robert Blake.

Until his death in 1657, Blake's history was virtually the Navy's history. He is universally considered next to Nelson the greatest of English admirals, and there are those who would drop the qualifying phrase. He had fought vigorously for the parliamentary cause and was a plain, blunt, outspoken, and inspiring leader. Though he had made some voyages as a young man engaged in his father's business, he had relatively little experience of the sea and none of naval warfare. There is a story, which is probably not true, that when he first went aboard his flagship and took his squadron to sea, he said to his signal officer, "Hoist the signal, 'By the right wheel, quick march.'" That is one of the few anecdotes about Blake, for in spite of several volumes of correspondence he remains a somewhat elusive character. The mental set of seventeenth-century Parliamentarians, with their constant consciousness of God's immanence, is sufficiently foreign that in spite of a colorful career Blake appears, unfairly, a colorless man.

The first task was to run down Prince Rupert. When Blake took up his commission, Rupert was in Ireland, blockaded at Kinsale by a Commonwealth squadron. Blake reinforced this, but he was blown off station in a gale, and Rupert escaped to Lisbon. He took refuge in the

Tagus estuary, where he was welcomed by the King of Portugal. Unable to violate Portuguese neutrality, Blake decided on the next best thing, and he stopped all traffic in and out of Lisbon. Since the city lived on maritime trade, Rupert soon outstayed his welcome and was asked to leave. Once again he slipped past the blockaders, and he swept through the Strait of Gibraltar and into the Mediterranean. Nothing daunted, Blake followed him in, and finally caught his squadron off Cartagena. One of the Royalist ships was taken; several others were driven onto the shore and wrecked. However, Rupert himself, who led something of a charmed life, escaped. Blake was recalled home to face other problems, and the Navy turned Rupert over to junior commanders. He eventually fled to the Caribbean, where for a time he maintained himself as a near-pirate, his squadron gradually dwindling away. His brother Prince Maurice was lost in a hurricane, and finally in 1653 Rupert brought his last ship back to Europe and lived quietly on the Continent until the Restoration.

Blake's foray into the Mediterranean marked the first appearance there of an English fleet, and, like the reorganization of the Navy generally, initiated a policy that was to be a guiding star for three hundred years. The Stuarts had suffered piracy in silence, but the Commonwealth would not. The British squadron not only chased Rupert; having entered the pirates' home waters, it also began to convoy merchantmen, first of all in the Levant trade. With this taking over of responsibility for the safety of merchant vessels at sea, the British Navy found its true mission in life, and the link between the British Navy and the British Empire was indissolubly formed at last. This practical link was formally recognized by the passing of the Navigation Acts, in effect a constitution for the first British Empire.

The dominant economic theory of the seventeenth century was known as mercantilism, and it received its fullest formulation from the great French minister Colbert. According to this idea, there was a fixed amount of wealth in the world, measured in bullion. Since the sum total was unalterable, wealth was something to be acquired, not created; and since it was all apportioned already, some to the King of France, some to heathens in unknown parts, the way a society gained wealth was to take it away from another society. This could be done either by war or by trade, and the two were thought to be essentially interchangeable, being simply different levels of the same competitive activity.

In war the matter was simple: Spain went out and took over the Inca Empire or the Aztec Empire and became rich. In trade it was a bit more complex. Here men assumed that each society was basically hostile to every other one and that their own society gained by selling goods to a neighbor, receiving bullion in return, and thus growing wealthy. The aim of every state was therefore to possess or create a closed, self-sufficient imperial system, producing not only all the goods it itself needed, but also generating a surplus that might be exported out of the system, to bring gold back in.

The theory was not entirely valid, though it did have more validity than has sometimes been thought by its detractors. Its invalidity, however, was less important than the fact that men believed in it and acted accordingly.

When Cromwell and his ministers looked at their world, they saw an almost satisfactory British system, with one glaring deficiency that drained off a substantial amount of wealth: The Dutch were masters of the world's carrying trade. In spite of Newfoundland fisheries and colonial coasting, most of British trade was carried in Dutch hulls. The result was both a chronic weakness of the British merchant marine and a drain of funds to the Netherlands to pay for Dutch services. The Commonwealth therefore decided to do what Spain and Portugal had done before them. They moved to create a closed sea, or, since by this time the sea itself could not be closed, a closed British Empire.

The first Navigation Act was passed in October 1651. Its provisions were simple: No goods could be imported into England unless they were carried either by an English ship, or by a ship of the producing country. This was obviously aimed at the Netherlands, but just to make sure no one mistook his target, Cromwell went farther. He insisted that taxes be paid on all herring caught within thirty miles of English shores, and he revived the ancient custom of demanding that all foreign vessels passing through the Channel salute the English flag by dipping their ensigns and lowering their topsails.

The Dutch already felt themselves sufficiently aggrieved by England not to brook further insults. During the Civil War numerous Dutch ships had been seized by forces of the Parliamentarians for trading with the Royalists. The Dutch particularly resented the limitations put on their herring fisheries. It took them no time at all to decide to fight. In May 1652 their great admiral, Tromp, was sent through the Channel with forty warships and orders not to salute anyone, orders he was delighted to obey. Off Dover he met Blake with twenty-three ships. Blake was outnumbered, but had some prospect of reinforcements, and his ships were bigger and more heavily gunned than the Dutch. Both sides were spoiling for a fight, the Dutch because they had a generation of success tending to arrogance behind them, the English because they had memories going back as far as Amboina to erase.

As the British ranged up, Tromp continued determinedly on his course. Blake in the *James* was slightly ahead of his squadron, while Tromp, who had the wind astern, had his whole fleet in immediate support. While they approached, both admirals fired at each other; each later insisted that these initial rounds were signal guns, but if they were, their message was far from diplomatic. The two flagships passed at close range, and Tromp in *Brederode* let fly a full broadside; the other Dutch ships, as they came up, followed suit. For some time the *James* alone was in action, and then gradually the other English ships came into the fray. During most of the afternoon they pounded away; toward evening reinforcements got out from the Downs, cutting the Dutch rear and taking two prizes. As nightfall came the Netherlanders bore away for their own coast, the English took the dismasted *James* in tow, and their prizes, and went home. Each admiral in his report put the blame on the other for opening hostilities.

It took two months for the mechanism of diplomacy to fall into gear, and it was July before war was declared. This First Anglo-Dutch War lasted until April 1654, though late summer of 1653 saw the last major fighting; the negotiations around the peace table took as much time as the actual combat phase of the war.

In July Blake was at sea again, seizing or dispersing the great Dutch herring fleet. Angrily Tromp sailed with his men-of-war to rescue his compatriots, but his fleet was scattered by a heavy summer storm, and public opinion at home mistakenly made him a scapegoat for the failure. He was relieved and command given to Admiral Cornelius de Witt. Though a bold sailor, he proved no match for Blake, who met him, about sixty ships a side, and thoroughly trounced him in September in the Battle of the Kentish Knock. De Witt was a bad-tempered man, and his subordinates failed to support him properly.

De Witt's failure brought Tromp back to office, while Blake's success led the Commonwealth government to halve his command, sending ships off to convoy duty in the Mediterranean and to the West Indies. Two months after the Kentish Knock, Tromp, with nearly a hundred ships and blood in his eye, met Blake off Dungeness, the English only forty strong. Once again the Dutch had the wind with them, and Blake, leading as always, took heavy punishment while the rest of his fleet straggled up. Two of his ships, *Garland* and *Bonaventure,* grappled Tromp's *Brederode,* and were then grappled in turn by other Dutch ships, so that for some time several vessels lay aboard each other, the men swarming back and forth over them with cutlass and boarding pike. At the end *Garland*'s captain set a powder train and blew off his own upper deck, and scores of English and Dutch with it, but both ships finally struck their colors. After five hours, the English drew off, two ships lost and three sunk. Tromp hoisted his famous broom to the masthead and sailed down the Channel, symbolizing that he had swept British power from the Narrow Seas.

By the end of the fighting season the laurels were about even, and both sides were satisfied to have the winter gales come on, keeping ships in port, where they might make good the hard usage of war. With spring, the English were ready first. The odds were really with them. The British Isles covered all the approaches to the Netherlands, and the Dutch were absolutely dependent for their prosperity on their seaborne commerce, while the same was not true of England. Also, the Dutch had to maintain a watchful eye on their land frontiers, while the Commonwealth had much lesser problems in that regard. The contest was bound in the long run to be unequal.

This inequality was now compounded by the Dutch instructions to Tromp: He was both to seek out and to fight the English and to bring home safely their great convoys of merchant ships, which were due in the spring. In February 1653 he was out with about eighty ships, convoying over two hundred homecoming merchantmen, when Blake came after him once again. The Battle off Portland lasted for three days, with Tromp trying to stand between the enemy and his convoy, and the English trying to break through his warship screen. Blake was wounded, but the English took seventeen Dutch and about fifty merchantmen and chased the rest over to the shallows on the continental side of the Channel.

While Blake recovered from his wounds, he spent some time thinking about naval warfare. Blake was not a sailor to begin with, but by now he had several years' experience at sea, and he knew pretty well what a ship, or a group of ships, could do. He and his fellow "generals at sea" therefore sat down and produced a set of rules for naval warfare, which they called the Fighting Instructions, and these became the basic text for naval warfare throughout the entire age of sail. Ships were to maneuver by squadrons, and to fight, generally, in line ahead, thereby bringing all their broadside guns to bear. The English also decided the advantages lay in having the weather gauge—that is, in having the wind in their favor so that they might dictate the course of the action.

Armed with these instructions plus their other advantages, the English pressed the war. George Monck, another great soldier-turned-admiral, beat Tromp off the Gabbard in June, the Dutch losing nearly twenty ships, and after that, for two months, the English were even dominant enough to mount a blockade off the Dutch coast. Late in July, however, De Witt skipped out past it, and at the end of the month, a combined Dutch fleet, a hundred strong, tried to break the blockade and fought the climactic battle of the war. The English had a larger fleet of bigger ships and were under better tactical control. Blake was still recuperating from his wounds, but Monck handled his command well, and by now the English had also a clear moral ascendancy. Several of the Dutch captains flinched and ran, Tromp himself was killed early in the battle by a musket ball, and after twelve hours the Dutch had lost over thirty ships. They were ready to give up at last and soon sued for peace. There would be no more brooms hoisted to Dutch mastheads in this war.

The general foreign policy of the Commonwealth, now abundantly proven in war with the greatest maritime power of the age, was to be self-confidently aggressive. Cromwell eventually took the title "Lord Protector" in England, Commonwealth became Protectorate, and with more accuracy than such names usually carry, England set out to protect her subjects both at home and abroad. With the Dutch humbled, Cromwell now turned to the West Indies and the Mediterranean.

England's American colonies had given relatively little trouble during the Civil War. New England had naturally declared for the Parliamentarians' side and remained a hotbed of Puritanism. Maryland had been split, but little had come of it. Virginia had been strongly Royalist, and when Charles I was executed, the colony promptly recognized and declared its loyalty to Charles II. However, a small naval force from the Commonwealth soon overawed the Virginians, who decided to be more discreet about their feelings, and there was no real trouble. Several of the island colonies were more overtly Royalist, but one by one they were forcibly called to allegiance to the new regime. For practical purposes, then, the shifts of English policy did not have a great effect on the colonies.

A simple reassertion of authority over colonies was hardly enough to satisfy the ambitions of the Protectorate, however, and the English now resurrected the old dream of a lucrative Spanish war. Cromwell demanded of Spain both free trade with its empire in America and exemption from the Inquisition for Englishmen. Tradition has it that the Spanish ambassador replied, "My master has but two eyes, and you ask for both of them." In 1655 Cromwell sent out a substantial naval and military expedition, led by Admiral Penn and General Venables, to conquer Hispaniola. But even the Protectorate was not immune to the usual ill fortune that dogged efforts in the West Indies. The troops were poorly handled, and the Spanish defeated their attempt to take the city of Santo Domingo. The troops next fell prey to yellow fever, which decimated their ranks. Finally, with ships full of dead and dying men, they sailed off, and rather than report complete failure, they occupied the island of Jamaica as a consolation prize to offset their larger disappointment.

They did far better in Europe itself. In the later stages of the Dutch war, English ships had been badly treated at Leghorn, whose duke still judged the Dutch to be the chief naval power. On the conclusion of peace, therefore, Blake was sent with a strong squadron to cruise the Mediterranean ports and inform their masters of the new order. This he did with characteristic thoroughness, and on several occasions he secured damages for earlier ill use by the threat of bombardment. Having cowed the Italian states, he then crossed over to the North African shore to deal with the pirate strongholds along the Barbary Coast.

These people, many of them Christian renegades, ex-slaves, or the scourings of Mediterranean ports, were still a scourge, especially of the Mediterranean but of the Atlantic waters as well. Blake's instructions were to negotiate first, then act if necessary. He approached the Dey of Algiers and got no satisfaction. A price for release of English captives could not be agreed upon, and no one was willing to make any efforts to accommodate Blake. Disgruntled, he sailed away to try his luck with the Dey of Tunis. When this ruler proved even more insolent and intractable than the one at Algiers, Blake's patience ran out. He threatened to attack the town, whereupon the Dey pointed to his shore batteries and his nine warships and invited him to try.

The position was strong; Tunis was at the bottom of a gulf, its entrance guarded by a major fortress, Porto Farina, and the Tunisian warships and land batteries were in mutually supporting positions. Still, the naval truism that men who attack stone forts with wooden ships must expect a difficult time had not been coined in Blake's day. On April 4, 1655, he sailed in, his ships divided into two squadrons. The lighter ships took on the Tunisian war vessels; the heavier ones anchored within musket shot of the walls of Porto Farina and opened up with full broadsides. The wind was with the English, and the gunsmoke, a major factor in days of black powder, drifted down onto the Tunisian gunners. The latter worked very poorly, while the English worked very well, and after a steady cannonade, the Tunisian batteries were smothered, guns dismounted, gunners dead or fled, and the shore silenced. Most of the pirate crews deserted the warships, and then Blake sent over boarding parties to burn the vessels.

Having done a good day's work, the English stood out of the harbor on the evening breeze, and the Barbary coast rulers suddenly became far more amenable to negotiation. Algiers signed a treaty, and the other rulers agreed to release captives on payment of a modest ransom and not to harbor pirates anymore. Their power was by no means destroyed, but it was certainly set back for the immediate future, and English stature rose accordingly.

This was all really but an interlude, and Blake now turned his attention to Spain as the peninsular counterpart to Cromwell's West Indian ambitions. The English had mounted the expedition to Hispaniola on the old comfortable assumption of "no peace beyond the line," but the Spanish, declining to play that game, went to war. This proved to be a mistake, for in September 1656 Captain Richard Stayner realized every English sailor's wildest dream by capturing the Spanish treasure fleet. Falling in with it off Cadiz, he sank four ships and took two others, bringing home more than two million pounds of booty to England.

Blake, however, was ordered to stay off the coasts of Spain, and basing himself in Lisbon, he blockaded Cadiz during the winter of 1656–57. Here yet another traditional practice of English naval strategy, that of blockading the enemy off his own coasts, was formed. Once again, as with battle formations, convoys, and the assertion of British power in the Mediterranean, what Blake was doing had previously been thought impossible. He was waiting for another treasure fleet, but in the spring word came that it had sought refuge in the Canaries. Blake therefore sailed for Tenerife; by the time he got there the treasure had been landed and was safely stored ashore, at the head of Santa Cruz Harbor, guarded not only by the batteries that lined the long, narrow approach, but also by six great galleons off the port as well as ten smaller ships behind them.

The British admiral, however, had figured his chances to a nicety. On the morning of April 20, 1657, the English squadron came in on the flood tide, and while the bigger ships silenced the batteries, the smaller attacked the galleons. The fire of the other Spanish ships was masked by the galleons until the English had taken the latter. At that the smaller Spanish vessels opened up, so Blake's men went on and took them as well. The British were too few in number to get the Spanish ships away as prizes, so they burned all sixteen where they lay. Then, to the joy of the crews, who were sure that day that God was a Protestant, the wind shifted, and a quite abnormal steady breeze filled the English sails and blew their ships back out of the harbor. The affair was one of the single greatest feats of naval history; it rocked Spain and all Europe and made Blake's name a household word in England.

Unfortunately, he did not live to enjoy his laurels. Worn out by hard and unending service, he was recalled home in August with those ships which, like himself, were too weak to stand another winter's blockade. He knew he was dying on the journey home and hoped he might settle his estates and die ashore. But he died peacefully two hours before his squadron anchored in Plymouth Sound. It would take England more than a century to see another sailor who was his equal.

The battle at Santa Cruz de Tenerife was the last great triumph of the Protectorate. Oliver Cromwell died in 1658, and the great problem-solver left a host of unresolved questions behind him. The two most pressing were money and the succession.

In the middle of the seventeenth century, states had not yet developed the concept of the national debt, whereby one generation lives beyond its means at the expense of its heirs. Kings could borrow either from their subjects or from bankers, on the strength of the order and continuity offered by the institution of royalty, but they were expected to pay back their loans, a charming conceit that has been given up in more progressive times. Revolutionary governments, however, be they English or American or French, were the antithesis of continuity, and they invariably had trouble borrowing or raising money. Cromwell, though his hand lay heavy on Englishmen's purses, still ran short of funds just as James and Charles had before him. Cromwell's vast expansion of the British Navy, beneficial though it might be in the long run, was very expensive, and that coupled with other equally costly policies left England almost bankrupt at his death.

Coupled with that was the overwhelming fact that he had never been able to legitimize his rule. Throughout the Protectorate, he had periodically produced constitutions that should have satisfied Parliament but never did; he remained a successful revolutionary, "playing Napoleon to his own Robespierre," but he never managed to convince England that he was anything more than that. No one had as yet conceived of the concept of the general will, the idea of social contract was barely in its infancy—the theory to support men's actions is always worked out after the actions have taken place—and therefore Cromwell could never find a peg on which to hang his sovereignty. When he died he left the Protectorate to his son, Richard, and Richard patently did not know what to do with it. After six months he resigned, earning the name "Tumbledown Dick," and by late 1659 there was open Army rule of the country, with a council of major generals sitting in control.

Meanwhile, ever since 1649, when his father had been executed, Charles Stuart, recognized on the Continent as Charles II of England, had been living quietly in exile, waiting for his day to dawn. Now he suspected it had and, cleverer than his father, he issued in 1660 the Declaration of Breda, in which he promised all things to all men, and was astute enough to tie those promises to their acceptance by a free Parliament. With England in a quandary, General Monck marched his Army down from the Scots border and called a free election of a convention Parliament; that in turn invited Charles back and proclaimed him King of England. On May 29, 1660, he entered London to general rejoicing.

Though Charles himself was a humane person and wished to let the past bury the past, a new Parliament, more Royalist than the King, wanted some portion of its pound of flesh. The regicide judges, those who had condemned Charles I to death, were persecuted, and some executed. A few escaped, however, and fled to New England, where in one instance they eluded pursuing authorities by hiding in a cave above New Haven, and that city's Whalley Avenue and Goffe Street still recall a connection with Puritan days. As for Cromwell himself, his exhumed body was mutilated, and the severed head was mounted on a pike for the edification of Londoners. It stayed there until at least 1684, and if it lasted five years longer, the skull would no doubt have been seen to grin.

England now embarked on the reign of the Merry Monarch, and good fun and bad morals came back into their own again. Yet all was not forgotten. The Navy and the Empire—and the Dutch—still remained.

4

"In Matters of Business the Fault of the Dutch . . ."

The trade of the world is too little for us two, therefore one must down.

—English sailor, 1664

In naval matters Charles II is best remembered for affairs. While in exile in the Netherlands, he had developed an interest in the new sport of pleasure sailing, and on his restoration, he introduced a special type of vessel, Anglicizing its name in the process. Thus the yacht appeared on the English scene. Charles was also a mighty seducer, and as he tended to name his yachts after his mistresses, he had scope for a considerable squadron; so H.M. Yachts *Katherine, Fubbs,* and *Portsmouth* joined the naval list, the latter two named after the same lady. At the time the word "fubby" meant "plump" or "cuddly," and "Fubbs" was Charles's nickname for the Duchess of Portsmouth. In all he built more than twenty of the lovely little sailing boats and firmly established yachting as an English pastime.

If what sticks best in the memory is the inconsequential, it was also true that Charles was deeply interested in the Navy and in maritime power generally, and during the quarter century of his reign the British Navy turned the corner into true professionalism. The Commonwealth establishment was kept up, and many more ships of new and improved design were added to the fleet. Even more important for the continuity and therefore the well-being of the service, the administration and organization of the Navy were put on regular lines. This was a period of bureaucratic development in western Europe generally, so much so that that activity appears as one of the hallmarks of the dynastic state. In Germany the Prussians and Austrians were building their state services; in France this was the great era of Colbert and Louvois, who gave the French government many of the characteristics it still retains. The same sort of thing was happening in England, with the result that what had hitherto been sporadic or accidental now became a regular function. Thus the work of creating an administrative structure for the Navy, which had its origins back in Tudor days, now reached its definitive formulation. There would not be another such major reconstruction until the twentieth century.

Charles appointed as his Lord High Admiral his brother James, Duke of York, and James was fervently interested in naval matters. Though his later judgment, when he was King, has not won him very high marks, he was an able man at this stage of his career. He installed an energetic group as Commissioners of the Admiralty, with young Samuel Pepys as Clerk of the Acts, and they began to attack the abuses that had either crept in during the last few years while the Protectorate was in trouble, or else had existed so long that even Cromwell had not managed to erase them. Dockyard and victualing services, which always offered peculiar opportunities for pilfering and corruption, were investigated and called to account. Records were more carefully kept and required of officers serving at sea. Sailors, whose wages were often many years overdue, were paid at last.

One of the most significant changes was in the character of the officer class. British naval officers at this time were still generally men who, like Francis Drake, had grown up at sea and had gained their commands by their ship-handling or fighting ability, even though the highest offices were reserved for royal appointees and favorites. Now there was a conscious effort to obtain officers from the gentlemen class. For a while there was considerable friction between the two groups, the seamen resenting the gentlemen, whom they considered ignorant of the profession, and the gentlemen effecting to despise the seamen, who knew everything about handling a line and nothing about manners. Gradually, however, such friction disappeared, largely because the seamen class finally gave way. Such men eventually dwindled off to warrant officer status, as masters and masters' mates, and the officer ranks became the preserve of the better classes, usually gentry and minor nobility. The rule of primogeniture and the ability of money to alter social status meant there were plenty of well-born younger sons available for naval or military careers. The trend could not have developed if the "gentlemen" remained ignorant of the mechanics of the business, but with the growth of the practice of sending young men to sea as midshipmen, together with the extension of half pay as a retainer fee to the intermediate officer ranks, a professional class of naval gentlemen soon developed. A society that habitually sent its sons off to school at six or seven saw nothing unusually cruel about sending ten-year-olds to sea as midshipmen, and whatever else the practice may have done, it produced the world's best naval officers for two hundred years.

Far less interest was taken in the men than in their officers, and the Navy continued throughout the seventeenth and eighteenth centuries to be manned by whatever it could scrape up. That often included the scourings of jails and poorhouses, though in a country where several hundred offenses were punishable by death, and jail was a common remedy for debt, prisoners were more likely to be simply unfortunates than hardened criminals. In time of emergency the Navy relied on the press gang, whereby a captain about to sail would send a party of trusted petty officers and sailors ashore to raid local taverns and brothels. Many a sailor home from the sea had time for no more than one quick drunk before he woke up with an aching head and a boot in his ribs, to find he had joined the Royal Navy. And many a merchant vessel, coming up the Channel after a long voyage, was boarded by the Royal Navy and stripped of her able seamen, leaving her just enough of a crew to limp into port, while the naval ship sailed off to foreign shores with a complement of prime new hands.

None of this seemed particularly unjust to the men of the times. Life was hard, and this was just another aspect of it. It would be another century before humanitarianism and labor reform made inroads on English ways of doing things, and even when they did, the lot of sailors was virtually the last aspect of working life to be reformed. In France the government had a regular maritime register, and men could count on an orderly sequence of work as civilians and call-up as sailors. Yet for years British seamen, pressed into the service and flogged until they learned their duty, would consider themselves "free-born Englishmen" and jeer at what they regarded as continental slaves and lackeys. If the irony of the situation was lost on them, the fact that they won their battles was not.

Reforms to the Restoration Navy cost a great deal of money, and that was one thing Charles did not have; like his father and grandfather before him, he was nearly always short of funds and constantly begging Parliament for more. Unlike them, however, he was a fairly clever politician. He was helped in his early days by the fervent royalism of his Parliaments, who were determined to demonstrate their love for the Crown by granting it money. Later, when the glow of novelty had worn off, Charles played his hands well; in his own oft-quoted words, "I have no desire to go upon my travels again," so he got what he could, and conceded when he had to. But the chronic shortage of money was often embarrassing and occasionally disastrous—as, for example, during the Second Anglo-Dutch War.

One of the first things the restored monarchy did was repeat the Navigation Acts. A new act, in 1660, was even more exclusive of Dutch shipping than the old one had been, and it was obvious that none of the major causes of dislike had been removed by the First Anglo-Dutch War. Indeed, as the decade of the sixties went on, the hatred intensified. The East India companies of the two countries continued to spar with each other, and there was overt hostility on the American coast and along the African coast as well as a new field of commercial enterprise opened up.

Strictly speaking, Africa was not new, for there had been rivalry in the slave trade since the days of John Hawkins. However, in 1660 Charles had given a charter to the Company of Royal Adventurers Trading to Africa, and this body had taken over the forts and factories of the East India Company along the Gold and Gambia coasts. Though it intended initially to be more than a slaving company, it soon boiled down to that, as slaves were far and away the most lucrative item of the area. From 1662 on, the company was almost completely concerned with black cargoes.

Slaves were the one indispensable item to the colonial empires of the seventeenth and eighteenth centuries. All of these especially desired to have the products of tropical colonies, sugar being the most important, but the Indian labor of the Caribbean and the Spanish Main had long ago been used up, and white Europeans did not last well in the climate. As far back as the early sixteenth century, importation of African labor had been recommended by such men as the great Spanish humanitarian Las Casas, who saw it as a reasonable alternative to the destruction of the Indian races. The idea was not as callous as it sounds now; slavery was widely accepted, both in Europe and everywhere else at that time, and Las Casas, who was a churchman, believed that in this way the Indians would be saved from anni-hilation, and the Africans would be marginally better off in America, and also brought to Christianity, than if left in Africa to be sold to the Moors or other slavers. In any case, no one saw anything reprehensible in this, and the western coast of sub-Saharan Africa became one of the great trading areas of the old colonial system. European rivalries were rapidly extended there, and Portuguese, Spanish, English, Dutch, French, and even Danes and Swedes all tried to set up slave trading factories and get in on a good thing.

In such places as this, the peace between England and the Nether-lands was not worth the paper it was written on, and by 1663, though the two countries were still officially at peace, the Dutch had seized most of the factories and nearly driven the English off the coast. The African Company, however, had friends at court, and Charles II was not the man James I had been. England decided that two could play the game of "no peace beyond the line," and in 1664, they struck back.

The Dutch had been in America, around the Hudson River area, intermittently since 1609, and they had built a fort at present-day Al-bany, New York, in 1614, and begun at the same time to settle on Manhattan Island at the mouth of the river. Gradually they built up a colony, not entirely realizing they were on one of the great gateways to the center of the continent. For years they fought sporadically with the Indians, and with the English settlers of Connecticut and New Haven, who slowly won mastery of Long Island from them. As they claimed the area from modern Philadelphia to Halifax, Nova Scotia, they were naturally often in trouble with their neighbors, and when the Swedes tried to plant a colony in Delaware, the Dutch sent an expedition, which captured it in 1655. At this time Peter Stuyvesant was governor of New Netherlands, and he was a rough, crotchety type who did not take kindly to infringement on whatever he regarded as his rights.

The English had already moved once to take the colony and had sent a force to Boston in 1654; it had recruited local troops and was on the point of sailing for New Amsterdam when news arrived that England and Holland had signed a peace treaty. By 1664, since the two countries were not yet at war, there was no such worry.

Charles granted the territory to his brother James, the Lord High Admiral and Duke of York, and the British rapidly moved to seize the colony. Taking it was not only a riposte for African affairs, but also a useful move in its own right, for New Amsterdam was a perpetual thorn to the English North American colonies and a definite hindrance to the enforcement of the Navigation Acts. James sent over a small squadron of four ships. Again they recruited troops in New England, where the men of Connecticut were especially anxious to be rid of the Dutch, and in August the little force sailed into the Hudson and dropped anchor off the Battery. Colonel Richard Nicolls, already appointed deputy governor, called on Stuyvesant to surrender. The latter would have preferred to fight, but he was unpopular, and he was also unprepared for defense. Grumbling about the injustice of it all, he gave up without firing a shot. New Netherlands became New York, a proprietary colony of the Duke, and the English congratulated themselves that the biter was thus bitten.

Such a resolution of affairs was far less satisfactory to the Dutch, so late in the year they sent Michael de Ruyter out to attack Barbados, and in March 1665 they declared war. Begun over commercial and overseas rivalries, throughout the war there was continuing activity in Guiana and the West Indies, where the European combatants were already beginning the policy of swapping islands during hostilities and trading them back at the peace table. But the main theater of the war was in the waters off the European coast as the English and Dutch navies both moved joyously to resolve questions left hanging a decade earlier.

The British Navy had been significantly improved since the later days of the Protectorate, and if it did not have a Blake to command it, it did still have Monck, now the Duke of Albemarle, the Duke of York himself, and Prince Rupert, the aging but still active *beau sabreur* of Civil War days. Massing their fleet, a hundred strong, they sailed over to the Dutch coast immediately on the outbreak of war and blockaded the enemy in the Texel.

However, the Dutch too had made improvements. Supported by the virtual ruler of the country, the Grand Pensioner Jan de Witt, Admiral de Ruyter had built up the Dutch warships and restructured the naval administration. Ten years before the Dutch had armed merchantmen and used them to supplement their men-of-war. Now they had a regular naval fleet.

The sailing warship had truly come of age, for there had been a rapid evolution since Elizabethan times. The later Tudor men-of-war were perhaps ninety to a hundred feet long on the waterline and mounted a main battery of twenty guns, seldom more than that, even though a few of the "prestige" ships of the century had been huge—and unwieldy—monsters. Through the first half of the seventeenth century, however, ship design had progressed markedly. The Swedish *Vasa* of 1628, for example, built by a Dutchman, had fifty guns. She was swamped and sank on her maiden voyage, in the harbor of Stockholm. A sudden squall came up, and as she had been designed with her lower-deck gunports too close to the waterline, the seas came in the opened ports and took her down within minutes of her launching, showing that designers—even the Dutch, who were the best in the world—still had a great deal to learn.

By midcentury, though, much *had* been learned, and the ships of the Second Anglo-Dutch War were as fine as any wooden vessels ever built. The towering castles at bow and stern were cut down, while masts grew taller, carrying topgallant sails as well as courses and topsails. Fore and aft sails, called staysails because they were rigged on the stays holding the masts straight, also came into use. Most important, the number of guns rapidly increased. H.M.S. *Prince,* launched in 1670, carried a hundred guns, and ships were now classed according to their gunpower—first-rate more than ninety guns, second more than eighty, third more than fifty. Anything above a fifty-gunner was considered strong enough to lie in the battle line and was therefore called a "ship of the line." The rates went down to a sixth-rate, which had between six and eighteen guns.

With improved design and increased homogeneity of ships, there had grown up considerable disagreement in the British Navy about the best way to conduct a battle. The Fighting Instructions were rewritten and issued again in 1665, but they remained essentially warmed-over Robert Blake. Sailors generally agreed that a fleet should obtain the weather gauge and close with the enemy while maintaining a strict line-ahead formation with hundred-yard intervals between vessels. They had also learned that it was easiest to maintain station if the ships were close-hauled—that is, had the wind as near abeam as they could. This made the ship slow but easy to steer and maneuver and therefore to keep in station. That was where agreement ended, for at that point two schools grew up, and this divergence lasted as long as the age of sail.

One school, called the Formalists, insisted that the line ahead should be rigidly adhered to as long as the battle lasted, that both sides ought to match up ship for ship, sail along on parallel courses, and slug it out until one side or another had enough. For these people, keeping the line intact became the ultimate aim of the battle, for they believed that only the concentrated fleet could be effective; to borrow a land analogy, possession of the field was more important than defeat of the enemy in detail. The second school, called the Meleeists, believed that once the opposing fleets were ranged together, the line should be broken, ships bearing down individually on their opposite numbers, and then fighting it out as best they might. Rupert, who had made his reputation as a hell-for-leather cavalryman, and Monck, who was always a hard fighter, favored the melee; James, who was more conscious of the need to retain control over his fleet, was a Formalist. Over the years the Formalists tended to become the admirals; the Meleeists tended to win the battles.

In the first battle of the new war the Formalists got their chance. When the English withdrew from the Texel to replenish, the Dutch fleet under Admiral Jacob Opdam got out and headed north, intending to cut off a large English convoy returning home from the Baltic. It and James's fleet met off Lowestoft on June 3, and James, who was outnumbered but had heavier ships individually, maneuvered to bring about a formal line-ahead battle. Unfortunately, Opdam refused to cooperate, so that every time James got his line up to and alongside the Dutch, Opdam reversed his course, and the two fleets passed each other going in opposite directions. Matters might have gone on indefinitely and indecisively, but on the third pass the Dutch flagship was hit by a full broadside and blew up, taking its admiral with it. Several of the captains of ships immediately following panicked at this and hauled their ships out of line, creating a large gap in their center. James quickly abandoned his formal tactics and cut through the enemy line to surround the next portion of it, taking or sinking some thirty ships. The remainder of the Dutch beat a quick retreat, their withdrawal covered by Cornelis van Tromp, son of the great admiral. James thought he had sufficient glory for one day and failed to pursue, a decision that caused so much complaint that he eventually gave up his command and went ashore. The fleet went to Edward Montagu, the Earl of Sandwich.

In this case well begun was not half done, for the English spent the next year trying to make up for the peacetime deficiencies of the fleet, shortages of men and materials, and failures of command and communication that even victory had revealed. While they were shaking down, the Dutch welcomed home their annual Mediterranean convoy, and then De Ruyter slipped in from his Barbados expedition as well and took over command of the Dutch war effort. They also sent a squadron off to blockade the Strait of Gibraltar, paralyzing English trade in the Mediterranean. In August Sandwich chased a Dutch Baltic convoy into Bergen, then part of Denmark, and was fired on by the Danish batteries there. Britain responded by declaring war on Denmark, which meant not only another fleet to fight but also the closing off of the Baltic and its valuable trade, especially in naval stores. For all the reforms of the early Restoration period, the British were not doing too well.

Things got worse. During the summer of 1665 the plague raged in London, and British life and government came close to breaking down. Funds were very low, and at the start of the new year, a suddenly assertive France joined in the war as well, and the newborn fleet of Louis XIV sailed with the Dutch against the hard-pressed British.

The new season was not any better. Monck took the fleet to sea early in the summer of 1666, then divided it in the face of the French threat. With about sixty ships he remained at the lower end of the North Sea, but he sent Prince Rupert with twenty-five to guard the Atlantic end of the Channel against the arrival of a French squadron reported to be en route from the Mediterranean. Therefore, when De Ruyter came out on June 1, Monck was heavily outnumbered.

In the Four Days' Battle that followed, the English had far the worse of it. Their casualties were heavy, and they lost more than twice the ships their enemy did. Monck was glad to get away with what remained of a whole skin, and he took refuge in the lower Thames estuary, where De Ruyter blockaded him.

He was still not finished, though. Rapidly repairing his ships and making up his crews, he sallied forth six weeks later, caught De Ruyter off the North Foreland, and soundly trounced him to the tune of twenty ships lost. Monck broke the blockade and rampaged over to the Dutch shore, where he attacked and took or destroyed 160 Dutch merchantmen anchored in the Vlie Channel.

Hit in their pocketbooks, the Dutch were about ready to give up. However, the British were in even worse shape. The plague was in its final stages, there was grass growing in London streets, the treasury was exhausted. To cap it all, in September, London burned in the Great Fire. Among war, fire, and pestilence, many people in London thought the end of the world had come.

Faced with all this, the government made a disastrous decision. They decided that, with the war as good as over, they could save money by disbanding the fleet. Monck fumed and expostulated, but the great ships were brought inside the Thames and anchored in the Medway, a little tributary stream to the southeast of London. Masts and yards were sent down, crews dismissed, and the ships put in ordinary, as the term was then, or decommissioned. The peace talks dragged on through the spring of 1667, the British government all the while congratulating itself that it was saving money on the fleet.

In June they paid a higher price than money for their folly. De Ruyter took eighty ships to sea and came in to Britain at the Firth of Forth. He then systematically ravaged his way south for a week, playing havoc with the coastal trade, especially the coal carriers for London. On the tenth he landed troops at Sheerness and burned or made off with all the naval stores there. The next day he sent a squadron crashing through the boom at the mouth of the Medway. While London listened fearfully to the distant crash of Dutch guns, the Netherlanders boarded and took the flagship *Royal Charles* and left six other great men-of-war burning at their moorings. They then sailed triumphantly downstream with a trumpeter playing jaunty airs on the quarterdeck of their prize. For another six weeks, until the English signed a peace treaty, the Dutch fleet sat at ease in the Thames estuary, and the price of coal in London increased 1,000 percent.

The Treaty of Breda illustrated the connection between affairs in Europe and overseas, where colonial counters might be used to offset losses or gains on the Continent. With the Dutch fleet masters of the eastern coast of England, the British gave up Surinam in Guiana to the Netherlands and their claims on Acadia to the French. They did manage to hold on to New York, but they also agreed to modify the Navigation Acts in favor of the Dutch, so that the latter might import into England not only their own products, but also those of all the territories whose rivers drained through the Netherlands. A sadder but slightly wiser British government decided to pay its sailors and repair its fleet.

· While the mother country was busy with the Dutch wars, affairs in the Empire continued in an abstracted way. There was considerable growth, if not quite as rapid as in the previous half century, and there was expansion in significant new directions. Through the decade of the sixties, Charles granted a charter to a group of proprietors who established colonies south of Virginia in an area called Carolina, and in 1663 New Englanders and Virginians settled at the mouth of the Albemarle River. The initial intent was that in this subtropical climate,

Englishmen might produce silk, wine, fruits, and other items that up to now had to be imported from foreign territories, so Carolina was an experiment in mercantilism.

The trickle of emigration from England continued, and by 1670 there were settlers in South Carolina, and Quakers, in trouble with the government at home, moving into Pennsylvania. By now England was becoming more tolerant, except of Catholics and in particular radicals such as the Quakers, and all of the new charters of the Restoration period allowed for religious freedom. The population of the colonies was also growing more cosmopolitan, with Scots, Irish, very substantial numbers of Germans, and some French Huguenots coming in. The New Englanders proved especially prolific, and many new settlements were founded by people who were already colonials, moving on to better pickings. Given a choice between farming rocks in New England uplands or going to sea, many younger sons went to the Carolinas or the West Indies instead.

The colonists demonstrated their independence at an early stage. The Navigation Acts, though they had provisions designed to benefit the entire Empire, were written from the point of view of the mother country first, and the colonies suffered under some of their regulations. This was particularly true of New England, for the whole system was intended to create an overseas empire that would complement the home islands rather than compete with them. But in climate and therefore products, New England was competitive with, rather than complementary to, England. The most blatant difficulty was over customs revenues; the Navigation Acts required that all trade going outside the system be channeled through England. But Massachusetts traders saw no reason to make an Atlantic crossing when their most lucrative markets were in the new French islands of the West Indies or in Acadia. British customs officials in New England were constantly seizing cargoes and arresting ships' masters, who were then released without punishment by their own elected officials. As early as 1676 reports home recommended the suppression of the charters of Massachusetts, Connecticut, and Rhode Island. Not only that, but in places where government was not to their liking, the colonists were quite capable of taking matters in their own hands; in that same year Nathaniel Bacon led a rising in Virginia, against the corruption of the royal governor, Sir William Berkeley.

There were growing pains elsewhere, too. Jamaica began to make progress at last, after ten years of being a neglected military outpost.

The British islands of the Caribbean were hitting their stride as sugar producers, swallowing an enormous amount of manpower in the form of African slaves and indentured or transported white labor, both terms being euphemisms for slavery. These colonies were already far more valuable to Britain than were the mainland North American ones, and for the next century and a half the West Indies was the heart of the overseas part of the Empire. The pirates and buccaneers of the area enjoyed their last great heyday as well, and in 1671 Henry Morgan marched a ragtag force across the Isthmus and sacked Panama. He was a year too late, for in 1670 England and Spain had signed a treaty by which the British agreed to suppress piracy in the West Indies. The pirates were soon hounded out of the area, though Morgan himself did well. Instead of a short rope he got a knighthood and became deputy governor of Jamaica.

In the North there were still colonists trying, in the face of all odds, to make a living in Newfoundland. About five hundred were settled there by now, and they were perpetually feuding with the fishermen who came every season and outnumbered the locals by ten to one. In 1675 the government ordered that permanent settlements be abandoned, but it changed its mind when it realized that this would probably throw the island into the hands of the French. As the Grand Banks fishery remained one of the staple items of the British economy, that would never do. So the royal government reversed itself and encouraged settlement, and slowly a permanent colony took root among the rocks.

There was now development in the Far North as well. The French by this time were well settled along the valley of the St. Lawrence River and were sending out tentacles farther westward and to the north as they extended the fur trade. Two French traders, Radisson and Groseilliers, found a route from the top of Lake Superior over the height of land to the bottom of Hudson Bay. When they sought a charter from their own governor to develop the new area, they were shrugged off; they had failed to touch the right palms with the right coin. Disgruntled, they went off to Boston, then Paris, and finally London. Here at last they received sympathy, from Prince Rupert. A trading voyage went out in 1668, and in 1670 Charles granted a charter to the Hudson's Bay Company, destined, like the earlier East India Company, to become one of the great trading ventures of world history.

. The East India Company itself, which had survived only with the greatest difficulty during the Civil War and Protectorate period, now entered on its most prosperous era. Immediately on his restoration Charles had reissued its charter. Even more important, in 1662 the King married Catherine of Braganza, daughter of John IV of Portugal. As part of her dowry Catherine brought England possession of Tangier, giving England a base for Mediterranean operations, and Bombay on the western coast of India. The latter was an unhealthy spot, and in 1668 Charles gave it to the East India Company for an annual rent of ten pounds. It finally supplanted Surat and grew to be the main British foundation of western India. More immediately effective was the fact that Catherine brought with her from Portugal a large train and a taste for what the Portuguese regarded as civilized fashions among the backward English. All sorts of exotic eastern products were suddenly in demand as the court and society quickly adopted the ideas of the new Queen; she became the arbiter of English taste, and the East India Company profited from it.

The company was slowly becoming a major factor in the Indian equation, for in 1658, with the accession of Emperor Aurungzeb, the great Mogul Empire began its decline. For the next half century there were widespread revolts in the subcontinent, and the Mahratta Confederacy arose in central India, partly a Hindu reaction to the Moslem Moguls. The British began to fortify their posts, providing a modicum of security that made some Indians look to them as increasingly desirable and useful elements. The British remained uninterested in political control, but how long they could do so was problematic, especially after the arrival of the French. The latter, under the driving energy of Colbert, founded a French East India Company in 1664 and began a mercantilist effort in the Indian Ocean.

All of this imperial growth was gratifying and prosperous, and in spite of the plague and the fire of London, and the poor end to the Second Anglo-Dutch War, Englishmen had reason to be pleased with themselves. The ideas of the time recognized, however, that their empire and its trade was of value to others as well as themselves, and if they were going to keep what they had gained and hoped to gain in the future, they must fight for it. The Netherlands was at its peak of success after the Treaty of Breda, and it was clear to commercial and political men that that treaty could only be a truce. In 1672 the Third Anglo-Dutch War broke out.

The Third (and last) Anglo-Dutch War was but a small part of a complex and convoluted chain of events taking place in the 1670s. The major factor in this development was the emergence of a strong and aggressive France. That country, under Louis XIV and his ministers Colbert and Louvois, embarked on a policy of winning the ultimate hegemony of Europe. Over the next twenty years the British recognized that France was the new enemy, replacing Spain and Holland, but such recognition came slowly, and not to everyone at the same time.

In 1668 England had joined with Holland and Sweden in a treaty known as the Triple Alliance, which John de Witt engineered as a check to the growing French threat. Some of King Charles's ministers were glad to adhere to this, but Charles himself heard a different tune. He solved his chronic shortage of funds by signing, behind Parliament's and his own ministers' backs, the Treaty of Dover in 1670. In this he accepted a pension of £200,000 a year from France. In return he promised to go to war against the Dutch and that he and his brother James would openly convert to Catholicism as soon as possible, and that they would try to carry the country back to the old Church with them. Louis offered them six thousand French troops to help in the good work of conversion.

How serious anyone was about all this is problematical. James converted at once; Charles died a Roman Catholic in 1685, but he never did find a convenient moment to convert publicly. For his part, Louis was far more interested in sending his troops into the Netherlands than he was in using them as religious messengers in England. Joseph Stalin, who had cause to know, once remarked that treaties were like pie crust, made to be broken, and that remark surely applies to the Treaty of Dover.

Having isolated the Netherlands—for he bought the Swedes out of their alliance as well as the British—Louis sent 130,000 men marching across the frontier in 1672 and called on Charles to do his part. The British had already tried to intercept the annual Dutch convoy coming home from the Levant, but they muffed it. Now they and the French fleet, slightly less than a hundred strong, concentrated at Solebay.

At the end of May de Ruyter found them there, and though he was outnumbered four to three, he came in to attack. The Dutch had not wanted to fight this time, but having had war thrust upon them, they were determined to do their best. This day it proved good enough, for the French admiral, d'Estrees, immediately took his thirty-five ships scudding out of the fight. That left the British outnumbered by the Dutch, who handed them a severe beating before more English ships came up and turned a defeat into a draw. The Duke of York was twice chased off his ship by ferocious Dutch attacks, and Lord Sandwich was killed in the battle. Pleas of contrary winds and apologies from the French were not entirely convincing, and the word in the British fleet was that the French were not really there to fight, but just to see that the English earned their pay.

For the next year they earned little. James's handling of the Navy was vigorously attacked in Parliament, though the real problem was less that than his open Catholicism, and finally he was forced to give up his office, being replaced by the still active and always popular Prince Rupert. More and more Englishmen were beginning to think that they were fighting on the wrong side in the war, and there was a growing disinclination to carry matters to a conclusion. Nonetheless, in the early spring of 1673, Rupert sailed over and attacked De Ruyter off the Dutch coast, in pursuance of a proposed English invasion. The Dutch responded furiously, drove Rupert away, then followed him back to England and blockaded him in the Thames. This in turn was broken, not by the Anglo-French, but by an outbreak of plague aboard their ships, and by midsummer the Dutch were back on their own coast, in trouble once more.

John de Witt had meanwhile been replaced by William of Orange, the bankruptcy of De Witt's policy illustrated by his death, for an infuriated mob dragged him into the street and tore him to pieces. William of Orange assumed the office of Stadtholder and, asked if he had any alternative to De Witt's policy, replied, "To die fighting in the last ditch." The Dutch cut their dikes against the French armies and held on. In the fall of 1673 their East Indies convoy was due home, and De Ruyter sallied out to escort it in. He met the Anglo-French fleet off the Texel and quickly drove off the French contingent. The English made more of a fight of it, but by the time the French got back, the convoy was safely in shallow waters, and the Dutch made off, the clear victors in a difficult affair.

As far as the British were concerned, that was virtually the end of the war. Public opposition to it was rising to flood levels, King and ministers were both unpopular, and the sailors openly said they were fighting the wrong people. Early in the new year, 1674, Charles signed a peace treaty with William of Orange, and the English dropped out. Louis fought on until 1678, but what he could not do with help he could not do without it, and eventually the war petered out, with the King of France's ambitions still unslaked.

Domestic affairs took precedence in England for the next several years. This was a period of resurgent political Catholicism, between the real menace of Louis XIV abroad and the artificial one of Titus Oates and the Popish Plot at home, and Englishmen got very excited, to the tune of riots and executions, over what they perceived as threats to the established order. In the closing years of Charles's reign, the matter settled around the question of the succession. The King had produced no legitimate heirs, and therefore the throne ought to pass, on his death, to his brother James. In himself James was not objectionable, but his Catholicism was. There had not been a Roman Catholic on the throne since Mary Tudor, and she was firmly enshrined in the public memory as "Bloody Mary." Therefore, in the late seventies factions grew up known as "Exclusionists" and "Abhorrers." The former wanted to exclude James from the line of succession, and eventually they became the Whigs; the latter abhorred the idea of tampering with the succession and finally evolved into the Tories. Charles himself fought a very clever rear-guard action, and when he died early in 1685 the crown passed undamaged to James.

Three years of turmoil followed. James had been a fairly competent Lord High Admiral; as a King he was so disastrous that historians have suggested his mind was failing prematurely. He was determined, against even the advice of the Pope, to bring some relief to English Catholics, and in seeking to do so, he rapidly alienated all shades of opinion, even that of the Catholics themselves, who feared that his excesses were going to land them in serious trouble and who generally preferred the sleeping-dog policy.

Once more the problem was perceived in terms of succession. James was an old man; in his younger days he had married an English Protestant lady, Anne Hyde, daughter of the Earl of Clarendon. They had had two children; the elder, Mary, married William of Orange, now Stadtholder of the Netherlands and the Protestant champion of Europe, and the younger, Anne, wed George of Denmark, another safe Protestant. After the death of his first wife, James had then married a Catholic princess, Mary of Modena, in 1673, after he himself had converted to the old faith.

From the point of view of the people who ran England, they could put up with James for a few years, sure in the knowledge that they would win in the long run; for on his death the crown would pass to Mary, the elder daughter, and Protestantism be safe once again. As James went on his rambunctious way, they gritted their teeth and waited their turn. Then, at the start of 1688, it was announced that Mary of Modena was pregnant. Leaders of English affairs received the news with dread; if the baby were a girl, all was well, for she would be but third in line for the throne; if it were a boy, he would take precedence, and there would be both a Catholic succession and a promise of continuation of James's policies. Seldom has the prospective sex of a child been of more interest to more people.

For this had ceased to be simply an English question. William of Orange was naturally vitally concerned. If his wife became Queen of England, he might expect to dominate English policy and use the country at least as an ally in his lifelong struggle against Louis XIV of France. For the same reason the French were equally interested in the matter. Many people believed it was all a Catholic plot, that the Queen was not pregnant at all but rather was parading around with a pillow in her dress, and when the baby was born, the Whigs spread the rumor that it was not hers but had been smuggled into the palace in a warming pan. On June 10, 1688, the birth took place, and all over England men anxiously counted the number as the salutes roared out. A girl rated twenty-one, but a prince, a new heir, got a hundred. As the twenty-second round fired, Englishmen looked at each other and wondered what they were in for now.

Less than three weeks later a letter was sent to William of Orange inviting him to come to England to save the country from the tyranny of a Roman Catholic regime. As he himself had engineered the dispatch of the letter—his agents had been visiting leading Whigs all summer—he made suitable expressions of surprise and accepted with alacrity. He immediately went to the States-General of the Netherlands and asked their permission and support for an operation to put him on the English throne. They dragged their feet; Louis XIV was about to march, and they feared a new French invasion. However, Louis' ministers misjudged the affair; they assumed William would get involved in a civil war in England and that this distraction would allow them a free hand farther south, in the Rhineland. They set their armies marching eastward. As soon as the Dutch knew that, they knew they were safe, and at the end of October, with fourteen thousand troops aboard his fleet, William sailed down the English Channel for the English coast.

As the Dutch fleet sailed through the narrows, no one knew what might happen. English and Dutch had been rivals for a generation, and their fleets had seldom met without fighting. But this time the Protestant wind that pushed William along kept the English ships in harbor, unable and unwilling to beat out against it and give battle. On November 5, the Dutch anchored off Torbay and began landing their forces.

James moved slowly to meet William, but James's army dwindled away. His supporters came in to make their excuses—illness, family affairs, and so on; one by one they left his camp and showed up a few days later making their obeisance to William of Orange. James returned to London, sent Mary of Modena and the baby prince off to France, and on December 11, he left himself. Even then the tragicomedy was not finished; the King was arrested at Sheerness and sent back to the capital, where everyone realized what an embarrassment he was. He spent one night in his palace guarded by Dutch soldiers; the next morning he walked down steps to a barge and sailed away. This time there was no awkward mistake; no one interfered. James heard Christmas Mass, an exile, at Ambleteuse in France. In England a convention Parliament declared that by leaving the kingdom, James had vacated his throne, and they offered it to Mary and William, who graciously accepted. The key to England's treasure was unlocked, and William and his Dutch advisers rubbed their hands with glee. They could now throw the greatest Protestant power in Europe into the lists against France.

It was almost exactly a century since Tudor warships had swept out into the Channel to challenge the assembled might of the Spanish Armada, and almost two since John Cabot had sailed off from Bristol in little *Matthew* to find Newfoundland. What had been accomplished in that time?

England itself had been through religious and political revolution, the death of one dynasty, the rupture of another. The country had been barely on the fringes of Europe in the late fifteenth century, and not much more at the center of it in 1588. Philip's great armada was not too different from Darius's invasion of Greece, a mighty force sent to chastise some upstarts beyond the frontier. By 1688 England had become one of half a dozen of the major states of Europe, and rather than seeking alliances and trailing her coat through French or Spanish courts, she herself was eagerly sought after as one of the dominant factors of the political balance. The world scene looked good to Englishmen in 1689.

They now had an empire as well. Hesitant and often unsuccessful as their early ventures had been, they had slowly taken root. There were English traders from Hudson's Bay to Spanish America, and solid blocks of settlement in the West Indies and along the Eastern Seaboard of North America. The white gold of the West Indies poured into England, and sugar magnates bought estates in the country and lived like minor kings, while many a London merchant could have bought and sold a half dozen German princes. There were ships flying the British flag all over the seas, on the fishing banks off Newfoundland, off the Guinea coast of Africa, in the Baltic and the Mediterranean, and along the coasts of India. In the great subcontinent the East India Company was gradually insinuating itself into the Indian equation, its goods and its influence sought by princes of political ambition. Of the five great colonial empires—Portuguese, Spanish, Dutch, British, and French—it was now the British that was most clearly on the way up.

Finally, tying a self-confident and assertive mother country to the empire that was an essential source of her wealth and strength, there was the Royal Navy, which was now an integral part of the national picture. Refined and reformed through successive reigns, it was Britain's first line of offense or defense, its ships well built and numerous, its officers and men reflecting the national mood of confident power. The Navy had discovered, largely by evolution rather than by conscious theorizing, its role in the national life, and the way to perform that role. Protecting trade, convoying the merchant fleets, and putting down piracy were day-to-day activities. In time of war the thing was to meet the enemy fleet and smash it if possible, if not to blockade it in port and watch it waste away. Such tasks were not easy, and the lessons would have to be relearned from generation to generation. But occasionally corrupt or abused or hard-pressed though it might be, the Royal Navy would never again see its flagships burned with impunity by the Dutch, or be spoken of slightingly by the Venetian ambassador as of no account.

So the essential links had been forged, the connections made. And none too soon. Those white-coated regiments of Louis XIV marching into the Rhineland were opening pawns in a game that was to last more than a century. At one point they would plant French banners on the Pyramids and the walls of Europe's cities from Lisbon to Moscow. But in that same period, while Frenchmen tried to conquer Europe, Englishmen would conquer the world. The struggle now beginning was ultimately for nothing less.

PART TWO

TOWARD THE ZENITH

5

"Three Cheers for King Billy . . . !"

. . . the most conspicuous success the French have ever gained at sea over the English. . . .
—Admiral Mahan

It would be difficult to imagine two characters more dissimilar than William of Orange and Louis XIV. The former was in his late thirties when he came to the English throne. Born a posthumous son, he had led a fragile existence for many years, partly because of poor health and partly because of his delicate political position. In 1672, on the collapse of John de Witt's policy, he had been called to the leadership of the Netherlands and discovered his great mission in life, the thwarting of France's ambitions. By 1689 he was at the height of his powers, a mature and cunning statesman but not a man to whom people warmed. Reserved by nature, he had learned by experience to keep his own counsel, and he might well, like his great-grandfather, have been called "William the Silent." He was never popular in England—rather, he was recognized as necessary—and he was suffered because his subjects wanted his wife as Queen; Mary's early death in 1694 hurt his political position. Nonetheless, what he wanted was what politically important Englishmen realized was desirable, and Parliament usually gave him most of what he asked for—in return for concessions that ultimately established the supremacy of Parliament in the national life. He himself did not care much for England, and less for Parliament, but he was primarily interested in his wars with France and in getting

English men, money, and ships to fight with. A poor field commander who got beaten in battle more often than not, he has gone down in history as steadfast, determined, and unexciting.

Things were quite different across the Channel in France. When Louis XIV moved, trumpets blew. The essential preliminary to empire was a strong mother country, with a viable economy and political system able to sustain long-distance operations. This had been achieved in Europe first by Portugal, then by Spain, and then concurrently by England and the Netherlands. France had been slow. The country had been late uniting, and for more than a century it had been wracked by religious or civil wars. In the intervals between these conflicts occasional Frenchmen had acquired bits of empire, and chartered companies had been set up to carry French goods and Bourbon power overseas, but their efforts had been intermittent and only marginally successful. Then the coming of age of Louis XIV changed all that.

Louis was born in 1638, and he succeeded his father five years later. For nearly twenty years, however, France was run by Cardinal Mazarin, Louis' mother's adviser, probable lover, and quite possible husband. It was not until 1661 that the King took over affairs in his own right. Louis saw himself, and was seen by his subjects, as the visible embodiment of France and of France's glory and destiny. Frenchmen had suffered a century of strife and troubles, and they were more than willing to resign power and responsibility into the hands of a sovereign capable of wielding them. It was no accident that Louis took the sun as his emblem. His father's great minister, Richelieu, had worked to make the crown supreme in France, and France supreme in Europe. He had not succeeded, but Louis intended to finish his work. He carried forward the growth of the bureaucracy and the central power, he destroyed the pretensions of the Church and the nobility, and he built Versailles as a showpiece for his glory. With his internal house in order, he embarked on conquest, initially of the Rhine frontier, eventually on much more than that.

Louis' first foreign adventure was in the late 1660s, the so-called War of the Devolution, thwarted by an alliance of England, Holland, and Sweden. He then bought the former and latter out of it, and in 1672 began the Dutch War, with the British on his side. This lasted until 1678, though the British dropped out after two years. Both of these wars had been directed toward France's northern frontier. In the next decade Louis turned his attention to the east and began meddling in the politics of the petty Rhineland states, a fertile ground for French politicians for well over a thousand years. It was also during these years that Louis, apparently under the growing influence of his mistress, Madame de Maintenon—she was a creature of the still vehemently anti-Protestant Jesuits, who believed the end justified the means—and of his war minister, Louvois, began the task of destroying French Protestantism in the name of Catholic unity. Louis was not, until the last decade of his life, a particularly religious man. He was rather the archetypal practitioner of the theory of absolute state supremacy, and he therefore thought that his own religion ought to be that of his subjects. His view was "one state, one religion, one king," the seventeenth century's equivalent of *"Ein Reich, ein Volk, ein Führer."*

So it was that when William of Orange, now William III of England, took his new country into the War of the League of Augsburg in May 1689, he was the leader both of an anti-French and an anti-Catholic alliance. It was not that long, after all, since the Popish plot, and James's Catholicism had been instrumental in his downfall. Anglican pulpits and Whig pamphleteers alike thundered death and destruction, and the British embarked on the best kind of war, one intended both to bring profit and satisfy conscience.

Not everyone entirely agreed with this, though. There was a revolt in Scotland, which still cherished residual loyalties to the exiled Stuarts, and a far more serious rising in Ireland. The exiled James landed there in March 1689, and the Irish, habitually unable to resist backing a loser, rose up for him and the Catholic faith. He entered Dublin in triumph, besieged Protestant Londonderry for three months, and set the island in an uproar. It was 1690 before William could turn his attention to this problem, but then he landed with thirty-five thousand steady troops and marched over the island like a plague of locusts. On July 1 his forces met the Irish Army of James at the Battle of the Boyne. As usual, the disciplined manner of the former, not to mention their eightfold superiority in artillery, was better than the untrained valor of the latter, and the Boyne destroyed James's real hope of holding Ireland, though it took another year of heavy fighting before the English wrapped up the campaign. The Battle of Aughrim, the final battle, was fought on July 12, 1691. One of the conditions of the subsequent Pacification of Limerick was that Irish officers and soldiers were free to immigrate to France, thus beginning the long saga of the Wild Geese, the Irish brigades in the French Army. It was a time when religion was as important as nationality; James's bastard son, the

English Catholic Duke of Berwick, became a Marshal of France, and William's field commander at the Boyne, Schomberg, was an exiled French Huguenot.

With his own kingdom secure at last, William could turn his attention to the Continent. In terms of results he would have done better to stay home, for fighting the regular armies of France was far less rewarding than taking on untrained Irish levies. In fact, by this time, France, thanks to a series of reforming ministers, was so obviously the first power in Europe that she more than held her own. A wide-ranging coalition of Spain, England, the Netherlands, the Hapsburg Empire, and a whole host of lesser German states was still unable to restrain her energies. Most of England's fighting on land was in the Low Countries, and here William repeatedly was defeated by superior French tactics and leadership. He was battered out of his entrenchments at Steenkerke and routed at Neerwinden. Not until he captured Namur in 1695 could he finally tote up a minor success, and it was virtually his only one of the war. The next year he secretly opened peace negotiations with Louis, and in 1697 the war ended by a general treaty, the Peace of Ryswick.

Far more important things happened at sea, and in terms of naval and imperial conflict the War of the League of Augsburg is a halfway house between the catch-as-catch-can affairs of the earlier period of empire and the struggles that immediately followed it, when there was something approaching world war, and a slowly dawning recognition of the connection between continental and imperial affairs.

For the Royal Navy, it might well have been a time of dire peril. The British, having taken the measure of the Dutch, had then been thoroughly distracted by the domestic problems that culminated in the Glorious Revolution. Therefore, when England went to war early in 1689, her Navy was far less prepared for serious battle than it might, or ought to have been, a condition that was to be repeated with distressing regularity for two and a half centuries. Not only was her Navy outnumbered by the French, but also a good part of it had to be sent over to Ireland. It was British naval vessels that raised the siege of Londonderry and that kept control of the Irish Sea for the passage of William's army. This necessarily left the Channel Fleet in a weakened state, and never before at a worse time.

When he assumed control of the French government, Louis turned over matters of finance, economy, and maritime affairs to his first minister, Jean Baptiste Colbert, and this remarkable man effected

a revolution in French seapower. Surveying the world economic scene
of the 1660s, he saw that the French Navy was inconsequential, that
France's infant colonies were languishing, that most of their trade was
carried by the Dutch, and that where Dutch merchant vessels were
counted in the thousands, France's were numbered only in the dozens.
All this was anathema to a thoroughgoing mercantilist, and Colbert,
who seems never to have slept but simply to have moved from office to
office, determinedly set about the reconstruction of the French imperial system. Unlike the haphazard English practice of independent
growth by private enterprise, the French proceeded from first principles. Colbert created or revived chartered companies and gave them
state subsidies and monopolies—for India, the Levant, the West
Indies, and North America. He built new ports and shipyards,
again with lavish subsidies; he imported the best ship designers and
builders he could get; he set up a marine register of seamen and officers; and he supervised the growth of the French marine from top to
bottom.

The result was that the merchant fleet grew remarkably, and the
Navy, which had numbered a mere twenty small ships in 1661, was by
the 1680s, when Colbert left office, bigger and better built than the
British and Dutch navies combined. Here was a classic example of big
government at work, and it seemed to work very well.

There were flaws in this approach, however, and one of them was
crucial. Louis XIV was not especially interested in ships and the sea.
He was a land animal, and as time went on, he became more interested
in the War Minister, Louvois, and his soldiers, and less interested in
what a navy might do for him. To him the Rhine was always more attractive than the Channel. Colbert fought against this tendency, but
not, ultimately, successfully. He collected plans and illustrations to
show Louis, and he had models built to sail on the pools of Versailles.
Once he arranged a tour of a shipyard; all the materials for a complete
ship of the line had been collected and prepared in advance, and while
the King and his courtiers watched from a gaily covered pavilion, an
entire ship was built, rigged, armed, and launched in the space of a
day. The King and his jaded court found this an amusing spectacle,
but it did not do much to develop an understanding of maritime potential.

Setting aside the King's preference for pursuing *la gloire* on land,
the French were still in a position on the outbreak of war to do the
English harm. It was they who landed James in Ireland, and seven
thousand French troops along with him, and had the French admirals

had their way, they might well have cut the British off from the restive island and thus changed the course of world history. But the royal policies, and preoccupation with affairs nearer home, turned an invasion into a raid—and James back into an exile.

If the French strategy was shortsighted, the English response was almost equally ill-directed. They not only had ships around Ireland, which was a necessity, but they also sent squadrons for convoy duty in the Mediterranean, but more to watch the French squadron of Admiral Château-Renault in Toulon. Unfortunately for them, he got out past them, cleared through Gibraltar, and joined the main French fleet under the great Admiral Tourville at Brest. In the summer of 1690, the British Admiral Torrington, in command of an Anglo-Dutch Channel fleet of only fifty-five ships, suddenly found himself face to face with a fleet of seventy-five French ships, almost all of them individually better than his own.

Torrington was a competent sailor if not a great one, and he proposed to counter the French essentially by avoiding battle, by keeping his fleet "in being." The concept, original with him, holds that as long as a fleet is in existence, it must remain the primary worry of an enemy, who is not therefore free to pursue other objectives, such as a cross-Channel invasion. This sensible view, however, was not shared by Torrington's superiors. England was in a desperate state, with campaigns afoot both in Scotland and Ireland, with no man entirely sure where his neighbor's loyalties lay, and with a new King and Queen very insecurely seated on their thrones. Queen Mary herself wrote to Torrington and told him he must fight if the slightest opportunity offered. He lay at anchor with his fleet divided into three squadrons, one Dutch and two English, off Beachy Head east of the Isle of Wight, and waited for the French to appear.

They did at the end of June. Tourville took his fleet out of Brest, the van commanded by the celebrated privateer Jean Bart, the rear by Château-Renault. Jean Bart as a young man had sailed into the Thames with De Ruyter and had now convinced the French that what the Dutch had done the French might do even better. A coarse, uncouth genius at irregular warfare, he had gained the ear of the King, and he blew like a fresh ocean breeze through the stuffy halls of Versailles. Here now was the first great test for Colbert's naval creation.

When the two fleets met on June 30, Torrington had worked out a plan that would give him the odds in spite of the three to two French numerical superiority. He had the wind; the French were sailing in line ahead, a little west of north. Torrington came up on them, with Dutch Admiral Evertsen leading the van. The British admiral strengthened his rear at the expense of his center, and he ordered Evertsen to lie off a little from the line of advance. In this way the heavier British concentration ought to be able to mass against the French rear, while the more distant Dutch could handle the French van. It was an admirable plan, and it went all wrong. Evertsen either misunderstood Torrington's signals or disregarded them. He went bowling along and ended up taking on the French center and van all by himself. To make a bad matter worse, the wind then shifted in the French favor and allowed Tourville to double back. Instead of the allies massing on the French rear, the French concentrated on the Dutch van, and the results were disastrous. Most of the Dutch ships were sunk, taken, or destroyed, and the French then were able to turn on the English. Torrington took a bad beating, and late in the afternoon he escaped only by ordering his ships suddenly to drop anchor. They did so, and the swift-flowing tide and current carried the French out of range to leeward before they realized what was happening. Torrington beat a hasty retreat into the Thames estuary, where he heaved a sigh of relief, happy to get away without being totally destroyed.

It is now generally agreed that by saving his fleet Torrington prevented an invasion of England. Public opinion at the time saw it differently. The militia was called out, the buoys were taken up along the coast and the Thames, and Torrington was relieved of command and lodged in the Tower of London. A court-martial later acquitted him, but William was sure he had sacrificed the Dutch fleet for his own and never trusted or employed him again.

The summer passed in an agony of expectation, but the French did not try their luck. William won the Boyne the day after Beachy Head; there were the usual complications in the Low Countries; the English fleet, though battered, was still there; and so the season was frittered away. Troops were not immediately available, and the French went off after convoys, most of which they missed. With the coming of autumn, the fleets were laid up for the bad weather, and it was time to relax again.

The next year passed while the British and their Dutch allies desperately made good their losses, and built up their fleets as they should have done earlier. They gained this breathing space largely because the French permitted it. The new French Minister of Marine, Pontchartrain, admittedly knew nothing at all about ships and less about directing a navy. All he really knew was that the King must be obeyed, a fact he repeatedly conveyed to Louis' admirals, who knew in turn that even the King could not order wind and tide and weather. And knew also that melting down the King's silver services to raise money did not make up for incompetent administration of the Navy. By 1692 the tide of war had definitely turned in favor of the British.

When Louis ordered preparations for an invasion of England that summer, therefore, just about everything went awry. Tourville was peremptorily directed to get to sea on April 25, which meant sailing with only forty-four ships, before the Toulon or Rochefort squadrons joined him. The idea was that he would catch the English and Dutch unprepared this early in the season, defeat them, and then convoy James and an army across to England. What he found instead was that Admiral Russell and sixty-three ships of the line had already joined with the Dutch Admiral van Almonde and thirty-six more. When the wind finally allowed them to get up the Channel, the French were outnumbered by better than two to one.

Nonetheless, on May 29, Tourville sailed boldly in and attacked the allied fleet. It was a cast either of desperation or defiance; Tourville's orders allowed no discretion, to such an extent that they cast doubt on both his competence and his courage. On the English side most of the leading admirals—Russell, George Rooke, and Carter— were all suspected of plotting with the exiled James, and so foolhardy did the French attack appear that the Dutch were sure they were about to be betrayed by their allies. They were wrong; the English were as anxious to prove themselves as the French were, and the result was a bitterly fought battle.

With the wind behind him, Tourville came down in line abreast, all his ships together. The allied fleet, in several divisions, awaited his coming. Then, just as the ships were within musket range, the wind dropped. The French were forced to hoist out boats and haul their ships around so their broadsides would bear on the enemy, and for a time the battle of the great ships was overshadowed by small-boat action between the lines as launches and pinnaces and gigs fought a miniature melee. Gradually the lines drifted close, and the great ships ground together, giving each other one broadside after another. The allies lapped around both ends of the French line and slowly, as the day wore on, threatened them with encirclement. A sea battle in a fluky wind was like a pavane, with ships slowly moving in and out of each other's range, going at different speeds depending upon how they lay in relation to wind and current, the whole complicated and obscured by the black powder smoke that hung in the air. To observers on the nearby headlands of France, there was but a huge cloud of smoke, with masts sticking out of it and occasionally falling and disappearing into it, and every half hour or so some beaten hulk would come creeping out of the murk, masts by the board and bulwarks shattered, perhaps a launch with dog-tired sailors towing her out of gun range.

The French, stung in their pride, more than held their own, and by the time the two fleets drifted apart at the end of the day, neither side had lost a ship to the other. The French thought they had won a moral victory, but unfortunately for them, that was not enough. The Dutch had not been closely engaged, and the allies therefore, even after withdrawing all the badly hurt English ships, were still far more numerous than their enemies. Over the next two or three days several of the harder-fought French ships were run aground on the coast around Barfleur and La Hogue—the battle is known by the names of either—and burned by the allies. In this way the French lost fifteen of their ships on the line. The English and Dutch then turned on the transports collected for James's army and rampaged along the coast of the Cherbourg Peninsula, destroying the invasion vessels with impunity.

La Hogue should not have been a disaster for France. The sailors had fought magnificently, and Tourville and his captains had every reason to pride themselves on their handling of the fleet. Admiral Russell, in the fashion of the time, wrote to his French counterpart and congratulated him on his performance. But at Versailles they were plunged into despair. Losing fifteen ships, Louis and Pontchartrain forgot that they had a hundred more. And like most men to whom the sea is not a natural element, they also forgot that ships were not an end in themselves but were made to be fought, and if necessary, lost. La Hogue, which ought to have been a triumph for French courage, was transformed into a turning point from which the French Navy never recovered. Louis gave up any thought of mastering the Channel or of invading England. He turned his back on the Navy and henceforth accepted that at sea the English must be masters, the French no more than second-rate challengers. Though his successors might occasionally attempt to reverse that decision, they had an uphill struggle for the next century and more. An otherwise inconsequential battle, with unimportant losses on either side, became a victory in the best Clause-witzian terms—a victory over the mind of the enemy.

None of which was to say that the French were finished, or about to give up the game completely. The next year Tourville swept down on the English Smyrna convoy, and harrying Rooke's escort unmerci-fully, took two of the British warships and ninety-two—nearly a quar-ter—of the merchant vessels in the fleet. Jean Bart returned to his old privateering game, disgusted with French officialdom, and romped along the Dutch coast, sinking Dutch ships of war and recapturing a hundred French grain vessels recently taken by the Netherlanders. Still, commerce warfare, as Mahan loftily pronounced, is the recourse of the inferior power, and for the rest of the war the Channel was English, William sat secure on his throne, and James resigned himself to exile.

These European dynastic conflicts were soon to be extended over-seas as British and French power was firmly established, and their ri-valry spread, to Africa, India, and the Caribbean. But by the 1690s there was only one serious overseas theater, in North America. Here already small groups of men were overcoming incredible natural ob-stacles in their eagerness to kill each other. The prototypes of such men were a New Englander, Sir William Phips, and a Frenchman, Pierre le Moyne, Sieur d'Iberville.

There are essentially three eastern gateways to the heart of the North American continent. One is Hudson Bay, in the Far North and hampered by climate. The second is up the Hudson and out through the river and lake system to the Great Lakes. Both of these, by the end of the seventeenth century, were in the possession of the English. But the third and greatest of them all, the St. Lawrence River, was claimed and settled by France, and ultimately the fate of the continent was de-cided along its shores.

French settlement of this potentially enormous empire had pro-ceeded only sporadically, in the rare intervals of peace at home during the sixteenth and seventeenth centuries. The original claim dated from the voyages of Jacques Cartier, made in the 1530s. These resulted in nothing more than an abortive attempt to found a colony at Quebec. France then got tangled up in the Wars of Religion, and little was done until they ended with the accession of Henry IV and his decision that Paris was worth a Mass. At the turn of the century Samuel de Cham-plain took up Cartier's work, and settlements were founded both at

Port Royal, in what the French called Acadia and the English Nova Scotia, and at Quebec again. Within a decade the French had traced the routes from Quebec as far as Lake Champlain to the south and Georgian Bay to the west, turning the first pages of the great fur trade saga.

Champlain's work overseas was paralleled by that of Cardinal Richelieu at home, and when he achieved power in the 1620s, he resolutely backed further attempts to develop overseas connections. Companies were founded not only to pursue the fur trade in New France, but to settle islands in the West Indies as well. Richelieu thought big, and the Company of the Hundred Associates was granted all the land between Florida and the Arctic Circle; the fact that Englishmen were already settled on substantial portions of this did not seem of any importance to the French. By the time the cardinal passed from the scene, the French were firmly based on the St. Lawrence, and through the century they pushed farther and farther into the interior. In 1682 Robert de la Salle reached the mouth of the Mississippi and grandly claimed the entire valley in the name of Louis of France.

Still, the work of making good these claims proceeded fitfully. The settlements around Quebec were secure by midcentury, but most of the exploratory work was done by the settlers-become-fur-traders themselves. Frenchmen at home were preoccupied with the Thirty Years' War, then the civil disturbances known as the Frondes, and then finally with Louis XIV's wars. Two other misfortunes dogged the empire. One was that the French, unlike the English, did not think they had a surplus of population at home. There was little push to send out colonies, and those who left "the beautiful land of France" often did so grudgingly. Perhaps even more important, the French conceived of their North American Empire not as a settlement empire, full of small peasant farmers, but as a commercial enterprise. They needed a base, true, but no more than a base. Beyond that they wanted the great forests left alone for the fur trade. They were more interested in converting and trading with the Indians than in dispossessing them, as their English counterparts were doing. In its claims the French Empire was very impressive; in actuality it was exceedingly thin on the ground.

The immensity of the continent was still not enough to keep French and English from disliking each other's presence. English claims were as all-embracing as the French, and the seaboard colonies had been given grants that ran all the way to the Pacific Coast, however far that might be. As early as 1628 an English expedition had sailed up and occupied Port Royal and Quebec, this when Buckingham was failing before La Rochelle, but nothing permanent had come of it. By 1689, however, when the League of Augsburg War broke out, both groups were ready to fight. To complicate matters for history students, the North American counterparts of all these European wars have different names; in the English colonies this was called King William's War.

Recognizing that they were outnumbered, the French took the offensive. Except for the tribes of western New York, the Five Nations or the Iroquois, the Indians sided with the French, not from any great prescience, but simply because of long familiarity with French traders, French priests, and French brandy. The colony's effort was directed by Count Frontenac, who was the only reinforcement Louis XIV could spare, and the best he could have sent. Fighting began with an Iroquois raid on the village of Lachine, but a few miles from Montreal, in midsummer of 1689. The French responded by encouraging Indian raids on the frontier settlements of New England and New York. Through the winter of early 1690 they terrorized settlers and wiped out garrisons and civilians alike at towns such as Schenectady in New York, Haverhill in Massachusetts, and Dover in New Hampshire. This was bloody and remorseless warfare, with soldiers ambushed, homesteads burned, women and children butchered or marched off to captivity and worse in the dead of winter.

If the French and their Indian allies were masters of the forest depths, the English thought in terms of blue water even then. Besides providing a few troops for New York and convoying ships home, the British did little to help. Therefore, under the leadership of Sir William Phips, the colonists reacted by themselves. Phips had been born in the district of Maine, as that part of Massachusetts north of New Hampshire was known. He had made a fortune, and earned a title for himself, by finding a Spanish treasure wreck in the Caribbean and getting its cargo to England, so he was practically the first of that characteristic New England type, the successful jack-of-all-trades. To the men of the time military matters were not especially arcane, and since Phips could find treasure, he ought to be able to beat Frenchmen.

Certainly taking Port Royal, up in Acadia, did nothing to contradict this view. The settlement was at most marginal, with perhaps a thousand people spread out over a hundred miles of dike and meadowland along the Bay of Fundy shore. Habitually neglected by France and living a subsistence life, the Acadian farmers wanted little more than to be left alone, a modest ambition that ultimately destroyed them. When Phips' squadron appeared in the Annapolis Basin off Port Royal, they responded by hastily surrendering. The English plundered the settlement, left a garrison, and looked for new worlds to conquer.

Port Royal was pretty marginal, and Quebec was obviously the root of all the trouble, so the northern colonies, thinking big, decided upon a two-pronged attack against the center of French power, an idea that was to be repeated regularly for the next sixty years. One expedition would proceed from Albany to Montreal, with Connecticut and New York state troops. Meanwhile, Massachusetts and the other northern colonies would send Phips and a fleet up the St. Lawrence to Quebec City itself.

This ambitious project proved far beyond the reach of the colonies at this stage of their development. It began well, with both forces finally under way in August. Yet both faced far more potent enemies than the French, for smallpox and dysentery, those great wasters of early modern armies, were soon at work among them. The land expedition was heavily dependent on the Iroquois, but smallpox hit them even harder than it did the Europeans, and instead of eighteen hundred men as promised, they mustered about fifty. By late August the expedition was back once more in Albany, having done nothing but raid the village of La Prairie, which was burned to the ground and its inhabitants slaughtered.

Meanwhile, Phips' squadron made a leisurely but uncomfortable passage north around Nova Scotia and into the mouth of the St. Lawrence, where they encountered bad winds and worse currents. Not until the first week of October did they anchor before Quebec City, a few hours after Governor Frontenac had arrived from Montreal with two thousand soldiers. The upstart New England nobleman and the arrogant French aristocrat glared at each other from deck and battlement.

Phips immediately demanded the surrender of the city and the colony. Frontenac replied that he would let his cannon answer for him and that if the English wanted his fortress, they were welcome to try to take it. For good measure he added that he thought William of Orange was a usurper and the New Englanders rebels against their lawful king, James Stuart, a jibe that was wasted on rock-ribbed Protestants such as these. In fact, Phips was far too weak to take by force what he could not get by bluster. He got some troops ashore, and they stayed there for four days and bitter October nights. Most of the naval ammunition was uselessly fired against the stone walls of Quebec, and when the soldiers were reembarked they went aboard their boats in a panic, which caused the French considerable satisfaction and no small amusement. After a week, the little fleet sailed dejectedly away, and smallpox, dysentery, and storms accompanied them all the way back to Boston, where their failure was attributed by Cotton Mather to a lack of religious conviction. It was all, he thought, God's punishment on New England for allowing an Anglican church to be built in Puritan Boston. Phips survived the disgrace and was soon appointed Governor of Massachusetts, just in time to be saddled with the Salem witch trials.

Pierre le Moyne took to the woods as naturally as his New England counterpart took to the water. A native Québecois, the third son of a wealthy seigneurial family, he had obtained a commission as a junior officer in the French Navy, made several voyages abroad, and returned home to New France in 1685. The next year he joined an expedition for Hudson Bay. This was three years before war broke out in Europe, but the French were playing the "no peace beyond the line" game, and they were determined to undo the mistake of Radisson and Grosseilleurs; their expedition was to reclaim the Hudson Bay area for France, and not at all incidentally, its fur trade for themselves. Seventeenth-century patriotism was expected to yield tangible rewards.

The first expedition started the Sieur d'Iberville on his career as one of the great North American practitioners of mobile warfare and perhaps the greatest irregular warrior this continent has ever produced. The force, commanded initially by the Chevalier de Troyes, consisted of thirty French regulars and seventy Canadian volunteers. They left Quebec in March, went up the St. Lawrence to Montreal, and then, on snowshoes, started up the valley of the Ottawa River, five hundred miles to the source of the river at Lake Temiskaming. They then had another hundred-mile hike across the height of land to Lake Abitibi. There they built canoes, then paddled three hundred miles farther, down the Abitibi River. It took them eighty-five days of unremitting labor, and only the strength of their officers kept them going. With the northern spring coming on, they were wet more often than dry, and hungry as often as not. In early June they arrived on the shores of James Bay.

Such a journey seemed almost impossible. Certainly it did to the seventeen Englishmen who represented the Hudson's Bay Company in the little stockade at Moose Factory, where the river emptied into the bottom of the bay. They were sound asleep when a hundred Frenchmen came screaming over the walls of their stockade, and the Englishmen surrendered immediately, a wise move under the circumstances.

Replenished and revived, the French swept from post to post. They took Fort Charles, and captured there a small sloop named the *Craven;* loading her with their loot, they sailed off to the main English post in the bay, Fort Albany, and this they subdued after a very short bombardment, when the Hudson's Bay men turned on their commanders and insisted they were traders and not fighters.

Fortunately for the English, the French campaign, after this auspicious beginning, was not pursued as effectively as it might have been. The English were all but cleared out of the bay, being reduced to two small posts, which were just as vulnerable as all the others had been but which the French left alone for no good reason. Finally the company was very happy to negotiate a treaty of neutrality for the area.

Iberville himself went off to France, where as a naval officer with colonial experience he could argue effectively for support of his efforts. He had a large vision, and had the men of Versailles matched it, North America might have been held for France. As it was, Iberville got a hearing but no action, and he returned home to carry on his own private war. In 1688 he raided the James Bay territory once more, in spite of the neutrality agreement. He then got caught up in the larger war blazing along the frontier, and he took part in several of the French raids southward. Most notably he took Fort Pemaquid in Maine, which had earlier successfully resisted a siege, and he ravaged the coast of Newfoundland, burning and destroying settlements there. In 1697 he was back in Hudson Bay, with a small naval squadron this time, and in several hard-fought little actions he again swept the English out of the area. Triumphantly he sailed over to France, sold his captured furs at a great profit, and proudly announced that the English company was destroyed, the northern flank reclaimed for France. In London the unhappy directors of the company agreed with him.

Faraway events, however, were of less importance in Europe than might have been hoped. The French government was nearly bankrupt, and the English were hugely in debt. The growing clamor for peace negotiations drowned Iberville's accomplishments, and when the Treaty of Ryswick was signed in 1697, Louis both recognized William of Orange as King of England and agreed to a restoration of all colonial conquests by either side. The colonies simply did not weigh that heavily in the scale, at least not yet.

So the war ground to an inconclusive halt, ended, as most wars of the period were, not by military victory or defeat, but by financial embarrassment. From the point of view of a total national picture, probably the most important event of the war was the founding, in 1694, of the Bank of England, which in the future would give the English a modern monetary instrument with which to pay for their wars. From now on, if the British Navy could preserve its occasionally tenuous control of the sea, then all the daring of the Tourvilles, the Jean Barts, and the Ibervilles was going to prove less important than the ability of money men in London to show a profit. Without realizing it at all, the English were groping their way toward a combination of Navy, Empire, and fiscal management that was going to make them a world power, for this first of the imperial wars had been merely a prelude: The great Spanish Empire was up now for grabs.

6

The Pillars of Hercules

... instead of seeing the navy of France riding upon our coast, we sent every year a powerful fleet to insult theirs. ...

—*Lives of the Admirals,* 1740

King Charles II of Spain was an unfortunate specimen of humanity, even by the poor physical standards of the seventeenth century. In an era when the prosperity and well-being of kingdoms depended upon the strength of will and body of the sovereign, he was an unmitigated disaster. Born in 1661, he had succeeded to the throne in 1665; he could not stand until he was six, nor speak until he was nearly ten. He was expected to die at any moment; in fact, he lived almost forty years. Though he married twice, he never produced any children, the marriages being for reasons of state only. He was the most unhappy of men, and even the prerequisites of royalty could not make up for the absence of good health.

The question of who would succeed him on the throne, and what might happen to Spain and her enormous possessions, became increasingly important as Charles's life dragged on. There were three claimants, all with almost equal validity to their cases. The first of these, unfortunately, was Louis XIV himself, for he was the son of Philip III's elder daughter and husband of Philip IV's elder daughter. Though Louis had repeatedly, in treaty after treaty, renounced his claims, there had always been conditions to the renunciations; eventually he passed on his case to his grandson, Philip of Anjou.

The second claimant was Leopold I, a Hapsburg, though his case was not quite as good as the French one, for he was son of the younger daughter of Philip III and husband of the younger daughter of Philip IV. Finally there was Joseph of Bavaria, an electoral prince of the Holy Roman Empire; he was Philip IV's great-grandson and Charles II's grandnephew. Obviously, his claim was legally the weakest of the three.

However, what might be legal might not necessarily be right. Spain and its enormous empire in Central America and South America was too big a prize for any of the powers of Europe to see it go to any of the other powers. If Spain and France were combined, then France, already full of pretensions to hegemony, would be virtually unmatchable; if Spain went to a Hapsburg, then the old German-Spanish combination of the days of Charles V would be re-created, and that was patently unacceptable to France, and the same argument held essentially true for the Bavarian possibility as well. The only viable political solution was some form of partition, with Spain going one way and her empire divided up among so-called friends and neighbors. The difficulty with this was that the one thing that might satisfy everyone else was anathema to the Spanish themselves. Inordinately proud and living on past glories, they hated to contemplate partition. As Charles's constant illnesses approached a conclusion, lights burned late in offices all over western Europe while ministers and plotters examined ancient treaties and legal documents, looking for the solution that would best suit their own interests.

The French found it. Though the country was nowhere near recovered from the War of the League of Augsburg, and though the King professed his own earnest desire to live out his life in peace, it remained clear that France would have to fight, either to put her own man on the Spanish throne or to keep someone else's man off it. Better the former, in that case; the wheels of French diplomacy kept grinding away, and there was certainly enough money to fill outstretched palms in the Spanish court. Virtually on his deathbed, Charles II signed a will in which he left his kingdom and empire to Philip of Anjou; Louis, with a pious show of reluctance, announced that he must support the claim of his grandson. Without much enthusiasm, the other states of Europe began to coalesce into an anti-Bourbon alliance.

Poor Charles died on November 1, 1700, whereupon Philip was proclaimed King Philip V. Louis said he would not attempt to interfere in the affairs of Spain, which would remain totally independent, but the word ran around the French court that "the Pyrenees no longer existed," and a whole host of French officials and civil servants, the most efficient in the world, began to move south with the new King.

By the summer of 1701 Great Britain, the Netherlands, the Holy Roman Empire, and various German states were putting their armies in motion. William of England was the architect of the alliance, closely seconded by the Emperor Leopold. William looked on this as the culmination of his life's work, but he did not manage its completion. In March 1702, preparing to go off to war once more, he was out riding for exercise when his horse stumbled on a molehill and threw him; the King suffered severe internal injuries, and within a week he was dead. The throne went to Anne, William's sister-in-law and the younger daughter of James II's first marriage, the nearest Protestant in the line.

At the accession of Queen Anne England was entering one of the great eras of her history. The price revolution had come to an end, population shifts were leveling off a bit, and a period of general stability and slow, manageable growth was beginning, to last until the advent of the Industrial Revolution and the population explosion at the end of the eighteenth century. None of the wars and upheavals for the next several generations had any great impact on English society or the English way of life. For the poor, life remained as miserable as it had always been. For growing numbers of rich and well-to-do, it was a supremely satisfying time to be alive. There was a general air of progress, without the preachy self-righteousness of the nineteenth century. Britannia ruled the waves, and all was well with the world.

Though there were bad harvests before the turn of the century, the economy was generally improving, shipping and imports and exports especially thriving. The population of England and Wales was estimated to be about six million, of which perhaps one seventh lived in London. Scotland, still an independent kingdom sharing a common sovereign with England, had under two million, and Ireland perhaps the same.

With all this, Great Britain was only a third as populous as France, and half the size of the Holy Roman Empire. What gave Great Britain power in the eyes of Europe was the depth of her financial resources, her growing imperial holdings, and her Navy. The empire consisted now of the American colonies, spreading north and south along the Atlantic Seaboard. They were more populous but less important economically than the West Indian islands, with perhaps three hundred thousand inhabitants scattered among them. Roughly another fifty thousand were settled on the islands of the Caribbean. Perhaps a hundred thousand of these British subjects were African slaves, highly concentrated, of course, the farther south one went. Emigration from England to the colonies slacked off during the early eighteenth century but was more than offset by the natural increase among the colonists themselves. With unlimited land available and apparently endless opportunity for the creation of new wealth, the colonists rapidly increased in number and provided a dynamic for imperial economic growth far out of proportion to their numbers.

The fringes of empire—Hudson Bay, the African slave coast, and India—were still seen only by scattered Britons; in numbers they were totally insignificant; economically, though, they grew amazingly in importance, and there are schools of thought that say the later Industrial Revolution was financed by the influx of capital either from the slave trade, or from India in midcentury.

At the opening of the war, therefore, William, before his sudden death, could offer potential allies major forces and resources. The fleet was Britain's first military asset, though the French had already conceded victory at sea. William could also offer a small but effective army, commanded after his death by a far greater soldier than he, John Churchill, the Duke of Marlborough. And most important, and also setting a precedent for every war England has fought since, he could offer money—money to Sweden to stay neutral, to German princes for raising troops, to Austrians as subsidies for their armies. Money, ships, and men, in that order, were becoming the holy trinity of English power.

The military course of the war also initiated a pattern that was to be repeated at least until 1940. Britain generally controlled the seas, and therefore the majority of the world's maritime commerce. War thus became a paying proposition, though that fact was often obscured by the inequities and inadequacies of the tax system. With the money this generated, Britain could afford to send a small army of her own to the Continent; far more important in an overall military sense, she could afford to subsidize continental allies against her enemy. Over the next two centuries there was hardly a country in Europe, from Portugal to Russia, that did not at some time enjoy a subsidy treaty with Great Britain. These allies invariably bore the brunt of the land fighting and absorbed the energies of the enemy, which in turn left the British free to mount overseas expeditions, to increase their naval predominance, to enlarge their empire, and to control more water and more trade, and generate more money, so that the thing might be done all over again.

In retrospect the progression is perfectly clear, and it seems the obvious course to have followed. At any given time, of course, events were far less clear and their potential results much less discernible. Relatively few British leaders over these centuries saw precisely the connection between different events and theaters, and there were many false, and some retrograde, steps. Not every British politician was the elder Pitt, nor every British sailor Admiral Nelson. Added to this was the simple fact that this took, in the case of the Anglo-French struggle, more than a hundred years. The nature of eighteenth-century warfare was such that few decisions were seen as irreversible; few, indeed, were decisive at all. An island or fortress taken in one war might be retaken in another, or even, as often happened, given back at the peace table. Naval strength lost in one decade could be reconstituted for the next. Neither Britain nor France fought to destroy the other— it was different when Germany became the primary enemy in the twentieth century, in a later, more violent world—but instead to improve their respective positions. For all its casual cruelty, society in the eighteenth century was in many ways more civilized than in the twentieth.

These wars also assumed a geographic pattern, with variations depending upon, in Europe, who was allied with whom and against whom, and overseas, what area of empire or potential empire happened to be the most active. In Europe itself armies marched and countermarched through the Low Countries, the Rhine and Danube valleys, and northern Italy, all of those classic areas of combat. There were periodic side trips—to the Iberian Peninsula, to Moscow, to Egypt. In the waters around Europe the question of world supremacy was decided, but occasionally the battling states would throw off squadrons or even whole fleets; many of empire's most important naval battles were fought within sight of the Continent, but many of Europe's important battles were also fought in distant corners of the globe, off Ceylon, or Singapore, or the Chesapeake capes. Finally, each of the imperial theaters—North America, the Caribbean, Africa, and the Indian subcontinent—saw its own wars, smaller in numbers but no less vicious in fighting, no less important in long-term significance, than what happened at home. And all of these were connected and made interdependent by the wide-ranging nature of seapower and im-perial considerations. During the American Revolution the French threatened the Indian Ocean. During World War II operations in Burma were tied to the availability of landing craft for Italy.

The linchpin for much of this was the Royal Navy, and the picture of it that emerges is one of "the silent service," steadfast and resolute, the lower deck consisting of jolly British tars with hearts of oak, the officer class tanned, stern, and weatherbeaten, professional to the bone marrow, always there, always reliable, a lion in battle, a complete gentleman out of it. This stereotype has been assiduously fostered by generations of novelists, and like most such pictures, has much truth to it. But it also leaves out a great deal, such as the fact that many of the men, especially in wartime, were either press-ganged or scoured out of prisons, packed in ships like sardines and worked and fought until they were used up, after which they were ignominiously dropped to beg or die on some inhospitable beach at home or abroad. Officers were occasionally cowardly, and more often incompetent. When Admiral Benbow attacked a weak French squadron in the summer of 1702, four of his seven ships' captains hung back, and two were subsequently court-martialed and shot. In 1708 Admiral Wager's captains deserted him en masse off Porto Bello, this in spite of the lure of attacking a Spanish treasure squadron. Throughout the entire period there were always captains who avoided battle, or took shelter behind the Fighting Instructions to excuse some dereliction of duty, and after virtually every battle, the captain who was thought to have done least was tried as a sort of booby prize.

All of this was matched by the naval administration, occasionally corrupt and often incompetent. After every war the fleet was virtually disbanded, the officers beached on half pay and the men thrown out to rot. Therefore, at the start of every war officers and crews had to be hastily found, and ships that might have been lying in ordinary for years to be brought out and refitted at enormous cost—and enormous profit to the cloud of suppliers, pilferers, and general hangers-on who pocketed as much as they could out of the process. About the only thing to be said for the Navy was that if it was bad, the Army was worse, the civilian administration worse still, and the various colonial administrations worst of all. Why, then, did the British win? Because everyone else was that little bit worse than they were. As that archetypal eighteenth-century man, Gibbon, said, "History . . . is, indeed, little more than the register of the crimes, follies, and misfortunes of mankind," and the historian, in recording it, imposes an order that is far more apparent to him than it ever was to the participants, and by the selection of his details and the emphasis he puts upon them, produces a reality that is true for him but not necessarily for those whose individual lives he describes en masse.

French troops were on the move as William died, French dockyards humming with activity. Queen Anne acceded peacefully to the throne of England, to grateful sighs of relief and occasional muttering in Scotland, Ireland, and among those who nurtured a taste for the past. Austrian regiments marched west from the Turkish frontier to the Rhine-Danube area, out-of-work professional gentlemen from the Hebrides to Lisbon to Warsaw packed their few belongings and set off to make the round of European courts, telling lies about their military experience and seeking commissions. German princes weighed the distance from France against the money offered by England and tried to decide which way to jump. In northern New England and around the Finger Lakes in New York tired women wondered if their men would come home from the fields, and lay awake at night listening for the sudden war whoop that meant death or outrage. It was only five years since the last war, and there was little enthusiasm for this one, but rather a wary calculation of chances. How little could one do, and what profit might be derived from it?

The British war effort, as far as the Continent itself was concerned, was tremendously enhanced by the death of William of Orange. In the years immediately before he died, William had been grooming John Churchill, the Duke of Marlborough, to be one of his leading ministers. Marlborough was an authentic political and military genius with an occasionally flexible conscience. He had, in other words, the sense to know when to leap, and the kind of scruples—or lack of them—that allowed him to leap in the right direction. He had been a favorite page to the then Duke of York as a boy, and a gift of five thousand pounds from the Duchess of Cleveland, Charles II's mistress and young Churchill's, too, got him started. In the 1670s he learned his military business under the great French soldier Marshal Turenne, and when James became King, Marlborough was one of his leading supporters, a position that did not prevent his rapid defection to William of Orange, which was what got him his dukedom. During the League of Augsburg War he played too clever a role for his own good, and his flirtations with the exiled James brought him under suspicion. By 1702 he had regained his place, however; he was William's right-hand man; more important, his wife, Sarah, was the best friend of the new Queen Anne. It was an unbeatable combination.

Fortunately, his military skill matched his political talents. Under Marlborough's command the small British Army that fought on the Continent, hampered by all the difficulties of waging war as part of a coalition, still repeatedly defeated the French and over the decade that active fighting lasted, the British Army added some of its most famous battle honors to its standards. In August 1704 Marlborough won the great Battle of Blenheim, to follow it up with Ramillies in 1706, Oudenarde in 1708, and Malplaquet in 1709. At the same time there were extensive campaigns both in northern Italy, where the Austrians were active, and in Spain, where a British expeditionary force, the little-known antecedent of Wellington's adventures, tried to unseat Philip of Anjou.

The results of all these were that by 1709 the French were exhausted financially and militarily. The aging Louis was willing to give up and would probably have done so had not the allies insisted on such harsh terms as to force him to continue. They demanded that he aid in deposing his own grandson, and faced with the choice of fighting to keep Philip on his throne or fighting to put him off it, Louis chose the former. The war dragged on until the Treaty of Utrecht in 1713, and for the last of the belligerents, was not concluded until the Treaty of Madrid in 1715.

The war at sea was equally lengthy, but much more decisive, especially from the British point of view. The French began the war with a conscious acceptance of their naval inferiority, so that, even with the Spanish fleet added to their own, they made little attempt to challenge British command of the sea. The Royal Navy around the coasts of Europe therefore spent most of the war in convoy duty, but two important events had a bearing on future developments.

Inheriting William's strategic plan, Marlborough had decided that the fleet might be best used in the Mediterranean to harass Spain, to shore up Austria, and to put pressure on wavering Italians such as the Duke of Savoy. To do this, however, the British needed a base from which they might operate. Tangier had been abandoned in 1683 as unsuitable for a major station, but lack of a replacement was still felt. Their first thought was to take the Spanish port of Cadiz, and Admiral Sir George Rooke attacked it in 1702. This particular affair exhibited most of the evils of what were then called "conjunct expeditions," with divided opinions among the commanders and poor behavior by the ill-trained troops. Eventually the British sailed away without having attacked the city, a failure that did a great deal to make the Spanish think Philip of Anjou's cause was likely to be the winning one. Fortunately, Rooke redeemed himself by picking off the annual Spanish treasure *flota,* which was unloading in Vigo Bay, so that his welcome home was far better than it might have been.

There still remained the problem of a Mediterranean base. By 1704 the British thought they might be able to seize Toulon, but nothing came of that; they had a look at Barcelona, whose taking might have had interesting subsequent results for separatist Catalonia, but again nothing was done. Finally Rooke and his fellow captains decided on Gibraltar. It was a perfect spot, weakly held but of immense potential strength. So on July 24, 1704, the British took, after one day's siege, the base that eventually became both the embodiment and the symbol of their empire.

The place was quickly garrisoned with British marines and a Dutch contingent; indeed, at this stage of operations the British would have been happy to make this an allied rather than an independent venture, but the Dutch and the Austrians both later refused to have anything to do with it. It was many years before Gibraltar was transformed into a full-scale naval base, but as soon as it was taken, the Spanish realized how much they had lost, and they initiated attempts to reconquer it. These brought on the only major naval action of the war in European waters.

The Spanish asked the French for help, and the result was that the Toulon fleet, fifty-two ships of the line, put to sea under the command of the Comte de Toulouse, a bastard son of Louis XIV. They sailed westward, and on the morning of August 13, Rooke met them off Malaga, sixty miles east of Gibraltar. Rooke had fifty-eight ships of the line, his own squadron and an Anglo-Dutch one under Admiral Sir Cloudesley Shovell.

The British had the wind but did not take much advantage of it. A year before, Rooke had rewritten the Fighting Instructions, basing his work on Torrington's of the previous war. As usual, when reworked by an admiral whose primary concern was maintaining control over his own fleet rather than getting at the enemy, the instructions tended more than before in the direction of formalism. Rooke wanted to keep his ships in a long line ahead and bring them down all together on the enemy, whereupon he would turn and the two fleets would then fight a battle with "coterminous" lines, each ship banging away at its opposite number. Old sailors might remember that this was what James had tried to do with Opdam in the Battle of Lowestoft, when the Dutch had refused to cooperate. The French now proved more obliging, and waited patiently as the British came down on them.

The matter did not go quite as well as Rooke had hoped. For one thing, he could not get his ships to maneuver all together. He approached in line ahead; he then had to turn to line abreast to go down into gun range, and once he got there, swing into line ahead a second time. However, each ship in his long line turned as it saw the one ahead turn, and since this took some time with nearly sixty ships in light airs, the leading ships were into action well ahead of the trailing ones. Rooke's van took a considerable battering while it alone was coming into range, but finally all the allied ships were in position, and the two lines sailed along under easy sail, with the broadsides rolling out at each other in fine style.

Since wooden ships were very difficult to sink, it might eventually have dawned on someone that they could go on like this indefinitely, or at least until they ran out of ammunition, for once Rooke had achieved his coterminous line, he did not have much idea what to do next. Sitting at the Admiralty drawing neat little diagrams and trying to work out the appropriate wording for all contingencies, it had seemed as if this were the culmination of the battle, and the enemy, pounded by British gunfire, ought to respond in the proper way by sinking, or striking his colors, or blowing up, or fleeing, or doing *something* besides sailing along, maddeningly firing back. To make matters worse, the allies were short of ammunition, having used a great deal of their supplies pounding down the ancient stone walls of Gibraltar. It finally became a question of what would arrive first, sundown or the bottom of the shot lockers. As evening came, Rooke took advantage of the light and fitful winds to draw off, glad to be let go. The allies had twice the casualties of the French, but neither side had lost a ship.

That night Toulouse, relatively inexperienced, held a council of war. His captains thought they had already done all they should. For the next two days the winds were so light the fleets lay within sight of each other, but both sides were happy to call it quits. The twenty-four galleys with the French remained completely inactive, and finally Rooke sailed off to Gibraltar. Both sides claimed a victory, the British because Gibraltar remained theirs, the French because they had inflicted heavier damage. The former thought, mistakenly, that their strategic victory had justified their inconclusive tactics, and the latter thought, equally mistakenly, that holding their own in the battle made up for their failure to retake the Rock. So both went home happy.

The French tried again the next year, but a smallish squadron was beaten by Sir John Leake off Marbella. After that the British were virtually supreme in the Mediterranean, and for the rest of the war operations around the Continent were either of the convoying variety or in support of land campaigns. The British undertook operations in Catalonia in 1705 and 1706. In 1707 a great imperial soldier, Prince Eugene of Savoy, marched from northern Italy into France and tried to take Toulon, and the British fleet supported him by landing sailors and marines. Though the attack on the port finally failed, the French thought it would succeed, and they scuttled fifty ships of the line in the harbor rather than have them taken by the allies. This cheap victory capped British efforts, and in the next couple of years they took both Sardinia and Minorca. They were now perfectly free to assert themselves in the Mediterranean Sea, though they lacked the strength to sustain their efforts on the Iberian Peninsula. As the war tailed off, Britain had the island bases she wanted; France, in the person of Philip of Anjou, now Philip V, had Spain.

There was more activity overseas. Marlborough, following William's lead, had seen that it was a logical extension of British power to move from the Channel and the Atlantic coast into the Mediterranean. He did not see as yet that it was equally logical to extend the field of battle overseas. There were those men of affairs in Britain who wanted the war effort concentrated in the imperial theaters, who were still lured, especially, by the possibility of robbing the Spanish Empire. But they saw this in opposition, rather than complementary, to the war on the Continent. England had not yet produced a statesman who could see both sides of this coin, so the imperial adventures were carried on in spite of continental affairs. Englishmen still fought two or three separate wars instead of one coherent whole.

Nonetheless, a semblance of unity was given to the war effort by the wide-ranging nature of seapower. Wherever there was blue water the Navy could operate, and warships crossed the oceans with surprising ease, moving from the Iberian Peninsula to the Caribbean almost effortlessly. Of these imperial theaters, the West Indies remained far and away the most important, and North America, for all its potential significance, was little more than an irritating sideshow as far as European rulers were concerned. For the British, the Caribbean offered especially rich pickings in this war, as they could attack both French and Spanish possessions. To the London merchants and their cronies in Parliament, there were not only French islands there for the taking; there was also the chance at last to break into the Spanish mainland trade in a big way. Such opportunities resulted in Wager's attack on Porto Bello in 1708, though the results were not all that might have been hoped. Offsetting the good prospects was the fact that large numbers of French warships were employed as commerce raiders, and men such as Forbin and Duguay-Trouin incessantly pestered British trade. Rising costs of seaborne goods, and skyrocketing insurance rates, led to demands from the merchant class for improved convoy protection, and the Navy that had mastered the enemy battle fleet found itself at full stretch protecting merchantmen from privateers and small French squadrons who carried raiding to a fine art. Risks for merchantmen were occasionally compounded by the Royal Navy itself; in the West Indies Commodore Kerr charged a private fee—a euphemism for blackmail—for allowing vessels to join homeward-bound convoys, and he was eventually relieved of his command because of it.

Throughout the war, then, the West Indies saw a series of small actions, ship against ship or little squadron against little squadron. Expeditions were mounted here and there, and no island was really safe; the sight of topsails on the horizon alarmed everyone, and only when they were clearly identified as friendly could the islanders, of whatever nationality, relax again. And, of course, far more dangerous than man himself, the tropic diseases, most particularly yellow fever, continued to decimate the Europeans of the area.

The war in Europe rapidly spread to the North American mainland. The Royal Navy provided a few ships, and the Army eventually sent some troops over. Most of the early fighting was done by the colonials themselves, however. Many of the leading men of the colonies were already worried by what appeared to them to be aggressive French designs, for in the years between the Peace of Ryswick and the outbreak of the new war the French had vigorously pushed their explorations and claims into the Mississippi Valley. They now had posts at Detroit, Cahokia, and in Louisiana down on the Gulf. Colonial land speculators, who thought big themselves, saw in this a threat of French encirclement and a loss of control over the Indian tribes. Though they deplored the expenses of war, they were ready to find some solution to the problem.

One such man was the governor of South Carolina, a former

Indian-trader named James Moore. He talked his colonial assembly into the idea of sending an expedition south to take the Spanish base at St. Augustine in Florida, and late in October 1702 eight hundred Carolinians and Indian allies besieged the little Spanish post, held by half their number of soldiers. The Spanish, with the entire population of the town crowded into Fort San Marcos, held off the English for seven weeks until a relief squadron arrived from Cuba. Moore abandoned his ships and retreated overland back to Carolina, to be greeted by a howl of protest that cost him, eventually, his job.

The next year, as a private venture, since the Carolina assembly refused to back him a second time, he gathered a force of several hundred Indians and a few whites and raided the Spanish mission territory in northern Florida, burning towns and missions, taking prisoners who were finally sold as slaves, killing, looting, and raping in a triumphant progress that destroyed Spanish credibility and thoroughly cowed the Indians along the frontier for the next several years.

In the North, affairs took a different course. During King William's War the New York frontier had seen heavy raiding, but the Iroquois, the Indian allies of the English, had by the end of the war been sadly disillusioned; they believed that they had borne the brunt of the conflict, especially as several French raids had been directed against them and their towns and crops. For Indians living at a subsistence level, the destruction of a year's crop was far more damaging than the loss of a few lives on the battlefield, for it meant starvation in the next winter. These memories, coupled with active French efforts during the interval between the wars, led the Iroquois to a neutral stance when hostilities broke out again. The French were happy to have them that way, and so, in the main, were the New Yorkers. As far as they were concerned, the French and the New Englanders could fight it out, and good luck to both of them. Trade between Albany and Montreal continued unabated right through the war, even when New York was later forced into hostilities, to the mutual profit and satisfaction of both sides.

The French in Queen Anne's War were outnumbered, as they had been in King William's, for the population of New England alone was now close to a hundred thousand, while that of New France still hovered around fifteen thousand. The new French governor, Vaudreuil, decided therefore on a policy of aggressive frontier warfare, designed more than anything else to cloak his weakness and keep the enemy busy at home. French traders, officers, and priests soon had the

Abenaki Indians in arms, and once more the frontier rang with stories of horror and death, isolated farms attacked, and the outer fringes of settlement recoiling against the Indian pressure. In February 1704 about two hundred Canadians and Indians came sweeping over the snowbound—and therefore unwatched—palisade of Deerfield, in western Massachusetts. Killing forty men, women and children, they set the village to the torch and marched more than a hundred half-naked survivors off to Quebec to be taken into slavery. Most of them, amazingly enough, survived the march, and as late as the 1720s, long after the end of the war, children and widows were still turning up, ransomed by relatives or sought out and released in one way or another. Men and women who were soft did not last long on the eighteenth-century New England frontier.

The English responded in kind. They garrisoned the frontier as best they could. They offered bounties for scalps—and undoubtedly paid for a fair number of their own peoples'—and they also took the offensive against the Abenakis. In 1704 Benjamin Church led a small-boat expedition along the coast of Maine and into the head of the Bay of Fundy, as far as the Minas Basin, ambushing Indians either separately or in their villages. He burned Minas to the ground and wrote a note to the Governor of New France telling him two could play the burning-village game and that if he continued he might expect to get worse than he gave.

After this the war temporarily quieted down. Neither side was able to continue such extended operations indefinitely; there was an unofficial truce in 1706; in 1707 the New Englanders undertook desultory expeditions against Port Royal, on the belief that it was a sort of primary base of operations that sustained the Abenakis, but the attacks were not pressed; the weak French did not have to defeat them, simply to wait them out, which they successfully did. In 1709 the British government itself was constrained to take a hand; New York was ordered to abandon its neutrality, and forces of about fifteen hundred men were recruited both in Boston and in Albany. For several weeks they drilled around the two towns, awaiting the arrival of the promised British forces, but in the end no British came, and they went home disgusted.

Next year, though, they tried again, not for Quebec, it is true, but for Port Royal, in Acadia. Colonel Francis Nicholson and thirty-five hundred troops, mostly New Englanders but including a regiment of British marines, sailed up the Bay of Fundy, through the gut into the basin, and overawed the meager garrison of Port Royal, which surrendered with considerable haste. Renamed Annapolis Royal, the little town, and all the surrounding shore of the Bay of Fundy, passed into English hands.

Encouraged by this success and by the expectation of further co-operation from the colonies, the British resurrected for 1711 the earlier plan of the two-pronged attack on Quebec. Francis Nicholson was ordered to raise troops at Albany once again, which he did, and Admiral Sir Hovenden Walker sailed over to Boston with a fleet and five thousand British soldiers and marines.

Almost everything went wrong. The colonies were slow to send in their money and to raise their troops. Once raised, though, the troops were quick to desert, and numbers of pressed British sailors or unhappy soldiers followed this example. The colonials found Walker nagging and pettish, and he found them nasty and penny-pinching. It was the end of July before Walker finally got away from Boston, though when he did he had a force twelve thousand strong in more than seventy vessels. If numbers alone counted, Canada was doomed.

In the third week of August, while Nicholson's men were getting into the valley of Lake Champlain and readying themselves for their final descent on Montreal, the fleet entered the St. Lawrence River. Walker had been told much of the fogs and treacherous currents and was in his mind half defeated before he got to Anticosti Island. Now the river finished the task. A hundred miles west of the island, where the river begins to narrow, his whole fleet blundered in the fog into rocks and reefs. Desperately the transports and warships hauled off, breakers all around them, and eight vessels went on the reefs, bottoms ripped out amid a swirl of breakers. Nearly a thousand soldiers and sailors were drowned in a few agonizing minutes, and what little heart was left went out of the expedition. A council of war quickly decided that Quebec could not be taken this late in the season, and the New Englanders sailed back to Boston, while Walker and his ships and sailors went home to England, French cheers and Yankee jeers following them in about equal measure. On the shores of Lake Champlain, Francis Nicholson tore his wig off and stamped it into the ground, vowing to have nothing more to do with British expeditions. Weak in men though it might be, New France was well guarded by its rivers, its rocks, and its forests, and its day was not done yet.

The Southerners had better luck. In 1706 a mismanaged French expedition against Charleston in South Carolina had been beaten off, hundreds of its men and even one of its ships taken prisoner. The next year the South Carolinians had raided Pensacola and had kept the eastern end of the Gulf of Mexico in a turmoil. And in 1711 the settlers had broken the power of the Tuscarora Indians, whose survivors trekked north to join the Iroquois, transforming the Five Nations into the Six Nations and adopting once more the posture of neutrality they had mistakenly given up in 1711.

So the war on the North American continent tailed off. The frontier raids lessened in intensity, and the men and women drifted back to their burned homesteads. Ships with no flags, but whose lines could have come only from Salem or Newburyport, dropped anchor in the French villages of Newfoundland, or off Martinique, not to raid but to trade. Colonial assemblies no longer heard deputations from their harassed western towns and happily cut their defense budgets. In Europe they were talking peace, and in the New World men were glad of it.

The Peace of Utrecht was a landmark for the British Empire, for its provisions clearly acknowledged that it was now the leading world power. Utrecht and the several other treaties associated with it marked the second great occasion when European diplomats tried to arrange a general peace settlement. The first had been the Peace of Westphalia, sixty-odd years before, at the end of the Thirty Years' War, and now once again men in lace, wigs, and high heels sought to resolve their differences and cloak their several ambitions and avarices in high-sounding language and not-so-genteel exchanges.

The war had lasted too long for either side to claim a whole-hearted victory. Louis did put his grandson on the Spanish throne, beginning the Bourbon line in that unhappy country, but doing so left France utterly exhausted. England and her allies on the Continent would have been better off to have quit in 1709, when they had been well ahead on points, rather than trying to push on to a complete victory that was beyond their grasp, an effort that left them as worn out as the French enemy.

But England herself did well. The problem of royalty between her and France was more or less reversed, for the French now acknowledged the validity of the Protestant succession in England. This meant that the Catholic Stuart cause was abandoned. James II had died in France in 1701, just before the war began, but France had recognized his son, James, known to history as the Old Pretender, he whose birth had set off the Glorious Revolution. The Pretender was now not only repudiated, he was also required by the terms of the treaty to leave France. He made a short and ill-managed attempt to claim his throne after Queen Anne's death, in the Scottish rising called "the '15," but it failed, as did almost all of the things that unfortunate family turned its hand to. After that James lived the remainder of his life in Rome, where in 1719 he married a Polish princess. So Anne and her Protestant successors were theoretically secure on their thrones, the more so since the English and Scottish crowns had been definitively united during the war, by the Act of Union in 1707, a far-reaching settlement designed specifically to prevent any return of "the King over the water."

On the other hand, the French were constrained to agree that the thrones of France and Spain would never be united, so the English felt they had scored points here. Actually, they had not; the French had been willing to concede that at the beginning, before all the people were killed and the money spent. Further, France and Spain were so closely allied in their foreign policies for the next century that they might as well have been united anyway; the whole issue was really academic.

More important than who had what throne was who held what piece of territory, and here the British were well in the lead. France recognized British control over Hudson Bay, so Iberville's old dream of the previous war was gone. That in itself was not unduly significant. What mattered far more was that France was also forced to acknowledge British sovereignty over Acadia, a potential stranglehold on the direct approaches to the St. Lawrence. A few thousand French settlers of Acadia became British subjects. There was some room for maneuver here, however, for no one knew what exactly Acadia was. The French had insisted in the past that Acadia was the entire area from the Maine settlements north to the Gulf of St. Lawrence, and the English that it was merely the actual territory settled by the French—that is, the Bay of Fundy shore of the Nova Scotia Peninsula. Now the position was reversed, each adopting the other's views, and the French continued to hold or claim Isle Royale, as they called Cape Breton Island, and Isle St. Jean, Prince Edward Island. Both now realized that this area was crucial for control of the whole continent; neither was willing to regard this as a final solution.

The British also got Newfoundland, though that rocky island continued in practice to serve as a temporary shelter for whoever was brave enough to fish its waters and settle its coasts, and French pockets remained. Down in the Caribbean the British also held the island of St. Kitts, which had changed hands during the war. In France, Dunkerque, nest of privateers, was to have its fortifications destroyed and its harbor filled up.

Setting another pattern for future development, Britain took almost more from France's allies that she did from France herself. Gibraltar was ceded to the British, and so was Minorca, which became a major base for the western Mediterranean; for many years it was far more important than Gibraltar, and its later loss was keenly felt by the Navy, and especially by Admiral Byng, who was shot for losing it. Most important of all, however, as far as Spain was concerned, the British got the Asiento Treaty. This allowed subjects of Great Britain, in the form of the Royal African Company, to supply slaves to the Spanish Empire in the New World for thirty years. The Spanish tried to interpret this treaty as strictly as possible, and the British as widely as they could. For practical purposes, it meant a foot in the door of the closed Spanish imperial system, and for the next generation, the British took full advantage of it, to such an extent that in that time British ships and traders became virtually indispensable to the Spanish colonials.

The quarter century after the Peace of Utrecht was therefore a good one for Britain and her Empire. All around the horizon there seemed to be an air of well-being, and the country rode on a crest of mercantile prosperity. It was not, of course, without its ups and downs. Anne died in 1714, and as none of her seventeen children survived her, she was replaced by the nearest Protestant in the line, who happened to be a German. This was George, the Elector of Hanover, a middle-sized but important North German state. Not knowing too much about England and being bored by cabinet meetings that he could only occasionally understand, George was happy to let sleeping dogs lie. He and his advisers easily survived the rising of the '15, and the Whigs were able, partly because of it, to cement themselves in power for the next half century. The fortunes of government were still tied intimately to the dynasty, or any person in it, and the sovereign, even one with so tenuous and parliamentary a claim as George, was still far and away the most important figure in the affairs of state. For fifty years the Whigs damned all opposition as Jacobite traitors and retained power by doing so. There were some residual dynastic bickerings after the Spanish succession, but they effectively ended when the British fleet took a hand and destroyed the Spanish fleet off Cape Passero in Sicily in 1718. After that, foreign adventures were over for a time; Englishmen could settle back to stock speculation and the delights of peaceful and uneventful government under the leadership of Robert Walpole.

The Empire continued to advance at a moderate pace. In North America, Acadia was garrisoned, and in the South, the new colony of Georgia was founded, conceived both as a barrier against the Spanish in Florida and as a humanitarian gesture to relieve the vast numbers of Englishmen imprisoned for debt.

Indeed, the American colonies were something of a problem for a mercantile empire. The whole tenor of the system, and the thrust of the Navigation Acts, was to keep the colonials as suppliers of raw materials to, and consumers of finished products from, the mother country. As early as the 1730s, however, this suit of clothes was beginning to pinch. The difficulty lay in two facts—first, that the French and Dutch West Indian islands were more efficient sugar producers than the British islands were, and second, that the American colonies, particularly New England, were beginning to produce manufactured goods of their own. The Navigation Acts required that Americans buy British colonial sugar, and they also required that colonial products be exported through Great Britain. The colonists in America thought this was ridiculous; if they dealt direct with the foreign West Indian islands, they could undercut everyone all around and still show a sizable profit. In other words, they preferred to smuggle.

In 1732 the British Parliament struck at colonial manufacturers by prohibiting the importation of hats and forbidding their being made overseas. A year later they took a far more difficult line: They put exorbitant duties on sugar and molasses imported into the colonies from non-British possessions. The British West Indian islands were in a depressed state, the planter interest was very strong in Parliament, and the planters, mostly absentee landlords, thought regulation by prohibitive duties was far easier than more efficient production, an attitude they would adhere to for another century, with disastrous results.

The immediate results were not very good either. Molasses and sugar were vital components of rum, and rum at this time was virtually the national drink of the colonists. It was also, and here was the rub, peculiarly the commodity on which New England merchants made their profit. There were literally hundreds of distilleries in New England in the eighteenth century, and this one item was the major factor in Yankee balance sheets. Because of this, colonial officials soon realized that the act was impossible, and though it was enforced in the southern colonies, where it was not a major item, in the northern ones the entire society simply disregarded it; the British government was forced to do the same, and a precedent was thus established whereby the colonists came to think that laws that did not suit them might be ignored. It was a dangerous habit of mind to get into. Even that early, prescient Frenchmen were suggesting that the best guarantee for the preservation of the British Empire was the threat offered by the existence of the French one.

The British quite naturally did not see the French in such a benevolent light. But the two did get along and even had a somewhat unnatural alliance for the 1720s and the 1730s. There were relatively weak sovereigns on both thrones, and the leading ministers, Walpole in England and Cardinal Fleury in France, were like-minded men who both thought their countries needed peace and prosperity. The French pursued a forward policy in India, but India was big, and the English company was still small. There were enough slaves on the African coast for both, and for twenty years western Europe and its empires enjoyed peaceful conditions. Walpole happily let the Navy rot, in the good old tradition. At the end of the thirties, it was not the French who upset the boat, it was the Spanish.

7

". . . And Planted Firm Britannia's Flag. . . ."

Now God be praised, I will die in peace. . . .
—James Wolfe, 1759

Captain Jenkins made a touching figure, standing there before the bar of the House of Commons, though there were those who thought, rather uncharitably, that he was much more used to frequenting other types of bar. With becoming humility in the presence of the great, he recounted his tale of woe. An honest English merchant sailor, he had been trading off the coast of the Spanish Main, perfectly legitimately, and of course he would not dream of smuggling, when his brig had been stopped and boarded by a Spanish *guarda costa*. The Spaniard, full of insolence and no doubt smelling of olive oil, had ransacked the British ship, and though he had found no evidence of wrongdoing, he had threatened and then even tortured Jenkins. He had, in fact, pulled out his sword and sliced off Jenkins' ear, suggesting that he take it home to his King as a present. With this Jenkins reached into a commodious pocket and waved aloft something that indeed looked like an ancient and grizzled ear and announced beseechingly, "And at that, sirs, I commended my soul to God and my cause to my country!" It brought down the house.

Robert Walpole, that pacifistically inclined Prime Minister, could not stand against this sort of amiable demagoguery; in vain did government ministers point out that Jenkins had gone through his ordeal seven years ago, or that he might well have lost his ear, as some said, not at sea but in the pillory as a common rogue. The simple truth was, England was bored. There had been peace and prosperity for very nearly two decades now, and pleasant as life might be, it was not at all exciting. The clamors for action, against Spain, against anyone, grew, and so in 1739 His Majesty's government responded by declaring war on Spain in what became known, inevitably, as the War of Jenkins' Ear.

Fortunately for the dignity of historians, this Anglo-Spanish struggle was soon subsumed in a larger, general European war, the War of the Austrian Succession. This was touched off by the failure of the male line of the Austrian Hapsburgs; after a very complicated diplomatic wrangle, one that in length almost matched the problem of the Spanish succession, France went to war with Austria. Most of the major German states sided with France, and Britain became allied with Austria, so by 1742 there was a full-blown war lasting until 1748. A peace, or more properly interlude, of exhaustion followed, but in 1756 war broke out once again, the Seven Years' War this time, lasting until 1763. Again it ended with virtually all the European powers financially drained, with one triumphant exception: Britain during these years found the secret both of empire and of European hegemony. She emerged from the midcentury wars the greatest empire and the strongest—and the most thoroughly hated—power in the world.

As all Britain's wars did, these began poorly. The mood of the public, and even of the members of Parliament, took little account of the condition of Britain's military forces. When the public wanted war, it did not stop to ask if it was ready to fight one. New regiments of regular soldiers and marines were hastily raised and sent off ill-trained to battle, and the Navy, which had shrunk by a good third in the years of peace, began the all-too-usual process of reequipping, putting ships back in commission, and scouring the seaport towns and the prisons with press gangs.

For a while successes were few and far between. Spanish privateers were active, and insurance rates went up markedly; the British blockade of Cadiz, initiated from Gibraltar immediately on the outbreak of war, was totally ineffective, for the ships were too poor to be maintained on station. The public was therefore delighted when, late in 1739, Admiral Vernon with a small squadron took Porto Bello on the Isthmus of Panama, and the government, pleased to have something positive to report, immediately decided on a larger expedition of the same type.

Now a popular hero, Vernon was given command of a major fleet and told to capture Cartagena, the chief center on the Spanish Main. In support he had an army of about eight thousand troops under General Wentworth. Vernon was most unhappy at the whole affair. The ships were ill-found, the troops raw and poorly disciplined, and Wentworth was a dolt with whom Vernon immediately quarreled. Preparation took so long that by the time the expedition was under way, it was late in the season. Just as Vernon had foreseen, the force arrived in the West Indies right at the height of the sick season, and the troops were soon in difficulties. To cap it all, the whole affair had been conducted so publicly that the Spanish had had plenty of time to send reinforcements out to their empire.

Mistake piled upon mistake. The ships could not get past the outer defenses of Cartagena, and the troops could not take the forts. Eventually, with both commanders firing recriminations at each other, they gave up and sailed off, to fail as miserably before Santiago over in Cuba. The fleet arrived back in Jamaica with yellow fever raging among the packed troops and with a trail of corpses bobbing in its wake. Eventually nine tenths of the soldiers died of disease, with absolutely nothing to show for it.

The condition of the English—and what some might accomplish in spite of it—was further demonstrated by the expedition of Admiral Anson. In 1740 he was commissioned to take several small ships and cruise the Pacific coast of South America, a Spanish holding that distance had kept nearly inviolate since the days of Drake. Anson was given five hundred soldiers to serve as marines, or five hundred of what the government of the day considered soldiers, for they took the men from the invalid pensioners at Chelsea Hospital and sent them aboard his ships. Half of them had the good sense to desert at Portsmouth before the ships sailed. Not one of the remainder lived to come home again.

It took Anson several months to beat past Cape Horn, and he lost six hundred men doing so, mostly from scurvy, some from the wreck of one of his smaller ships. He then cruised the Pacific coast, taking several prizes, but doing nothing serious to the Spanish. In the spring of 1742 he started across the Pacific, losing men all the way. Nonetheless, he made his crossing, refitted at Macao, and in June of the next year he fell in with and captured the Manila galleon, the annual Spanish trea-

sure ship from the Philippines to America. Refitting again, he sailed
for home in his flagship, *Centurion,* the only vessel left, and he finally
got home in the summer of 1744, after sailing right through a French
squadron in a fog off the English coast. He and his surviving crew were
hailed as heroes, and they and their treasure were paraded triumphantly through the streets of London.

By now the Spanish war had merged into the larger War of the
Austrian Succession. British armies were fighting once more on the
Continent, as adjuncts of larger allied forces. At Dettingen in 1743
King George II led his army personally in battle, the last time an
English sovereign did so. Actually, he retired from the field after mak-
ing a few ceremonial flourishes in the direction of Louis XV, who was
also there, but "the Prince of Wales was seen to draw his sword in a
most affecting manner," and all in all it was a satisfactory occasion.

This was the era when warfare was at its most formal, and all the
movements of battle were carefully worked out, very much like the
dances of the time. Three years after Dettingen, for example, the Battle
of Fontenoy was fought, one of the most famous encounters in British
military history. The British, fourteen thousand strong, marched
steadfastly between two fires up to the French line; there they paused,
and Lord Charles Hay, colonel of the First Foot Guards, pulled out his
silver flask, drank a toast to the French some forty paces in front of
him, and called out that he hoped they were going to wait for him and
not run, as they had at Dettingen. They not only waited, they also
fought like mad, Gardes Françaises and Irish Brigade against British
and Hanoverian, and after three hours of toe-to-toe slugging, the British fell back in good order, leaving seven thousand dead and wounded
behind them. The courtesies of the day served only to mask the brutality of the fighting, and the great Marshal Saxe, touring his battlefield
with Louis XV after it was over, remarked, "You see now, sire, the
fruits of victory. Next to a battle lost, the saddest thing is a battle won."

Fontenoy, fought in 1745, was the last major battle of the war on
the Continent for British soldiers; that year also saw the last Stuart attempt to regain the throne of Britain. Prince Charles Edward Louis
Philip Casimir Stuart, son of James Edward and Princess Sobieski, was
the last hope of the exiled dynasty. In France they saw him as a useful
pawn, and after fighting bravely at Dettingen, he was appointed to
head an invasion army in 1744. As usual, however, the French could
not gain command of the Channel, the troops were taken off for other
duties, and the Young Pretender was left to cool his heels in French

anterooms. Finally he had had enough of this kind of help, and he sailed from Nantes with seven comrades. He spoke French with a Polish accent and could barely speak English at all, but when he raised his father's standard at Glenfinnan in mid-August, the clansmen flocked out for the old cause. On September 17 Edinburgh opened its gates to him, and though the Castle held out, he still set up court in Holyrood, and the Scottish lairds came to bend the knee as they had to his great-grandfathers. His Highlanders easily beat a weak British force under General Cope at Prestonpans, and in November they moved south, with the pipes playing "The Blue Bonnets Are over the Border" and the men singing laughingly, "Hey, Johnny Cope, are ye runnin' yet?"

But the English of the northern counties would not rise. It was one thing to meet visitors in the dark of the moon and drink vaguely worded toasts to the Jacobite cause; it was another to hazard life and property with a bunch of wild men from the northern hills, barefoot and hungry-looking and eyeing the cutlery. Charles took Carlisle and moved on south, as far as Derby.

Meanwhile, where French ships might not sail, British ones could. Back from the continent came those steady red regiments of Fontenoy, led by the Duke of Cumberland, and there was no joy in the Scottish camp. Charles might have tried for London, and the gamble might have worked, but his commanders cried caution, and they began a retreat. The Highlanders went sullenly north, cursing shuttered English windows, and in April Cumberland's troops caught up with them at Culloden Moor. Impatiently, the Scots charged with all their undisciplined fury, and the English stood in ranks and shot the heart out of their charge, then moved among the moaning masses with their bayonets and musket butts. A despairing Charles fled for the mountains, and after months of being hunted, got away to France. Cumberland marched through the Highlands carrying fire and sword and British law, so that he went down in Scottish folklore as "Butcher" Cumberland, and the last hope of the Stuarts flickered and died.

The hand of the Navy could be seen in all this. Charles could not get across with his French Army, but Cumberland could with his British. In this war as in earlier ones, the French had given the game away early by accepting naval inferiority. By now, in fact, they had come up with strategic and tactical doctrines that rationalized what they were doing, telling them that their mistakes were the right ones. Strategically they invented the idea of the ulterior objective, which said that the control of the seas was unimportant if one could occasionally get a fleet out to take islands or bases, and turning a conveniently blind eye to the fact that while they did not command the seas, any overseas base was a mere hostage held at the pleasure of the enemy. Tactically they chose to fight with the lee gauge, which they said allowed them to break off the action at pleasure; in gunnery, where the British shot for the hull, to kill, the French shot for the rigging, to disable and leave themselves free to maneuver. So the French had a complete, coherent doctrine, with only one thing wrong with it: It did not work.

But then the British were very much in the same condition, for by now, after a generation of peace, they had firmly settled in a traditional mold as well. The Fighting Instructions had become an absolute Bible for British captains, and even admirals disregarded them at their peril, as was shown in the one big naval battle of the war, off Toulon.

Here Admiral Thomas Matthews, commanding a blockading fleet of twenty-eight ships, had been watching the joint French and Spanish squadrons in the harbor. In February 1744 they got out, twenty-eight strong, and headed westward, presumably for the Strait of Gibraltar. Matthews followed, but the winds were light, and his ships were foul from being long on station. It took him three days to come within battle range. The situation was peculiar, for neither side was a happy fleet. The French and Spanish thoroughly distrusted each other, and the French commander, Admiral de Court, an old man of eighty, had wanted to mix the Spanish ships in with his so he could control them; the Spanish had indignantly refused, and when the allied fleet sailed, the French took the van, there was a mixed center division, and the Spaniards took the rear. On the English side, Matthews had quarreled with his captains, and especially with his rear admiral, Richard Lestock; in fact, the two hated each other. As the English caught up with the allied fleet, Lestock's rear division was several miles behind, in the windward position.

Matthews hoisted the signal for line ahead, and he bore down to meet the enemy. His original intention was to come even with them, the old coterminous line principle, then go down on them all together. However, he soon realized that his ships were not good enough to catch up, so he hoisted a second signal, "Engage the enemy," and turning with the wind, he and the ships in his immediate vicinity closed with the allied line, where they were soon involved in a ferocious firefight.

In the rear Lestock chose to obey the signals literally and conformed to his admiral's movements, coming down against nothing but keeping the purity of the battle line. His entire division sailed serenely alone through the battle. The three ships in the British van, seeing that if they did conform the French would be in a position to double back and surround Matthews, disobeyed the signal, maintained course, and thus stood off, with heavy fighting, the entire French van of some eleven ships. The brunt of the battle was therefore borne by Matthews and the few ships ahead and astern of him; several of the ships even in his center division kept their line and failed to support the admiral. Under these circumstances only one enemy ship was taken; Captain Edward Hawke took the Spanish flagship *Real Felipe.*

The battle then further disintegrated, and at day's end the two fleets stood off, eyeing each other but not doing much more. Matthews followed the Franco-Spanish for two more days but did not renew the action.

The climax came later, for of the twenty-eight English captains and two admirals involved, court-martial charges were laid against both the admirals and eleven of the captains. Matthews himself was convicted of not doing his utmost to destroy the enemy, while Lestock, who did his utmost to destroy Matthews, was acquitted on the technical ground that he had correctly followed signals, even if they meant taking him out of the battle. Of the eleven captains, one died; Captain Norris deserted rather than face trial; two were acquitted; and seven were found guilty, including the captain of the van who by his presence of mind had held off the enemy van and probably prevented a disaster. He was convicted of not obeying the admiral's signals. The whole thing was a badly needed shock to the Navy's sense of itself, showing, as Mahan pointed out, that Britain controlled the seas more by her enemy's weakness than by her own strength.

The same kind of thing happened elsewhere, for in the Indian Ocean the British lost Madras in 1746 largely through naval ineptitude, too. Since the turn of the century the British East India Company had been generating steady profits out of India and slowly improving its position in the increasingly chaotic political scene there. In 1717 they were granted exemption from customs duties by the declining Mogul Empire, and they continued to establish factories and to spread along the coasts of the subcontinent.

They now faced European competition, however, for the French, whose East India Company had been founded by Colbert in 1664, had also gained concessions and factories, and by the 1740s they were ready to put on a major drive for control. It was at this point, in fact, that the entire complexion of European contact with India was changed, a new direction initiated largely by one man. Joseph François Dupleix had been in India for twenty years, and in 1741 he was appointed governor general of the French Indies. As Europe's new war spread to India, Dupleix decided on a bold new departure. Where the English had always done their best to remain aloof from Indian politics, Dupleix chose instead to create a French Empire in India. He believed he could pick the right Indian princes, and French resources and military skills could guarantee that they would be winners; the result ought to be a series of grateful client states that would shut the English out of the subcontinent and make it a preserve of the French.

This was a tall order, for the English were far stronger than the French were. The English were now solidly entrenched at Bombay, at Madras, and in Bengal, with a network of subordinate factories radiating from each of the three centers. They had also extended their trade through to China; even more important, they had a good naval dockyard at Bombay and enjoyed the support of a substantial Royal Navy squadron. The French holdings were still confined largely to the Coromandel coast, with their capital at Pondicherry, and their nearest naval station was on the island of Mauritius. Even then there were no ships there, for over the protests of the governor, Labourdonnais, French men-of-war had been recalled home on the outbreak of war in Europe. Nonetheless, Dupleix was determined, and his determination changed history, though not in the way he had hoped.

Throughout the period of European contact with India, the primary factor of control was seapower; whoever dominated the Indian Ocean, or even at some times the Atlantic Ocean, could get his troops to India and keep a rival's from getting there. The great strength, as well as the chief peculiarity, of seapower lies in its potential ubiquity, and overseas territories might be won or lost by a battle that occurred off the coast of France. The increasing oneness of European and imperial affairs was graphically illustrated in the War of the Austrian Succession by events on opposite sides of the world, in India and in North America.

It was 1746 before either French or English undertook any serious action in India, but in that year La Bourdonnais raised a squadron of his own, part East India Company ships, part impressed merchantmen, and with it he threatened to turn the tide of affairs. There was a superior English squadron under Commodore Peyton off the eastern coast, and the two fleets met off Negapatam in July. Though they fought a drawn battle, the British had slightly the worse of it, and Peyton used that as his excuse for withdrawing from Coromandel altogether. This left the French a free hand, and La Bourdonnais capitalized on it by sailing for Madras, which he took after a short land and sea investment in September. He then offered to ransom the place for several million pounds, and his offer was quickly accepted. Dupleix, however, with whom the sailor was not on good terms, claimed that once taken, Madras was within his jurisdiction as Governor General of the Indies, and he disallowed the deal. La Bourdonnais, furious, was subsequently recalled to France, where he was imprisoned, the price of having exceeded his instructions and actually accomplished something, and he died soon thereafter.

With Madras in his control, justly or otherwise, Dupleix then turned on the British factory at Fort St. David, but had to raise the siege when the British naval forces reappeared. In 1748 he might well have lost the entire game, for a substantial enemy fleet under Admiral Edward Boscawen attacked Pondicherry itself. Dupleix managed to hold them off, partly with the aid of a typhoon, and then news arrived of the end of the war before they might do further damage. As far as the fighting went, then, the French were well ahead on points.

The connection of India with North America was more real than apparent. Here the major operation of King George's War, as it was known in this part of the world, was in the North, once more over Acadia.

After the Peace of Utrecht and the cession of Nova Scotia to the British, the French had continued to hold Cape Breton Island (or Isle Royale, as they called it). They decided to build here a great fortress that would serve as a guardian for the approaches to the St. Lawrence. The work was begun in the 1720s, and on the gray shore around Louisbourg a huge fort on the best European models slowly took shape. It was planned along the principles laid out by a great military engineer, Vauban, with covered ways, scarp, counterscarp, batteries here and bastions there. When someone suggested that stone and mortar did not stand up well to the moist, salty climate of Cape Breton and the local extremes of heat in the summer and cold in the winter, the French builders scorned such nonsense. Surely what was good enough for Europe was more than good enough for someplace in the back of nowhere. So they built it of beautiful dressed granite, with mortar that weakened and crumbled away winter after winter. It was still very impressive and very expensive; Louis XV one day grumbled that he expected any day to look out the western windows of Versailles and see the battlements of Louisbourg rising over the horizon. Like a later, greater French fortification, it was never entirely finished, and it was never fully garrisoned, either. The French had hoped that under the guns of Louisbourg, the French population of this new Acadia would flourish; but Cape Breton was not the Annapolis Valley, and the town remained a small fishing settlement, a scraggle of poor houses and a large number of taverns where disgruntled soldiers off duty might drown their sorrows. Ironically, Louisbourg survived its winters and its shortages because illicit traders sailed up from Massachusetts to sell their rum and their grain to the French.

When war broke out, then, the Yankees knew all about the "Dunkerque of North America," and they quickly decided to take it. The chief instrument of this decision was the Governor of Massachusetts, William Shirley, a London lawyer who had found colonial society more suited to his budget, if not his tastes, than the capital. Unfortunately, the colony was in no position to undertake large military operations, for it was bankrupt. Shirley was not put off by that; he asked London for money and vigorously campaigned in the other colonies to get them to contribute. In London the ministers thought the colonials might be getting a bit above themselves but that the whole was worth a try. They gave the go-ahead, and Commodore Peter Warren brought a small squadron up from the West Indies to support the attempt. The colonies as far south as Pennsylvania raised men, or money, or ships, or all three. The actual command went to William Pepperell, a Maine man of many parts. Colonel of the Maine militia, though he had no military experience, Chief Justice of Maine, though he had no legal knowledge, his chief qualification was that he was a rich merchant and therefore a man who knew, presumably, how to get things done.

In March 1745 all was ready, and the expedition set off, four thousand strong, in a hundred transports, with fifteen armed colonial ships and Warren's sixty-gunner and three frigates. It was a motley fleet, brigs and snows and pinks and schooners, and the troops in all manner of uniforms and more often none at all, yet it was a portent of things to come. Setting aside the little forays of the previous wars, really nothing more than raids, this was the first major Anglo-

American "conjunct expedition"; two hundred years later the descendants of these men crossed the Channel to Normandy.

They mustered at the Strait of Canso, between Cape Breton Island and the mainland, and then sailed on to Gabarus Bay, where they landed unopposed and set up their camp a couple of miles from the great brooding fortress. The French held out for six weeks, while the amateur soldiers outside their walls ran around like a disturbed beaver colony. They seized one isolated battery the French had left unmanned and turned its guns on the fort. They tried to take an island bastion in a night attack; unfortunately, the stormers had been issued too much rum as a stimulant. On landing below the bastion's walls, they gave a cheer for their safe arrival, whereupon the suddenly aroused French shot them to pieces. They next hauled guns up on a height the French thought unscalable, and bombarded the fortress with plunging shot. In mid-June the French had had enough and negotiated for a surrender. The Yankees had taken the greatest fortress in North America with a loss of a hundred men.

It actually proved more costly than that, for after taking it, the Americans had to garrison it. At the end of the siege they already had ten times as many men sick with camp fever as had been hurt in combat; over the next several months they lost nearly a thousand to disease. Still, they had done it all by themselves, or with just a little help from the Royal Navy, and they were very pleased with the affair. Pepperell was rewarded with the first baronetcy ever granted to an American, and he and Shirley each became colonel of a regiment, a very lucrative sinecure in those days. Warren was promoted to admiral, made governor of Cape Breton, and got several hundred thousand pounds' prize money.

This was practically the only real success of the war for British arms. Naval affairs continued to bumble along for a couple more years, with attacks on convoys and a few inconclusive, if occasionally hard-fought, battles between escorts and attackers. But the war was running down. On the Continent the King of Prussia, who had started the whole thing by invading Austrian territory, had dropped out of the war, then come back in, then dropped out again, each time betraying his French allies. Everyone was tired, the financial drain was heavy, and no one seemed able to achieve anything decisive; eventually the major parties opened negotiations, and in October 1748 they signed the Treaty of Aix-la-Chapelle.

The essential futility of this war, as far as Britain, France, and

Spain were concerned, was shown by the provision that all their captures should be mutually restored. After nine years of effort, none of them had gained anything. The British East India Company was given back Madras, to the intense chagrin of Dupleix and the very real loss of standing of his company with the Indian princes; and the French were given back Louisbourg, to the even greater disgust of the New Englanders. About the only one who came out of the war with gains was the King of Prussia, whom his subjects now began to call Frederick the Great.

Under these circumstances, peace did not last a decade. All of the powers were shopping for new advantages and new allies, and in the midfifties, in a game called at the time the Diplomatic Revolution, there was a general post of alliances. Britain and Prussia ended up allied together, against a coalition that initially included Austria, France, Russia, and some of the lesser German states, and finally Spain as well. In part this was engineered by Queen Maria Theresa of Austria, who was determined to get her stolen possessions back from Prussia, in part by Empress Elizabeth of Russia, whom Frederick had publicly referred to as a fat pig. Faced by a coalition that his own intemperance had created, Frederick opened the war with an invasion of Saxony in August 1756.

Overseas, the peace had been largely illusory anyway, for in both India and North America, the rivalry between France and England was now reaching its climax. The French in Canada had seen their position steadily eroded away. The New Englanders were encroaching more and more on the St. Lawrence gateway, and traders and settlers were seeping across the mountains of Virginia and Pennsylvania into the Ohio Valley. Nor could formal peace in Europe prevent the East India Company of either country from attempting to improve its position at the expense of the other.

No sooner had the British given back Louisbourg than they realized that they needed it. Just a year after the peace treaty was signed, therefore, they sent a large expedition to Nova Scotia, and it established a colony on the shores of a beautiful basin, Chebucto Bay, about midway along the Atlantic coast of the peninsula. The spot itself was inauspicious. Late in the last war, the French had sent a naval expedition to recapture Louisbourg; it had carried the plague with it and had gotten as far as this spot, where it had hastily buried thousands of wretched corpses. Skeletons poking out of shallow graves welcomed the British as they came ashore.

Yet the site itself belied this grim meeting. For the little colony—Halifax, it was named—proved one of the best and most strategic spots on the entire North American coast; it opened on one of the finest natural harbors of the world, Bedford Basin, and within months it was a thriving garrison town, attracting trade and settlers. Halifax, in fact, was the only colony ever founded by direct action of British military forces, and for two hundred years it well lived up to its name of "the warden of the North."

The English were equally concerned with the isthmus that connected Nova Scotia to the mainland, and they built a fort there, Fort Lawrence, named after the governor, to balance the French holding at Fort Beausejour. It was obvious that in this area things were shaping up to a conclusion, and that brought to a head the problem of the Acadians. There were several thousands of them now, industrious and determinedly French peasant farmers, scattered along the Bay of Fundy shore around the Minas Basin. After the Peace of Utrecht, they had been required only to take an oath of allegiance to Great Britain; most had refused to do so, partly under the strong influence of their priests, but mostly because they just wanted to be left alone. Successive governors of Nova Scotia at Annapolis Royal had tried to enforce the oath without much effect. At midcentury, this anomalous condition came to the attention both of Governor Shirley in Massachusetts and of the new governor at Halifax, Lawrence. The latter, especially, possessed a bureaucratic clarity of mind that saw everything except the human issue. He decided to give the Acadians one more chance, and when they evaded it as they always had, he then decided to deport them.

New England troops, who made up much of the garrison of the area, moved in and rounded up the Acadians. They were held prisoner while their farms and homes were burned and ships were collected; they were then put aboard ship in lots and sent off, to be broken up as a people. Each of the British colonies was supposed to take a set number, according to Lawrence, but he had not bothered to check that the other colonies agreed to this. Some were imprisoned, some were thrown out to beg, some were further deported. Those who managed to get away from the English colonies and make their way to Quebec were treated as badly as they had been along the British seacoast. A large portion of them eventually found refuge in Louisiana, then a Spanish colony, and many stayed there. Back in Nova Scotia, their diked meadows and farmlands were settled by New Englanders, a colony of a colony, and Windsor, Nova Scotia, is named after Windsor in Connecticut and not in England.

It was events in the South as much as his immediate problems that had triggered Lawrence's actions, for the Anglo-French struggle was heating up in the Ohio Valley, too. In 1754 a young Virginian named George Washington had been chased back over the mountains by the French, and the next year, when the British decided to send an expedition to the forks of the Ohio, it was ambushed by French and Indians. Braddock's defeat, in which regular English soldiers were mown down by the forest skills of their enemies, occurred in a time of ostensible peace; it was therefore easy to make the transition to war.

Peace was equally illusory in India, for in the years between wars, both sides tried hard to improve their position. The thrones of the Deccan and the Carnatic were each available, and by 1751 the French dominated both, with Dupleix being the power behind the throne in the latter, and another French officer, Bussy, in the same place in the former. It looked as if the French might well achieve their ambitions when they were suddenly faced, at last, with inspired British opposition.

Robert Clive had arrived penniless in Madras at the age of eighteen, to serve as a clerk in the East India Company. Friendless and depressed, he had tried to commit suicide, but the pistol he held to his head misfired. Deciding that Fate meant him for better things, he took part in the scrabbly fighting of the War of the Austrian Succession, and in 1751, as French fortunes were at their peak, he suddenly rose to stardom by seizing the great fortress of Arcot with 215 men and holding it against 7,000 Indians and a few French for eleven weeks. This turned the muddied tides of Indian politics, and in 1754, when Dupleix was called home, British fortunes were on the rise.

The actual outbreak of war in 1756 was merely an intensification of a conflict that was now gathering its own momentum. The world had become too small for the imperial rivalries of England and France, and everywhere there was contact between the two systems, antagonism was a matter of course.

It peaked first in India, for though Dupleix was never to be replaced by a man of similar caliber, his legacy lived on. Both companies were now thoroughly embroiled in native politics, and the British found that even if they had been disposed to do so, they could no longer avoid territorial imperialism. The company fell victim to its own success.

It was a success hard won, for the affairs of India were labyrinthine indeed, and it was always difficult to know who was on whose side. But British naval control kept France from interfering more than marginally in the area, and superior British technology and military organization finally won the day. The great turning point came in Bengal. In 1756 the Nawab of Bengal, Siraj-ud-Daulah, a twenty-year-old wastrel, attacked and took the British factory at Calcutta. The Governor and many of the senior officials got away by ships, leaving behind slightly more than a hundred of their compatriots. These surrendered and were casually herded into a cell in the local jail, where many of them died from overcrowding, heat, suffocation, or wounds; the story of the Black Hole of Calcutta thus passed into the legend of empire.

The East India Company responded to this by sending up Robert Clive and a few hundred European soldiers with a Royal Navy squadron. The force was numerically insignificant, and there was a fair amount of time spent bargaining back and forth, until it was apparent to Clive that the Nawab was a fool about to collapse of his own weight. All Clive had to do was pick the right plotter to back, and he finally sided with a former court official and distant claimant to the throne, Mir Jafar. In June 1757 the fate of Bengal was decided at Plassey. For one of the decisive battles of imperial history, it was not much of an encounter; Clive had eight hundred European troops and twenty-two hundred Indians to pit against fifty thousand of the Nawab's men. But very few of the fifty thousand wanted to fight. There was an inconclusive cannonade; several of the Indian princes, including Mir Jafar himself, sat it out waiting to see which way the wind might blow. Finally Clive's European infantry, impatient, advanced against orders, and the entire Bengal Army dissolved in flight, led by the Nawab himself. Siraj-ud-Daulah was soon captured and executed, Mir Jafar seated on his throne, and the British, though it was not immediately apparent, had both a puppet regime and a firm base in northeastern India.

In the intervals while he waited for plots to mature, Clive also managed to take the French Bengal post of Chandernagor, effectively squeezing them out of the area. But events in Bengal were considered at the time to be secondary to the fighting farther south, along the Coromandel coast, where the center of both British and French power still lay. What happened there depended largely on naval power, and that in turn was chiefly influenced by events in Europe.

Though Frederick the Great's invasion of Saxony in the summer of 1756 officially initiated the Seven Years' War, this only served to formalize the battle already going on between the English and French for their imperial possessions. Braddock had been defeated at the forks of the Ohio the year before. In the same year the French had sent a large squadron to Quebec, with substantial reinforcements for the garrison there. A British government that was ordering troops to the Ohio Valley was not going to stand for that, peace or no, and Admiral Edward Boscawen was ordered to intercept and destroy the French. Lying in wait for them off the Strait of Belle Isle, between Newfoundland and the mainland, he actually did take two ships, but the rest got past him in the constant fogs of the area. The French recalled their ambassador to London but did nothing more about what was clearly an act of war. They were not ready yet, and between Braddock's failure and Boscawen's, they seemed to be doing well enough anyway.

The British ministry under the Duke of Newcastle was equally vacillating; a month after the Belle Isle affair, it ordered Sir Edward Hawke to cruise off the coasts of France and to take any French ships he could. In six months he took three hundred merchant ships and captured six thousand French sailors. Still the government at Versailles bided its time.

As the next year opened, however, they began to move. Activity at the Channel ports picked up, and noisy preparations were made for an invasion of England. Newcastle, who knew everything about packing Parliament with his supporters but nothing about world affairs, allowed his attention to be fully absorbed by this spectacle. Then, at the last moment, the French sent a small squadron and a large troop convoy out of Toulon, landed it on Minorca, and immediately besieged the weak British garrison there.

Hastily the British sent Admiral John Byng, a distinguished sailor from an old naval family, off to lift the siege. By the time he got past Gibraltar Byng had thirteen ships of the line to match against the French twelve. The Battle of Minorca, fought on May 20, 1756, was the usual inconclusive affair of the period. Byng was unable to get his ships in good order, and his van took a heavy pounding while he, in the rear division, was hardly engaged at all. The French might have done real damage and even taken several ships, but they were excessively conscious of the landing force behind them and were content to see the British withdraw. This Byng did, sailing away for Gibraltar, disappointed in his failure but sure he had followed the Fighting Instructions to the letter and feeling it was not his fault that they failed to work.

In England they thought differently. The government decided to court-martial Byng, thinking that in showing his dereliction of duty they could disguise their own stupidity. The admiral was charged with cowardice in the face of the enemy, disaffection, and "failing to do his utmost" to bring the enemy to battle. He was acquitted of the first two, but the latter was unbeatable, and the penalty for it was specifically enjoined in the articles of war: death. Byng was therefore sentenced to death, and though a recommendation for mercy was made by the court, who were after all naval officers, knowing the same thing might someday happen to them, the King declined to be merciful. On March 14, 1757, Byng was executed on the quarterdeck of his own flagship, *Monarque,* in Portsmouth Harbor, prompting Voltaire's famous remark that "every so often the English shoot an admiral to encourage the others."

Shooting admirals was all very well in its place, but it really did little to forward the English situation. Two months after Byng's execution they finally got around to declaring war on France, so that the fighting was now generally joined. There was already a British army on the Continent, operating out of Hanover under the command of the Duke of Cumberland and generally protecting Frederick's western flank by keeping the French busy. As a rule this army's operations were overshadowed through the war by the larger affairs of Prussia, but one event was particularly noteworthy. In 1759, then under the command of the Duke of Brunswick, it met a larger French army at Minden. At that time the allied force had only six British regiments of infantry, and a force of British cavalry under Lord George Sackville; the majority of its troops were made up of contingents from the western German states. Largely as a result of misinterpreting orders, the British infantry advanced in formation against the overwhelming French cavalry, and by steadily plowing ahead, at heavy cost, broke the French and drove them from the field. For infantry to do this to unhampered cavalry was virtually without precedent. As the French turned to go, Brunswick, expecting to turn a retreat into a rout, ordered Sackville and the cavalry to charge. In spite of repeated urging, Lord George refused to move forward, and after the battle, he was court-martialed for cowardice and cashiered. Obviously he got off much more lightly than Byng; not only did he live, he also became Lord George Germain, and from 1775 to 1782 he was Secretary of State for the colonies—that is, the man who presided over the loss in the American Revolution.

One reason for the small size of the British forces on the Continent by 1759 was that Britain had at last found a leader who could put together a wide-ranging but still coherent plan of imperial war. The advent to power of William Pitt in 1757 marked the dawn of a new era. The Elder Pitt, as he is called to distinguish him from another Pitt, of the Napoleonic period, was also known as "the Great Commoner," a useful political misnomer, for he was related to everyone who counted in the English establishment. He had entered politics from the Army in the 1730s, taking up vigorous opposition to Robert Walpole, who had one day muttered, "we must muzzle this terrible cornet of horse." This was a view fully shared by King George II, and his dislike kept Pitt from power for years. Gradually, however, he worked his way into the inner circles, even George became reconciled to him, and as the bumblings of Newcastle's government grew to unbearable proportions, Pitt slowly took over the war effort. In the end they made a good combination, the amiable humbug, Newcastle, adroitly controlling a corrupt Parliament, and the acerbic and unpopular Pitt managing the war effort.

At last there was a man who could see the war, and the world, as a whole. The vision was so clear it was a wonder no one had seen it before. English trade and money enabled Britain to subsidize allies on the Continent—in this case, Frederick the Great. That kept France busy. France's preoccupation with Germany allowed Britain to rule the seas, and command of the seas enabled her to build up her own empire overseas and destroy the French in the process. The greater the empire, the greater the volume of British trade, and the more money, a self-perpetuating circle that would go on indefinitely and make Britain the chief world power. Pitt not only had brains enough to see it, he also had character enough to do it. It took a while for the ship of state to feel the firm hand on the wheel, but when it did, the effects were miraculous.

It was under Pitt, too, that the British at last began to discover an affinity for combined operations. The country was numerically weak compared to her enemies and never tried to match the great armies of France, or later Germany, with one notable and tragic exception. But Britain's small army did have the mobility conferred on it by sea control; militarily, the "power of Britain" might be negligible, but "the amphibious power of Britain" was a different matter, and that was a phrase that might be heard increasingly.

In 1758 matters began to take shape for Britain. Pitt devised the idea of amphibious raids along the coast of France to keep the French busy and distracted; these were not very successful, for such raids are heavily dependent upon natural conditions and are difficult even when a force is not at the mercy of wind power; the opposition in Parliament characterized such pinpricks as "breaking windows with guineas," a costly waste of effort. But though Pitt was still feeling his way, he was also finding the kind of men who could do what he wanted done. The year 1759 went down in history as the *annus mirabilis*, the "year of miracles," and it was said that Londoners, instead of wishing each other good day, asked what news of victories had come in during the night. In that year it all came together at last.

The French, as usual when they got sufficiently bothered by the English, were planning an invasion of the island. And equally as usual, they went about it backward. They simply refused to accept the vital nature of sea control, and they devised an elaborate plan to make up for this deficiency. The new French minister, the Duc de Choiseul, decided that the Toulon and Brest squadrons, united, would land a force of twenty thousand on the western coast of Scotland. Then they would sail around and enter the North Sea from the north, pick up a second French army in the allied Austrian Netherlands, and transport it across to the southeastern coast of England, from which it would march on London. Meanwhile they would also invade Ireland, where the Irish might be expected to rise up in revolt. Choiseul was no fool, and all in all it was an ingenious house of cards.

The British as well as the French recognized that the Toulon squadron was the first order of business. Its preparations were the most advanced, and it must initiate the whole sequence of events. On August 12 Commodore de la Clue got out of Toulon with twelve ships of the line and sailed for the Strait of Gibraltar. Unknown to the French, however, Admiral Boscawen had been sent with reinforcements to Gibraltar. "Wry-neck Dick," as he was known in the fleet, was lying in the harbor refitting with fifteen ships of the line. Late in the evening of August 17 De la Clue sailed through the Strait; he was just congratulating himself on hoodwinking his adversary when the station frigate sighted him and began firing signals. While the French disappeared in the darkness, the British hastily finished their work and sailed out of the harbor.

During the night De la Clue lost contact with several of his ships which eventually put in to Spanish ports. Morning found him with only eight ships left, and he sailed westward. Boscawen, determined not to let him get away, took advantage of the one loophole in the Fighting Instructions that gave room for independent action: He signaled for a "General Chase," and the British took off after their adversaries, each ship sailing as fast as it might.

The chase went on through this second night, and at dawn De la Clue had only five of his own ships still in company but was well within sight of the English fleet. Faced with the prospect of a long day ahead, he decided that if he could not fulfill his mission, he would at least deny his ships to the enemy. He turned for the coast of Portugal and sailed into Lagos Bay, where he ran his flagship, *Océan,* full on a rock, a total wreck. His other captains were less determined, or put more faith in Portuguese neutrality, for they carefully anchored inside the bay, under the guns of a Portuguese fort, and breathed a sigh of relief.

Boscawen was not to be put off by the neutrality of a little place like Portugal, however, not when there were four ships of the line sitting there for the taking. Disregarding warning shots from the Portuguese, he kept his "General Chase" signal flying and sailed boldly into the bay, with the rest of his squadron after him. He took two and burned two, and then sailed happily out to sea. Later he wrote to Pitt that he assumed his action would be approved and that it was easier to satisfy Portuguese protests than it was for the French to build four new ships of the line, a point with which Pitt readily agreed.

With the Toulon survivors under close blockade in Cadiz, the great combination was in ruins. Choiseul persisted in his idea, and though he dropped the cross-Channel aspect of his scheme, he still hoped to bring off the Scottish invasion. There were twenty-one ships of the line in Brest, under Admiral Conflans, while a British squadron of twenty-five ships of the line, plus several smaller ships, cruised to the west. Their commander was Admiral Hawke, who had captured the Spanish flagship off Toulon in the previous war, and Hawke fully lived up to his name. Faced with a major threat, he had developed a new idea. Up to this point, the British had watched the French Breton ports during the fair season, but when the winter gales came on, they retired to harbors on the southwestern coast of Britain, believing that a westerly storm that drove them off station also kept the French landbound. Hawke decided this was not sufficient watch, and he initiated the practice of keeping the blockade manned in all kinds of weather, winter and summer. From now on, year in and year out, through fog, gale, or fair weather, British ships cruised steadily back and forth off the approaches to Brest, from Ushant to the Saints, their topsails a permanent feature of the French seascape. It could be deadly work, men washed overboard, a couple of ships a year run aground on the treacherous rocks that dotted the Iroise Channel, but it worked. It made the British the best sailors in the world, and their belief in their moral and psychological ascendance over their enemies made them even better. This was the year that the great actor Garrick wrote "Hearts of Oak," the Navy's march ever since.

In mid-November a tremendous westerly gale came up, so strong that even Hawke's ships could not stand before it, and the British bore up and sailed for Torbay, leaving but a couple of frigates sheltering behind Ushant. As the gale finally moderated, Conflans seized his chance and put to sea, and while Hawke was desperately plunging back from Torbay, the French admiral headed south and east, toward Quiberon Bay at the bottom of the Brittany Peninsula, to pick up the transports for the Scottish invasion. When he reached Belle Isle, off the mouth of the bay, however, what should he sight trailing him but Hawke and the whole British fleet. Utterly surprised that they should be back so soon, he lost his nerve; he had put his twenty-one ships in line for battle, but now he signaled them to flee into Quiberon Bay. The seas were increasing yet again, as another storm took shape, Quiberon was an even worse place than the Brest approaches, full of rocks and shoals known only to the local fishermen, and Conflans was certain the British would not dare follow him in. Gratefully the French ships fled before the wind.

Hawke had been waiting his opportunity for months now, and he intended to seize it. Like Boscawen, he hoisted "General Chase," and his captains, one eye on the wind and another on their straining masts, set extra sail and took up the pursuit. Through howling wind and crashing surf, the French sailed into Quiberon, the British right after them. Hawke's van caught the rearmost Frenchman as she entered the bay; boldly she opened her lower gunports to give a broadside and immediately flooded and went down, eight hundred French sailors drowned in an instant. Hawke's *Royal George* swept by another French ship, gave her a full broadside, and she blew up. Admiral Hawke stood on his quarterdeck brimming over with exhilaration, and when his pilot screamed a warning at him, he roared back, "You have done your duty by warning me! Now lay me alongside that French ship!" As darkness came on to complicate things further, the British took two quick prizes, and lost two of their own to the reefs. Finally they could see no more, and anchored for the night, carefully watching their cables and listening to the breaking storm waves.

In the morning the French were gone. During the night seven ships had slipped out, along the coast and down to Rochefort, where they were laid up for the next year. Seven more had thrown their guns overboard and lightened themselves sufficiently to run up the Vilaine River, where they finally grounded on mudflats at high water. It took a year's work to float them again. At that they had done better than Conflans himself. He ran his flagship, *Soleil Royal*, of eighty guns, on the rocks and tore her bottom out. The French Navy was finished for this war.

The conclusion of affairs in North America was equally satisfactory, and followed much the same pattern, defeat and delay in the beginning, but increasing effectiveness and triumph in the end. Boscawen's failure of 1755 meant that the French at last got a substantial number of troops out to Canada, something near three thousand, and the next year they managed to send another thousand, together with a new commander, the Marquis de Montcalm. The northern frontier blazed up yet again, and columns, no longer so little, threaded their way through the forests all the way from the forks of the Ohio around in a great arc to Louisbourg. The French were determined to hold their claims, and for a while it looked as if they might well do so. The colonies continually wrangled among themselves, and the new British commander-in-chief, Lord Loudoun, found that he spent more time fighting the Massachusetts Assembly than he did his official enemies. In August 1756 the French took Oswego, advancing their control of the northwestern New York region, and a year later they took Fort William Henry, at the bottom of Lake George and only fifty miles from Albany. Their Indian allies got out of hand and massacred the survivors after the garrison had surrendered, providing James Fenimore Cooper with one of the more memorable scenes for his novels of the Old French War.

But by 1758 the British were taking hold once more. Montcalm's support from home dried up, for the French could no longer ship reinforcements across the ocean, and he was left to fight with what he had. The British and colonials planned a four-pronged drive against New France, all things they had tried before. One expedition was to march on the forks of the Ohio, repeating Braddock's route with, one assumed, better success at the end. Second, Colonel John Bradstreet was to move west out the Mohawk Valley to Oswego, cross the lake, and take Fort Frontenac, where the St. Lawrence empties seaward

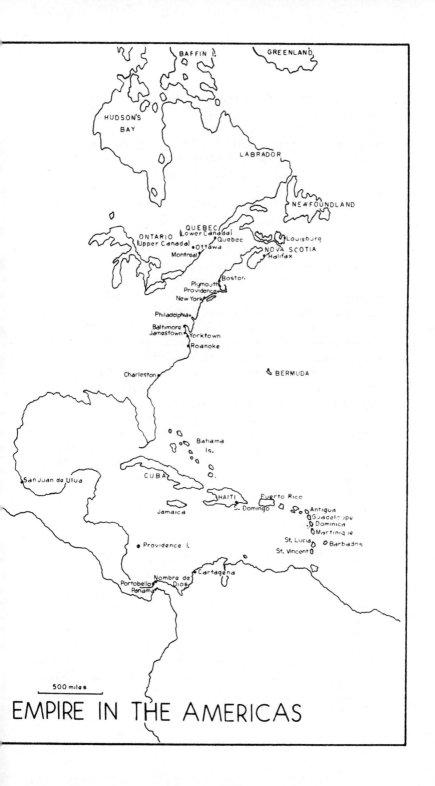

EMPIRE IN THE AMERICAS

out of Lake Ontario. General James Abercromby would advance with the main British effort straight up the old Lake Champlain route, taking the major French post at Ticonderoga and heading for the heart of New France around Montreal. Finally, an amphibious operation commanded by General Jeffrey Amherst, who replaced Loudoun as commander-in-chief, was to capture Louisbourg, then move up the St. Lawrence to Quebec. There were more British soldiers in North America than in all the British garrisons and field armies in continental Europe, and Pitt was heavily criticized by the opposition for scattering forces far from the center of action.

The year went almost, but not quite, as well as might have been hoped. A dying John Forbes painfully dragged himself, with an army behind him, over the mountains to the Ohio Valley and took Fort Duquesne, or the ashes where it had stood. The French left without much fight, and Forbes renamed the spot Fort Pitt and built a stockade there. In part the French gave up because Bradstreet had cut their communications with his successful strike against Fort Frontenac, and the western tribes began to drift into the British orbit.

Both of these successes were overshadowed by failure, though, for Abercromby made a thorough botch of the main attack. With fifteen thousand men, an enormously large force for the time and place, he marched north from Albany early in the summer. The general was at best an amiable dolt, and most of the work of managing the expedition was done by his subordinate, Lord George Howe. By July the British had reached the fort, which the French called Fort Carillon. Montcalm himself was here, prepared to make a determined stand, and he had thirty-six hundred men with him, all he could spare from his many other fronts. On July 6, as the British were reconnoitering the place, Howe was killed in a skirmish, and this left Abercromby with little idea how to conduct his business. The fort was formidable, and the French had further enhanced it by felling a great number of trees in front of the works, so that there was a tangled abatis protecting the walls themselves. Without bothering to look at the place or bring up his artillery, the British general could think of nothing better to do than to order a straight frontal assault, which he then observed from a couple of miles away. While the colonial troops, who were not heavily engaged, stood by in utter amazement, the regular British infantry spent the entire afternoon trying vainly to struggle through the abatis under the uninterrupted fire of the defenders. Not until it was nearly dark did Abercromby finally send orders to desist, by which time his soldiers were a ruined mass of bodies tangling the trees. He lost sixteen hundred men and most of his regimental officers. Then, with his nine thousand colonials still unused—and his artillery still unlimbered—he decided that if the true British bulldog spirit could not take the fort, nothing else could either, so he turned around and marched back to Albany.

As a memoirist once wrote, "there are hazards to all military service, but truly it must be said that the hazards in the British service are rather more peculiar than most." None of which prevented Abercromby from being promoted to lieutenant general the next year, or dying as a full general in 1781.

Matters went far better at Louisbourg, for Amherst was no Abercromby but a solid soldier who knew his business thoroughly. He was ably seconded on the military side by one of his brigadiers, James Wolfe, and the naval command went to Admiral Boscawen. Indeed, Boscawen did most of the preliminary work, collecting the thirteen thousand soldiers at Halifax and even drilling them in landing operations there. He had twenty-three ships of the line on the North American station, and Halifax was packed to bursting with ships and soldiers, drum and fife competing with boatswains' pipes for men's attention. When the great fleet sailed at the end of May, its numbers were better than four times those of the French. More importantly, this was a thoroughly competent force, professional from top to bottom.

Perhaps for that very reason, the second siege of Louisbourg lacked some of the inherent drama of the first, when the amateur soldiers of America took it twelve years earlier. This force was Royal Navy and regular Army, it was expected to perform well, and it did. Only a colonial would add that the same expectation might have attended Abercromby, too.

Once more the attackers landed at Gabarus Bay, an opposed landing this time, for the French had also learned some lessons. They lined the shore with entrenchments and fired vigorously, and the British might have been beaten off had not Wolfe gotten some men ashore on steep rocks and then flanked the lines. After that the siege pursued its normal course. It was a slow affair, though. The weather was chancy, and for a time it prevented Amherst from getting his guns ashore and set up. Boscawen sealed off the harbor tighter and tighter, and the French hung on grimly. There was smallpox among the besiegers, and the French Governor knew that even if he could not save himself, he might delay Amherst long enough to preserve Quebec for another year.

That was what finally happened, for the siege dragged through the summer. It was July 26 before the French surrendered; then all of Cape Breton and Prince Edward Island passed from their hands, while Amherst sent out small expeditions to sweep up isolated outposts as far away as the Gaspé Peninsula. However, the season was too far advanced now for the great assault on New France itself. Between the long siege and Abercromby's disastrous failure, the French got one more breathing spell. The British, firmly in possession of the St. Lawrence gateway, could afford to wait. With Halifax established, they did not need Louisbourg, and at the end of the war they blew it up, leaving great piles of granite, like the bones of some half-buried prehistoric animal, to lie among the encroaching dune grass. For years coastal traders loaded the cut stone as ballast, and some found its way as far south as the Carolinas, used for front steps and mantelpieces.

New France now felt the constriction of death, for there was no help from the mother country; the British blockade saw to that. The messages that got home, beseeching help, were answered with no more than heroic platitudes: Montcalm and his men must hold on, that was all. France itself was in a depressed state, its armies beaten, its ships rotten, and its government worse. At Versailles ministers and mistresses vied for power; drawing-room heroes made gibes at the expense of better men than themselves, there was a sense of all-pervasive decay, and Voltaire casually dismissed an empire with the remark, "Who worries about the barn when the house is burning down?"

In 1759 the outposts of New France were all gone, and the British could aim at the heart itself. Amherst marched slowly up the lake route, levering the French out of Ticonderoga and showing how easily Abercromby might have done the same. Amherst then drove them from Crown Point, a few miles farther up Lake Champlain, and there he settled for the winter, building a fort and a fleet of gunboats that held control of the lake for him. The discouraged French fell back to Isle-aux-Noix at the top of the lake.

But the main blow was amphibious; Wolfe and about nine thousand regular soldiers sailed up the St. Lawrence in an impressive British fleet. Admiral Sir Charles Saunders, a quiet, efficient sailor whom many authorities think should have the real credit for taking Quebec, commanded forty-three warships, more than a hundred transports, and altogether about thirteen thousand men. The force gathered at Louisbourg, got an appropriately early start, and appeared below Quebec late in June. Careful piloting avoided the disasters that had

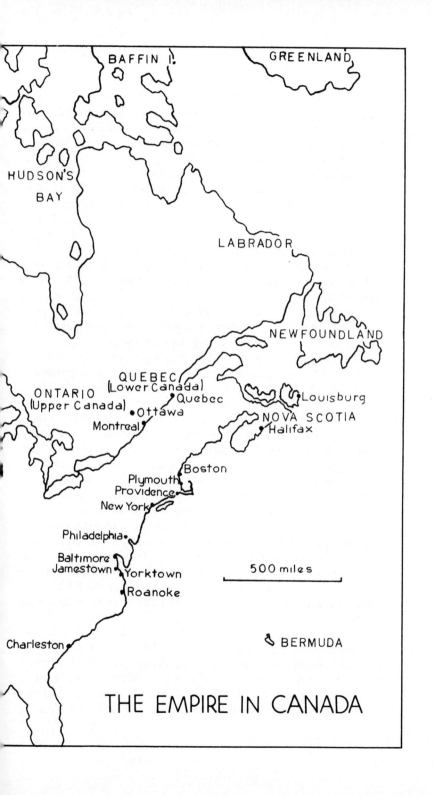

THE EMPIRE IN CANADA

beset Walker's earlier attempts, and this time the British scoffed at the supposed dangers of St. Lawrence navigation. They set up camp on the Isle of Orleans, then moved some of their forces to the southern shore, Point Levis, and began raiding up and down the river while Wolfe figured out how to take the city.

Quebec was a very formidable place, both because of natural difficulties and because Montcalm had done his best to enhance them. From a colony of roughly sixty thousand souls, he had managed to call up twelve thousand men and boys, so in quantity if not in quality, his forces actually outnumbered the British soldiers. July and August dragged by while Wolfe tried in vain to find a weak spot; nothing seemed to work. The general, a hypochondriac, fretted over his health, and pestered his brigadiers with ideas that led nowhere. The French sent fireships down the river, but the British sailors handily boarded and towed them off, and it looked as if there might be a stalemate. That would be a French victory, for if the winter came, the British ships must flee before the ice, taking their army with them.

But during the siege the sailors had managed to run ships upstream, past the city and its batteries, and they were in a position to threaten Quebec's communications with the interior. Late in August Saunders and Wolfe's brigadiers came up with an idea: Take the troops upstream, land them on the north shore, and advance directly on the city. It was somewhat desperate, but no one could think of anything better. On the night of September 12–13 the Navy took Wolfe's men in boats and landed them at a small cove, from which they climbed the steep bank, quickly overpowering a French picket. On the morning of the thirteenth there they stood, a line of red clumps on the Plains of Abraham, inviting the French to come out from their walls.

No one knows why Montcalm accepted the invitation. He had good defenses, he had enough provisions to stand even a close investment, and he also knew French troops from Montreal were marching to his assistance and would soon be able to harry the British rear. He also knew that in a mere month winter would drive the British away without his help. Nonetheless, he mustered his troops and marched out to give battle.

It did not take long. The French formed their ranks and charged gallantly forward; the British held their ground and then, firing rolling volleys by sections of platoons, shot the charge to pieces. The French militia, especially, soon became disordered, and the troops began to fray away. A stray shot hit Wolfe, and as he tried to rally his men, one hit Montcalm as well. Both commanders died, Wolfe at the climax of the victory, Montcalm during the night. The battle itself lasted but half an hour, a short period to seal the fate of a continent.

That might not have been so; the French could still have stood a siege, but the heart had gone out of them with Montcalm's death, and they surrendered with what almost looked like indecent haste. A British garrison marched in and took over, and Saunders and his ships stood back downriver, safe from the ice and victorious at last.

The next year the positions were reversed, and a small French force marched down from Montreal to besiege the British garrison of Quebec. Again the defenders came out to meet them and again were defeated. But within a week, topsails were sighted coming up the river, and, almost inevitably, they were British and not French. The French attackers fell back to Montreal, hoping for rescue, and at the end of the summer, in 1760, they surrendered at last. New France was finally finished.

It was the same in India. The capture of Bengal, and the revenues that that brought in, enabled the British to meet the French on more or less equal terms. While the company forces and the Indian allies of both marched back and forth and besieged each other's factories, the real decision was reached at sea. For two years a small British squadron under Admiral George Pocock sparred with an equally small one under Commodore d'Ache for command of the Bay of Bengal. D'Ache arrived off the coast in April 1758, escorting nearly two thousand French troops, a sizable force for India, as well as the new governor, Baron Thomas Lally. They immediately besieged Fort St. David, and when Pocock met them off that place, there was an indecisive battle in which the French gave slightly better than they got. Pocock was forced to draw off, and the British factory, deprived of relief, surrendered shortly thereafter.

D'Ache was hampered both by the fact that he and Lally disliked and therefore distrusted each other, and the more important fact that D'Ache had no base nearer than Mauritius, two thousand miles away. This made him extremely reluctant to risk a full-scale, stand-up battle, while Pocock had no such difficulties. The two met again, off Negapatam, in August, and this time the French got the worse of it. D'Ache, conscious of the difficulty of refitting, gave up fairly quickly and sailed away for Mauritius, leaving the land forces to take care of themselves. When the monsoons came later in the year and Pocock was driven off the coast too, Lally took the opportunity to besiege Madras, but as soon as the season changed, Pocock was back again, and the siege lifted.

So it went. D'Ache returned later in 1759, and he and Pocock met a third time, off Pondicherry itself, in September. They fought a fairly bloody action, though in this as in both the previous encounters neither side lost a ship. The Frenchman had had enough by now, and he left the Bay of Bengal for good. In doing so, he also left India to the British. Soon after the turn of the year, the British, led by Eyre Coote, met Lally and several thousand Maratta cavalry at Wandiwash. The French fought well, but the Indians, sensing the trend of events and disliking Lally as much as his naval commander had done, held back. At the height of the battle, as British and French were locked all along their line in hand-to-hand fighting, a lucky shot blew up a French ammunition wagon. British cavalry charged among the momentarily disorganized French marines, and the tide suddenly turned.

Lally could do little more. In August he was besieged in Pondicherry, and he surrendered early in 1761. The French government at home had tried to get reinforcements out to him but again were foiled by the ubiquitous British Navy. With those all-important sea links severed, French India withered on the vine and died.

By 1759, the year of miracles, Britain's triumph was assured. Minden, Lagos Bay, Quiberon Bay, the naval battle off Pondicherry, the crowning mercy of Quebec, one victory after another had come crowding in, in full vindication of Pitt's ideas on how to manage a war. The country was sated with glory.

And therefore began to tire of it. Taxes were high, for all this war had still to be paid for. Worse, it had to be paid for by an inequitable revenue system, so that if the City merchants grew fat on war profits, the country squires thought they were growing poor through high land taxes. Men were therefore ready for a change, and when George II died in October 1760, change could not be far off.

It was a noted peculiarity of the Hanoverian kings of England that they all hated each other, father and son. George II's heir presumptive had been his eldest son, Frederick Louis, and Frederick had quarreled so violently with his father that he had moved his laboring wife to a new home rather than have the baby born under George II's roof. Frederick had then become the focus of opposition to George's policies, and all the dissatisfied elements of English political life had gathered around the Prince of Wales in the 1740s. Supporting a young heir rather than an aging monarch was obviously to be on the winning side, but Frederick died in 1751, before his father, and never made it to the throne. The opposition therefore gravitated to the little grandson, who was to become George III, only thirteen on his father's death, and the boy grew up surrounded by people who hated his grandfather and by extension his grandfather's ministers. Young George was especially under the influence of his mother and his tutor, the Scottish Earl of Bute, who was also his mother's confidant, adviser, and, most people thought, lover. He was a shy, unintellectual boy, uncertain of himself and therefore very stubborn when he made up his mind, and when he ascended the throne in 1760, he was determined, like many uncertain people, to assert himself. Not knowing exactly how to go about it, distrusting the ministers his grandfather had left him, he turned to those people he knew best, and the Earl of Bute became the gray eminence behind the throne. Bute and George were both concerned "to do good," a fashion that was just coming in in late eighteenth-century Europe, and so, in his first speech from the throne, in the midst of all England's victories, George spoke passionately of bringing an end to "this bloody and expensive war," an attitude that hardly endeared him to William Pitt.

What finally finished Pitt was trouble with Spain. The great minister held on for a year, while the war rolled merrily along. By midsummer of 1761, it was obvious to everyone that Spain was about to declare war on England. This piece of supreme folly had been engineered by a Frenchman, the Duc de Choiseul; the Spanish, so far had their diplomacy fallen from the great days of old, allowed themselves to get sucked in by the promise of territories in Italy, among other things. Pitt, knowing of this, wanted to get in the first blow, while the Spanish were still dithering. The cabinet under the influence of Bute and the King refused to back him, and in October he resigned, emphatically stating reasons that ought to be engraved on every official's heart: "Being responsible I will direct, and I will be responsible for nothing that I do not direct!" Pitt passed into a very formidable opposition, and Spain, having gotten its annual treasure fleet home safely, then declared war.

Even without the master's hand at the helm, the British war effort was now so well organized that it went right on winning victories, while King George and Bute, who officially became Prime Minister in 1762, tried to negotiate a way out of their embarrassment of riches. Early in 1762 Admiral Rodney took the last major French station in the West Indies, the great sugar island of Martinique, and followed that up by sweeping over Grenada, St. Lucia, and St. Vincent. Even more important, the British then in midsummer sent a great fleet against Cuba, the heart of Spanish power in the Caribbean. Admiral Pocock, back from the Indies, commanded thirty-seven men-of-war, and General George Keppel, the Earl of Albemarle, had an army of about twelve thousand soldiers and marines. The force came through the Old Bahama Channel, a dangerous eastern approach that took the Spanish by surprise. Albermarle got his men ashore neatly, and they then besieged Morro Castle, at the mouth of Havana Harbor. It took forty days of mining, but the British finally broke in and overran the weary defenders. The city surrendered a few days later, and the British captured with it enough gold to pay for the entire war that year. This was the richest single distribution of prize money in the Royal Navy, and Admiral Pocock's share of it was £122,000; the ordinary seamen got £4 each.

Still, the British were not entirely satisfied. In India the Royal Navy hired troops from the East India Company and set off to take the Spanish possessions of the Philippines. Admiral Sir Samuel Cornish sailed into Manila Bay, where he brought the news of the war with him and overpowered the small Spanish garrison there after a very creditable resistance. The British ransomed the city for four million pounds, accepting that much to keep their troops from looting it, and they also captured the annual Manila galleon for Mexico, with a cargo worth three million more.

This sort of thing was the equivalent of a gold rush, or harked back to the days of Drake. It seemed so easy that a London consortium outfitted a private expedition to take Buenos Aires, a logical extension of privateering of the day. But amphibious operations were a bit more complicated, and this one failed miserably, suggesting that these things were better left to the Army and Navy.

With that it was time to quit; more than time, the government thought. Britain's ally on the Continent, Frederick the Great, had all but gone under; the only thing that saved him was the fortuitous death of his archenemy, Elizabeth of Russia. When she died, her successor, Peter III, who was an ardent admirer of Frederick's, immediately took his country out of the war, and was in fact preparing to come back into it, on the other side, when he was deposed and assassinated. Frederick had already several times suggested that England make peace, as part of a general toning down of the war. Finally, when George and Bute did so, they left Frederick in the lurch. In view of the Prussian record, this was just a case of the biter bit, but Frederick ever after referred to "perfidious Albion" and looked with delight on her future difficulties.

Peace finally was signed, early in 1763, at Paris, among the British, French, and Spanish; the continental side of the war took a while longer to burn out. George wanted a general peace, and he was willing to make concessions to get it; he and Bute told each other it was undignified to haggle like tradesmen over this or that bit of territory. As a result the Bourbons came off a little better than they might have, but it was still bad enough. France ceded Canada and Cape Breton Island and recognized the Mississippi River as the western boundary between French and English territories. In the Caribbean the British gave up all their conquests but Grenada, though that was largely a matter of British economics. The sugar planters of the British West Indies did not want the competition of the French planters in the Empire's economic system, so the islands went back, causing a great outcry from Pitt, who condemned the government for keeping "a few acres of ice and snow" in Canada when they could have had Martinique, the pearl of the Antilles. The French also gave up Senegal, on the slave coast in West Africa, in return for Goree, and the British gave back both Pondicherry and Chandernagor in India, under conditions that guaranteed the French would no longer have any more than a minor trading company there.

The Spanish, already having paid for the war, did better. They ceded Florida to the British, but the French gave them Louisiana in return. And the British gave back both Cuba and the Philippines, probably because they had already taken everything portable out of them.

So the war came to its glorious conclusion. Sharp-eyed fur dealers from New York began moving up to Montreal, and land-hungry Pennsylvanians filtered across the mountain gaps to the Ohio. Officers on half pay settled back in Cornwall and Norfolk to enjoy their prize money, and sailors suddenly on the beach signed on for slaving voyages or to make the trip to the fishing banks. Red-coated Irishmen were mustered out to farm if they were lucky, beg if they were not, and regiment after regiment was disbanded. In India the Honorable Company settled down to make money once again instead of spending it on armies. Normal intercourse with the Continent reopened; Edward Gibbon, discharged from the Hampshire Militia, sat musing among the ruins of the Capitol in Rome, listening to the friars singing vespers, and decided to write on the decline and fall of the Roman Empire. In London the great Samuel Johnson met his Boswell, and Almack opened a gaming house in Pall Mall. After a successful war, men had money to spend. All was well with Britain's world.

8

The World Turned Upside Down

*You cannot conquer America. . . . I rejoice that America
has resisted.*

—William Pitt, Earl of Chatham

In 1763 the British Empire bestrode the world like some revived and
enlarged Rome. The British Isles themselves, since the union of Scotland and England, were the largest free-trade area in Europe, and into
that area poured wealth from all the far-flung territories of the Empire.
North America east of the Mississippi was under the Union Jack, as
were most of the rich Caribbean islands. Slaving stations in Africa and
factories in India contributed their profits to London bank accounts,
and Englishmen basked in the feeling that they had taken on most of
the world and won. Across the Channel the French were on the long,
slippery slide to national bankruptcy; the Dutch had settled back to be
a contented second-rate power. In the Iberian Peninsula they might
still cherish memories of imperial grandeur, but the ruling houses of
Spain and Portugal were decadent, their days of glory long over. But
Britain was well into her Augustan age, and there looked to be no end
to it.

These were most exciting times. The Enlightenment was in full
swing, and some men believed, or professed to believe, that Utopia was
just around the corner. In fact, this view was not correct at all, and just
as most people thought the stability of the eighteenth century would
last forever, it was about to end. The old benign equation that allowed

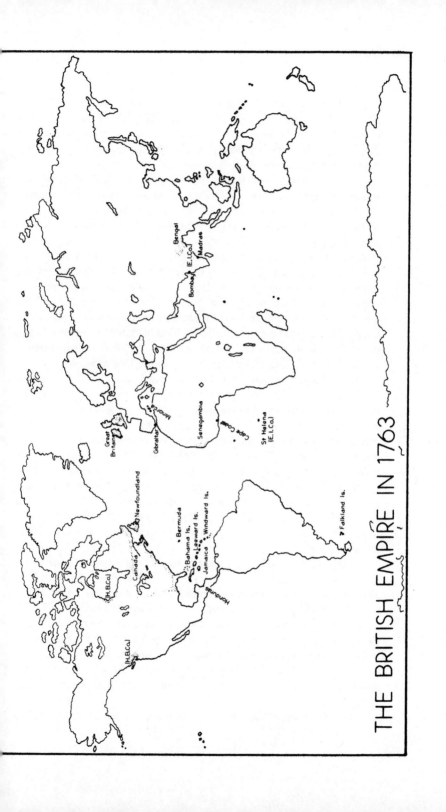

THE BRITISH EMPIRE IN 1763

the upper and middle classes to run affairs while the other 80 to 90 percent of the population worked so that they might do so, was coming under attack. In the next century the common man was going to take over. It was the very beginning of what R. R. Palmer has called the Age of Democratic Revolution.

Hardly anyone saw this in the 1760s; indeed, even those who wanted change would have been shocked at the thought of democracy, for at that time the word still had its original classical meaning—rule by the masses, or more properly, by the mob. The middle-class radicals who set the process in motion wanted rule by themselves and had no thought of extending their power, once they got it, to those farther down the social scale. But just as the logical end of Protestantism was independence in religion, so the logical end of expanding the political spectrum was democracy. Or that was one end of it; the other end was dictatorship, as Rousseau found when he had to invent a Legislator to tell people what their general will was. Young men who discussed radical politics in London clubs and cheered for "Wilkes and liberty" would live to see Jacksonian democracy in the United States, and Napoleon I, Emperor of the French, across the Channel.

In the sixties these things were hardly perceived even as clouds on the horizon. Englishmen thought their constitution was as near-perfect an instrument for governing man as had yet been developed; it needed, true, a little tuning up, but that was the advantage of unwritten documents; you could tune away, you might even change them out of all relation to the original, and no one would ever really notice. The British have been perhaps the most revolutionary people on earth, and they have done it all in the name of restoring the good old ways. The politicians in Westminster settled down to a decade of bickering and squabbling, and it was almost purely by chance that in the process they lost an empire.

King George III had conservative inclinations. He believed, rightly so, in the context of his day, that the King had a vital role to play in running the country, and he set out to play it. He found ministers who would support him, and he in turn supported them. Opposition to this gathered for several years, and there were attempts to put the Crown in commission and to remove the King from the business of politics. Some authorities say that this happened; in fact, George fought a very successful campaign to preserve the royal prerogative, and actually did so until age and infirmity caused him to slacken his hand.

This fascinating internal fight absorbed the attention of English politicians, and in their concentration on it, they forgot that many of the tactical ploys they used had effects of far greater moment; in their efforts to solve domestic problems and to score points against each other, they neglected the fact that the most populous part of their overseas empire was increasingly alienated and disaffected. Imperial policies were used as means to the end of preserving or destroying ministries, and it was this incredibly short sighted view that brought about the American Revolution.

Change would undoubtedly have come anyway, but it might perhaps have come by evolution rather than revolution, as it did in most of the later empire. The Americans did it the hard way. The problem was basically twofold; one aspect was that the Navigation Acts did not entirely fit the imperial system by this time; the other was even more fundamental: The colonists in America were not Englishmen anymore, they were Americans.

The Navigation Acts had served Britain well for a century. Behind their protective shield the empire had grown and had outshone all its rivals. A fairly well-balanced creation had emerged, with tropical commodities produced in the West Indies by slave labor from Africa, and with temperate products generated from America. However, as early as the time of the Molasses Act of the 1730s, the American colonies were feeling cramped by a system that assigned them a permanent second place in the imperial scheme. They did not, of course, see themselves being first, but they did see themselves being equal. Economically, Britain thought the empire, as her creation, existed for her convenience, and units within it ought to conform to her views. Politically, the British idea was that Parliament legislated for the entire unit and represented the views of all the Empire. Their theory, in the days of rotten boroughs and an unreformed franchise, was that it made no difference what a member of parliament's constituency was, for once elected, he was supposed to think not only for all Britain, but for all her territories, too. So when Americans said they were being economically disadvantaged by the Navigation Acts, British politicians replied that that was for the good of a greater whole, and they ought to be willing to put up with occasional inconvenience in return for general benefits. When Americans said perhaps they ought then to be represented in Parliament, Britishers replied that they *were* represented in it, and indeed they were, just as much as any farm laborer in Suffolk or tin miner in Cornwall or slave in Jamaica. If there was some justice to the former reply, there was less to the latter.

This question was even further aggravated by the results of the late war. First of all, it had been expensive, and British ministers not unreasonably decided that since Americans had been among the prime beneficiaries of the war, they ought now to help pay for it. A series of attempts to generate taxes in America from 1761 to 1774 was what finally led to armed conflict. Paradoxically, the same war that had generated the expense had removed the necessity of it, for the French threat no longer existed. The Americans were highly reluctant to pay its removal costs, and when the British proposed to keep a substantial defense establishment in America, the colonials refused to support it on the grounds that it was no longer needed. The Empire was falling victim to its own success, as foresighted Frenchmen had seen it might. Americans felt themselves thoroughly aggrieved, penalized by the Navigation System that had created them, asked to pay for its continued maintenance, and then denied any political voice in changing it.

The more profound truth was that the colonials were simply ceasing to be Englishmen. After a century and a half, some of them were the sixth generation of Americans, and they were a different group from the home-grown product by now. During most of that century and a half they had been left pretty much alone by the imperial government—the years of "salutary neglect," as some historians have called them—and they had developed their own ways and habits of thought and action. Their tradition of local government was extremely strong, as an early royal governor noted when he reported home regretfully that "an assembly has broken out here." Now that the period of salutary neglect was over and the British showed all the signs of wanting to neaten their operation, the Americans came slowly, and for many of them painfully, to the realization that they really were not very much like Englishmen after all.

So the government in London, busy with its own affairs, passed one act after another to regulate matters in the colonies. In 1764 it was a tax on sugar, to raise money for the war debts; the colonists protested that they were obliged to pay regulatory duties but had never before paid revenue taxes. The next year the government brought in the Stamp Act, requiring a fee for all legal documents, pamphlets, newspapers, and playing cards. Had they tried they could not have chosen a worse device, for it angered lawyers, writers, editors, and gamblers. The colonials replied with a Stamp Act Congress in New York and riots in Boston.

In 1766 the British thought better of it, and they compounded their mistakes. They repealed the Stamp Act, which made the Americans think they could win, and they then passed the Declatory Act, saying, in effect, "Well, we won't tax you this time, but we have the right to if we want to." The colonials saw red once more.

On it went. In 1767 the British brought in the Townshend Acts, duties on glass, lead, tea, and paper imported into the colonies. The colonies, ominously concerting their actions, replied with nonimportation agreements, and British exporters saw their incomes dwindle. In March 1770 an undignified brawl between a Boston mob and British soldiers resulted in the guard firing into the crowd, an event mythologized as "the Boston Massacre." The colonies saw this as hirelings of the Crown mercilessly shooting down sober citizens about their peaceful affairs, but the courts acquitted the officer of the guard, defended by a Boston lawyer named John Adams. The British repealed all the Townshend duties except the one on tea, which they retained partly because they wanted to take a stand on principle, partly because the East India Company was in financial trouble and needed the money. In 1772 a Rhode Island mob boarded and burned the revenue cutter *Gaspé,* and the different colonies formed committees of correspondence to inform and encourage each other. Late in 1773, when the East India Company got some tea cargoes to Boston at last, the local citizens dressed up as Indians, boarded the ships, and threw the tea into the harbor in a night of jolly fun.

At this the British ran out of patience. They closed the port of Boston, took away many of Massachusetts' rights from its charter, enlarged the power of the royal governor, and passed an act for the quartering of troops on the citizens. At the same time, and quite independently, they passed the Quebec Act, which enlarged the boundaries of that province at the expense of the recalcitrant Americans, and guaranteed the Roman Catholic religion to the French, a step that added a mighty thunder from New England pulpits to the growing anti-British clamor. September 1774 saw the Continental Congress meet at Philadelphia to draw up a Declaration of Rights and Grievances.

In England old William Pitt, now the Earl of Chatham, took a long view and saw in America the modern counterpart of the England of a century ago, of the Glorious Revolution. He proposed compromise and conciliation, but he was long out of power now, and the King and his ministers were determined on a firm line; every time they had given an inch, the Americans had stolen a yard. General Thomas Gage in Boston knew the local citizens' committees were collecting arms and ammunition. He was ordered to stop this, and in April 1775 he acted. He sent troops out on a night march from Boston to Lexington and Concord to seize the stores. The Americans were warned, and when the British troops got to Lexington, there was a line of militia tumbling out of the houses around the green. The two forces drew up and growled at each other a moment, like suspicious pups, and then someone—no one yet knows who—fired a shot. The British then fired a ragged volley; the Americans got off a few shots, then broke and ran before the advancing bayonets.

By the time the British got to Concord the entire countryside was aroused, and by the time they got back to Boston at the end of a long, bad day, they had lost about 250 men out of a total of roughly 1,800 engaged. The news spread like wildfire, and within a day men were slinging haversacks and cleaning muskets, contingents and individuals setting out from as far away as the Connecticut River Valley and the Hampshire grants to besiege Boston. Once blood was shed the time for talk was over, and both sides had blundered into a war that few men wanted, a war whose consequences were incalculable.

The task of subduing the rebellion was far more formidable than the British ever acknowledged, which was one reason why they failed to do it. There were in 1775 approximately three million people in the British territories of North America. Probably no more than a quarter of them were ardent rebels, another quarter were firmly loyal, and the 50 percent in the middle just wished the two extremes would go away. British generals always made the mistake of assuming that the vast mass of the population was really loyal at heart and would rally to them if once given a chance. This, like the underestimation of the enemy, was a constant with them, and it led them into some notable disasters.

During the course of the war, the Americans managed to raise nearly four hundred thousand men, but that figure is highly misleading. The largest number for any one year was only eighty-nine thousand, of which nearly half were militia. The American commander-in-chief, George Washington, never commanded more than seventeen thousand troops at one time. The British, who preferred to count only those enemies they thought were roughly their equivalents, regular soldiers, therefore always took the view that they were facing but a few thousand hard-core rebels; and since they persisted in the fallacy that most people were loyal, the militia they often counted on usually turned out on the other side.

The Americans were hampered by the divided nature of their political structure, for every colony—or state, as they now called themselves—consistently went its own way, and cooperation among them
was minimal. They thoroughly distrusted each other and were jealous
of their rights and privileges. Only when faced with dire emergencies
would they overcome their suspicions, and while New Englanders and
Virginians might get along because they did not know each other well,
it was very hard to get men from Connecticut and New York to work
together; after all, they had years of feuding about Long Island Sound
to overcome. But this very divisiveness also worked to their advantage,
for the British found the revolution to be a hydra-headed monster.
Used to European-style warfare, they assumed that there must be a key
point, usually the capital city, at which they might strike. Initially Boston was the center of discontent, but in spite of their holding Boston
for several months, the rebellion went on. Next they moved to New
York, already the greatest city of North America. They occupied that
for most of the war; it made no difference. They then decided that since
the Continental Congress sat at Philadelphia, that was the place to be,
so they marched down and took it. Still the rebellion continued. In the
South they tried Charleston, with as much luck as they had had every-
place else. They tried to cut off New England from the rest of the states
and failed, and it would have done no good anyway. What they never
did realize was that this was not a war of posts, that the revolution had
happened long before and that its heart was not in any one or any
dozen cities but in almost every little village and hamlet. The true
capital of the American Revolution was the meeting hall in a thousand
towns from Maine down to Georgia, and the war was not the Revolution; the Revolution had already taken place, and the war was just to
adjust the political scheme of things to what was already a fact of life.
Even if the British had occupied and held every one of those town
meeting halls, the Revolution would still have been an accomplished
fact.

If such things were recognized at the time, society would not have
wars. So the British persevered in their attempt to subdue the rebels,
and they marched here and they sailed there, and they conceived this
plan and that ploy, and they won battles all over the place. They practically ruined the youthful American Army around New York, and
they chased its battered remnants across New Jersey. But they could
not stamp it out, and every time the flame was dampened in one place,
it sprang up strongly in another. The Britons' own army was inadequate, both in numbers and in skill, to do what was demanded of it,

and the German auxiliaries they hired never won one battle in which they alone faced American troops.

Given the failure of the British Army to stamp out the Revolution in a hurry, the thing then became a matter of staying power. Could the Americans last until the British got sick of the war and quit, or until one of Britain's ancient enemies on the Continent decided the time was ripe for intervention and revenge? Or could the British isolate the rebellion, shut it off from outside help until it sickened and died, as it eventually must if the Americans ran out of money and were forced to rely on their own too-meager military resources? In other words, barring a quick military decision, the Revolution was to be decided by seapower.

Here at least the odds were clearly with Great Britain, for she had the greatest Navy in the world; the Americans had none. The Royal Navy faced three main tasks, in order of their appearance. The first was the support of military operations along the American coast. Then there was the growing necessity of convoy work and putting a stop to the depredations of privateers and occasional American naval vessels; finally, as the war widened, the British were forced to fight all their former foes, and the war at sea took on the pattern of the former imperial wars.

The Americans could never challenge the general British control of North American waters. They could not prevent the British from loading their soldiers and supporters aboard ship and sailing away from Boston to Halifax in March 1776. No more could they interfere with the great armada that brought Sir William Howe and his invasion army back to New York in midsummer, nor the approach of an invasion force to Charleston at the same time; the latter's failure occurred on land, not at sea. And it was general British control of the sea lanes and the routes to North America that preserved Nova Scotia for the Crown and allowed the British to hold and operate south from Quebec. Denied New England timber, especially for masts, the British might be short of wood, but the Americans were short of everything else that made for seapower. Their minuscule navy never provided a major challenge to the Royal Navy, and throughout the war, with one vital exception, the British moved by sea pretty much where they wanted to.

Privateers were another matter, though. In 1775 there were about 2,000 American vessels afloat, scattered all over the seas. Hundreds of them were caught in the British net, by ships of the Royal Navy or by

British privateers. The whaling fleet of Nantucket alone lost 150 ships early in the war. But these losses were soon made up. Within weeks of the outbreak of the war merchants were bidding frantically for the small supply of guns in the colonies, and soon, in every creek from the Penobscot to the Savannah rivers, one heard the sound of hammers, adzes, and caulking mauls. Pinkies and schooners with names like *Hannah* and *Charming Molly* put to sea with six men, a boy, and a dog, armed with a couple of old muskets from the French War and a rusty swivel or two, and before the war was weeks old, British supply vessels bound for beleaguered Boston were coming into Salem and Marblehead under prize crews, their flags upside down and their cargoes destined for sale to the rebel army.

The privateers had one glaring weakness: They did not like to fight. They were in business to make money, as private enterprise, and faced with a British man-of-war, they would run for it if they could. So however difficult it might be, if the Americans were going to challenge the Royal Navy at all, it had to be with a regular navy of their own. Several of the states produced their own miniature navies, some of which did fair work for a time, and the Congress too formed a navy. They could never manage ships of the line; they were too costly and consumed too much manpower, and though they tried to build some, they were not very successful. But they could build frigates, sloops, and brigs, and they did, and soon the strange striped flag with the multitude of odd devices—the rattlesnake was much favored—was seen not only off the American coast, but in British waters as well, an impudence the British thoroughly resented, as if somehow the natural order of things was being challenged. And where the privateers usually ran, the naval ships often fought.

The first frigate of the Continental Navy to get to sea was the *Randolph,* of thirty-two guns, a pretty little ship that was also the first to fly the Grand Union flag. In early March 1778, under the command of Captain Nicholas Biddle, she met a small British two-decker, the *Yarmouth,* of sixty-four guns. The Americans were in a squadron of six, but the *Yarmouth* ran down on them anyway. Instead of fleeing, the *Randolph* opened fire, and for about fifteen minutes the two unequal ships went at it hammer and tong, with the big Britisher getting somewhat the worse of it, when suddenly the American blew up. The British captain reported bemusedly to the Admiralty that he did not really understand the American's motives.

May 23, 1778: The British sloop *Drake* lay at anchor in the small harbor of Carrickfergus, on the Irish side of the Irish Channel. Another vessel appeared off the mouth of the harbor, and the *Drake*'s captain sent an officer out in a boat to see who she was and what she wanted. When the boat did not return, the *Drake* weighed anchor and sailed out. The other ship was unidentifiable, lying stern to. As the *Drake* came up and hailed, she suddenly bore around, hoisted American colors, and fired a full broadside. It was the sloop *Ranger,* commanded by a former Scot named John Paul Jones, who had for some weeks been making a pest of himself in the area. The *Drake* replied handily, and for better than an hour the two ships sailed along at little more than pistol-shot distance, broadsides rolling out at each other. Soon after midnight, her captain and first officer both mortally wounded and forty men down, the *Drake* struck her colors, the first vessel of the Royal Navy to surrender after a fair fight so far in the war.

That was bad enough. A year later, Jones did it again; in the most famous single-ship action of the war, his *Bon Homme Richard* took the first-class frigate *Serapis* off Flamborough Head in Scotland, and Jones, calling out that he had not begun to fight, while his ship was already a sinking wreck under his feet, started a rival tradition that would someday match that of the Royal Navy itself.

But single-ship actions did not win or lose wars then. Though the Americans, privateer and regular Navy together, took more than three thousand British vessels in the course of the war, they never once by themselves shook the bulldog grip. Their Navy got but one squadron to sea, in an early expedition to New Providence in the Bahamas. For the rest, the blockade did its slow work of strangulation, and American frigates were increasingly trapped in their ports, with British squadrons off the Isle of Shoals, off Cape Ann, off Newport, off the entrance to Long Island Sound, all the way down the coast. Slowly, port by port and ship by ship, the old formulas were working, and the Royal Navy, if left alone, would win its war.

The key was "if left alone," for, of course, the Royal Navy was not going to be left alone. Great powers, as they invariably learn to their surprise and dismay, have few friends, and Britain in the 1770s had none at all. France remained her inveterate enemy, and the two states Britain customarily subsidized to distract the French were both alienated, Prussia in the previous war and Austria in the one before that.

To make matters worse, the French had had another of their periodic naval renaissances, spurred by the humiliations of the previous war. By 1775 the French were just waiting for an opportunity, and they saw it in British troubles with America. Right from the start the French were sympathetic to the rebels and supported them with surreptitious arms and funds, all the while loudly proclaiming their neutrality. American privateers found refuge in French ports, where they rearmed and sold their prizes, over strong British protests. The French government, however, played its cards carefully; France was not going to jump in prematurely on a losing side. Let the Americans prove they were worthy of support—that is, capable of winning—and then France might act openly.

Late in 1777 the Americans proved just that, when word sped to Europe that an entire British army had been surrounded. General John Burgoyne, "Gentleman Johnny," playwright, light cavalry specialist, man-about-town, had led an expedition south from Canada down the Lake Champlain route toward Albany. Between the bottom of the lake and the Hudson he had gotten enmeshed in a wilderness of swamps, little ravines, and tangled trees, made worse by the Americans, who cut more trees across the path and blocked streams to impede his progress. Weary and worn, his army had staggered into the Hudson River Valley, to meet more Americans swarming over the hills. Doggedly, the British had tried to fight their way through to Albany and had been incapable of doing it, and on October 17, Gentleman Johnny surrendered five thousand British troops at Saratoga. The news caused wild rejoicing throughout the American states, and a sober assessment in France that perhaps the rebels could win after all and that therefore it was time for France to enter the game. In February of the new year the French signed a treaty of commerce and alliance with the new American government, the prelude to declaring war on Britain. At the same time the British offered terms to the Americans, but it was too late for terms now; the rebels were set on independence. What would have saved the Empire and eventually been seen as an act of great statesmanship in 1774 was seen only as an act of desperation in 1778.

Fortunately for Britain, the blockade of America was being carried on by smaller ships. The largest Admiral Richard Howe had with him was a small ship of sixty-four guns; most of his seventy-odd vessels were frigates. This meant that all the heavier British ships of the line were available to meet the French, provided, of course, that they could be commissioned and manned in time to do it, for the government, fighting an unpopular war, had tried to do so as cheaply as possible.

Faced with these new hostilities and already deeply involved in

America, the British Navy decided on a defensive stance. Lord Sandwich, the First Sea Lord, gave up the idea of close blockade of France
of the previous war and concentrated what ships he had available off
the Channel approaches. Though this was a retrograde step strategically, it was to become a constant of British naval policy: Keep the
close blockade when possible, but when not, fall back on the Channel,
the one area where control remained absolutely indispensable.

The French were soon at sea under these conditions, but unfortunately they remained preoccupied, as in the past, with secondary concerns. They did, however, get a squadron over to the American coast,
twelve ships of the line commanded by the Count d'Estaing. Under the
threat of the arriving French, the British had evacuated Philadelphia,
General Henry Clinton marching his troops across to New York, while
Admiral Howe took his ships, and the Army's heavy equipment,
around by sea. Howe barely beat D'Estaing back to New York, and the
American hopes skyrocketed, for if the French attacked boldly, the
Revolution might end right then and there. Instead the Frenchman
contented himself with some mighty posturing, after which he sailed
off to harass the British at Newport, Rhode Island. Not daunted, Howe
followed him and was prepared to attack with his far weaker ships
when an early hurricane blew up; Howe returned to New York, and
D'Estaing, after visiting and wearing out his welcome in Boston, sailed
for the West Indies. There might be rich pickings there, and the French
were not in the war, after all, because of their love of liberty, or even of
Americans, however much they might profess to care for either.

For the rest of his period of command D'Estaing did little to en-
dear himself to the Americans. He took St. Vincent and Grenada in the
West Indies, and in July he fought Admiral John Byron off the latter
island. The outnumbered British got very much the worse of it, but instead of pressing his advantage, the Frenchman sailed off to South
Carolina, where he failed dismally to take the city from its smaller
British garrison. Having thoroughly deflated American hopes of any
substantial help from him, he then left happily for home, with everyone wishing him good riddance.

French diplomacy was more successful than French arms, for in
July 1779 the French succeeded in bringing Spain into the war with the
old lure of recovering Gibraltar and Minorca. The Spanish besieged
the former for nearly two years, one of the great if lesser known sieges
of history, and they also put their ships at the disposal of the French.
Having their own great colonial empire, however, they were even less

enamored of abstract liberty than their allies, and they refused to have much to do with the Americans. They did combine with the French fleet to threaten invasion late in the summer but acted so poorly, with little real cooperation and less naval skill, that the risk of invasion was more apparent than real.

The war dragged on. Most of Britain was sick and tired of it, but George III, who had called the Seven Years' War "bloody and expensive," was determined not to give up. George was far from the tyrant, or even the fool, that old American histories used to portray him as being; he was simply a stubborn man who was convinced he was right. Poor old Lord North, his Prime Minister, wanted desperately to retire and be done with the whole painful business, but George would see it through. In the end he was the last man in England to feel that way, the last to acknowledge that no matter how right you think you are, you still may not be able to win.

Early in 1780 the neutral Baltic powers, harassed by British searches, formed the Armed Neutrality, and Russia, Denmark, and Sweden agreed to resist with force if necessary any further British violations of what they considered their rights. It accomplished so little that Catherine the Great of Russia nicknamed it the "Armed Nullity," but it meant that British standing, and British ability to maneuver, had slipped again. At the end of 1780 the Dutch, more incensed than the other neutrals, declared war on Great Britain, so there was yet another enemy to face. The next year the British lost Pensacola down in Florida, and in the West Indies Tobago, St. Eustace, Demerara, St. Kitts, Nevis, and Montserrat; and more important than all of these, they lost command of the seas off the American coast, opening the way for disaster.

That disaster came in the fall, the result of the one great strategic combination of the war—indeed, one of the greatest of the century. It just happened that all the players were in exactly the right place, and for the Americans and French everything worked as it should.

The French had landed a force of nearly five thousand men under General the Comte de Rochambeau at Newport in Rhode Island, and they had been there for months. Eventually, early in 1781, the French commander concerted with Washington, and they decided to operate against New York. Meanwhile, a French fleet, with a strong military contingent commanded by the Comte de Grasse, was in the Caribbean.

The British had for the past year or so carried out their major military operations in the southern states; except for occupying New York, they had tacitly surrendered the North but hoped to hold the Carolinas, Georgia, and perhaps Virginia. There had been wide-ranging sweeps back and forth across the countryside, with now the British, now the Americans holding the advantage. In the spring of 1781 General Lord Cornwallis had moved his forces up into Virginia, chasing the Marquis de Lafayette, France's most famous contribution to the American Revolution, and various other bodies of American troops, mostly Virginia militia. In New York, Sir Henry Clinton was preparing an amphibious operation against Newport, and he sent orders to Cornwallis to detach some of his troops to join this expedition. Cornwallis moved toward the seacoast and his rendezvous with the expected British vessels.

While this was going on, Rochambeau had moved his army westward and linked up with Washington at White Plains, New York. Soon after they joined they received a letter from De Grasse saying that he was coming North, that he had to return to the West Indies by late October, and that therefore he could not help them in an attack on New York; he was instead sailing for Chesapeake Bay, and could they meet him for some kind of joint action there? The soldiers immediately decided that they could, and masking their intentions by feints against the New York perimeter, they began to sidle their troops west and south. Late in August, they took off across New Jersey, heading for Philadelphia and then Baltimore and passage down Chesapeake Bay.

De Grasse represented their trump card. It made little sense to pin Cornwallis to the seacoast if the Royal Navy, as it always could, came in and lifted him off. The British, for their part, were satisfied that they could do just that. Admiral Graves had a substantial squadron in New York, and Admiral Hood was following De Grasse up from the West Indies. The Fates worked against them, however. Hood took a faster route than De Grasse did and reached the Chesapeake capes before the Frenchman. Believing his enemy was heading for New York anyway, he simply looked in at Yorktown and then went on to New York, where he joined with Graves on August 28. There was a small French squadron at Newport, and the two British admirals decided to destroy it first and then deal separately with De Grasse when he reached New York.

Unknown to them, two days after Hood reached New York

De Grasse reached Chesapeake Bay, anchored, and immediately began landing troops to support the thin American forces already there. Early in September Washington and Rochambeau arrived, and Cornwallis and the main British field army in America were firmly caught in a trap.

All now depended upon the Navy. A thoroughly outnumbered Cornwallis could not fight his way clear by land, and if he were to be rescued from surrender, Admiral Graves must sail south and defeat the French. With nineteen ships of the line, he reached the Virginia capes on September 5, to be presented with an opportunity beyond the wildest dreams of Hawke or Boscawen. There at anchor, in no sort of order, with large numbers of men ashore on fatigue duty, lay De Grasse's fleet of twenty-four ships of the line.

Unfortunately, Graves was not the man to seize the unforgiving minute. Still hampered by the Royal Navy's inadequate signaling system and unwilling to risk a general action against a superior enemy, however disadvantaged, he simply herded his ships into line ahead and waited for the French to come out. Short-handed though his crews were, De Grasse knew he could hardly be in a worse position, so he hastily weighed anchor and offered to do battle.

For one of the decisive battles of history, that of the Chesapeake capes was rather disappointing in its details. The French got out in three straggling divisions—van, center, and rear. Graves intended to dispose his slightly smaller fleet in equal divisions as well and then to have each division attack its opposite. Again the signal book failed him, however, and when he had made his dispositions and finally ordered his attack, late in the afternoon, he found that no one had understood him. The two vans came together, more by accident than by good management, while the rest of both fleets sailed leisurely along under battle canvas, occasionally exchanging fire at long range. What might have been a deadly swoop turned into a stately promenade. The French shot high and the British low, but at this distance hull shots did little damage, while the British, with their rigging cut, slowly lost the minimal cohesion they had possessed at the start of the fight. At nightfall the two sides separated.

For the next five days they remained in sight of each other, De Grasse leading the fuming Graves slowly out to sea. Then the wind shifted, and De Grasse turned around and ran back for the capes. While he and Graves had sailed east, Admiral Barras had arrived with the Newport squadron. Graves returned westward to find the French strength now thirty-six, nearly double his own. If he could not win before, he could not win now; he sailed off to New York, leaving Cornwallis to his fate. The British general held on until October 19, but then, with no prospect of relief in sight, he surrendered. After toasts and mutual congratulations all around, De Grasse returned to the West Indies. For all the good it might do them now, the British could reclaim command of the American seaboard. Having lost it once, they had lost the war.

More precisely, they had lost the war of the American Revolution. The larger, imperial war went on and assumed its old pattern of British vs. Franco-Spanish, lasting until the general peace of 1783. After Yorktown the British realized that for practical purposes they had lost America, and they reduced their effort there to a holding operation. They kept New York for a time, they kept Canada and Quebec, and they continued to foster Indian activity along the frontiers. For the rest, it was a naval war, and this, as always, could be fought wherever the water was blue.

What the British might achieve in their own element, under an able commander, was shown in the West Indies, where Admiral Hood, freed from the moribund hand of Admiral Graves once more, handily maneuvered De Grasse away from St. Kitts, held the anchorage there against him, and kept him pinned down until Admiral Rodney, Hood's senior who had gone home on sick leave, returned to the theater. Rodney brought a fleet back with him, and now, early in 1782, thirty-six ships of the line strong and with blood in their eye, the British set out to make up for lost time.

There were fifteen Spanish ships in the area, and De Grasse hoped to avoid an action until he might join with them, for the French were now worn while the British ships were fresh. But Rodney was determined to fight; the disasters of the past year had finally reawakened the old spirit of dogged enterprise and unusual invention. Many of the British ships had improved gunnery techniques, including a new type of gun, the carronade, which greatly enhanced their fighting power at short ranges. Therefore, when the two fleets met off the Saints, little islets between Dominica and Guadeloupe, on April 11, the British gave chase while De Grasse sought to delay a battle. Two or three of his ships were soon disabled, however, and he gallantly decided to stand by them. On the morning of the twelfth, the stately dance began once again, the two fleets approaching in line ahead and firing broadsides as they passed each other.

This time there was a difference. When the lines were very nearly even, a fluky shift of the wind threw the French into confusion and sent some of their ships crashing right into the British. This sudden break caused several of the British ships to come through on the opposite side of the French formation. Breaking both lines was the unpardonable sin of the formal fight, but suddenly it dawned on Rodney and Hood, and several of their captains, that here was the real answer to the sterility of current naval tactics. While the French were thoroughly dismayed by the sudden shift, for the British it was as if a light had suddenly shone on them. The broken French line sped off to the west, and the elated British took up hot pursuit. They soon overhauled the slower of the French ships and by the end of the day had taken five, including De Grasse's magnificent flagship, the 110-gun *Ville de Paris,* which they battered to a pulp. De Grasse was a broken man, and Rodney overnight a hero in an England desperate for some good news at last.

The French still had thirty-odd ships in the West Indies, and the Spanish squadron was still there as well, but they never managed to regain the initiative for the rest of the war. The sparring and the combinations continued, but for practical effects the Battle of the Saints remained the decisive event in the theater.

The British did equally well in European waters. They lost Minorca after a heroic siege, but they managed to hold Gibraltar. Franco-Spanish fleets in the Channel in 1781 and in 1782 both acted as ineptly as had the one in 1779. In August a small British force under Sir Hyde Parker and a small Dutch one fought each other to a standstill off Dogger Bank, the only Anglo-Dutch action of the war. They also managed to hold on in the Indian Ocean, and therefore British skill and tenacity at sea seemed just about equal to the superior numbers of French, Spanish, Dutch, the residual American, and the Armed Neutrality. It was clearly time to call a halt.

Britain came out of it far better than she should have. The Americans were let go, of course, their independence acknowledged and a fairly generous settlement made. The British minister who engineered the peace, Lord Shelburne, hoped to win American support by his magnanimity and then tie the new country back into the British orbit by a trade treaty. Unfortunately for him, he was known in British politics as "the Jesuit," the implication being that he was too clever for anyone else's good. Since he could hardly divulge his plan publicly, he fell over the generous peace before he had recouped it by the

9

Leopards Driven into the Sea

Those far distant, storm-beaten ships, upon which the Grand Army never looked, stood between it and the dominion of the world.
—A. T. Mahan, 1892

With the loss of the American colonies, Britain now entered upon a paradoxical and contradictory period in which revulsion against the imperial idea went hand in hand with the acquisition of vast new overseas territories. In the public mind, empire was no longer worth the effort. As the colonies reached some degree of security and self-assertion, all the money, effort, and care lavished on them would be repaid only by rejection. Look at the Americans! Had not Britain founded them, nurtured them, defended them, adjusted her policies to their wants and needs? And what was the result? A long, wasting war, insurance rates up and stocks down, disarray at home and defeat abroad. So Britain would get along with what she had but would not bother with any more. As is the habit of states that have just lost a war, the British turned inward and thought themselves no longer interested in the larger world.

This neglected several facts. The Empire after the American Revolution was far more homogeneous than it had been before it, and it fit much better into the mercantile mold for which it was ostensibly designed. India, the African stations, the Caribbean islands, and the residue of British North America nicely complemented the perceived needs of the mother country, supplying the raw materials she wanted and taking the excess products she produced. The British no longer had to stifle internal competition from New England, nor try to collect revenues from American smugglers, nor to garrison and defend American frontiers. And ironically, it would not be long before Britain was doing more trade with an independent United States than she had ever done with the thirteen colonies.

Second, the removal of several thousand Loyalists from the United States to British North America—Nova Scotia and Canada—meant that the remainder of the Empire on the continent was more firmly loyal to the mother country than it had ever been before. At the time of the Revolution, Nova Scotia, though it had a few French, some Scots, and some English, was largely a colony of New England. Sea-power more than loyalty had held it for the Crown. Now its population changed; American emigrants and disbanded soldiers made it truly a British holding, which soon hived off yet another province, New Brunswick. Similar development took place in Canada; it was transformed from a French island in the British Empire into a determinedly Anglo-French bloc. The linguistic duality has caused problems in Canada ever since and brought about all kinds of attempted solutions to the problem—Upper and Lower Canada, a united province, and finally the two Canadian provinces of Quebec and Ontario. But whatever they were to be, they were not to be American.

Another fact left out of consideration by the anti-imperialists was that the empire kept right on growing in spite of them. India was still there, and British officials of the East India Company found it impossible, having once become involved, to avoid further extension into Indian politics. The French extended the war of the American Revolution to India, and in the course of subduing them, the British took some of their small remaining possessions, fought with the local rulers such as Haidar Ali and his son Tipu Sultan, and gained indirect control over more of the Indian states. In 1788 Travancore, at the bottom of India, became a protected state and came under the British umbrella. The company's interference in India was matched at home by the government's interference in the company. Several hotly discussed acts of Parliament resulted in the Crown setting up a board of control that functioned as a super board of directors. India was simply too rich a plum, and now too vital a part of the empire, to leave it entirely to the discretion of a private firm. Just how rich a plum it was, and the degree to which it had become part and parcel of British life, was illustrated by the political trial of Warren Hastings, the former

Governor of Bengal and the first Governor General of India. Hastings was impeached before the House of Lords for corruption in one of the most famous political trials of the century. Though he was acquitted, the trial took seven years and in legal fees cost Hastings most of the eighty thousand pounds he had brought home from India. His remark that, given the opportunities for corruption put before him, he was amazed not by the extent to which he had succumbed but rather by the degree to which he had restrained himself, may well stand as a general summation of the whole of British rule over India.

Yet the greatest acquisition of empire in the decade of the 1780s was not on the dusty plains of southern India but rather five thousand miles to the southeast where, as a direct result of British seapower, the smallest and least known of the continents was opened to British settlement.

In 1616 a Dutch navigator by the name of Dirk Hartog landed on an island, subsequently named after him, on the western coast of Australia. His predecessors had already explored the East Indies and sailed through Torres Strait, the water separating New Guinea from northern Australia. In the next ten years they investigated the western coast, part of the northern coast, and in 1627 part of the southern coast of the continent. In the 1640s Abel Tasman sailed east from Mauritius, discovered Tasmania, touched New Zealand, and sailed right around Australia without ever sighting it, thus proving that whatever it was, it was not part of Antarctica, as had been suspected till then. The first Englishman to reach the area was William Dampier, who coasted western Australia in 1699. It was another three quarters of a century before any more interest was sparked, with the appearance on the scene of the greatest of the Pacific explorers, Captain James Cook.

Cook was the son of a farmer and came to the sea service through the eastern coast of England and the Baltic trade. He joined the Navy in 1755, and became a master in 1759, spending the next several years in surveying work around Newfoundland and the St. Lawrence. In 1768 he was given command of a converted merchant ship, the *Endeavour,* and sent with a scientific expedition led by Sir Joseph Banks to explore Tahiti and the southern seas, and, in the first instance, to take observations of the transit of Venus across the sun, a major astronomical event occurring less than once a century, and in this instance fully observable only in the South Pacific.

After the observations were taken, Cook sailed southwest from

Tahiti and spent six months circumnavigating New Zealand, which he claimed for Britain. He then bore away for the eastern coast of Australia. Thinking his landfall looked like the Welsh coast, he named the southeastern part of the continent New South Wales. He coasted the Great Barrier Reef, a feat of consummate seamanship and a great deal of good luck, passed through Torres Strait, and returned home by way of the Cape of Good Hope. He also claimed New South Wales, like New Zealand, for Britain, but the home government ignored both claims.

Cook made two later voyages, but this first was the most fruitful in terms of development. His second voyage was chiefly concerned with Antarctica, still called Terra Australis, though he did visit the New Hebrides and New Caledonia, the former already discovered and claimed by the great French explorer Bougainville. On his third voyage Cook was looking for that old chimera, the exit of the famous Northwest Passage, still firmly embedded in Europe's imagination. He discovered Hawaii, or the Sandwich Islands, and sailed through the Bering Strait before returning to Hawaii, where he was killed in a scuffle with natives.

For nearly twenty years Cook's claim to Australia lay dormant. The British government had some vague thoughts of using the new land as a refuge for American Loyalists, but the expense was too great, and the distance too far, and nothing came of it. Through the mid-1780s, however, another problem nearer home became more pressing. The southern American colonies had served as a dumping ground for convicted Englishmen, and in the past, thousands of them had been transported to America to serve out their sentences as plantation labor. After the Revolution, the British were denied this outlet. They tried some short-lived penal settlements on the western coast of Africa, but the climate was so difficult that transportation there was a virtual death sentence. For several years the government debated the problem in a desultory way, while conditions in British prisons grew increasingly horrible. Often sentenced for minor offenses, hundreds of men, women, and children crowded aboard prison hulks, old, worn-out men-of-war lying in the rivers and harbors of England, where these people fought, bred, starved, and terrified each other. Finally in 1786 Parliament passed an enabling act, appointed Captain Arthur Philip of the Royal Navy as the first Governor of New South Wales, and launched an expedition. Philip's ten ships, with some seven hundred convicts, about two hundred of them women, and two hundred marine guards, arrived in New South Wales in January 1788. Philip's orders were to establish a colony on Botany Bay, a name that stuck to the whole colony for many years, but he rejected it after one look and settled in a harbor a few miles to the south. Cook had called this harbor, which he had not explored but merely noted, Port Jackson; eventually it was named after the then British Secretary of State for Home and Colonial Affairs, Lord Sydney. Eighteenth-century seamen could tell a good anchorage when they saw one; Sydney was the antipodean equivalent of Halifax, both of them among the finest natural harbors in the world.

Subsequent pride and nostalgia have considerably romanticized the convict settlements of Australia. They were in fact very grim. The Governor officially enjoyed absolute power. A body of guards, the New South Wales Corps, was set up to assist him; though inordinately proud of itself, this force was only marginally better than the convicts it was created to watch. Many of its officers drifted into speculation that would today be considered conflict of interest of the worst sort. Its most famous member, Captain John MacArthur, made a fortune by introducing sheep to Australia. The convicts were used as contract labor, a euphemism for slavery, and on the completion of their terms were given small grants of land. Discharged members of the corps got larger grants, and officers were allowed a monopoly on imports, so that they controlled the entire settlement. Some idea of living conditions in New South Wales may be gleaned from the fact that at one time rum was the official currency of the settlement.

As did most other colonies, New South Wales went through the familiar patterns of early development. It soon threw off splinter settlements, first on Norfolk Island and then on Tasmania, the latter for fear of rumored French claims. There was ongoing conflict between the Governor, until 1809 a naval officer, and the dominant economic group, the officers of the New South Wales Corps. In 1804 the Irish convicts, large numbers of whom had been transported after the Irish risings in 1798, rose up and were brutally suppressed by the English. The home government then sent out as governor Captain William Bligh, famous for the mutiny on his ship *Bounty* and therefore well known as a stern disciplinarian. Bligh fulfilled his reputation so well that in 1808 he was arrested by the garrison commandant, at the instigation of Captain MacArthur and the money men of the settlement. Bligh was the last of the naval officers to serve as Governor there. Britain replaced him with a Highland colonel and his men, and under Lachlan MacQuarrie the colony turned in a new direction. He broke the New South Wales Corps, encouraged the free settlers, who had been trickling in for fifteen years, set up civil courts, and pursued an uphill fight to move the colony away from its penal settlement origins and stigma.

This continued for the next generation. Other settlements were opened up: Perth in Western Australia in 1829, South Australia and Victoria in the 1830s. The last convicts landed in 1840, by which time some seventy thousand people had been transported from England. When the last ones arrived, however, free settlers far outnumbered the total of prisoners or ex-prisoners. The home government attempted to resume a modified form of transportation, the conditional pardon system, but there were such protests from the people who were now Australians that the idea was soon abandoned.

This was more than half a century after the original foundation of Australia, and that half century saw changes of incomparable magnitude at home. When the first convicts landed near Botany Bay, the Industrial Revolution was just beginning to make inroads in English life. When the last arrived, it was not only a different century, it also was a different world. Sometime about the middle of the eighteenth century there began to be a transformation of English life. Developments in technology in a variety of industries, especially cotton manufacturing and iron founding, and in transportation, began a process of acceleration; one invention necessitated and then built upon another. Roads were surfaced, railroads and canals built; steam power was applied to pumping out mines, to driving railroad and ship engines, to making looms and spinning machines work. There was a similar, and slightly earlier, revolution in agricultural processes so that more food could be produced for more people by fewer farmers.

All these developments required venture capital, but England was rich. There were profits from India, from the slave trade, from the sugar plantations, from war contracts. This surplus money could be invested in turnpike trusts, in canal companies, in mining monopolies, in foundries and factories. Rich merchants married their daughters to the sons of the landed nobility and invested their money on improving estates. Younger sons went into business; "business" was respectable, "trade" was not. Poor men with brains and ideas—for better cotton machines or for new ways to bore out cannon—met men with money. A great many people were fleeced and cheated, but some were made rich beyond the dreams of their fathers.

The social effects were enormous. The changes in agriculture displaced thousands of poorer farmers and drove them and their families off the land and into the slums of the cities and growing factory towns. Here they became fodder for the new industries. It is customary to contrast the England of "dark, satanic mills" with an idyllic agricultural, preindustrial society. This overromanticizes the old ways, which were brutal and callous enough in themselves, but it does not paint too darkly the new ways, for it would be impossible to paint them too darkly. It was half a century before the English social conscience awoke to the evils that were rampant in its own house, but when it did, horrific tales came out. Men worked in the mines and never saw the light of day. Women crawled half naked along mine tunnels, towing carts of coal behind them; three-year-old children sat in the tunnels for twelve and fourteen hours at a time, opening and closing the safety doors as the women and miners crawled through. Child labor was used in the factories in less skilled tasks, because that way the machines could be placed closer together. Six-year-olds darted between hurling piston rods and whirring belts, squirting oil on the machines, and every once in a while a careless or exhausted child would lose a limb or have his skull cracked by a machine. Parents would waken their children before dawn, spoon food—such as the food was—into them, march them off to work, and put them to bed after dark, too tired to eat. Young girls were whipped for falling asleep over their jobs, and deformed from sitting, at age ten, in one position, for twelve hours a day, six days a week, fifty-two weeks a year. Typhus, tuberculosis, alcoholism, dysentery, all the diseases of slum populations tried, but did not succeed, in keeping the birth rate down. Thomas Malthus wrote his dire prophecies of population growth spiraling out of control, and Jane Austen's soft, green England lived side by side with conditions as bad as any humanity had yet endured. English power and progress as an industrial and commercial power was paid for by sweat and blood.

Yet the power and progress were there, undeniable for all to see. As the last decade of the century approached, this "nation of shopkeepers" was far ahead of the rest of the world in its production of goods and services. In absolute numbers, the French might make more of some particular item; that was far less significant than the fact that the English item was produced at a lower unit cost and with fewer man-hours. English factories were becoming the producers for the world. English cotton could be bought in St. Petersburg and Philadelphia, English pots in Vienna and Santiago, even if they had to be smuggled into the latter. Perhaps more important, in the next quarter century, Frenchmen were going to march to Moscow in British-made overcoats and boots, and Russians were going to drive them out with British-made bayonets; for just as the full impact of the Industrial Revolution began to be felt, France made its last and greatest bid for the hegemony of Europe, and the last round of the great Anglo-French struggle began.

The energies that were harnessed and exploited in England were frustrated in France. The age-old compromise that allowed the Crown to hold a balance between the privileged estates—Church and nobility—and the Commons or Third Estate, broke down in the eighteenth century, partly because of the inadequacies of the royal government, partly because of the rising claims of the bourgeoisie (the leading element of the Commons), and partly because of the reassertion of ancient rights by the privileged orders. Where in England Parliament and primogeniture provided some sort of safety valve for the assuaging of frustrations, in France the time-honored formulas simply ceased to correspond to reality. King Louis XV, that much-maligned ruler who is always remembered for his shrugged "After me the deluge," made a valiant effort to restructure his state—and failed. His successor, the well-meaning but inept Louis XVI and his charming wife, Marie Antoinette, who was a political disaster all by herself, made far less effort and failed far more disastrously.

By 1787 France was bankrupt, and the great governmental machine created by Richelieu and Colbert ground to a halt. Two years later the country was in the throes of a revolution that was still, with some unfortunate excesses, essentially gentlemanly. But by 1792 the provincial lawyers and dissatisfied priests who had thrust themselves into prominence were being elbowed aside by men willing to go farther. Beset by internal difficulties that were not as amenable to solution as they had naïvely thought, the new rulers of France tried the classic resort of failing politicians: They declared war on virtually all of Europe. The mere fact that revolution was not working at home was no reason not to export it to the rest of the world—if necessary on the points of bayonets.

In Great Britain, the outbreak of the Revolution across the Channel had been greeted with very real enthusiasm. The British tended in the first instance to be flattered by events, for much of what the French said they wanted was couched in terms complimentary to the islanders. The British constitution and Parliament were held up as models of what a government ought to be, and Englishmen thought that Frenchmen were working in the right direction, that of making themselves like Englishmen. The drama in France also tended to obscure domestic difficulties among the British. In 1788, for example, the King had had his first attack of illness, diagnosed as insanity, and there had been acrimonious discussion about a regency until George III suddenly recovered in the midst of it and resumed his normal life. There were also more profound dissatisfactions than the King's health; George had by now withdrawn from much of the day-to-day routine of government anyway and left it in the hands of his capable Prime Minister, William Pitt the Younger. But there were demands for reform in England, just as there were in France. The population shifts of the Industrial Revolution and the growth of new centers of commerce and industry had left the British electoral system more glaringly deficient than ever. Cities of several thousand people had no representation while grass-covered mounds of ruins sent two members to the House of Commons. If Americans twenty-five years before had thought the British system needed updating, there were many Englishmen now who agreed with them.

Naturally, the members of the government were not among them. Except for a few dedicated radicals, such as Charles James Fox, most of those securely in place were interested only in keeping themselves there. The clamor for reform outside Parliament was but a muted echo inside. Many Englishmen of the middling sort soon began to think that a dose of French medicine would do England good. It was this sort of thing that prompted the twenty-year-old Wordsworth to write, "Bliss was it in that dawn to be alive, But to be young was very heaven!"

Enthusiasm for affairs in France soon began to wane, however. The more perceptive among English observers noted that the Revolution, begun with such high aspirations, was sliding downhill into bloodshed and the tyranny of King Mob. In 1790 Edmund Burke published his *Reflections on the French Revolution,* and within a year or two Burke, once a leading liberal, was advocating the suppression of free speech in England lest the continental disease get a foothold on the island. The rapid evolution of Burke's ideas was matched by the government. All demands for reform and change were condemned as treasonous. Laws were passed against "seditious" writings and meetings, and Charles James Fox noted that the same ideas that brought William Pitt to the Prime Ministership in 1783 would send a poor man to Botany Bay for life a dozen years later. For a quarter century reform in England was stopped dead in its tracks by fear of revolution in France.

Yet when war came, early in 1793, the British government did not immediately recognize that it was involved in a great ideological struggle. The French abolished the monarchy and declared a republic in September 1792. They celebrated their new order by overrunning the Austrian Netherlands—Belgium. In January 1793 they executed poor, harmless Louis—Citizen Capet, as he was now called—and on the first of February they declared war on England. William Pitt's government was distressed at the execution of the King of France—it was a long time since the English had done that sort of thing themselves—but what really bothered them was that the French opened the rivers of the Netherlands to international trade, a direct threat to British commerce and markets. To the extent that he had a foreign policy at all, and up to now he had had very little, Pitt was interested more in overseas affairs than in continental ones. His concerns with Europe were mainly that British trade should flourish and therefore that Britain should be free to exploit the commercial arteries, the North Sea, the Baltic, and the Mediterranean. It was for this reason that the French incursion into the Low Countries prompted such alarm. "Antwerp is a pistol pointed at the heart of England" was an adage known on both sides of the Channel; Antwerp in the hands of a distant and nonmaritime Austria was one thing; Antwerp in the hands of France was another. Britain went to war.

The British government did not expect that the war would be very long or very difficult. France looked as if it might collapse at any moment. There was Royalist revolt down in the Vendee, the Austrians recaptured Brussels in March, and France's best general, Dumouriez, defected from the Revolution and surrendered to his opponents. Pitt's government, all unknowing that the Terror was about to burst on France and galvanize its energies in a wave of blood and patriotism, prepared to play the by now classic British game. The Army was small and would stay that way, but there were more than a hundred ships of the line available, and the French Navy was rotten with the Revolution and poor discipline. Britain need not make any real continental commitment; instead she would sweep up the overseas possessions of France. When peace came Britain would sit down at the table with the best pile of counters and come away the handy winner in a short, inexpensive war. The British had made that misassessment before, and they were to make it again.

This view of what the war was about was to be rudely shattered, for it turned out to be not a trade war in the graceful pattern of the past. This was a war between the eighteenth century and the modern era. Pitt's world of gentlemanly debate was far from Nantes, where the representatives of the Terror were crowding "counterrevolutionary" men, women, and children into the holds of ships and scuttling them in the mouth of the Loire, or from Paris and Saint-Just's desire to strangle the last King with the guts of the last priest. "Death is of no account, so long as the Revolution triumphs!" It took Pitt ten years to learn what he was up against.

In those ten years Britain clung, without notable success, to the classic formula. She subsidized allies on the Continent; she reasserted her general control of the seas; she landed occasional expeditions on French-held coasts; and she undertook a series of overseas expeditions to expand her territories and diminish her enemies'.

On land Britain's allies were no match for the new French armies. Their tactical and strategic doctrines reworked by a series of military thinkers before the Revolution, their ranks reinforced by a successful mixture of old professionals and new patriots, and their leadership provided by a group of brilliant rising young stars, the French armies proved nearly unstoppable. They cleared the Austrians out of the Netherlands in 1794, they drove Prussia and the German states into peace in 1795. Spain soon gave up the struggle. That left only Austria and some of the northern Italian states, and Britain. The Italians, then the Austrians were bludgeoned out of the war by the military genius of a young unknown named Napoleon Bonaparte, and by 1797, only Britain was still under arms. Bonaparte's invasion of Egypt brought the eastern European powers back into the field once again, and from 1798 to the general peace in 1802 the forces of the Second Coalition waged yet another war against a France that had turned the corner from revolution to military dictatorship. But once again French arms bore out the old motto of Louis XIV, "Not inferior to many," and under a series of hammer blows all the members of the coalition gradually succumbed and one after the other dropped out: the Ottoman Empire, Naples, Portugal, Russia, and finally Austria all made peace. Pitt alone would have fought on, but instead he retired temporarily and a war-weary Britain signed the Treaty of Amiens in March 1802. So much for short wars.

The British did far better at sea relying on their own resources than they did on land relying on their allies. At the outbreak of the war twenty-five ships of the line and nearly fifty frigates were in commission, and the Admiralty, having wisely adopted a policy of keeping reserves of stores on hand, was able to bring fifty more ships of the line into commission in a relatively short time. Manning the ships was as usual difficult, and the Navy resorted to the press gangs, stripping incoming ships of their seasoned hands and making the rounds of seaside taverns and brothels. Where in the past the French maritime organization had been superior to the British, this time the Royal Navy was soon at sea, while the French were distracted and demoralized by the upheaval of the Revolution. Possessing about seventy-five ships of the line, the French could get fewer than half of them to sea. Often they had to be commanded by merchant-ship officers, and these might well be dispossessed by their crews, who had been as affected as everyone else by the current craze for democracy. What man would want to furl topsails in a Bay of Biscay gale if he could vote not to do it?

In the naval war, therefore, the odds were all against France. Not only did she have the deficiencies of her political situation, but initially all Europe was against her. Counting only the ships of the line, France had some 75. Britain alone had 115. Spain had 56, which were not very good. The Netherlands could put 50 to sea, good, if smaller than most. The minor naval powers—Portugal, Naples, Austria—could contribute another 12 or so. On a straight numerical basis, the French were outnumbered 3 to 1.

The allies did not in fact count for much; the Dutch fleet eventually fell under the direction of France, and the Spanish switched back and forth and fought on and against both sides during the long course of the war. In this first decade of war, it was mostly Britain vs. France; in the second decade, it was Britain vs. the world.

For some time there was little more than ineffectual sparring between the two great naval rivals. Not enough French ships could get to sea in 1793 to matter. The first general action came the next year. In June 1794 the French slipped a huge grain convoy past the British. As part of this operation, the two battle fleets met in an inconclusive engagement hailed in Britain as "the Glorious First of June." The seventy-year-old British Admiral, Sir Richard Howe, took only six French ships and was lucky to do that. He never sighted the grain convoy, which got by a hundred miles to the south and reached France with relatively little trouble. The British celebrated a tactical victory, the French a strategic one.

The first of June was less glorious to knowledgeable sailors than it was to the general public. The British Navy knew that the French had not done too badly, had done better, in fact, than might have been expected, given conditions in France itself. The war dragged on, with combinations here and excursions there. The British sponsored an *émigré* invasion of France that came to naught in 1795, and the French tried to invade Ireland, being foiled more by bad luck and bad weather than by the British. There was extensive commerce raiding on both sides, and the French badly mauled the Grand Banks fisheries fleet, while a young naval captain named Horatio Nelson made his reputation in the Mediterranean, annoying the communications between southern France and northern Italy. Events on land went against Britain, for in 1795 the French armies overran the Netherlands, and the Dutch fleet fell under French control, and the next year, in August, the Spanish agreed to ally with France. Faced with this triple threat to maritime supremacy, the British were forced to pull their fleet out of the Mediterranean, for the first time since Blake had carried the Union Jack into those waters nearly a century and a half earlier. As a result, 1797 was a year of crisis; it saw two fleet actions, and far more threatening, a mutiny at Spithead just off Portsmouth.

The first of the fleet actions was off Cape St. Vincent, in Portugal. Admiral Sir John Jervis, the strictest disciplinarian in the Royal Navy, was in command of the Mediterranean fleet, now operating outside the Strait of Gibraltar, and cruising off the coast of Portugal with fifteen ships of the line. The Spanish Admiral Cordoba got through the strait with twenty-seven ships, heading for the age-old chimera, a junction with the Brest fleet and an invasion of Ireland. The battle between the British and the Spanish, fought on February 14, was finally a definitive victory, not over the Spanish, but rather over the Fighting Instructions, which had so long held the British Navy in their paper shackles.

As Jervis sailed on a southerly heading toward the Spanish, who were split into two groups, Cordoba turned his main body northward. Jervis tried to bring his line around to meet them, but the British turned late. When it looked as if the main Spanish element might escape, Horatio Nelson, in H.M.S. *Captain,* the third ship from the rear of Jervis' line, hauled out of position and crossed the Spanish bows; Captain Collingwood in *Excellent,* who prided himself on his reputation as the hardest hitter in the fleet, followed him in, and together they threw the Spanish into such disarray that the rest of the British were able to get at them. The battle disintegrated into a murderous melee in which Nelson took two ships, boarding the *San Nicolas* and passing right over her to take the massive *San Josef,* of 112 guns and already disabled by Collingwood's smashing broadsides. The Spanish finally got away, after losing four ships. With that, they still outnumbered Jervis, who burned his prizes rather than risk their being retaken. He fully expected to fight again the next day, but Cordoba, his courage now shown to be no match for his earlier confidence, turned and ran for Cadiz.

England was deliriously grateful; the threat of invasion was removed once more, and the government, which after five years of inconclusive war badly needed a victory, showered honors on the sailors. Jervis became Lord St. Vincent, and Nelson was knighted and promoted to rear admiral. When one of Jervis' senior captains mused that Nelson had disregarded the Fighting Instructions, Jervis replied that with such results, anyone who did the same might well be forgiven. At last the dead hand of formalism was removed from British naval officers, the fear of court-martial replaced by the spirit of initiative.

Before the victory could be enjoyed or its lessons developed, a thrill of fear ran through the Navy and the country. At Spithead in April, the fleet mutinied.

This was not red revolution, as had happened across the Channel. Like the French military mutinies of 1917, this was simply a desperate reaction by men who had been pushed farther than humanity and decency could stand. The sailors were ready to fight the French if they should come out, but they had finally had enough of rotten conditions, meager pay and rations, and officers who were often martinets and occasionally brutes. They took over the ships and either put their officers under guard or escorted them ashore. It was in fact less of a mutiny than it was a sit-down strike. The grievances the sailors presented were truly pathetic. Their pay had not been changed in more than a century, and what little they received was usually held back on the excuse of one regulation or another. Once entered on a ship's books, they were there until the ship's commission was over—that is, until she "paid off," or for life, more often the latter. There were only three ways to get out, and they were summed up on the ships' muster rolls: "D" for "discharged," "R" for "run," and "DD" for "discharged dead." In any given muster roll, the R's and DD's were far likely to outnumber the D's. During the Seven Years' War, for example, out of 180,000 sailors, only 50,000 had been discharged; a mere 1,500 had been killed, and nearly 130,000 had either deserted or died of sickness. Truly, as Dr.

Johnson said, no man would go to sea who had sense to buy a rope and hang himself. Cooped up in intolerable conditions with but a few inches to sling a hammock, kept aboard for years at a time, the sailors were far from the jolly jack tars of the later music halls and sea novels. Their life was unremitting toil and misery, and the more sensible, thinking officers had to acknowledge the justice of their complaints. It was a good six weeks before the mutinies were over and many of the sailors' grievances redressed.

The infection then spread to the Nore, off the mouth of the Thames, and the squadron guarding the North Sea. This time it did have political overtones, and the government dealt more firmly with the second mutiny; here men were hanged at the yardarm. The Nore mutiny was less dangerous than the Spithead one, but it came at a more awkward time, for the French now knew about England's problems and were trying, in combination with the Dutch fleet, to put together a force for a quick invasion.

This danger was resolved by Admiral Adam Duncan, one of the few Scots to rise to high rank in the old Royal Navy, a big, tough, hard sailor who brooked no nonsense in his immediate vicinity. With most of the North Sea fleet in a state of mutiny, he sailed across to the Texel with his flagship and one frigate. Leaving the frigate on the horizon to relay his signals to an imaginary fleet beyond view from the shore, he boldly anchored in the main channel in full view of the Dutch fleet and for two weeks he sat there, hoping no one would call his bluff.

It was not until October that the Dutch got their battle squadron to sea, fifteen smallish ships of the line. By then the invasion threat had passed as the French gave it up for another year, and the mutinies were over, too. So when Duncan met the Dutch off Camperdown with his sixteen ships, he and the Dutch Admiral de Winter were fighting largely for the sake of fighting, which carried one back almost to the days of the Anglo-Dutch wars. In the space of five hours, the British came down against the Dutch line in two divisions and broke through it. A general melee followed, in which the heavier British construction and weight of metal told markedly in their favor. Not one British ship lost a mast. That was not to say the Dutch did not make a fight of it, for they finally lost all but five of their ships, most of which were battered into rolling hulks, and Camperdown turned out to be proportionately the bloodiest naval battle of the entire Revolutionary and Napoleonic wars, with the British suffering 12 percent in casualties, and the Dutch, counting all the men they lost as prisoners, losing close to 75 percent.

Between Cape St. Vincent and Camperdown the British had neutralized both of France's important naval allies and should, therefore, have enjoyed the initiative for a period. England was weary from the war, however, and had been thoroughly scared by the naval mutinies; in fact, she had tried unsuccessfully to negotiate peace through the summer of 1797. French conditions proved unacceptable, and the war dragged on. There was still no British presence in the Mediterranean, and in 1798 the French tried the one great strategic combination of the Revolutionary War: They invaded Egypt.

In retrospect, after it had failed, the invasion of Egypt looked to be an act of supreme folly. At the time it had something to commend it. There was, in the first place, no British squadron in the Mediterranean, and the French could therefore expect to be unmolested in their passage. There had also been French contacts with the Levant for centuries—even the term "Levant" is French—and the commercial classes considered the shores of Egypt, Palestine, and Syria to be a profitable field of activity. Egypt was already an important way station on the Mediterranean route to India, and the French government readily accepted the view put forth by the hero of Italy, General Bonaparte, that this was the most likely way to pressure England and bring her to the peace table. The General, when he returned triumphantly from Italy, had been assigned up to the Channel coast to consider the prospects of a direct invasion of Britain. He had not liked what he saw, and he thought Egypt the better plan. The current government of France, the Directory, was wisely wary of having an unemployed military hero on their hands, and they accepted his suggestion with alacrity. The Channel was a better place for him than Paris, and Egypt was better yet.

There were difficulties. Though it was ruled by a semiautonomous and dissolute military caste called Mamelukes, Egypt belonged officially to the Ottoman Empire. Never mind, said Bonaparte; we shall take Egypt, and we shall send our Foreign Minister, Talleyrand, to Constantinople to tell the Turks we are simply reconquering Egypt for them. There was no money for the expedition, but that was not allowed to become an impediment either. In the way of self-proclaimed champions of freedom, the French occupied Switzerland and stripped it of its ready funds to pay for their new campaign.

Both these solutions backfired. Talleyrand, a former bishop and a radical of the early revolutionary period, was a cautious old fox. Many years later, when asked what he had done during this era, he remarked with a smile, "I survived." A mission to the Sublime Porte was not the way to do that, and he stalled so successfully that he never got there at all. The Turks declared war on France. Nor were they the only ones. The invasion of Switzerland touched off a rash of declarations of war as the European powers decided there was no sating French ambitions. They held their hands out for English gold and recalled their ambassadors from Paris. To satisfy Bonaparte's ambition of playing Alexander the Great, the Directory found itself at war again with most of Europe.

French trouble was British opportunity. Bonaparte left the southern French and Italian ports in May 1798. The British remained uncertain of his destination. The French cover plan was of an invasion of England, but the Admiralty was certain this was merely a ruse. They were worried over Ireland; they thought the French might possibly head for the West Indies. But the most pressing threat was to Portugal. If the French and their Spanish allies took Lisbon, the British would be left with no viable base in Europe south of England itself, Gibraltar not being large enough for a major fleet base.

Admiral Jervis, now Lord St. Vincent, was stationed in Portugal, watching the Spanish fleet still shut up in Cadiz and worrying at a distance about the French in Toulon. He could do nothing about the latter but send Admiral Nelson with a small squadron to keep an eye on things. Given full freedom to act, Jervis finally took the risk of splitting his fleet. He kept some of his ships off Portugal, but he sent another ten ships of the line to Admiral Nelson, so the British were at last back in force in the Mediterranean, for the past two years virtually a French lake.

Nelson's ships were the best St. Vincent had, and that meant the best England had, but there was one glaring deficiency: Nelson had no frigates to serve as scouts; there was simply none available. Had there been, the entire history of the nineteenth century might have been different.

In mid-May, before his reinforcements reached him, Nelson was blown away from Toulon by a gale. Bonaparte and his naval commander, Admiral Brueys, took the opportunity to slip out. They had thirty-five thousand soldiers and hundreds of transports and supply vessels. Their naval force was not too impressive, thirteen ships of the line and nine frigates; most of the ships were poorly equipped and undermanned. Several of the frigates were commandeered from the Italian states. All had supplies sufficient to get to Egypt; getting back was their own problem.

The French armada was sailing for Malta as Nelson was meeting his reinforcements off Toulon. With the new British ships coming from the west, they now knew Bonaparte was not heading for Gibraltar. But where was he heading? The ensuing campaign proved a fascinating example of the problems of naval warfare and strategic intelligence in the age of sail. While Bonaparte was at Malta, which occupied him for about a week, Nelson was at Civita Vecchia in Italy, just north of Rome. A week later, learning where the French had gone, he reached Cape Passero, the southeastern point of Sicily. But by then the French had left Malta, and the latest news was that they were sailing east. After that, nothing. Brueys was keeping any sail he sighted with him, thus imposing a news blackout on the eastern Mediterranean.

Where could the French be going? Nelson, thinking it over, decided that they must be heading for Alexandria. He believed they were perhaps a week ahead of him, when in fact they had left Malta with only a couple of days' lead. Making their best speed, the British, thirteen ships of the line strong, set off directly for Egypt.

The French, meanwhile, with four hundred merchant ships and transports, were making a leisurely passage to Crete. Bonaparte and his corps of savants discoursed on the sciences and the arts, and the troops gambled, joked, and whiled away the hours of a tedious but not unpleasant ocean voyage. On the night of June 15, as the French ghosted along, the British fleet, full of bulldog determination, passed them and crossed their track some sixty miles ahead. Had Nelson possessed a scouting line of frigates, he must surely have fallen in with them.

Nelson reached Alexandria on June 29 and was devastated to find he had guessed wrong. The port slept under the African sun. No French. Nothing! Now in a perfect quandary, Nelson rocketed and richocheted up the Levant coast, past Greece, and eventually all the way back to Syracuse in Sicily, before he finally met a merchantman who told him casually, "Oh, yes, the French are in Egypt; they landed at Alexandria on July first."

By now Egypt was already French. Bonaparte had fought the Battle of the Pyramids and entered Cairo on July 21 and was now busy organizing the country and flirting with Islam. He had insisted, however, that Admiral Brueys keep the fleet in Egyptian waters. Brueys wanted to go home. When Bonaparte ordered him to stay, he anchored his fleet in Aboukir Bay, east of Alexandria, and sat there for a month while his crews were depleted by sickness, heat, and drafts to help the

French Army. It was there, on the afternoon of August 1, that he received word of the arrival of the British.

Brueys immediately held a council of war, which decided that little could be done, and therefore nothing need be done. The French commanders chose to give battle at anchor, hard against the shoal line of Aboukir Bay. After a month of being at the army's beck and call, it was all they could do to clear their decks and fight one side of their ships at a time. The British view was different. Sizing up the situation, Nelson concluded that if there were room for the French to swing at anchor, there was room for the British to sail. He came right on in through the failing light of late afternoon. His leading ship, *Culloden,* ran aground on a shoal at the entrance to the bay, but the rest kept clear of her. With a favorable wind, they came down on the head of the French line. Maneuvering expertly, the result of long practice and perfect understanding of each other—this was Nelson's "band of brothers" at work—they doubled the French line, half outboard and half on the unprepared inboard side of the hapless French. From there they simply moved on down the line, smashing, burning, sinking as they went. At ten the French flagship, *Orient,* blew up with a huge crash, the climax of the battle. As dawn broke over the bay, two French ships were sunk, nine more were prizes, and the bay was full of floating junk and corpses. It was the most crushing naval victory of the age of sail. The night before, Nelson had remarked at supper, "By tomorrow, either a peerage or Westminster Abbey"; his victory made him Baron Nelson of the Nile.

From Nelson's victory at the Nile to the Peace of Amiens in March 1802, the naval war around the coasts of Europe was almost, but not quite, anticlimactic. The British remained active in the Mediterranean, and it was their control of the sea that eventually foiled Bonaparte's expedition up the coast to Syria. Late in 1799 he barely slipped home through their blockade. That year saw British and French squadrons at sea, but the French, true to their traditions, did their best to avoid action and concentrated on assorted "ulterior objectives." In March 1801 the British, in their best-planned and best-executed amphibious operation before the Normandy invasion, landed in Egypt, in Aboukir Bay itself, and subdued the dispirited remnant of Bonaparte's deserted army there.

By then Bonaparte himself was the First Consul of France. He had taken over the French Navy as he had everything else, but without significant effect. Meanwhile, British economic pressure against France and the Continent had created hostility among the neutral trading nations, as it had in the American war. Once again the Scandinavian countries formed a second Armed Neutrality, and in April 1801 Nelson, under the ostensible command of Admiral Sir Hyde Parker, sailed with a fleet up to Denmark and reduced the Danish fleet to lumber in the bloody Battle of Copenhagen. Since the Danes wanted principally to be left alone, the victory, hard-won though it was, was not one in which the British took a great deal of pride, and the conflict was soon resolved.

Having failed to get their neighbors to take on England at sea, the French went back once again to the old invasion game. They began building gunboat flotillas for a quick dash across the Channel. The British in turn went back to worrying about them, and launching attacks, mostly ineffectual, against them. They were still at it when peace broke out.

In terms of William Pitt's long-term strategy for the war, all these operations around the coasts of Europe were less an end in themselves than they were means to a larger prospect: the securing of British sea communications, both for trade and to gain new holdings overseas. The holdings, in this instance, were to be temporary; they were the leverage Britain would use to gain a favorable peace. From the start of the war, therefore, the British mounted distant expeditions to take enemy territories. The results were mixed.

As always, British attention focused on the Caribbean as soon as the war broke out. The security of the British islands there was thought to be essential, especially by those absentee landlords whose fortunes derived from them, and it seemed perfectly logical to send most of the few troops the government had available off on a spree to capture potential French bases. This reasoning was supported by the chaotic condition of the West Indies, for the Revolution in France had had repercussions in her Empire; on some islands, planters had declared against the new government at home; on others, the slaves had seized power. The British had both the chance to take new islands and the need to prevent the spread of revolutionary contagion.

In 1794, therefore, Sir John Jervis sailed over with seven thousand soldiers, one third of Britain's Army at the time, and easily occupied Martinique, St. Lucia, and Guadeloupe after little or no fighting. They then went on to Haiti, where they added yet another strand to the tortuous history of this unhappy island.

The second largest of the Caribbean islands, Haiti was formerly known as Hispaniola. In the eighteenth century, it was also called Santo Domingo; the western third of the island had been French since 1697; the larger, eastern part remained Spanish. When the British expedition arrived, already seriously depleted by garrisons left on the other conquests, it was warmly welcomed by the forty thousand white settlers, for they were sitting on a powder keg, and the fuse was already lit. In Paris, the Republican government had announced the freeing of the slaves and had proclaimed the equality of all men, white or black. A servile insurrection had begun as early as 1791 and had found a leader in Toussaint L'Overture. As there were half a million blacks on the island and they had every reason to hate their white masters, the British were seen less as conquerors than as rescuers by the whites.

The rescuers were soon in serious troubles themselves. For one thing, there were not many of them. Pitt at home was spreading his little army all around the map in penny packets, supporting royalists at Quiberon and Toulon, sending detachments here and frittering them away there. The British naval blockade of France was far from complete, and the forces in the West Indies were soon faced by three major threats. The most obvious of these—but as it turned out the least dangerous—was the French themselves. A force six thousand strong sailed from Brest in spite of British efforts and recaptured Guadeloupe by the end of the year. From then on both sides sparred back and forth through the Lesser Antilles, taking an island here and losing one there. The British remained slightly ahead, but no more than that, on points.

A second and potentially more dangerous threat came from the political activities of the French, for the new government sent out subversive emissaries to preach the pernicious doctrines of liberty, equality, and fraternity to the slaves and to suggest that they manifest their interest by overthrowing their masters. Such preachings naturally fell on fertile soil and caused whites throughout the Caribbean, of whatever nationality, to respond with all too reasoning fear and very open-eyed hatred. The slightest suggestions of slave unrest were fiercely put down before, as in Haiti, they could get out of hand.

The most deadly enemy of all, however, was indigenous to the area. Having once committed troops to that theater, the British then raised new forces and shoveled them in as if it were a bottomless pit. It was; by 1796 they had had forty thousand men killed by yellow fever and a further forty thousand absolutely ruined in health. In two years in the West Indies they lost twice the number of men Wellington lost in the entire Peninsular War.

Meanwhile, the island-swapping continued. In 1795, as part of the

Peace of Basel, when Spain temporarily dropped out of the war, she ceded to France the eastern part of Santo Domingo-Haiti, probably relieved to be rid of it. The French made futile efforts to conquer it, killing off nearly as many troops as the British had, including among them Napoleon's brother-in-law, General Leclerc. The French also used Haiti as a dumping ground for politically hyperactive army regiments, recognizing that there was nothing like a bout of yellow fever to cure political aspirations. In 1797 the British sent an expedition to take Trinidad from the Spanish; the islanders were delighted, and the takeover was confirmed at the Peace of Amiens. Trinidad became a permanent part of the Empire and an important toehold in the door of the closed Spanish imperial system. It flourished both as a trading center and as a refuge-*cum*-base for aspiring revolutionaries along the Spanish Main. Just because the British did not want revolution in their own territory did not mean they were opposed to it among their enemies.

As with earlier wars, the Caribbean might be the most important overseas area, but fighting was not confined to it. Once again British and French battled each other, in a small way, for control of the slaving coast of West Africa, without reaching a definitive conclusion. The French no longer had much in the East, but their allies did. In overseas terms, it was almost a bonus for the British when France overran the Netherlands. As the Dutch became allies or satellites, this meant their colonies could be attacked by Britain, just as the British had hastened to gather in the Spanish colonies at the end of the Seven Years' War.

Amsterdam was occupied by French troops early in 1795. By September a British force reached the Cape of Good Hope and was received with little opposition. The Cape Dutch had no use for French revolutionaries, or for their own home government that had succumbed to them. Here as elsewhere the British were welcomed as rescuers. They then pretty well swept through the Dutch East Indian Empire, taking Ceylon and securing a treaty with the King of Kandy, still ruler over the inland parts of the island. From there it was on to Malacca, Amboina, and Banda, and control of all the major stations of the East Indies.

In India French agitation contributed to the Fourth Mysore War in 1799. By now French influence in the land was well on the wane, but there were still Indian princes who hoped to play off one European power against another. That, after all, had been the Indian game ever since the British had first appeared to challenge the Portuguese two centuries earlier. But it no longer worked. The Governor General of

India, Richard Wellesley, demanded that French troops in the service of the Indian states be disbanded, and he made his demands stick. In southern India the Sultan of Mysore resisted, and Wellesley sent his younger brother, Arthur, marching through the land with two armies. At the Battle of Seringapatam the Sultan was killed, and Mysore came under British control. Arthur Wellesley was thought to be the less promising of the brothers, and his Army career was to this point only average. Napoleon would one day contemptuously dismiss him as "a sepoy general."

These conquests, satisfying though they might be, were simply not enough to make a winning war for Great Britain. British troops were in Capetown, but French were in Amsterdam; the British held Trinidad, but Madrid was allied with Paris. Pitt's style of eighteenth-century warfare was not dynamic enough to balance the energies unleashed by the Revolution and later personified by Napoleon Bonaparte.

In fact, a curious juxtaposition had taken place. The French for better or worse had entered the modern world of popular government, even if it was eventually embodied in a dictator. Through the Terror they had channeled the ambitions and the power of the nation, and those ambitions and that power found fullest expression in the Army. It was here that the "career open to talent" held sway, and the marshals of the Empire, and Napoleon himself, were the archetypal expressions of those aspirations. Through these wars, it was indeed true that every French soldier carried a marshal's baton in his pack. The bloody but fresh wind of revolution blew across the Continent and militarily created a force that had not been seen before in Europe, the force of the nation-state in arms, "half God and half monster." It was ironic, and fortunate for Britain, that the one aspect of the French state it touched least was the Navy; here, until too late, old ideas held sway, and even when Napoleon turned his attention to the Navy, his reforms were organizational and administrative rather than tactical and doctrinal. In naval terms the French made the same mistakes under the Empire that they had made under Louis XIV; they just made them more efficiently.

Britain in this curious period went the other way. Where the French government became revolutionary, the British became reactionary. Englishmen clung to their traditional ways of doing things all the more tenaciously the more they were challenged, whether the challenge came from across the Channel or from workingmen in Birmingham or peasants in Ireland. And where the French Army was the point

of the new order, the British Army during the Revolutionary and Napoleonic wars remained determinedly eighteenth-century. It never attempted conscription, its drill and discipline remained as they had
been; there was no infectious enthusiasm disordering the ranks here.
Marlborough would have been proud of it.

On the other hand, where the French Navy was the element least
touched by the new forms, the Royal Navy was the most revolutionary
part of Britain. Not in its manning or its organization, but in its officers. Nelson's band of brothers was the British equivalent of Napoleon's marshals, and the discarding at last of the Fighting Instructions
in the Navy was like the French abandonment of the old military constraints. If Napoleon had had both his Army and Nelson's Navy, then
he would indeed have been another Alexander the Great.

As it was, by 1802 both sides had reached a standoff and exhaustion. Napoleon was master of most of western Europe, Britain of most
of the world's oceans. Under these circumstances, the peace negotiated
at Amiens could be little more than a truce, but each was willing to
make a few compromises to get it. Napoleon, who could be as clever
and as unscrupulous at the peace table as on the battlefield, did slightly
better. He gave Malta back to the Knights of St. John and made a few
minor concessions. Of all her conquests from the other imperial states,
Britian retained only Ceylon, which had been Dutch, and Trinidad,
which had been Spanish. That was her net imperial gain for ten years
of war.

A treaty that addressed none of the basic issues of contention between the two belligerents and to whose few provisions neither side
adhered faithfully was a truce rather than a peace, and it was pretty
well recognized as such by both sides. Napoleon always insisted that
he genuinely wanted peace, and perhaps he did, but he always wanted
it on his terms. The British insisted the same (that is, peace on their
terms), but they could not really tolerate a dangerously engorged
France, one that all too obviously thought of itself in terms of universal
empire. A flood of British tourists swarmed across the Channel in the
summer of 1802 to have a look at Paris and the Great Man, but men of
affairs kept their own counsel and were not yet prepared to relax. A
scant four months after the signing of the Treaty of Amiens, Napoleon
became Consul for Life, a long step toward the establishment of empire, and by May of the new year of 1803 the British ambassador had
left Paris, and the two countries were back at war.

It was a curious war, rather like the "Phony War" of a later, similar era, for the French could not get to sea, and the British could not get to shore. Napoleon therefore talked invasion of England and ostentatiously collected troops along the Channel coast. He set up a headquarters for his vast Army at Boulogne, and he held glorious reviews; in the intervals between his visits, the French built invasion barges and gunboats, and the soldiers practiced clambering into and out of them and looking stern and warlike.

How real the threat was was problematic. There is no doubt Napoleon wanted to invade England, but for an islander he was an oddly landbound creature. He never acknowledged that ships could not maneuver as regiments could. Since the sea was an element he could not master, he was simply not much interested in it. The preparations marched forward, but there was an air of underlying skepticism about them.

The British, of course, had to take them seriously, and they did. The Navy maintained its blockade, day in and day out, month after month. In October 1804 Admiral Sir Sidney Smith launched a fireship attack against the invasion flotilla on the coast of the Low Countries and set back the French schedule. After Napoleon was crowned Emperor in December 1804, British sailors were probably the first foreigners to hear the deep-throated roars of *"Vive l'Empereur!"* from the Grand Army, for when Napoleon held grandiose reviews of his troops, Royal Navy ships stood impudently close to the shore, just to remind the French that he who rules the land does not necessarily rule the waves.

Such a standoff could not last indefinitely, and the British were not merely passive in their approach; British money and diplomacy were hard at work throughout the courts of Europe, and slowly they, and Napoleon's imperial arrogance, began to take effect. As the summer of 1805 came, central Europe began to stir. Austria, Prussia, and Russia all felt threatened by an engorged France, and a Third Coalition against her now matured. Even before it did, Napoleon had lost patience with Britain. All through 1804 and into 1805, he had considered plan after plan for combining his ships in overwhelming numbers that would gain him command of the Channel for a few hours or a few days, long enough to pass his invasion force across. One after another, the plans fell apart before the determination of the British—Nelson off Toulon, Cornwallis off Brest, Keith in the Channel; wherever there were French ships in port, there were British ships offshore, hoping only that the enemy would sally forth. The British compounded their difficulties by attacking a Spanish treasure flotilla in late 1804—shades of Drake—and Spain entered the war on France's side, bringing Napoleon a gift of thirty more ships of the line.

The French plans never did reach a definitive stage; they were modified, corrected—and mixed up—until they finally ended in disaster. The initial idea was for a mass breakout of all the French and Spanish squadrons from all their various ports, a combination in the West Indies, and then a massive return to the Channel, where they would convoy the invasion fleet across to England. The French were still so wedded to the idea of the ulterior objective that they somehow convinced themselves they might do this without fighting. Then failing to get most of their squadrons to sea, they decided that those who did get out should rendezvous at Martinique, sail back to Spain, and from there sweep northward, adding ships from successive ports as they moved along the coast. Once again, they hoped to do it without a fight, as if the Royal Navy were somehow to look the other way while all this was going on.

The British were delighted with the prospect of the French coming out; anything was better than perpetual blockade duty. Nelson off Toulon deliberately kept his squadron far out at sea, to give the French every opportunity. This finally allowed Admiral Villeneuve to sail at the end of March 1805. Nelson then misjudged his direction and followed him correctly only after several weeks' delay. Villeneuve took his ships across to Martinique and waited for someone to show up to join him.

Nelson chased all the way to the West Indies, and when the Frenchman learned that, he headed back to Europe. Nelson chased him back. Not knowing where his quarry was going, Nelson fell back toward the Channel, while the Frenchman, after an inconclusive action with Sir Robert Calder's squadron off Ferrol, finally took refuge in Cadiz. The end result of affairs by early August was that the French and Spanish were still scattered, if in Atlantic rather than Mediterranean ports, and the British had a fifty-ship concentration off the approaches to the Channel.

It was too late now. Austrians and Russians were on the march, and Prussia was threatening. The Emperor turned his attention from these maddening sailors and their talk he could not understand and sent the Grand Army crashing off across northern France to the upper Rhine. He casually sent his final orders to Villeneuve: Get back to Toulon. It was all over.

Not quite. The British force outside Cadiz was now commanded by Nelson, and for the next month he talked endlessly with his captains. He knew many of them personally, for some had been with him since the days of Cape St. Vincent and the Nile, and all knew him by name and reputation. Nelson had had his ups and downs, a long career in low-level tasks, and several wounds in his country's service—he lost an eye in Corsica in 1794, an arm at Santa Cruz in 1797. But St. Vincent had brought him fame, and the Nile glory, so quickly that public adoration, concentrated especially in the person of Lady Hamilton, had nearly ruined him. In some ways he was an almost archetypal Romantic hero, out of Goethe or Byron. But now, here and among his fellow officers, he was precisely what Mahan called him, "the embodiment of the sea power of Great Britain." Night after night, the captains hammered out their ideas of what should be done in any given situation, and by the time the French and Spanish came out, they understood each other as well as men can ever do. All strong men of single minds, they were absolutely confident that whatever could be done with a ship of war, they were capable of doing.

It was hardly the same inside Cadiz. Villeneuve eventually fought because he read in the papers the announcement of his relief from command. His ships were worn, his men's morale questionable. The Spanish were in worse condition, and neither ally really trusted the other. The allied fleet went out to sea because it had nothing better to do, or because Villeneuve, a brave man in a fight, lacked the moral courage to tell the Emperor he was wrong. On October 20 they got to sea, thirty-three strong, hoping to get through the Strait and into the Mediterranean without a fight.

Nelson cut them off, and on the morning of October 21 the Royal Navy found the Franco-Spanish drawn up in a long, concave line to leeward. Their formation looked fairly sensible; actually, it was the result of accident and their inability to form a better line. The British sailed down to meet them in two divisions, Nelson leading one in the hundred-gun *Victory*, and Collingwood leading the other in *Royal Sovereign*. It was late morning as the ships came close to each other. Suddenly the *Victory* spouted signal flags from her mastheads and yardarms, and Nelson produced his famous signal "England expects that every man will do his duty," as fitting a summation of British naval attitudes as he himself was.

The French and Spanish opened at long range but did little damage while the leading British ships, still silent, swept slowly and majestically down on them. Collingwood was first into action, and *Royal*

Sovereign's opening broadside was delivered at pistol range. From then on, one after another, the great British ships came into action and broke through the allied line. Fighting was general by noon, with the superior skill of the British more than a match for the despairing bravery of their adversaries. Soon after one o'clock a French marine from the mizzen top of the *Redoubtable* put a musket ball through Nelson's chest, and he was carried below to die among his wounded seamen while his captains went on to win the most famous of their naval victories, a victory most would gladly have given up to have had Nelson survive.

By late afternoon, it was all over. Villeneuve surrendered at four-thirty; the Spanish Admiral Gravina made off with those ships he could gather about him. Of the thirty-three allied ships, only eight made it back to Cadiz, and only two were worth repairing. At the cost of Nelson and seventeen hundred sailors, Britain ruled the seas unchallenged.

The day before Nelson won Trafalgar, the Austrian General Mack surrendered Ulm to Napoleon. Six weeks later, on December 2, while Britain was still celebrating its triumph and mourning its loss, the Emperor defeated the Russian Army at Austerlitz. When he heard the news, William Pitt remarked, "Roll up the map of Europe; it will not be needed these next ten years." Two months later he too was dead. It was said the grief of Austerlitz killed him before he could savor the joy of Trafalgar.

If the British had now removed virtually all opposition to their power at sea, Napoleon went on to do the same on land. Austria collapsed after Ulm and Austerlitz; in the fall of 1806 Prussia was driven out of the war at Jena and Auerstadt, and finally, at Friedland in June 1807, the French finished off the Russians. Napoleon and Tsar Alexander of Russia met on a raft in the middle of the Niemen River, and by the Peace of Tilsit they divided continental Europe between them. Britain was once more alone against the world.

Britain and France were, in fact, back where they had been three years earlier, except that the situation had hardened for both sides. The French now had no hope of doing anything on the water, and the British could no longer anticipate, at least for the foreseeable future, that there would be any viable opposition to Napoleon on the Continent. Both sides were therefore forced to resort to less direct forms of warfare. For the British this meant the continuation of their policy of blockade, not only of France and her immediate satellites, but of practically the entire Continent as well. Eventually the British, through their Orders in Council, declared a blockade of all ports from which English trade was excluded—that is, of all ports under French domination, direct or otherwise; they announced that any ships attempting to run their blockade were subject to seizure, and they insisted that any neutral shipping intending to trade with Napoleon's French Empire must first stop in a British port and receive a license to continue. Napoleon countered with the Continental System, enunciated in the Berlin and Milan decrees. In this he declared a counterblockade of British commerce, and he closed off the Continent to British imports. Neutrals such as the Americans were caught in the middle: If they did not have a British license, they were subject to capture by the Royal Navy; if they did have one, they were liable to seizure by the French.

Each side intended to ruin the other. The British believed that the Continent could not subsist without British goods, and they encouraged their own merchants to break the French system, which they did with great success; trade through neutral Sweden, for example, rose several hundred percent, and while Napoleon was trying to shut his enemies out of Europe, he was at the same time creating markets for them, not only surreptitiously in Europe itself, but also by driving them into the overseas territories, especially in South America, of those states he held hostage. His intention was to clog the British distribution system, and he believed that if he denied her avenues of export, eventually the economy of the island would collapse. He was nearly correct; 1808 was a very difficult year, and in 1811 the British were near bankruptcy. However, Napoleon himself needed British goods, and he could not keep his system inviolate. He attempted to replace Britain with France as Europe's major producer, but the French economy could not supply the markets, and non-Frenchmen resented having their own interests so obviously subordinated to those of France.

Both sides tried to extend their power. Early in 1807 a British squadron under Admiral Sir John Duckworth forced the passage of the Dardanelles and threatened to bombard Constantinople. The Turks responded very firmly, and Duckworth was lucky to get away with an almost whole skin. Later in the year, when Napoleon demanded that Denmark join his new system, the British sailed into the Baltic and repeated Nelson's ploy over again, attacking and then carrying off the Danish fleet from Copenhagen. The Danes not only joined with Napoleon economically, they also declared war on Britain.

So did Russia. At Tilsit, Alexander's opening remark to Napoleon had been, "Sire, I hate the English as much as you do." It was an opinion he was eventually to revise, but only after five years of finding out what he should have known already, that Napoleon was not the apostle of peace he claimed to be.

If the constraints of the Continental System forced the British into wider ventures, their blockade also forced Napoleon to overextend himself, and this was finally a major contributor to his undoing. He annexed the remaining Italian states as well as the Papal States, and he finally pushed down the Dalmatian coast to Ragusa; he took over the North German states. But his real problem was the Iberian Peninsula. Spain had been one of his more or less consistent allies, but Portugal was an economic satellite of Britain. When he called on her to close her ports to Englishmen, therefore, the Portuguese refused, not from any heroic vision, but because it meant financial ruin. Napoleon next sent an army into the peninsula, and in November 1807 his troops occupied Lisbon. They arrived just in time to see the royal family sail down the Tagus for refuge in Brazil, protected, of course, by the ubiquitous Union Jack.

That was all right, but in the process of taking over Portugal, Napoleon got tangled up in the family politics of Spain, and the Spanish Bourbons were such dolts that they virtually invited him to take over their country. He was ill advised enough to accept. In March 1808 a hundred thousand Frenchmen filtered into Spain and seized the major towns and fortresses. However, the decadent Bourbons were not Spain, and two months later the population rose, practically en masse. Revolutionary juntas were set up, the most brutal fighting Europe had seen since the religious wars began, Spain asked for help from Britain, and all of a sudden Napoleon was faced with a people's war.

The British injected an army, at first under Sir John Moore, later under Arthur Wellesley, home from India and on his way to becoming the Duke of Wellington, and with this, the "Spanish ulcer" began the process of eating away at the Napoleonic Empire. The Peninsular War lasted until 1814; in fact, its last battle, at Toulouse in southern France, was fought after Napoleon had already abdicated. For years it went its repetitious way. Every time the French dispersed to pacify the countryside, the small British army marched in from Portugal and made a nuisance of itself; every time the French concentrated to face the British, the countryside rose around and behind the French. It was like trying to put out a fire in a peat bog. The Iberian Peninsula turned out to be the one place in Europe where the British could face the French on advantageous terms. They could sustain themselves by sea across the Bay of Biscay far more easily than the French could by land across the Pyrenees. At last they had found the Achilles' heel of the Empire. The Iberian Peninsula became what the Dardanelles expedition was supposed to be in 1915, or the invasion of Italy in 1943, a distant theater where seapower could negate the enemy's overwhelming manpower odds.

The British did not entirely understand this, and they continued to play—and to make mistakes—around the fringes. In 1809, when Austria fought Napoleon again, the British landed an expedition of forty thousand men on the island of Walcheren, hoping to take Antwerp. Instead they lost fifteen thousand men to sickness and withdrew without ever getting onto the mainland. As late as 1811, the government was still asking Wellington, as he now was, if it would not be best to withdraw from Spain and give it all up as a waste of effort.

That, however, was slightly premature. For the next year Napoleon's relations with Russia finally curdled. Once again the proximate cause was economics; pressured by his nobles and his merchant classes and squeezed by blockade, Alexander announced he was reopening his ports to Britain. Napoleon decided to invade. He would show the world, and the British, that there was to be no change; his system was how things would henceforth work. He told his troops that by defeating Russia they would "drive the leopards into the sea"—referring mistakenly to the lions on the British coat of arms—and then, at last, there would be peace. Most of his army found peace, all right, but it was the peace of death. Few of those Frenchmen who marched all the way to Moscow ever came home again. By 1813 all of the Continent was springing to arms against France; Prussia turned around and signed subsidy treaties with England, a British adviser rode with Tsar Alexander, and a token British rocket battery fought at the Battle of the Nations in 1813. Worn out, deserted by his marshals who no longer equated his interests with those of France, Napoleon abdicated early in 1814. The victorious allies gave him the tiny island of Elba for a kingdom.

During these years the British had been as active overseas as they had been in the waters around Europe. They had taken the Dutch colony at the Cape of Good Hope a second time, and this time they kept it. They had once more occupied the French islands of the Caribbean, and they had taken Mauritius and Réunion in the Indian Ocean. They had extended farther their control in India, and finally they had run into trouble both in South America and then in North America.

In 1806, while Napoleon was defeating Prussia, the British had taken Capetown. They then sent Admiral Sir Home Popham and fifteen hundred men under Colonel William Carr, Viscount Beresford, across to capture Buenos Aires from the Spaniards, who were at the time allied with France. This was indirect war with a vengeance, but the men who ran the government had visions of opening the entire Spanish Empire to British trade, which would more than offset economic problems in Europe itself. Popham and Beresford quickly occupied the Argentine city. Before they could enjoy it, however, the inhabitants regrouped, rose up, and captured the British garrison in its turn. Popham's grandiose visions of ruling the continent came crashing down, and he was called home for a court-martial.

The British then had a second try. General Sir John Whitelocke sailed for the Plate River, and with ten thousand men this time, he surrounded Buenos Aires and attempted to storm the city. After he had almost succeeded and lost a third of his force in the process, his nerve gave out. He called off the attack, negotiated a cease-fire, and sailed away to his court-martial. The British then gave up trying to liberate the Spanish from themselves.

In North America they got involved in a full-scale, if fairly low-level, war. Angered by high-handed British practices at sea and casting covetous eyes on Canada, the United States declared war on Great Britain on June 1812. American invasions of Canada failed ignominiously, but at sea, the Americans gave the Royal Navy some severe shocks. The British were now, after Trafalgar, used to regarding themselves as lords of the waters, and when American ships consistently won a series of bitter single-ship actions, the British were outraged and dismayed. However, an American Navy of fourteen ships, no matter how brilliantly handled, could not make much impact against a Royal Navy of a thousand ships, no matter how distracted the latter were by their major war. The defeats were embarrassing, and Wellington at one point bitterly complained that American privateers were denying his troops their supplies, but eventually the entire American coast was blockaded, the United States ships run down one by one, and American seaport towns themselves raided. Finally even Washington was burned. With the defeat of Napoleon and the patent inability of the United States to conquer Canada, most of the causes of the war disappeared, and in December 1814, peace was signed at Ghent in Belgium, two weeks before the final battle of the war was fought at New Orleans.

There was one last act. Early in 1815 a bored Napoleon escaped from Elba and was welcomed back by a restive and dissatisfied France. All Europe moved against him, but it did not take all Europe to defeat him. After beating the Prussians at Ligny, he met Wellington at Waterloo in June. For a long day his frantic legions tried to batter their way through to Brussels. The French General Foy, veteran of the Peninsular War, had said, "The British infantry is the best in Europe; fortunately there is not much of it." This day there was just enough of it, and in the gathering twilight of June 18, the shattered battalions of the once Grand Army fled down the road into history. Napoleon abdicated, tried to flee from France, and on July 15, in an act whose dramatic fitness he never fully realized, he surrendered to Captain Frederick Maitland aboard H.M.S. *Bellerophon* in Rochefort Harbor. There would not be another general European war for a hundred years, and the Royal Navy and the British Empire sailed serenely into the nineteenth century.

PART THREE

THE SUN NEVER SETTING

The fundamental difference between Britain and the European powers was that the latter perceived their security and stability in terms of acquisition of territory, while Britain saw hers in terms of a generalized European peace that would prevent upheaval and guarantee attractive commercial conditions for the future. As an island, her territorial interests lay outside Europe; as a trading and industrial power, she wanted a prosperous, peaceful Continent.

The settlement toward which the British delegates, Castlereagh and later Wellington, worked reflected some if not all of Britain's desires. A barrier of states was built around France, but the great enemy was not punished unduly. Austria gave up her part of the Low Countries to the Netherlands, a deal that lasted only fifteen years, and she was compensated in northern Italy. Prussia was enlarged at the expense of other German states and Poland, and Russia got the lion's share of Poland, storing up trouble for the future. All the powers agreed to support the idea of legitimacy—that is, to keep the kings on their thrones and to put down liberalism lest, as in France twenty-five years before, it should get out of hand.

Compared with these shifts, the British seemed to get little. In fact, what they got suited them nicely. The held on to most of the French islands in the West Indies and the Indian Ocean, guaranteeing their control in both areas. They kept the Cape of Good Hope, another link in the chain to the East. And around Europe itself they gathered a series of quite crucial bottlenecks, a recognition of the desirability of naval control over European waters. They already had Gibraltar, and for years they had played around with Minorca and more recently Corsica. Now they kept Malta, right in the heart of the Mediterranean. To add to that, they also claimed and garrisoned the Ionian Islands, giving them a stranglehold on the Adriatic; Napoleon, after all, had worked his way down the Balkans as far as Dalmatia. In the North Sea, crucially located off the mouth of the German rivers, they held the island of Heligoland. None of these was of much interest to anyone except a seapower, and Britain was the only seapower, and likely to be the only one for as far ahead as anyone could see. If those mad islanders wanted these sorts of things, land creatures such as Metternich and Alexander of Russia were quite willing to let them have them.

There were a few more extra-European by-products. In the 1670s a British astronomer, Edmund Halley, after whom the comet was named, had used the island of St. Helena in the distant South Atlantic as an observatory. Since then it had been an occasional way station for East Indian Company ships. The British decided it was the appropriate place for the modern Prometheus. To make sure he did not escape, they also held the nearest islands, Ascension to the north, and lonely Tristan de Cunha far to the south, which they "garrisoned" with a retired corporal and three families. Ascension, with its thirty-odd square miles, the Admiralty treated as a warship in commission. Important or significant though some of the British acquisitions might become in the future, none of them could be considered in any way a disturbance of the balance of Europe so eagerly sought by Castlereagh and Wellington.

At home the peace and what might be gained by it were overshadowed by domestic distress. Not realizing, or at least not wanting to acknowledge, the extent to which the war had fueled British prosperity, Englishmen confidently expected a great postwar boom. In actuality, without the stimulus of war, they got a depression instead. Ports and country towns were crowded with discharged sailors and disbanded soldiers, nearly a half million of them. Civilian workers were also thrown onto the unemployed labor market by the cancellation of war orders. Agriculture was equally hard hit, and the usual response of employers and owners, to cut back on wages, served merely to increase dissatisfaction. The government reacted negatively; to the extent that it was answerable to public opinion, that opinion was still expressed far more by the middle and upper classes than by the lower. The only recourses of the mass of Englishmen to their frustrations were in drink and riot, and those merely served to reinforce the possessing classes' view that they were sitting on the lid of a potential revolution. In 1817 Parliament enacted a series of "Coercion Acts," which were as repressive as anything done at the height of the war, and in 1819 the yeomanry cavalry charged a crowd of workers during a political meeting at St. Peter's Fields outside Manchester. Reformers contrasted "Peterloo" with "Waterloo," and the lower classes, increasingly despairing of any help from Parliament, grew more and more bitter.

Parliament and the government had their own problems, not the least those of the Crown, for this was the period of Regency England, and whatever that connoted for Beau Brummel and other gentlemen about town, it meant a constant headache for the cabinet. Poor old George III had long outlived his usefulness. He lasted until 1820, sixty years altogether on the throne. Until the 1780s he was an active and a powerful sovereign, but he grew infirm as the years went on, asserting himself less and less as time passed, though when he did, as on the occasion of the great question of Catholic emancipation in 1801, he could still bring down a government as strong as William Pitt's. From 1810 on he was considered insane, though actually he seems to have had some illness that put pressure on his brain. For the last ten years of his life he was blind and out of his senses, a pathetic relic of the vigorous young man whose mother had always told him, "Be a king, George." From 1810 on, the throne was for practical purposes occupied by his eldest son, the Prince Regent, George IV to be, a wastrel and ne'er-do-well, considered by his friends "the first gentleman in Europe," considered by the rest of the world to be a fool and perhaps a cad. Whatever else he was, "Prinny" was not the man to provide leadership in a time of real distress, and his scandalous quarrel with his equally doltish wife provided distraction but no relief to Englishmen of the day.

Ironically, the mildly reactionary political climate at home was not matched in foreign policy. When it came to the affairs of other states, the British were far more liberal in attitude than they were when they dealt with their own workers. Into the 1820s the Continent was dominated by what came to be known as the "Congress System," in which the major powers combined to prevent liberalism anywhere. Under the leadership of the Austrian Prince Metternich, the rulers and governments adopted Benjamin Franklin's adage that they must either all hang together or all hang separately. A threat of reform or revolution in one country was seen as a threat to all, and throughout this period kings called upon each other's armies to bail themselves out of trouble. At first the British were prepared to go along with this, but their ideas soon diverged. Since most of the "radical revolutionaries" in one country or another wanted something close to the constitution the British already possessed, they found it difficult to lend themselves to suppression of reform movements. Even to fairly conservative British ministers, most of the kings of Europe were such patent fools as to be undeserving of support anyway.

The sticking point for Britain came over affairs in Spain and especially Portugal. Both the Iberian empires in America were restive; both had been opened to British trade during the Napoleonic wars, and by about 1820, America was a major source of materials and a market for finished products in the British system. The United States was Britain's largest single customer, and exports to non-British North and South America equaled Britain's exports to her entire Empire. Therefore, when the restored kings of Spain and Portugal announced their intention to reestablish their old closed mercantile systems and to shut their colonial markets to Britain, there was a howl in London. As these kings were similarly reactionary at home, they were soon faced with domestic revolutions. The other European powers moved to support the kings, and the British found themselves caught in a dilemma: They did not particularly want to see rulers, however foolish, overthrown, but they certainly did not want to see their own economy crippled by those rulers. They tried to follow some sort of middle line, best illustrated by their involvement in a triangle consisting of themselves, Portugal, and Brazil.

King John of Portugal had fled to Brazil on the French invasion of his country in 1807. He liked life there so much that he refused to return, and if he had had his way, Portugal would have become a dependent of its own colony. However, the Portuguese rose up in the first wave of revolutions, in 1821, demanded his return, and he reluctantly agreed to go home. He left his son Pedro to rule Brazil for him. By the time he got home the Portuguese were already moving to reassert their colonial control over Brazil, and the Brazilians were not prepared to stand for it. In 1822 Brazil declared its independence, with Pedro as its Emperor. Whether this might work depended largely on foreign recognition, and that brought in the British.

The conservative powers, meeting in Verona in 1822, decided to invade the Iberian Peninsula, and early in 1823 a French army crossed the Pyrenees, marched south to Madrid, defeated the Spanish rebels, and restored King Ferdinand VII to his throne—minus the constitution forced on him by the revolution. They then turned toward Portugal, but John quickly revised his own constitution in an absolutist direction, and the British publicly supported him, so that actual military intervention by the Congress was held in abeyance.

For more than a year the affair hung fire. Neither Portugal nor Spain would recognize the independence of their colonies, and as long as they would not do so, the other Congress powers also refused to do so. Britain was in the awkward position of supporting both the Brazilians against King John, and King John against the other European states. Meanwhile, Brazil was seething, there was now open war in the rest of Latin America, and British merchants were being hurt by the economic dislocation of their trade. Finally the British cut the Gordian knot. They simply accorded de facto recognition to the various revolutionary regimes in Spanish America—in Argentina, Colombia, and Mexico. The British then turned on Portugal and informed King John that if he did not acknowledge Brazilian independence, they were going to leave him in the lurch. The sequence of treaties was interesting. An Englishman, Sir Charles Stuart, negotiated the treaty in which Portugal recognized the independence of Brazil. Immediately following that there was British recognition of Brazil, followed by an Anglo-Brazilian trade treaty, and the whole was then capped by an Anglo-Portuguese treaty of friendship and support. The same followed all over Latin America. The continent's independence was compounded of its own military efforts, British diplomacy, and the silent command of the sea exercised by the Royal Navy, exercised in this instance on behalf of liberalism for the colonial world and trade for Britain, two things that Englishmen tended to regard as synonymous.

They were not, of course, quite that blatant about it. As part of his plan, the British Foreign Secretary, Sir George Canning, intimated to the Americans that he would welcome an initiative by them. This led the U.S. President, James Monroe, to issue a statement saying that the United States would not permit the establishment of any non-American power in the Western Hemisphere. It was this that enabled Canning to remark, in 1826, "I called the New World into existence, to redress the balance of the Old." He did not need to add, for everyone at the time knew it, that it was the Royal Navy and not the minuscule U.S. Navy that put teeth into the Monroe Doctrine. Canning's diplomatic ploy became a cornerstone of United States foreign policy until 1962, when President John F. Kennedy guaranteed not to invade Cuba in return for the dismantling of Soviet missiles there, thus allowing the first new non-American power to get a foothold in the hemisphere in nearly a century and a half.

Naval power was more blatantly displayed, in an even thornier situation, at the other end of Europe. It was one thing to intervene on behalf of legitimate rulers against their obnoxious subjects, but what did you do if the subjects were Greeks, the descendants of Pericles and Socrates, and the ruler was the villainous Turk? Who wanted to carry the support of legitimacy that far?

In 1821 the Greeks rose up against their scattered Turkish masters and went on an orgy of blood and massacre. The next year the Greeks declared their independence. The Turks responded with equal ferocity, invaded Greece in force, massacred the inhabitants of the island of Chios, and overran the country as far as the Isthmus of Corinth. Russia was willing to intervene on behalf of the Greeks, but no one else in Europe trusted her motives, and the western powers combined to create a diplomatic cordon around the area. The Greeks fell to fighting among themselves, and the Turks hired their most important vassal, Mehemet Ali, the ruler of Egypt, to subdue the rebels. Mehemet sent his son Ibrahim with a substantial navy and a well-trained army and systematically overran the Morea. In Europe there was a wave of panhellenism; Delacroix painted pictures of heroic Greeks, Byron went out to fight for them and to die at Missolonghi. Most of the important men of Europe were brought up with a classical education, and in the Greek Revolution they saw echoes of the Persian War and remembered the Spartans at Thermopylae. The more successful the Egyptians were, the more aroused Europe became. Still, it was not until 1827 that the powers could overcome their mutual distrust enough for Russia, Britain, and France to agree to intervene. They sent a combined naval squadron under British Admiral Sir Edward Codrington to cruise in Greek waters, with instructions to exert pressure on the Turks and Egyptians, and the Russians began to move troops to their border.

On October 20 Codrington met the Turkish-Egyptian fleets in the Bay of Navarino. They were numerically superior to his by three or four to one, but his ten ships of the line—three British, three French, and four Russian—were substantially more powerful. Codrington anchored close to the enemy, intending to overawe them while negotiating. However, the negotiations collapsed, mostly because of continued action by the Greeks, and Ibrahim's ships opened fire. That turned out to be a mistake. The allied ships replied with stunning efficiency, and within a short time they had sunk fifty of the smaller Turks and Egyptians and run even more of them aground. In the space of a couple of hours, Ibrahim's fleet was reduced to matchwood. It was an impressive display of what was then modern firepower and techniques against a more or less backward foe; it was also the last fleet engagement between wooden warships.

The British government that had put Codrington in this situation was dismayed that it had led to a natural conclusion; they protested that they really had not wanted to fight at all. The admiral was recalled, court-martialed, and eventually placed in command of the Channel Fleet, which might be construed as the admirals showing the politicians what they thought of contradictory orders. It took another five years and a Russian army for the Greeks to become fully independent, but after Navarino the Egyptians were finished, and the rest of the war was a rear-guard action by the Turks. Once more naval power had demonstrated its versatility—and its volatility—as an instrument of imperial policy.

Foreign liberalism and domestic conservatism were only superficially irreconcilable, for the tide of reform was swelling in Britain itself. In the 1830s and 1840s Britain underwent a near-revolution, carried out as always in the name of sensibility and moderation, which transformed the entire constitution and carried over as well into fundamental questions about the organization of the Empire and its relation with the mother country. A great groundswell of reform that had begun back in the late eighteenth century finally reached its culmination. In Parliament it brought reform of the franchise in 1832, the ruination of the House of Lords and therefore of the landed classes as opposed to the commercial and industrial classes. Various other acts soon followed; the old and vicious poor laws were changed, if only marginally for the better. Parliamentary commissions investigated the horrible conditions in factories and mines, and the first labor legislation was passed. And in three vital areas Britain moved toward a new concept of its Empire. Free trade came in, slavery went out, and hesitant steps were taken toward the idea of local self-government.

A closed mercantile system, most of whose markets and sources were external to it, did not make a great deal of sense, and the idea of free trade had been around for three quarters of a century. In the 1760s there had been a group of ministers in France who called themselves physiocrats, and their basic idea was that the natural economic forces of supply and demand would work to produce the most prosperous society possible. Their catchphrase had been, "To govern better, govern less"; they believed that the basis of economic society lay in land and its use. In 1776 a Scots professor named Adam Smith, who had known many of the physiocrats, published a work of his own, building on their ideas but attacking many of them, especially the idea of the primacy of land. The *Inquiry into the Nature and Causes of the Wealth of Nations,* destined to become the first classic of political economy, was thus published in the same year as the American Declaration of Independence; the one was almost as significant as the other. Smith believed that labor and not land was the mainstay of a nation's prosperity. Most important for the idea of empire, he attacked the closed imperial system as inhibiting the natural growth of trade and the accumulation of capital. Mercantilism, he said, simply put obstacles in the way of the free flow of goods and thus retarded what it was supposed to advance.

This was prophetic in 1776; fifty years later, when Great Britain had an industrial lead miles ahead of the rest of the world, when more of her trade was outside her Empire than inside it, Smith's ideas were only common sense. The British were diligently undermining the Spanish and Portuguese mercantile systems. How could they defend their own? Yet mercantilism was so firmly entrenched in the British view of the world that it lasted another generation. The first breach came in 1823, when William Huskisson as President of the Board of Trade lowered the duties on a wide range of imports: iron, wool, silk, wine, coffee, sugar, cotton, and others. The producers of many of these products had been protected by prohibitive duties against foreign imports for as long as anyone could remember. Now they were considered to be so far ahead of any foreign competitors that the duties were useless. And if they were not, too bad about them, for free trade eventually evolved into a rampant laissez-faire individualism, sink or swim and the devil take the hindmost. Huskisson was a convinced and far sighted free trader, and had he lived, he undoubtedly would have pushed for further changes. He was killed, however, in a railroad accident in 1830, an early and ironic victim of the kind of progress he himself represented. For nearly twenty more years the liberals picked away at the protectionist duties and mercantile regulations. Agitation finally became intense as the "Manchester School" of political economists led the fight for change. They insisted that free trade meant cheap food and better wages for industrial workers, and cheaper raw materials and wider markets for their employers. Landowners cried that they would be ruined, but when free trade came in definitively in 1846, it marked the triumph of the town over the country, of the manufacturer over the farmer, of the businessman over the landed gentry. For the final demise of the old England, 1846 would be as good a date as any.

One of the main lines of the great reform period, and one of the noblest struggles of modern history, was the fight to abolish slavery. The slave trade had made John Hawkins rich, then it had made the ports of Bristol and Liverpool rich, and some authorities say it fueled the entire Industrial Revolution. For many years, a society that transported men for stealing a loaf of bread, that put men, women, and children in debtors' prison, that pressed sailors and enlisted soldiers for life, saw little objectionable in slavery or in the slave trade, and it was possible to rationalize the institution with the dictates of the Christian conscience. The famous hymn, "How Sweet the Name of Jesus Sounds," for example, was written by a captain off tl e coast of Guinea

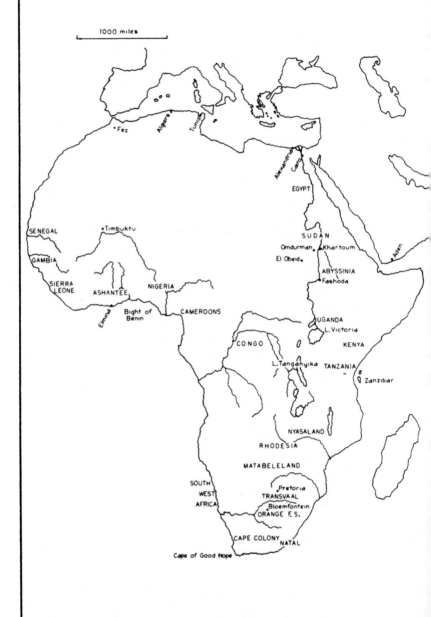

while he was waiting to fill his holds with slaves. As late as the middle of the eighteenth century, the slave trade was still considered one of the great props to English prosperity.

Gradually, however, opposition to it arose. The Quakers were the first to speak out against it, as early as 1727, but they were generally a despised sect, and opposition from them almost guaranteed its continued respectability. Dr. Johnson was opposed to it, to the surprise of his friends. The first real champion of the African slaves, however, was Granville Sharp, and in 1772, after several tries, he succeeded in getting Lord Chief Justice Mansfield to declare that it was illegal to hold slaves in Great Britain itself. The cause was then taken up by Thomas Clarkson and a young member of Parliament, William Wilberforce, and for twenty years a devoted little band of humanitarians tried to carry abolition of the slave trade through Parliament, blocked at every turn by the antagonism of the sugar interests or the uninterest of William Pitt. Pitt saw himself as a great reformer, but Africans dying on the Middle Passage were not high on his list of priorities.

Slowly the abolitionists gained adherents. A society was formed. The great pottery magnate, Josiah Wedgwood, joined and produced a cameo seal showing an African in chains with the motto, "Am I Not a Man and Brother?" Shakespeare had pointed out that a Jew bleeds; the abolitionists had to show their countrymen that Africans bled, too. Opposition was philosophical; some men held that if a man had the right to sell his labor, which was after all the root of the whole economy, then he had the right to sell himself as well, and therefore slavery was part of the natural order. Others said that if you freed the slaves, you deprived their owners of their legitimate property, and property was one of the other roots of English life. Had not the great John Locke written that the inalienable rights of man are life, liberty, and property? The question was to reconcile the slave's liberty with the owner's property, but the owners were articulate and respectable Englishmen, and the slaves were poor and illiterate Africans.

Year after year Wilberforce fought his lonely battle in Parliament. Meanwhile, the abolitionists founded Freetown in Sierra Leone on the West African coast and settled it with freed slaves from England and black Loyalists from Nova Scotia. The settlement eventually went broke and was taken over by the Crown as a colony in 1808. During the Revolutionary and Napoleonic wars, with French and Spanish trade disrupted, the slavers made money as never before. Even so, by the first decade of the new century, antislavery was an idea whose time had come. Its adherents were not strong enough to have slavery outlawed entirely, but slavery's defenders could no longer maintain their intransigence. In March 1807, the slave trade was outlawed. The government hoped that ending the trade, and thus the source of supply, would eventually end slavery itself. For the next several years, therefore, they attempted to get other maritime states to outlaw the slave trade as they themselves had done. As that often proved impossible, they tried to get other states to concede the right of search. But other countries, particularly the United States, which thought it needed the trade more and disapproved it less, were extremely reluctant to cooperate.

The abolitionists took several years to realize that the end of the trade did not guarantee the end of the institution, and only in the 1820s did they take up the battle against slavery itself. It required yet another decade of agitation to succeed, and once again proslavery interests argued that the government had no right to interfere with property. In the West Indian islands the colonial assemblies protested the imposition of British controls on their freedom to handle their slaves as they chose, and they raised the specters of riot and revolution. There was a slave rising in Jamaica in 1832; the planters charged that it had been set off by all this inflammatory nonsense about emancipation, and they suppressed it so brutally that they destroyed much of their own case. Flooded by horror stories, Parliament at last was forced to act; the bill went through in August 1833, and slavery in the British Empire became illegal on August 1, 1834.

That took care of the legal problem. It did not solve the matter as far as the Royal Navy was concerned, for expression of good intent in London had to be given practical impact by sailors off the coast of Africa. The Navy's battle against the slavers continued; and where William Wilberforce gained justly deserved fame for devoting his life to a noble cause, hundreds of ordinary seamen over the years gained only lonely graves for doing their job no less nobly than he had done.

The Royal Navy fought the slavers along the Atlantic coast of Africa for sixty years. It was a tiresome, tedious, thankless task, and in the end it was completed successfully not so much because of what the Navy was able to achieve, as because Britain—and events—finally forced the closing of the great markets. British pressure got the Brazilians to cease importing slaves; the Spanish eventually closed down Cuba. In the United States, importation officially became illegal at the end of 1808, but only the American Civil War finally stopped the trade.

On the African coasts the British stationed a fleet of small vessels, for this was not work for the great ships of the line, and even a frigate was too slow, and too readily recognizable from a distance, to accomplish much against slavers. The work was done by sloops and brigs and topsail schooners. Small ships meant young commanders, and this was a place, after 1815, where a junior officer might see some action—if he did not die from one of the many voracious tropical diseases, or go insane, or become an alcoholic.

There were two ways to go about suppression, and the Navy tried both. One was to destroy the infrastructure along the slaving coast. The British bought off the chiefs who traded their own people, burned their slave pens, and alternated carrot and stick in an attempt to wipe out the market. Success was slow to come; the trade had been part of Africa since long before the Europeans arrived, and Arab and Indian dealers had spread its tentacles through and across the entire continent. Local chiefs were not disposed to give up a lucrative business at the behest of some distant power they had, initially, no reason to fear or respect. This aspect of naval activity came to consist of endless tedious negotiations, punctuated every so often by a boat raid in the dark of the night, sudden attacks on slave markets, and little fights in the mouths of sluggish creeks or among the mangrove swamps, where a man could be just as dead from a rusty musket shot, or an infected wound, as if he had died gloriously at Trafalgar.

The other aspect of breaking up the trade was to drive the slavers off the sea, but that too became difficult. In the early days of the naval patrols, it was fairly easy to catch slavers, for their ships were frequently worn-out tubs no longer good for anything else. However, as the Royal Navy's presence was felt, slaving vessels became better and faster; they were always cheaply built, for they were not expected to last long, but their design improved over the years, and some of the best shipbuilders in England or North America turned to finding the optimum combination of speed, handiness, and cargo-carrying capacity. Such vessels were far faster than the clumsy naval brigs with their heavy armament and could be caught only when trapped against a lee shore or perhaps come upon surreptitiously in the night. For many years as well, all the odds were against the Navy. Many countries, especially the United States, refused to concede the right of search. Even when that right was finally granted, the slaver had to be caught with slaves actually aboard, so that even if every bit of construction and hardware shrieked of the trade, there was nothing the Navy could do about it. Slavers kept a good watch, and they could easily jettison their human cargo—which they readily did—before a patrol vessel could close with them. Faced with such limitation, the Navy adopted its own solutions, and many a ship seized "for inspection" was run on the rocks by a prize crew who knew that the law would allow the ship to go free again. Humanitarian business could not be conducted in a humanitarian manner.

The costs were heavy. Year after year there was a steady toll of men and materials. Boats were swamped in the surf, ships ran on uncharted reefs or shifting bars, and always there was sickness, a steady wastage of from 5 to 25 percent per year in men and officers. Even during the Napoleonic wars as many as a quarter of the Royal Navy's vessels were engaged in patrolling against the trade, but finally the task was accomplished. Between loss of markets on both sides of the ocean and constant harassment by the Navy, the slavers gradually gave it up. The Atlantic trade was stopped at last. On the other side of Africa it lasted even longer, and well into this century the Royal Navy was still trying to close down the Indian Ocean slave trade with its great center at Zanzibar.

The campaign against the slave trade was fought by the old Royal Navy of wooden ships, and it was not until the 1840s that the first auxiliary steam vessels appeared in African waters. But in the meantime, the Navy had begun the remarkable process of change that culminated just before World War I. The transition was slow and often painful.

The idea of applying steam to propulsion at sea was current in Napoleon's day; the American inventor Robert Fulton had offered steam-powered vessels to the Emperor and had been turned down. For all his military genius, Napoleon was not very innovative technologically, and he did not see much value in what was a chancy thing at best. Neither at first did most sailors. The early engines developed relatively little horsepower and used a lot of fuel; they broke down constantly; paddle wheels interfered with the gunnery, and on and on. The sailors who resisted steam were looked on, after steam had won, as a bunch of old fuddy-duddies, as those who resist change always are. But they did have what they regarded as valid reasons, and there was more to it than the simple fact that engines were ugly and dirty, while ships were clean and beautiful, though there was, of course, that as well. At one point the First Lord of the Admiralty, Lord Melville, solemnly proclaimed it was the Admiralty's "bounden duty to discourage to the utmost . . . the introduction of steam vessels, as . . . [this] is calculated to strike a fatal blow at the naval supremacy of the Empire." Men later would say the same about iron hulls, about the all big-gun battleship, about oil fuel, about the submarine, and about the airplane. And maybe they were right, but that did not mean they could stop time in its tracks.

For steam did come in. Like many revolutionary changes, it sneaked in by the back door. No one trusted it for use on the high seas, but even the most determinedly reactionary had to admit that it would be useful to have some way to get out of a windbound harbor. And so the first steam vessels acknowledged by the Royal Navy were tugboats, to be used for towing the great ships out to sea, where they could find their true element, the wind. The trouble with innovation is that once you have admitted it in principle, it becomes very hard to stop. From steam tugs sailors went to steam supply and dispatch vessels. The Americans built a steam-powered patrol boat; the French used auxiliary steam-powered warships in their landings in Algeria in 1820. The big breakthrough came in the mid-1840s. By then marine designers had been working for twenty years on the screw propeller. At the stern of the ship and below the waterline, it was far less vulnerable than the paddle wheel and did not interfere with the fighting of the ship—unless one believed, as did Sir William Symonds, Britain's leading naval architect, that a vessel with such a propeller could not be steered.

In 1845 the Admiralty built two ships identical except that H.M.S. *Rattler* had a screw, H.M.S. *Alecto* a paddle wheel. Hitching them up stern to stern, they gave the command, "Full speed ahead," and let them fight it out. Slowly *Rattler* gained headway, and finally she was towing *Alecto* backward at a good two to three knots in spite of all the paddle-wheeler could do. That clinched it. Steam and the screw propeller were in to stay. The days of the hybrid Navy had arrived, and ships, still built as ships with tall masts and white sails, also carried collapsible funnels and raisable propellers. Under sail they could telescope the funnel so it would not interfere with the sailhandling, and raise the screw out of the water to improve the run of the ship. The British might in many ways deplore the change, but these things could no longer be avoided; the French were innovating; so, to a lesser extent, were the Americans. As with almost all the vast changes in naval technology in the nineteenth century, the British, with the greatest Navy in the world, preferred to let others take the lead and force them to follow, confident that British industrial superiority could catch up with and surpass anyone else when necessary. Steam was only the beginning.

As in materials, so in manpower and organization. After Waterloo the Navy shrank by three quarters, and whereas there had been more than a thousand ships in commission in 1810, there were but three hundred in 1830. Sailors were released by the thousands, and officers, full-time professionals by now, were left to grow old in minor appointments. Only when an officer made the rank of captain did he get on the seniority list and float up from there as his seniors and elders died. Until then, officers could be put on indefinite half pay and might wait forever for a position. By 1825 there were 5,539 commissioned officers in the Royal Navy, but only 550 of them were actively employed, leaving 90 percent of the professional naval officers of Great Britain growing old and sour on half pay. In 1841 the senior lieutenant of the Navy had held that rank for sixty-three years.

Most simply waited it out and either got promoted eventually or died. Some became adventurers. For example, one of the most famous nineteenth-century sailors, Thomas Cochrane, Earl of Dundonald, had been an admiral in the British, Chilean, Brazilian, and Greek navies before he died. Cochrane was a stormy petrel, and at one point he advocated the use of a "secret weapon" to ensure British naval supremacy. The weapon was gas, and several investigating committees turned the idea down, for no civilized state in the nineteenth-century world would contemplate the use of such an inhuman weapon.

The clogging of the Navy with overage officers continued into the second half of the century, though from the 1840s there began to be some regulation of the problem. Meanwhile, there had been a serious attempt, under Sir James Graham as First Lord of the Admiralty, to revamp the administrative services of the Navy in the early 1830s. Hampered though it remained by the economies of peacetime and burdened with an unwieldy and unimaginative officer corps, the Navy still functioned adequately. It was a naval vessel that took Darwin on his voyage; it was the Navy that bombarded pirate strongholds in North Africa in the 1810s; it was the Navy whose power and presence helped to hold together and add to the Empire.

Even without the stimulus of foreign war, the Empire continued to grow and to be transformed. The little-Englanders at home did not reckon with the dynamics of the imperial urge. The anti-imperialists might fulminate against the acquisition of territory, and the Colonial

Office might constantly instruct its officials in the field that no more was to be added, but the empire kept right on growing. Other men wanted to trade, or to conquer, or just to have a farm where they were not crowded by their neighbors. A hundred fifty years ago, the world was still vast, and much of it lay waiting empty for the taking.

In this post-Waterloo period, the imperial units also began the process of transformation from colonial status to nationhood. From the British point of view, the eighteenth-century experiment in imperial constitution-making had ended in failure with the American Revolution. The second time around, in the nineteenth century, they did it better. The peculiar contribution of Canada was to be the testing ground for a new concept of empire, a new relationship between mother and daughter countries.

In virtually all of the white-dominated colonies—Canada, Nova Scotia, Australia, even South Africa—there was a range of common problems. There was always antagonism between old settlers and new settlers, between the official Church and the more radical religious sects, between the frontiers and the settled towns—between, in other words, the "ins" and the "outs." The former were in because they had been there first, and they had built their communities in their own way and for their own benefit. The latter were in the colonies to begin with because they wanted a better deal in life, and having made the move, they were not content to see themselves frustrated by some local copy of the same sort of establishment they had left home to escape.

This difficulty arose first in Canada, and it reached the point of rebellion in 1837. At that time the colonies had progressed as far as what was known as controlled representative government; in this system, which was more or less analogous to the system in eighteenth-century Britain, there was an elected assembly, but real executive power remained in the hands of the governor and an appointed council. That was all right as long as the council could dominate the assembly, but there was obviously potential for conflict when the assembly answered to its electors, and the council answered to the governor, who answered in turn to the Crown. By 1837 there were enough frustrations in the two provinces of Upper and Lower Canada, modern Ontario and Quebec, that rebellions broke out simultaneously in each. In Upper Canada a fiery Scots newspaper editor named William Lyon Mackenzie led a rising against the domination of the "Family Compact," while downstream around Montreal his Québecois opposite number, Louis Joseph Papineau, rose up against the "Château Clique." Both rebellions soon fizzled, and the leaders fled to the

United States, which was thought by responsible British officials at the time to be more or less appropriate punishment. But the events shocked the home government out of its complacency; no one wanted another American Revolution, and clearly something had to be done.

The British solved the problem by sending out one of their own. Lord Durham—"Radical Jack," as he was known to his contemporaries—was a nuisance in British politics. He held advanced parliamentary ideas, and he had enough money—it was Durham who said a man ought to be able to limp along on ten thousand pounds a year—to be influential. Lord Melbourne, the most gentlemanly of prime ministers, had gotten him out of the way by appointing him ambassador extraordinary to St. Petersburg, but now he was home again and looking for a cause. Melbourne appointed him Governor of Canada and packed him off once more.

Durham lasted only five months in Canada. Some of his legislation was disallowed by the House of Lords and he came home in a huff without being officially relieved. However, in the time he was there, he alienated the local leaders by talking to all the wrong people, most important of them Robert Baldwin, one of the great unsung constitutional heroes of the British Empire. Baldwin helped convince Durham that responsible government—that is, the modern idea that the executive is ultimately answerable to the electors—must come, and that was what Durham recommended in the famous *Report on the Affairs of British North America,* better known simply as Durham's Report. For some years the matter hung fire, but in 1849 Lord Elgin, as Governor of the united provinces of Canada, simply accepted the principle of responsible government, at least in local affairs. What the Americans had not been able to get inside the Empire, and the Canadians got only by rebellion, thus became an acknowledged aim of colonial development. The rest of the Empire, first the white-dominated colonies or dominions and ultimately the black, eventually followed the same sort of pattern. A free-trade mother country accepted the idea with little reluctance, without perhaps even much interest, that the colonies would finally grow up and become independent. In the nineteenth century, that did not seem to make much difference. No one foresaw that in the twentieth such offhanded generosity would be repaid by Australians at Gallipoli or by young Canadians in the skies over England itself.

Any general imperial patterns were subject to wide local variations. In Canada the new elements in society won; in South Africa the old elements simply moved out. The Cape Dutch had welcomed the British during the Napoleonic wars, but after them they were disturbed by a slow influx of British settlers, and even more so by British justice and interference with their own customs, chief of which was that of enslaving the natives. The British settlers moved eastward along the coast and established Natal. English language and laws gradually replaced Dutch. But what really bothered the Dutch—Boers, as they called themselves—was the vacillating policy toward the natives, trying at one time to be conciliatory toward them, at the next to take their land away. The Boers were particularly incensed at the abolition of slavery in 1834, and the next year they voted with their feet.

The frontier Boers were semimigratory anyway, hitching up their great wagons and following their herds of cattle across the plain or veldt. They were a rock-ribbed, Old Testament people, as self-reliant and as potentially stubborn as any in the world. They had a very low saturation point, and when British interference became intolerable to them, they got out. About ten thousand Boers packed their wagons and headed north and east in the great heroic event of their people, the Great Trek. They crossed the Orange River and established the Orange Free State, a minimal republican government with a few thousand white people spread across two hundred thousand square miles. Those who found that too confining went to the next river, across the Vaal, and set up the Transvaal Republic, half again as big as the Orange Free State and with fewer white people. There they were sure they would be left alone; all they had to do was fight the Zulus, the Kaffirs, and the British in Natal whenever anyone threatened to crowd them in. It was their version of paradise; they remained unaware of the gold and diamonds under their soil.

Finally in this period there was a totally new foundation, an island and therefore another manifestation of the far-reaching ramifications of seapower. When the first white men visited New Zealand, it was a heaven on earth. By the 1810s, it was closer to hell. Traders from New South Wales had visited the islands, and in return for flax and wood, had given the natives guns. The Maoris, a race of highly intelligent cannibals, had gone to war, one tribe against another. Then the whalers, sealers, and escaped convicts from Australia had arrived. Vice flourished unchecked for a generation. However, if the Europeans corrupted, they also redeemed. The first missionaries arrived in 1814, and by the late 1820s large numbers of Maoris had been converted. The Bible was translated into Maori, and there was an Anglican bishop of

New Zealand in 1842. The missionaries wanted to keep New Zealand for the natives, and for their own work, but the magnificent islands were too tempting for that. There were settlement schemes as early as 1826, but it was not until 1840 that the first British colonists landed. This was a private venture, organized by Edward Gibbon Wakefield, one of the great colonial theorists of the period, a latter-day version of Sir Walter Raleigh. Wakefield's idea was that cheap land in the colonies led to such diffusion of the settlers that local development was nearly impossible. There should instead be regular organizations, and settlers should buy their land. This would both guarantee a good class of settler and provide the colony with necessary funds for public services. His theories had already been tried, with some success, in South Australia, around Adelaide in 1836. Now he applied them to New Zealand as well.

The home government was, as usual, disapproving; it had several times since the days of Captain Cook disavowed claims to New Zealand, but that made little difference. Official opposition was disarmed by the rumor that the French were thinking of founding a colony, and under that threat, Wakefield's New Zealand Association founded the town of Wellington. Where settlers went, government could not be far behind. A month after the settlers landed, Captain William Hobson of the Royal Navy signed the Treaty of Waitangi with the Maori chiefs and proclaimed British sovereignty over the islands. With the advent of British law and order, the new colony progressed rapidly. Infringements on native holdings caused a long, low-level Maori war in the 1840s, in which the British troops had a hard time subduing the tribes. In 1848 Scottish Presbyterians founded Dunedin, the Gaelic name for Edinburgh, and two years later, an Anglican organization settled Canterbury. By 1856 New Zealand had responsible government and was for practical purposes a little England set down in the South Seas.

If New Zealand was a bit of nineteenth-century England overseas, there were more exotic places than that added to the Empire during this period. The expansion of the British, not only in India, but from India now as well, gathered momentum. In the subcontinent itself, the same pressure and dynamics that were influencing the rest of the Empire were also at work; the British, as the dominant power, simply became more and more intrusive into the affairs of lesser states. Any kind of trouble meant less security for British commerce and therefore for British interest. As long as the Napoleonic wars lasted, the British were forced to be on guard against French influence and subversion of the

Indian princes. From the firm base in Bengal, British tentacles crept out to the northwest, west, and south. There were treaties with Sind, Persia, and Afghanistan and a war with Nepal. The last of the Maratha confederacy was broken up, and by 1820, almost all of India was either directly ruled by the British, or by its own native princes, who acknowledged indirect British control. Many of the states remained incredibly rich and still powerful, but at each of them there was a British resident, a polite but firm adviser who was concerned that their attitudes should remain pro-British.

British control meant British culture, and a veneer of English ideas began to spread over the welter of India's languages, religions, and customs. Universities were founded, newspapers started, and an active publishing industry grew up. The British began building roads, controlling floods, and seeking ways to get rid of disease and famine. They were in India to make money, and they never forgot it, but making money for them meant prosperity and order for the Indians. The British now felt sufficiently secure that they could take some interests in the Indians as Indians, and it was British Orientalists who sparked the Hindu renaissance in Bengal and the publication of many ancient Hindu texts. Under the Governor Generalship of Lord Bentinck in the 1830s, the current British itch for progress really reached India with a vengeance. Bentinck was supported by a member of his staff, Thomas Macaulay, later the archetypal British historian of the century, and the two pushed Indian reform at a rapid pace. Bentinck started suppression of the Thugs, bands of thieves who committed ritual murder, and he also took action to stop the practice of suttee, where a widow threw herself, or was thrown, on the funeral pyre of her husband. When Indian religious leaders complained to Bentinck that this was a time-honored custom and that widows had to be burned, he replied that in England it was the custom to hang murderers, and that if he allowed them to follow their customs, they must allow him to follow his.

The cynic might have pointed out that that was all very well, but Bentinck was not in his own country, but someone else's. Bentinck did not see it that way. And neither, at this time, did most Indians, for Indian nationalism had not yet begun any real development; for the vast mass of Indians, the British were simply very distant and occasionally glimpsed rulers, perhaps a little strange, but not much more. The princes, of course, were the ones who found the British objectionable, and there were periodic wars in one part of the subcontinent or another. In 1827 the British abandoned the fiction that they were subject to the rule of the shadow Emperor at Delhi; in 1831 they took over di-

rect control of Mysore, whose native ruler had been scandalously mis-
governing his territory. And sometimes they made mistakes. In 1839
Lord Auckland's highly exaggerated fears of a Russian takeover of
Afghanistan prompted a British preemptive intervention. But Afghanistan was a distant, forbidding land, and foreigners came to grief there.
After three years of occupation of Kabul, the British agreed to withdraw. General Elphinstone left the city with forty-five hundred troops
and a train of twelve thousand civilians and began the march back to
the Indian frontier. A mid-January trek through the mountains was
bad enough, but the tribes rose up in an orgy of ambush and massacre.
One sole survivor staggered into Jalalabad to tell the tale of disaster.

War on the frontier was endemic, and sometimes there was war
inside India itself. The British were not always high-minded in their
approach. In 1843, for example, they decided that they should annex
Sind, virtually the last independent Indian princely state. So they pro-
voked a war, and General Sir Charles Napier marched an army into
Sind, defeated the local troops, and proclaimed British control. Napier
himself had second thoughts about his actions, and he cabled home
news of his success with a single Latin word, *Peccavi,* which is a fairly
elegant pun, "I have sin[ne]d."

The home government had problems as well with this empire
within the British Empire. The conscience that had been awakened at
the time of Warren Hastings' trial was still troubled by the spectacle of
a vast conglomeration of people ruled by a private company for profit.
In 1813, when the charter of the East India Company came up for discussion, Parliament renewed it, but for only twenty years; free trade
was running a strong campaign at that time, so the company's trade
monopoly in India was abolished, and missionaries were allowed into
the company territories. Twenty years later, the company's trading
function was taken away from it altogether, and the East India Company, still a private firm, became purely a government, an anomaly
that perhaps only the British could have developed.

One of the reasons that India had been desirable to begin with was
its trade connection with the East Indies, where the British had been
too weak to sustain themselves against the Dutch. During the war with
France, British expeditions had taken over most of the Dutch Empire;
they had held Java for a time and had twice occupied Malacca, on the
strait that led from the South China Sea to the Indian Ocean. In 1818,
however, they returned that territory. As early as 1786 they had established a naval station in Penang, up the western coast of the Malayan

Peninsula, but that was not much of a trading center. By the end of the Napoleonic wars, they still did not know to what extent they might be involved in the East Indies. The decision was made for them by Stamford Raffles.

Raffles had been secretary to Lord Minto when the latter was Governor General of India. In 1811 Minto occupied Java and appointed Raffles as its administrator. Raffles was a young man in a hurry, and he rapidly overhauled the old Dutch administration, thinking the British would retain Java. When they did not do so, he began looking around for a British commercial foothold in the Indies. He settled on the island of Singapore, right at the bottom of the Malayan Peninsula. Once a great trading city and now utterly decayed, this seemed to Raffles the ideal spot. On his own initiative, Raffles signed a treaty with the Sultan of Johore, and Singapore was ceded to Great Britain. More correctly, it was ceded to Raffles, for it took the government five years to decide that it really wanted the new station, and it was not until 1824 that Britain officially sanctioned what Raffles had done. That year he went home, was shipwrecked on the way, and lost his life savings and his botanical collections. He arrived in England penniless and was presented by the East India Company with a bill for twenty thousand pounds, which they claimed he had spent without authority. In such a way did Britain gain the greatest center of Southeast Asia.

One of the great commodities of the East India Company was tea. It had become the national nonalcoholic drink in Britain. In 1668 the company had imported a hundred pounds of tea; in 1786, fourteen million pounds. Tea came from China, and the company had long had a small but important factory at Canton, where the British, with other foreign merchants, lived on sufferance from the Chinese. The Manchu Empire refused to acknowledge the existence of other states, but it found trade with Europeans mildly convenient and was thus willing to allow it under certain restrictions. Until 1773 the East India Company had paid for the tea it took from China in silver, as there were few European commodities the Chinese wanted. In that year, however, the company discovered that the Chinese did want one external item: The British began carrying opium from Bengal to Canton. Opium was then recognized for medicinal purposes, but some years later the practice was introduced from the Dutch East Indies of using it as an indulgence. This spread so rapidly that the Chinese prohibited it in 1800, without any noticeable effect.

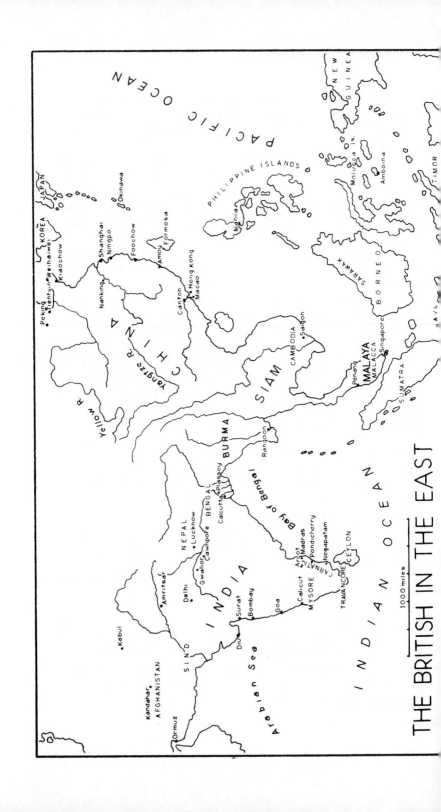

THE BRITISH IN THE EAST

So the situation continued for thirty years; then in 1833 the British government took away the East India Company's monopoly of trade with China. The word rapidly spread that a man could make a fortune in the Far East taking opium in and tea and other goods out. Within five years the South China Sea was one of the most exciting, and deadly, places on earth. Fortunes were made and lost on one ship, or the changing of the tide. There were pirates of all colors and nations. Small, fast, handy ships called opium clippers were built to handle the local drug cargoes, and larger tea clippers to race home to England with the yearly tea crop.

In 1838 the Chinese government decided that opium had become a plague, and it moved to stop the trade. The British had already tried to establish official relations with China, but had failed due to the latter's insistence that foreigners could not be equal with the government of the Middle Kingdom. The East India Company and its servants had been willing to put up with occasional humiliation for the sake of profit, but with the monopoly gone, unregulated British merchants were now subject to Chinese government pressure, and they howled for protection and redress from their own government. East and West were meeting on the China coast but were not communicating with each other. In 1834 the British had sent out Lord William Napier as an ambassador, but he had not even gotten past the Governor of Canton, let alone to the throne, and he had finally died in despair on the Portuguese island of Macao. His successor, Sir Charles Elliot, arrived with a British naval squadron, determined that Britain was not going to be treated high-handedly any longer.

Elliot did his best to negotiate, but again the Chinese would have nothing to do with him. Finally some Chinese junks attempted to seize several British sailors off Hong Kong, and the Royal Naval vessels fired on the junks. This was the era of Palmerston's ebullient government in England, and if the Chinese wanted to keep out opium merchants, that was their business; if they tried to apprehend British sailors, that was the Royal Navy's business.

So the imperial machine swung into motion. A brigade of troops under General Sir Hugh Gough came out from India, the Navy reinforced its squadron, and early in 1841 the troops stormed and captured the forts at the mouth of the Pearl River leading up to Canton. Moving upriver to the city itself, they then took and occupied it. The Chinese, whatever they thought of their superiority to foreign devils, were no match for British organization and European technology, even when manifested in a shoestring operation run at long distance by the East India Company. There was a cessation of hostilities during the summer while both sides thought matters over. Then, putting more pressure on, the British operated along the coasts. They bombarded and took Amoy, across from Formosa, then moved north and took Ningpo as well; having done that, they settled down in Hangchow Bay for the winter, where the consequences of their inadequate logistics arrangements took a far heavier toll of them than enemy action had done. They lost numbers of men to sickness, and several ships to typhoons. It was June 1842 before they were ready to move again, when they seized the great port of Shanghai. Then they began a slow advance up the Yangtze River toward Nanking, which was the southern capital of the Empire. Finally the Chinese were forced to acknowledge the existence of the outside world, and commissioners came to ask for negotiations. The result was the Treaty of Nanking, regarded by the Manchus as something beneath their notice and by the British as the opening wedge in the great market of China. The British got an indemnity, and the right to trade in five treaty ports: Canton, Amoy, Foochow, Ningpo, and Shanghai. More important, they got in perpetuity the cession of the barren island of Hong Kong, off the mouth of the Pearl River, a physical counterpart of the treaty itself. Traders were soon building their warehouses and their mansions there.

In this way another of the great outposts of the British Empire was founded; another segment of the world, containing a quarter of the people on earth, was opened up, primarily to the British, but as well to anyone who cared to come and compete with them. Most of the world has called this little conflict the Opium War; the British have preferred to call it the First China War. Like everything else they did in this period, their little war was pregnant with consequences for the future.

11

Lesser Breeds Without the Law

No man has a right to fix the boundary of the march of a nation.
—Charles Stewart Parnell, 1885

The British Empire in midcentury presented a phenomenon unique in modern history. Even at that point, long before it reached its greatest extent, one could boast that the sun never set upon the Union Jack, which flew from New Zealand west all the way to British Columbia, and from the Falkland Islands in the South to the barren wastes of the Hudson's Bay Company in the North. Red-coated garrisons stamped and wheeled on green parade grounds in Halifax and across the dusty plains in India. Ships of the Royal Navy patrolled the coasts of Africa and the Persian Gulf and carried explorers to the high altitudes of both the North and the South. Chinese listened to the skirl of bagpipes, and in Brazil people made appointments either "on Brazilian time," which meant they would be late, or "on English time," which meant they would be punctual. There might be 430 million Chinese on earth, and Russia might claim territory from Warsaw to Alaska, but there was still only one great empire in the world, and it was indisputably British.

For empire consisted not merely of people, or even of space, but of all those items, both visible and invisible, that went to make up power. At the midcentury census there were only 27 million people in the British Isles, slightly more than there were Americans in the United States or Italians in Italy, slightly less than the total population of France, or what is now Germany. A better measure was that of the number of inhabitants in the capitals of the great states. Berlin, still the capital only of Prussia, had a mere 300,000, Vienna somewhat more. Paris was close to 1 million, but London had 2¼ million and was truly the capital of the world, or at least of an empire that, with no income tax and no national debt, could afford to spend £70 million a year on government expenses.

The British were in this enviable position because they were so incredibly productive. The lead given them by the Industrial Revolution was going to last for another generation, and in the meantime, they had it all their own way. Britain produced as much pig iron as her two nearest competitors, France and Russia, combined. The Americans dug 7 million tons of coal annually, the French 12 million. In 1851 Britain mined 60 million tons. Textiles was a major industry; Britain clothed the world. In 1853 she imported 740 million pounds of raw cotton; she exported 1.524 billion yards, followed by 165.5 million yards of wool, 133 million yards of linen, and more than 1 million pounds of silk. The cotton industry alone employed 400,000 workers.

And not only did Britain clothe and arm the world, she also financed it and carried it. British money built railroads in Germany and Argentina, established ranches in Colorado, and built dams in Rio de Janeiro. Almost everyone who went anywhere traveled on a British ship, and anyone who sent goods by water shipped them in a British hull. In 1846 there were 131,000 steamships carrying the red ensign, and countless sailing vessels, from little West Country smacks in Devon to huge lumber schooners in Canada. Sail could still hold its own with steam, even though ten years later the number of steamships had trebled; in 1856 there were 387,000 British steamships plying the seas, more than 4 million tons of them. It was said that you could yell, "Hey, Jock!" down the hatch of any engine room on any ship in the entire world and a Scot would poke his head out from the pipes and valves to answer.

Outsiders were somewhat at a loss when confronted by the magnitude of things British. It was difficult for a German who had never seen the sea to comprehend how vast a seaborne empire might be; frustrated Germans from Wurtemburg or Saxony told themselves that if their country were united, it too would be great, and they studied the British Parliament and talked about customs unions and brooded about the day when the flag of a German Empire might fly over great ships at sea. The French, as usual, cast a jaundiced eye on things British. France already had something of an empire, in Algeria, for what it was worth. Life in France was too sweet to bother about adventuring, and Frenchmen joked that the British Empire was founded by men searching for a good meal, or trying to get warm. Americans alternated between vociferous independence, or slavish imitation of things British. In many parts of the United States, and among certain elements of the population, people felt very British still. In the twenty years of the middle of the century, 700,000 Englishmen had immigrated to the United States, very close to one American in twenty-five. They still retained ties with home. But at the same time more than twice that many Irish had left the old country for the United States, and they had little cause to remember Mother Britain with anything but loathing. It was they more than the British who became a voice in American politics, especially in the cities; it was they who put their pennies aside and gave to the cause of a free Ireland. Yet in spite of them, British tastes and ideas remained dominant. Cuffs on trousers were introduced in the United States by an Englishman who turned up the bottoms of his trousers one day when crossing a muddy street in New York, and ladies waited for news of the latest English fashions.

The British themselves had not yet reached the apex of complacency and pride that they would attain later in the century. Englishmen had always thought they were better than most other people. Even back in the sixteenth century the Venetian ambassador had reported on their charming conceit, so that whenever they saw something pleasing they asked him if there could possibly be anything that good where he came from. So now they moved through the world armored in the consciousness of their own superiority but without the necessity for strident assertion of it that they later developed. Still, a country whose foreign policy was run by Lord Palmerston could be infuriating to its neighbors.

For example, when a shady Portuguese moneylender named Dom Pacifico had his house pillaged by an Athenian mob, he claimed protection from the British on the grounds that he had been born in Gibraltar and was thus a British subject. Palmerston, without checking too carefully in the matter—he was at the moment fed up with the Greeks—sent the Mediterranean fleet to blockade Athens until compensation should be paid. Palmerston's defense of his action before the House of Commons was one of the high points of his career and illustrated at least one view of what Britain was all about. He closed with, "As the Roman, in days of old, held himself free from indignity when he could say, *'Civis Romanus sum,'* so also a British subject, in whatever land he may be, shall feel confident that the watchful eye and the strong arm of England will protect him against injustice and wrong."

All of this vastness of territory and view was presided over by a still-young woman who was the epitome of nineteenth-century life and ideas, so much so that she gave her name to the age. Alexandrina Victoria had become Queen of England in 1837 on the death of her uncle, William IV. Serious, moderately intelligent, rather plain, she had been groomed, like her grandfather George III, to rule. Not only that, she had been carefully tutored by her governess and a group of European relatives, chief among them her uncle Leopold of Belgium, in such a way as to react against the immorality and licentiousness of the court of George IV. Victoria took the business of being Queen, and of living, seriously. So did her husband, the Prince Consort, Albert of Saxe-Coburg and Gotha, a German, a pedantic but attractive stick with whom she was madly in love. She sent him notes full of underlined phrases and exclamation points—she was far more exuberant in her correspondence than in public—and they placed their desks side by side while they attended the many duties of ruling the Empire, not least of which consisted of producing nine children, so that eventually half the crowned heads of Europe, including the Tsar and the Kaiser, called her Grandmother.

Taking herself seriously, Victoria did rule, not alone or absolutely by any means, but she was the most active sovereign in years. George III had become incapacitated, George IV had been a dolt, and his brother William IV, the "sailor king," had done little except try to hold back the reforms sweeping the country in his seven-year reign. Victoria knew every inch of the royal prerogative, and she exercised it to the full. In the early years of her reign she necessarily went slowly, but eventually she had been Queen for longer than most of her ministers had been alive. From being the embodiment of the Empire in her early years, she was virtually the apotheosis of it in her later ones.

There were, of course, problems; life remained hard for most people, wages were low and hours of work long, the poor were always there, and social welfare at the time was dominated by the idea that if the poor were made too comfortable, they would choose to remain poor, which meant that charity was cold indeed. And in the 1840s, a natural disaster of immense proportions, comparable only to the plagues of the Middle Ages, hit Ireland. The potato crop failed.

Originally imported from North America, the potato had replaced wheat as the staple food for millions of Irish peasants. An intensively cultivated acre of potatoes would support a family who had required four or five acres of wheat, and some authorities maintain that it was the widespread adoption of the potato that touched off the population explosion of the late eighteenth century; in Ireland the population had grown from five million to eight million in the forty years from 1801 to 1841. Of course, Irish conditions were aggravated by an entire host of evils, absentee landlords, rack-renting agents, short leases for tenants who could not improve their holdings, a priest-ridden peasantry, and a distant government that responded only to the interests of the wealthy Anglo-Irish establishment. Lord Palmerston, who was one of the better Irish landlords, owned several thousand acres that he seldom visited, and he thought the best remedy for his tenants' problems was that they be driven to emigrate.

Under such marginal conditions, the failure of the potato crop was unmitigated catastrophe. The blight, which killed the plants and turned the potatoes black and rotten in the ground, first showed up in southern England late in 1845. It rapidly spread to Ireland, and the next year practically the entire crop was touched by July. The government estimated that three of every four acres were totally ruined; as it also estimated that four million Irish, or half of them, lived entirely on the potato, this meant that unless something drastic was done, three million Irish were going to starve to death.

Very little was done. There were shortages of grain in Britain, and as the government was extremely reluctant to interfere with normal trade channels, Irish peasants died in ditches while grain convoys, under armed escort, passed by them on their way to ports for export to Britain. Private charity broke down. The government did extend help and tried to institute substantial public-works schemes. But it was not very experienced at this—the men who knew how to react to famines were doing their job in India, not in Ireland—and the schemes were woefully inadequate. No one who held more than a quarter of an acre of land was eligible for government assistance, which both gives an idea of the government's view of help and the conditions under which most Irish lived.

The Irish were left with not very attractive choices: rebellion, emigration, or death. Many chose the former, and especially in the more distant areas there was considerable agrarian violence, burning of haystacks, and hamstringing of cattle. A radical party calling itself Young Ireland tried a rising in Tipperary in 1848, but starving men do not make revolutions, and these eruptions of frustration were put down by the constabulary. Millions chose the second alternative, most of them going to the United States, but numbers also heading for Canada and Australia. Families mortgaged themselves and their pathetic holdings, and sold whatever they could, including their daughters into "service," to raise enough money to get a son to America. In 1850 Irish laborers in America sent home two million pounds, accumulated a penny at a time, to help relatives get away from their homeland. Many of those who went overseas died on the way. "Emigrant ship" was often a euphemism for "plague ship"; conditions were almost as bad as those for slaves from Africa, rations were totally inadequate, and among the debilitated passengers, cholera and typhus frequently broke out. In the St. Lawrence River at Montreal, ships unloaded cargo after cargo of dying Irish, who never saw any more of the New World than a freezing warehouse full of their fatally ill countrymen.

Between emigration and death, the population of Ireland dropped dramatically. From more than eight million in 1841, it was down to six and a half in 1851. Nor were the losses made up; if the famine passed, the other troubles remained, and the habit of emigration became ingrained. By the end of the century the population of Ireland was still dropping, to below five million in 1901, to four million by 1921. After America, Ireland remained Britain's greatest failure as a colonial enterprise; the British did far better with French Canadians or Indians or Malays than they ever did with Irish Catholics.

Whatever the difficulties in Ireland, the British could still congratulate themselves that they were spared the kind of thing that went on across the Channel, for 1848 saw another series of revolutions in Europe. The July Monarchy came tumbling down in France, to be replaced by a short-lived republic. Central Europe was aflame; Garibaldi made his name in Italy, Louis Kossuth in Hungary; the Austrian Army suppressed the Italians, the Russian Army the Hungarians, and the Prussian Army the Danes and Saxons. For a year liberal speeches and marching boots were heard, and the roar of cannon. But in England there was simply a great petition for reform handed in to Parliament. The Chartists, as they called themselves, respectfully asked for a greater share of government, including such shocking innovations as universal manhood suffrage and a secret ballot. Their petition had several thousand signatures; in fact, Queen Victoria and Prince Albert were found to have signed it several times. It was all a great nothing; English politicians were willing to declare that the constitution as presently constructed was "as perfect an instrument as the mind of God had devised," and they were all conscious how far above the goings-on across the Channel they were. When Prince Albert opened the Great Exhibition in London in 1851, his own pet project, the theme chosen was "Prosperity," and few of the thousands who gaped their way through the Crystal Palace could doubt that prosperity indeed was what lay ahead for Britain.

What lay ahead was war, for three years later an obscure disagreement over the holy places in Palestine somehow became the Crimean War. The British interest in the Middle East, though it oscillated, had never entirely declined since the days of the Napoleonic wars. There had been the problem of Greek independence, and all through the 1830s and 1840s there had been periodic squabbles with Mehemet Ali, the too-ambitious ruler of Egypt. The British did not want Mehemet Ali to get too strong, nor the Ottoman Empire to get too weak. They particularly did not want the Russians to reach Constantinople, so even at a fairly early stage they were feeling their way toward the late-nineteenth-century policy of shoring up Turkey. This both protected their own commercial interests in the eastern Mediterranean and illustrated the growing importance of the area as a way station on the route to India.

Unfortunately for them, the British were not the only major power concerned over the Levant. The French and the Russians were equally involved; all three western powers kept making deals, two against the third, while the Turks tried to play them all off against each other. It was suitably Byzantine, and therefore it slid downhill into war. The Russians moved troops into the Danubian principalities of the Ottoman Empire, the British and the French sent ships to Constantinople. With this kind of support behind them, the Turks, in a burst of jubilation, declared war on Russia on October 4, 1853.

Little happened for two months. Then, at the end of November, the Russian Black Sea squadron, consisting of several ships of the line armed with the new shell-firing guns, steamed into the Turkish harbor of Sinope. A Turkish fleet of several smaller vessels was sheltering here while carrying troops to the Caucasus theater. The Russians, in overwhelming strength, virtually massacred the Turks. While the latter fought valiantly with their old-fashioned solid-shot cannons, the Russians blew up ship after ship with their exploding shells. Then, not content with that, they shot up the lifeboats and the survivors swimming the harbor. When Admiral Nakhimov sailed away, he had killed three thousand Turks, with a loss of thirty-seven of his own men. In Britain and France there was wild indignation, not only at the brutality of the attack but also because the Russians had failed to be impressed by the presence of the Anglo-French squadron at Constantinople. It was a long time since Europe had had a real war. Early in January the Anglo-French fleets sailed past the Golden Horn into the Black Sea, and in March 1854 the two allies declared war on Russia.

As a rule, historians make their reputations by proving that the conclusions of earlier historians are for some reason invalid. No one has yet, however, seriously challenged the general idea that the Crimean War was a small masterpiece of muddle and confusion. The British and French, having declared war on Russia, were then at a loss over how to fight her, for if geography presents enormous frustrations for Russians trying to get out to open water, it presents equally enormous frustrations for an enemy trying to get in.

The allies did not really know they were fighting the "Crimean" War; they were fighting against Russia and had to start by looking for ways to do it. For both Britain and France, it was more convenient to fight in the Baltic than in the Black Sea, and they sent a combined fleet through Danish waters, toward Russia. The British commander was Admiral Sir Charles Napier, who had been a dashing middle-grade officer but who was now tempered by advancing age (he was nearly seventy) as well as by inhibiting instructions from the government. His French colleague, Admiral Parseval-Deschenes, was slightly more bellicose, but unfortunately his fleet did not match his manner; whereas the British had mostly steamships, the French were all in sailing vessels, so throughout the campaign the slow-acting British commander was delighted to wait for the slow-moving French ships.

Under these conditions the admirals decided that little could be accomplished, and then set out diligently to justify their prediction. There were only three possible targets anyway: Kronstadt, the naval base near St. Petersburg; Sveaborg, another naval base in Finland, which was then part of Russia; and a small fortress on the Aland Islands, at the mouth of the Gulf of Finland. They decided that this latter was just about what they could handle; it was August, six months after the declaration of war, before they attacked and took the fort of Bomarsund. They then realized that when winter came, the Russians could recapture it over the ice of the gulf, so they abandoned their conquest and sailed away for the winter.

Napier had now fulfilled his instructions so well that there was a public outcry in Britain over his doing nothing, and he was relieved of command. Another squadron under another commander operated in the Baltic the next year and bombarded Sveaborg. The government was careful to present this as a great accomplishment, so that, though nothing came of it, as Southey said of Blenheim, " 'twas a famous victory."

The war was indeed full of those, for the logic of supporting Turkey had meanwhile dictated that the major allied effort should be in the southern theater. Once the Anglo-French fleet had passed through the Bosporus into the Black Sea, the Russians simply withdrew to their great naval base at Sevastopol and refused to come out. The allies bombarded Odessa without a great deal of result, and they then transported an expeditionary force up the western coast of the Black Sea to Varna, where the allied presence was to put pressure on the Russian Army in the Danubian principalities. It did this all right, but the troops got infected with cholera in the process and died by the thousands.

With the Russians withdrawing, the allies were ready to talk peace. Unfortunately, since no one could figure out why they were fighting in the first place, it became very difficult to negotiate, and the Russians obstinately rejected the allies' offers. Deciding that more action was needed, the British and French governments instructed their field commanders to do something, and looking over their maps, these gentlemen decided they might as well attack the Crimea and the base at Sevastopol. They had not reconnoitered their objective, and they had no idea what they might encounter, but this seemed as good a thing as any to do.

So the two navies loaded up the cholera-stricken troops and sailed off, about a hundred fifty ships strong, for the Crimea. The best that can be said for the naval arrangements is that they were slightly superior to those of the soldiers, though the French so overloaded even their warships that they were incapable of fighting at sea. But at least the naval commanders, Admiral Dundas and Admiral Pernaud, sent scouts ahead to find a landing place, something the soldiers were not interested in, thinking the landing was purely the Navy's problem. Of course, the spot they did pick, just north of Sevastopol, was rejected by the military leaders, and the landing was finally made over open beaches thirty miles north of the city. The Russians neither opposed the landing nor tried to interfere with the transports while they were disembarking. In fact, the Russians simply sank their ships in the mouth of Sevastopol Harbor and left it to their land forces, supplemented by fifteen thousand sailors, to stand a siege.

The siege lasted from late September, when the troops got ashore, for almost a year. It witnessed several battles notable in military history: the Alma, Balaclava, Inkerman, and the storming of the Redan. The courage of the troops and the incapacity of their commanders were best summed up by the remark of a French general watching the famous Charge of the Light Brigade: "It is magnificent, but it is not war." Meanwhile, the navies were occupied trying to supply the troops, which they did totally unhindered by the Russians, with only mixed success, and later on, in cutting some of the Russian supply lines. In October 1855, for example, the Anglo-French ships bombarded the Russian port of Kinburn, employing for the first time ironclad floating batteries. Finally the allies succeeded in breaching the defenses of Sevastopol, and the Russians withdrew, burning the ruins of their city behind them. Everyone had now had enough, more especially as this was the first war in which news correspondents' reports were sent rapidly home, and the utter incompetence with which the war was being fought threatened the security of ministries. It was therefore time to make peace. Both sides had lost about a quarter of a million men; the allies had had about seventy thousand deaths in combat, the rest mostly to cholera. That was enough to satisfy the public craving for excitement, and in March 1856, a peace was finally negotiated at Paris. It was a war everyone was well out of.

The Crimea touched off a spate of demands for reform of the armed services, but before this could be effected, Britain was faced with another explosion. The Crimea was a tale of muddle and disaster redeemed only by the dogged heroism of the men in the trenches. The Indian Mutiny, begun in the same kind of confusion, ended by being the great epic of imperial history.

There were many causes for the rebellion, running back into the past several years, though the Mutiny was not an early manifestation of nationalism, as some Indian historians have since claimed. One of the factors was that the British were perceived to be weak; they had now settled down as the ruling class of India, they had brought their wives and children, and they had done their best to transform their stations into little British islands in the midst of an Indian sea. In their spoiled and lazy families they had given hostage to fortune, and in their recent poor performance in the Crimea they had shown that perhaps they could be defeated after all. Their military power certainly rested on a slim foundation. There were three types of troops in India. The vast majority of them were Indians in the service of the company, some 233,000 native troops or sepoys divided among the armies of the three presidencies—Bengal, Bombay, and Madras. Then there were British regiments in the company service, and finally there were the regular British Army regiments, but these had been thinned by the demands of the Crimea. There were less than forty thousand European soldiers in the whole of India, and of these, relatively few were in Bengal, which was the center of the Mutiny. The Indian troops, not very efficient, had become distant from their officers and had for some time been disaffected by a series of innovations that seemed to them to strike at the root of their caste system, such as the new enlistment provisions that after 1856 required them to serve anywhere. This made practical sense to the British, but to many of the military classes of India, crossing salt water was a loss of caste and therefore forbidden.

Of more concern to the Indian princes was the fact that the British, under the Governor Generalship of Lord Dalhousie, had pursued a very aggressive policy. This had come to be known by the name of "paramountcy," and in this view the British, as the dominant or paramount power, had the right to intervene in the affairs of the Indian states to preserve their position. Up until the middle of the century, the British had preferred to exercise this power only in controlling the external relations of the Indian states, but under Dalhousie they began to take the greater role in internal matters as well. To paramountcy he added the idea of "lapse." The British insisted on the right to recognize the successions to the various princely thrones. Indians were polygamists, and they often either adopted their heirs, or chose them from among the children of favored wives. By disallowing this and insisting on inheritance by primogeniture in strict English terms, Dalhousie maintained that various Indian lines had "lapsed" and that their states should thus come under direct British rule. Many of the leaders of the Mutiny were claimants dispossessed by the new British policies.

For some time these various muddied currents had roiled beneath the apparently placid and complacent Indian scene. In May 1857 they burst open with shocking violence at Meerut, twenty-five miles from the ancient capital of Delhi. The British had issued new minié cartridges for use with the Enfield rifle; the loading drill required the soldier to bite the end off the cartridge and pour the powder down the barrel of the piece. The cartridges were greased, and the Indians believed that the grease was a compound of pig and cow fat; pigs were anathema to Muslims, and cows were sacred to Hindus, and use of the cartridges was seen as a deliberate attempt to destroy the Indians' caste system. When a cavalry troop refused to perform the drill, the entire unit was placed under arrest.

On the morning of Sunday, May 10, 1857, the rest of the Indian garrison rose up, freed the troopers, and then, before the stunned British could recover their wits, went on a rampage of murder and arson. After practically destroying the station, the mutineers marched off to Delhi to proclaim old Bahadur Shah the Emperor of India once more. The rising rapidly spread through Bengal, in most cases abetted by the incredulity of the British officers, who simply refused to believe that their men might be unfaithful. There was a massacre at Delhi, though a small garrison held on outside the town. At Cawnpore and at Lucknow the British garrisons and their dependents were put under siege. In lesser stations the sepoys slaughtered their officers and families brutally. Ladies who a week ago had not had to lift a finger now found themselves running through swamps, hiding in ditches, or hauling sandbags in a desperate attempt to remain alive.

Had all India risen, the British might well have been driven out. But there were no answering echoes beyond Bengal. The Bombay and Madras armies remained loyal, Nepal sent ten thousand Gurkhas to help out the British, and as the British pulled themselves out of their initial shock, they reacted with a ferocity that, on reflection, astonished even themselves. Within weeks relief columns were forming, and reinforcements began to come in by sea, first in a trickle, then in a stream. Cawnpore surrendered in June, on a promise of safe passage for the garrison. The Rajah of Bitpur, Nana Sahib, then betrayed the British, massacred most of them, and threw two hundred English women and children into close confinement. Two weeks later, as a relief column neared the city, Nana Sahib ordered his captives killed. They were hacked to pieces by butchers brought in for the task, and their remains were thrown down a well. When the British under Sir Henry Havelock defeated Nana Sahib's army and entered the city, they went mad. From that time on, very few Indians with weapons were taken alive. Many of those who were were tied across the mouths of cannons and blown to death. But for most it was a minié bullet or a quick thrust of a bayonet, and no questions asked or quarter given. The carefully constructed codes of Victorian society were sloughed off like a rotten husk, and the British swept through the land as vengefully as the conquerors of old. Delhi was stormed. A relief column fought through to Lucknow, only to be besieged again. A second column, under Sir Colin Campbell, destined to be one of the great imperial soldiers—it was Campbell who once told his Highland regiment, "If any man fails in his duty, I will have his name read out in the kirk of his home parish, to be disgraced forever!"—crashed through to the rescue. Lucknow was definitively freed in early 1858. Meanwhile, Sir Hugh Rose was marching and countermarching in central India, and at Gwalior in June he defeated the last Indian field army. From then on it was a matter of hunting down dwindling bands of rebels, who gradually subsided into banditry. By late 1858, with nearly a hundred thousand British troops in India, British rule was refastened with an iron grip.

The Mutiny finished off the Honorable East India Company. Though it led a shadow existence for another twenty-five years, it was formally divested of its governing powers by the Government of India Act, passed by Parliament in August 1858. The Governor General now took the additional title of Viceroy of India, and at home the cabinet post of Secretary of State for India was established. The India Office became an integral part of the British government; by royal proclamation, the Queen also gave up most of the policies of Dalhousie that had alienated the princes, and the British settled down to put their Indian Empire on a firm footing. It would never be quite the same again, though. If the Indians were appalled and thoroughly cowed by the British vengeance, the British themselves were chastened by their experience. No one who lived through the Mutiny would ever forget it; it had revealed to Englishmen not only the dark side of India, but the dark side of themselves as well.

As the greatest trading and industrial power in the world, Britain was necessarily interested not only in her own affairs but also in those of her customers. And since her customers were everywhere, this meant that most events in the world were of some concern to the British. This held true whether the incidents involved some distant petty chieftain or an almost major power such as the United States of America.

In 1860 the United States was Great Britain's single biggest customer. British attitudes toward the Americans were as ambivalent as were the Americans' toward them. Through the years there had been a variety of disagreements over boundary claims with British North America, and there were residual antagonisms about the American view of neutral rights at sea vs. the British view of the right of search.

The vast majority of Britons were opposed to slavery, yet the prominent classes in Britain tended to empathize more closely with the aristocratic planter society of the American South than with the pushy industrial society of the North. Also, no matter how much the British might deplore slavery in the abstract, the greatest part of their raw cotton came from the southern American states. *Uncle Tom's Cabin* was the most popular book in Britain in the 1850s; that did not lessen the need for slave-grown cotton.

The attitude of Britain toward the outbreak of the American Civil War was crucial. As soon as the southern states seceded, they placed an embargo on their cotton, believing that the British economy could not survive without it, that Britain must therefore grant them diplomatic recognition, and that this in turn would guarantee their winning the war. On the other side, if President Lincoln had announced that the war was being fought to free the slaves, he would almost certainly have had unequivocal British support. Lincoln, however, could not afford to alienate the loyal slave states along the border, and he had to insist vehemently that the war was *not* over slavery but rather over the differing interpretations of the U.S. Constitution. Lincoln was therefore forced to do without any real British support. He further harmed his cause in their eyes by the proclamation, in April 1861, of a naval blockade of the southern coasts.

This was an ironic case of the biter bit. The United States, during the entire Civil War, practiced exactly those maritime tactics to which they objected so vigorously when the British employed them in the Napoleonic wars and later, in World War I. The British, who insisted absolutely on their right to blockade, search, and seizure in the Napoleonic and First World wars, protested loud and long that they were illegal when used by the Federal forces during the Civil War. A month after Lincoln's blockade was announced, the British government responded, very carefully, by recognizing the "belligerency" of the "states styling themselves the Confederate States of America." But they did not recognize Confederate independence, and they announced their own neutrality. If recognition of belligerency was a blow to the North, nonrecognition of independence was a far greater blow to the South.

Though the British government did not propose to pull Rebel chestnuts out of the fire, it was still primarily sympathetic toward the Southerners, and as always the British were prepared to make a profit out of the war. Between British chicanery around the fringes and

Union actions at sea, the two parties came close to blows on several occasions. The first of these was the famous *Trent* affair. The South sent two commissioners to Europe, gentlemen by the name of Mason and Slidell. They successfully ran the Union blockade, still a token matter, in the fall of 1861, and reached Havana. There they took passage for England in the Royal Mail Steamer *Trent*. On the morning of November 8, the *Trent* was plowing up the Bahama Channel when a steam sloop, the U.S.S. *San Jacinto,* fired a shot across her bows. Captains of Royal Mail packets simply did not acknowledge shots across their bows, and the *Trent* kept on. A second shot came closer, and the *Trent* disdainfully hove to. At this the *San Jacinto* sent a boat across, and an officer climbed up the side and silenced the British captain's protests by producing a warrant for the arrest of Mason and Slidell. When the Britisher pointed to the privileged Royal Mail pennant, the American pointed to his cannons. The two southern gentlemen went over the side and into the Union ship's brig.

The Union was ecstatic; this was twisting the lion's tail with a vengeance, and Captain Wilkes of the *San Jacinto* was deluged with ceremonial swords of honor. In Britain, however, there was unbridled fury; how dare these Yankees act like Englishmen! War talk among the public was unrestrained, and the government, which really did not want to fight, sent a stiff note to Washington and ordered fifteen thousand reinforcements for Canada. But a dying Prince Albert softened the tone of the British message, and Lincoln's cabinet realized they could hardly do what they had always insisted the British not do. They apologized, handed over the Southerners, and offered Britain the use of Portland, Maine, as a disembarkation point for their troops in the Canadian winter. By the time the American reply reached London, cooler heads had prevailed there too, and when the manager of the Drury Lane Theater interrupted a play to announce, "The Americans have thought better of it ..." the entire crowd cheered themselves hoarse. No one really wanted a war over two men who proved to be "the most worthless booty we could possibly have extracted from the Americans." When Mason called on the Foreign Secretary, Lord John Russell, the latter refused to receive his credentials.

Still, private Britons were more than willing to help the South and to make money. Both sides bought extensive arms and equipment from British manufacturers, and most of the blockade runners were British ships. The British government simply washed its hands of them and looked the other way. A more delicate problem was of Confederate commerce raiders built and bought in Britain, where the government admitted there were unfortunate loopholes in British legislation. The most famous of these vessels was launched on the Mersey at Liverpool in May 1862. The builders called her *No. 290;* she sailed on trials in late July, one day ahead of a detention order, and once at sea, she hoisted Confederate colors and changed her name to the C.S.S. *Alabama.* In the next twenty months she ranged every ocean in the world and destroyed seventy-one Union ships; she caused American insurance rates to skyrocket and the U.S. Navy to dispatch dozens of ships to hunt her. She was finally run to earth in Cherbourg, and when she came out to do battle, the U.S.S. *Kearsarge* sank her after an hour's hard fight.

The *Alabama* was but the most noteworthy of several ships produced in British yards. The U.S. government insisted from the start that it would hold Britain responsible for such damages as they inflicted, and the dispute, known as "the *Alabama* claims," went on for almost a decade. In 1872, the British agreed to pay fifteen and a half million dollars in settlement.

Even before the war ended the British had reluctantly recognized that in their position, they were setting a dangerous precedent by allowing a neutral power to equip warships for a belligerent, one that might well be used to their future disadvantage. Early in 1863 the U.S. ambassador, Charles Francis Adams, protested that the Laird yards outside Liverpool were building two iron ram-type vessels, which could be used only against the Union blockade. Lord John Russell professed innocence, at which Adams produced his famous retort, "I am ignorant of the precise legalities of the matter, but it is superfluous to point out to your Lordship that if these rams are allowed to sail, it means war." Britain did not want war, not with a United States who looked increasingly like winning the Civil War, a United States with the biggest and best Army in the world at the moment, and with a large, modern Navy. The British government bought the rams for the Royal Navy.

The cotton embargo hurt, and there was great distress in the manufacturing areas. But it was the very people who were hurt, weavers and workers, who understood intuitively what the American Civil War was all about, who could set aside the political intricacies and realize that the war was over government of, by, and for the people, who most vigorously supported the Union. Once Lincoln had issued his Emancipation Proclamation after Antietam, the cause of the Southerners was doomed in Britain. The *Times* of London might print the news of the fall of New Orleans in mourning borders, but the *Times* was not England, even if it occasionally thought it was. When the war finally ended with a Union victory, it was a victory for ordinary Englishmen as well as Americans, and the British government was relieved to have been able to steer a successful middle course.

The most direct effect of the American Civil War was not on the people of Britain generally, but on the Royal Navy. The test of war forces men to discard the conceits and inhibitions of the past, and in this case, the Civil War proved definitively that the day of the wooden ship was gone. The work of the French iron floating batteries at Kinburn was reinforced by the events in American waters, and most especially by the famous battle between the ironclads *Monitor* and *Virginia* (formerly known as the *Merrimac*). The ironclad was just that, a wooden ship built in the traditional way, with iron plating added for protection. The Russians at Sinope had shown what the new shell-firing guns would do to wooden ships; the *Kearsarge,* when she fought the *Alabama,* had armored herself by flaking down her anchor chain outside the hull. As early as the 1830s the first iron-hulled merchant vessels appeared, but the navies of the world had clung to traditional construction methods. The British Admiralty had tested iron before the Crimean War but had found that in many ways it was more brittle, and therefore more vulnerable, than good old English oak. It took another twenty years of refining metalworking techniques before useful iron for warships was produced. That development was assisted by the fact that by 1860 the British were at last running out of suitable ship timbers. Huge oaks were only a marginally renewable resource, and the building tempo of the Napoleonic wars meant Britain was short of timbers by 1860.

In 1859 the French launched the first seagoing ironclad, the *Gloire;* her sides were 4½ inches of iron supported by 17 inches of wood. The British responded with their first ironclad, *Warrior,* with the same thickness of iron and a bit more wood. Both of these looked like "real" ships, and neither was as revolutionary as John Ericsson's new American *Monitor,* which looked exactly like what the Confederates said—"a cheesebox on a raft." That was what it was, except that the raft was iron and the cheesebox weighed 140 tons and carried two 11-inch Dahlgren guns, the most powerful ordnance available at the time. She was not very seaworthy; in fact, she nearly foundered on the trip from New York to Chesapeake Bay, but she was all new, and between them, she and her Confederate counterpart opened a new age of naval warfare in March 1862. The ship of the future was going to be made of iron. By the time the Civil War ended, the United States Navy, ship for ship, was the most powerful and most advanced in the world. It was also the ugliest, with its beautiful tall sloops and frigates giving way to squat, dumpy little toads of monitors and rams and river vessels. The rest of the world was forced to follow suit, and at Lissa in 1866, during the war between Prussia and Italy on one side, and Austria on the other, the Italian and Austrian navies fought the first fleet battle of ironclads in modern history. By the mid-1860s, the naval revolution was well under way. The competition involving propulsion, hull form, guns, and armor that began then continued until the end of World War II, and the technical stability of the age of fighting sail faded away, never to return.

The problems of imperial policing remained, however, and whatever the big ships might do, or be, in the waters around Europe, in the farther reaches of the globe naval matters went on as they had for generations. Events in Abyssinia illustrated the march of the Empire.

Abyssinia in the 1860s was ruled by a man who styled himself King Theodore. Originally of some abilities, he had gradually alienated most of his followers by capricious cruelty. The British, of course, had a consul in the country, and early in 1864, when Queen Victoria failed to answer a letter sent to her by Theodore—it was mislaid by the Foreign Office—the irate monarch threw the British consul and his entourage in jail. They were allowed to write home, which they did, asking for rescue. The home government responded with an emissary, and he and his staff were also thrown in jail. After that, in a rather ponderous way, the machinery of government slipped into gear, and preparations were made for an expedition.

The major problem was not Theodore himself, since no one was expected to fight for him, but rather that his capital was nearly four hundred miles inland over some of the worst terrain in the world. The British organized a force in India and moved the force to the Red Sea coast. Sir Robert Napier, whom all authorities agreed waged a model campaign, needed close to a quarter million tons of shipping, fourteen thousand troops, and upward of fifty thousand laborers to construct a base on the Red Sea coast, march his men inland, and finally defeat Theodore's ragtag army at Magdala. It was a lovely campaign, and it caused a boom in shipping circles from the South Atlantic to Australia. Of the three hundred vessels employed, a mere twenty actually belonged to the government; the rest were taken on time charter and happily sat for months being paid while doing nothing. The campaign was almost as profitable for shippers as it was for mule dealers, for Napier had to have transportation, and inexperienced officers unfamiliar with the intricacies of the mule bought every animal they could find from Syria to South Africa. The campaign took almost eleven months of preparation and about two of actual operations, and it cost nine million pounds. The Secretary of State for India, whose office carried it out, justified the expense by saying the government had pretty well given Napier carte blanche and told him to do the job, which may well explain why the Army regarded Abyssinia as a model of what a campaign should be.

A campaign such as that in Abyssinia typified British activities in the third quarter of the century. The possession of the Empire conferred advantages on Britain unsuspected by other states, not only in the way of trade, but also in the varieties of military and naval operations. French and German soldiers met on the battlefields of Europe, but British military men were likely to meet all sorts of enemies in all sorts of odd places. Sir Garnet Wolseley, for example, caricatured by Gilbert and Sullivan as "the modern major-general," fought in Burma in 1852, the Crimea, the Indian Mutiny, and in the Second China War of 1860. Ten years later he put down the Red River Rebellion in western Canada, then fought in Ashanteeland in 1873. He served in Natal in 1876, Cyprus in 1878, and conquered Egypt in 1882. He led the Gordon Relief Expedition in Sudan two years later, and eventually he was commander-in-chief of the British Army in the 1890s. A naval opposite number, Admiral Sir Beauchamp Seymour, known to his contemporaries as "the swell of the ocean," served in the Second Burmese War with Wolseley, in the Baltic against Russia, and in New Zealand. He was made a peer for commanding the bombardment of Alexandria in 1882. The British might not have experienced some of the massive battles of the Franco-Prussian War, but they had experienced just about everything else in the military or naval line, from Arctic expeditions to tropical ambushes.

By the 1870s the momentum of the Empire was quickening. Much of the map of the world was already painted red for British, and much more was potentially open to British expansion, for they held the most favored starting points for the penetration of Africa, or China, or whatever they wanted. Their cable networks and their shipping lanes were the arteries and veins of the world's economic system, as London was the heart of it. And if there was a significant spot they had missed, a remedy for the oversight was always possible. The Suez Canal was the final proof of that.

For many years Egypt had been recognized as a vital crossroads of the world; Napoleon had seen this, and so had others after him. During the early part of the nineteenth century, when the country had been ruled by Mehemet Ali, Egypt had become a local power. A railroad had been built linking the Mediterranean and the Red seas, and many British traveling to or from India did so via Alexandria and Cairo. This was obviously the shortest and therefore most profitable route, but the necessity of transshipping was a nuisance. That was all changed in 1869, however, when the French consul in Egypt, Ferdinand de Lesseps, after many years' work succeeded in his dream of opening the Suez Canal. Now ships might sail the entire way from Europe to the Far East without the long trip around Africa, and the canal bid fair to become one of the most important links of the world.

The British remained suspicious. They did not care for the government of Egypt, run at the moment by the Khedive Ismail. He had grandiose ideas about modernizing his country, and he ran heavily into debt to do so. As many British investors bought his bonds and got a poor return for their money, they were not too enamored of him. They were displeased that the canal had been built by a Frenchman; relations with France were chancy at best, and it seemed somehow an affront that an important waterway should be built by anyone but a Briton, almost as if De Lesseps were meddling. For some time the British government refused to use the canal and continued to offload, transship, and reload through Egypt, as if by pretending the canal were not there, they could make it so.

Slowly, though, it dawned on them that for once they had missed the boat. The advantages of the canal were becoming so obvious that something had to be done. In 1875 the Khedive was so deeply in debt that he decided to sell his shares in the Suez Canal Company, 176,000 of the existing 400,000. He was secretly negotiating with two French groups for the sale when a British journalist found out about it and told his government. Most of the cabinet were not interested, but the new Prime Minister, the flamboyant Benjamin Disraeli, was. Parliament was not in session; Disraeli went to his banking friends, the Rothschilds, and got them to stand good for the money. He then bought the Khedive's shares for £4 million in one of the most spectacular financial coups of modern history. Most Englishmen were delighted; it seemed a good joke that after De Lesseps had done most of the work, Britain should simply buy in to the action. Not that De Lesseps himself cared; he thought it was a fair deal. The Kaiser wrote his English mother a note congratulating her: ". . . England has bought the Suez Canal. How jolly!" Fifty years earlier, Canning had "called the New World into existence." Now, in 1875, when Britain wanted a new world, she bought it. The very next year, Queen Victoria assumed the additional title of Empress of India. The world's greatest empire was nearing its apogee.

12

A Temporary Thing

Her Majesty's Government contemplate shortly com-
mencing the withdrawal of British troops from Egypt.
                                        —Earl Granville, 1882

For close to a century now, historians have debated the reasons why, after 1875, there was a revival of the old imperialist urge and Europe entered a period of intense nationalistic rivalry. The development was all the more startling because it appeared to be such a complete turn-about from earlier attitudes. Of all the great powers, the British alone for the previous half century had added substantial imperial holdings, and generally they had done this reluctantly at first and in the face of official policy. The British Empire had grown in a purely *ad hoc* way. Even Gladstone, four times Prime Minister and the man who added more to the Empire than any other, insisted to his dying day that he was a "little-Englander" and wanted if anything to diminish rather than increase British territory. France was the only other power with substantial colonies, and at the end of the Franco-Prussian War she offered to give all of them to Bismarck if only he would leave her Alsace-Lorraine. Bismarck contemptuously spurned the offer; Germany, he thought, had no interest whatsoever in overseas empire. Yet ten years later Germans were scrambling for a piece of New Guinea.

What happened to change men's minds so quickly? There have been almost as many answers as there have been historians. The favorite explanation has been economic, first advanced by J. A. Hobson and then modified by the Marxists. In this view, imperialism was a penultimate stage of capitalism. Capitalistic society produces an excess of wealth, and since it fails to distribute it properly, there must be some outlet for this surplus. It therefore seeks sources of materials and markets overseas, and from that, political control follows. This creates further conflicts and imbalances, and then capitalism falls into internecine war and destroys itself. So some economic historians have seen the imperialism of the period as an example of the frog trying to become as big as a bull, and in the process blowing itself up, the explosion being World War I.

The process was much more complex than that, and Europe's imperial drive was compounded of a great variety of causes. Europe's was not only the most productive society of the world in economic terms, it was also the most advanced socially and politically. Its domination lay not simply in one category, but in all of them. Civilization like water seeks its own level, and it is difficult to think of an advanced social system in world history that has been able to restrain itself from expanding into less-developed neighboring territories. In the late nineteenth century, man's technological level reached the point where the entire world became "neighboring territory." Steamship routes and cable lines made it possible to tie the world together, and medicine at last made the penetration of hitherto inaccessible places such as Africa feasible for Europeans.

To this technological capability was added a frame of mind in which it was imperative that European countries take over other areas. For one thing, European nations were peculiar among the world's powers. In spite of Popes and Holy Roman Emperors and more recently Napoleon, no one had ever unified Europe. There was therefore a group of competing states, all sharing in significant degree a common heritage. The French and the English might not like each other, but they had far more in common with each other than either had with the Chinese or the Hottentots. In pursuit of their own nationalistic rivalries, European states extended a generalized European culture over the rest of the world. Britain occupied Burma in the Third Burmese War, for example, because France had already occupied northern Indochina, and the British feared further French extension in Southeast Asia.

Nor was this attitude couched solely in nationalistic terms. The religion of Europe and the dominant social thought also encouraged expansion. David Livingstone was a medical missionary and thus combined in one person two of the great European drives: to bring the aborigines the benefits of both European science and European religion. Throughout the century the missionary movement was cresting. There had been an enormous revival of faith after the Enlightenment and the Napoleonic era, and thousands of men and women of the nineteenth century devoted their lives to good works at home or abroad. If to a post-world war generation their attitudes and pronouncements seem complacent or even hypocritical, that is our loss rather than theirs. In the midst of all its crassness and materialism, Europe produced a great number of people who risked and often gave their lives to practice a Christian ideal throughout the world.

As the century aged, the religious impulse was reinforced by the ideas of the social Darwinists. The theory of evolution was applied to societies as well as species, and the idea of survival of the fittest seemed peculiarly apt when viewed in an imperial context. A state demonstrated its fitness to survive by competing with its rivals. The more territory it gained and the more people it controlled, obviously the more it deserved to hold. This was a satisfying, self-fulfilling prophecy. The world was there for the taking. Europe wanted to take it, needed to take it—indeed, *ought* to take it, not only for Europe's benefit, but for the rest of the world's benefit as well. Conscious of their superiority to the rest of the world, Europeans set out to control it. The great race was off and running.

Almost all of the European powers, including two who were of but not in Europe itself, were competitors. There was Britain, naturally. France was interested.

The Third Republic, child of humiliation in the Franco-Prussian War, sought solace overseas, and bold explorers on leave from the Army and Navy extended French holdings in Africa and Southeast Asia. The Germans were a new entry. After the Wars of German Unification, Bismarck had thought his new German Empire a satiated power. He soon decided otherwise, and by the late 1870s he was playing the age-old game of disarming opposition at home by encouraging expansion abroad. German businesses and German shipping lines were soon pushing their way into markets the British had long considered their own. Italy, also newly unified, had aspirations but not much more. For years she cherished Tunisia, and a bridge across the Mediterranean narrows. But France got Tunisia, and the French jokingly referred to Tunis as "our largest Italian colony." Later the Italians failed dismally to take Abyssinia, and eventually they settled for

Libya. The Russians, thwarted in the Balkans by western support of Turkey, turned their eyes eastward. Vladivostok, "Dominion over the East," was founded in 1860, and there were Russians in the Amur Valley north of China and in Afghanistan, northwest of India. If they sold Alaska to the United States, it was obvious that they were staking out most of Asia for themselves, a point Kipling never tired of making nor Britons of hearing. So of all the major powers of Europe, only Austria-Hungary did not enter the race for new colonies overseas; she had enough trouble holding on to what she had in Europe itself.

By this time too, Europe, like a spider plant, had thrown off other centers of power. In foreign policy the Americans were European in all but location, and they became as imperialistic as any of the older European states. They had finally settled their boundaries to the north with Canada and to the south with Mexico, but there was still no natural limit envisaged to the west. Many Americans saw the Pacific Ocean as a highway rather than a barrier. American businessmen connived at making Hawaii a republic and at its eventual annexation. At the end of the century the United States took the Philippines away from Spain, and President McKinley, after a night of anguished prayer, decided the United States must keep and civilize the Philippines. It was an American expedition that opened Japan to the outside world in 1853.

And once opened to outside—that is, European as well as American—influence, the Japanese transformed themselves with a vengeance. Onto their traditional attitudes of duty, loyalty, and courage they grafted European technology and organization. China tried to reject the West; Japan adopted what she wanted so that she might remain essentially Japanese. It proved an enormously potent combination, and Japan, a partially European-style power that happened to be in Asia, soon joined the march of imperial conquest.

None of these new developments, in their early stages, bothered Great Britain. By now free trade had become as sacred a doctrine as mercantilism had ever been, and if the British believed that what was good for them was good for the world, they also believed that what was good for the world was good for them. They welcomed the advent of new powers. If Germany was united and pushing ahead economically, that meant more markets for British trade and opportunities for British investment. When the Japanese built a navy, they contracted their ships to British yards. British goods poured into the bottomless markets of the United States. Even when other countries raised protective tariffs, the British remained confident that the superiority of their production methods, and therefore the quality and cheapness of their products, would continue to give them an edge. But they were mistaken in this view. Their manufacturing plants were now beginning to age, while other countries were just starting up, and Britain herself was short of natural resources, whereas other lands had surpluses. German and American steel production crept up on, and then ahead of, British, and by the end of the century Great Britain was a net importer of food. But these things were not immediately apparent. In the 1880s it was inconceivable that the natural, God-given order of things might someday be upset. Britannia, after all, did rule the waves; in the music halls they sang with cheerfully bumptious pride, "We don't want to fight, but by jingo! if we do, we've got the ships, we've got the men, we've got the money too . . . ," and they introduced a new phrase into the language. Rudyard Kipling, the archpoet of empire, advised the rest of the world to "Walk wide o' the Widow at Windsor, For 'alf o' Creation she owns." If the rest of the world wanted an imperial race, Britain was ready and willing to join in.

Not only willing, but must. Other countries, in the flush of revived mercantile imperialism, now known as economic nationalism, took territories to keep closed for their own exploitation. The British must thus take new holdings to keep them open. They had also to retain their traditional supremacy at sea, and that meant gathering islands and other critical spots to use as bases and coaling stations; for in a new world of steamships, bases became an even more necessary adjunct to seapower than they had been in the age of sail. British cruisers had to be able to get coal anywhere they might be sent; the best way to guarantee that was to own the coaling station. Preservation of access to or control over the world's great waterways brought both problems and opportunities. The takeover of Egypt in 1882 was a classic case in point.

When Disraeli bought the Suez Canal shares from the Khedive Ismail in 1875, it provided no more than a temporary fix for the Egyptian finances. By the next year Egypt was broke again and defaulted on interest payments on her bonds. Most of those bonds were held by British and French investors, and they howled. A hundred years ago governments believed they had some responsibility to their citizens, and even to their money, so the French government forced the Egyptians to set up an external control mechanism for their country's finances, known as the *caisse de la dette publique*. Because the French wanted to avoid the suspicion that they were plotting to assume control of Egypt itself, they asked the British to appoint commissioners, and as there were substantial British investors involved, the latter agreed; in 1878 the *caisse* became an Anglo-French condominion. The same year the powers, still unable to change Ismail's spendthrift ways, got his nominal sovereign, the Sultan of Turkey, to depose him in favor of Ismail's son Tewfik. The son proved an amiable enough nonentity. The economies forced on the country by the control commission alienated many native Egyptians, especially in their large and otherwise useless Army. A group of middle-grade officers staged a mutiny in 1879, brought down the ministry, took over the running of the country, and soon ran into trouble with the British and French commissioners. By 1881 Egypt was rife with xenophobia, its currency was collapsing, and there were riots in the streets of Alexandria.

The normal response of great powers to this sort of trouble was to send warships, and by the spring of 1882 there were ships or squadrons from nine different countries in Alexandria Harbor. The most important contingents, naturally, were British and French, and several of the others were there as much to watch them as to watch the Egyptians, for everyone expected that someone else was about to pull a land grab. In fact, no one wanted the country, but no one wanted anyone else to have it, either. The Egyptians, now led by a Colonel Mohammed Arabi, who can be seen as the first great Egyptian nationalist, began building batteries along the harborfront. Europeans were mobbed in some ugly riot scenes in mid-June, and the ships landed parties of marines to restore order. The British reluctantly went along with the French view that intervention was now well-nigh inevitable.

Just at that point, however, the French government fell, paying the penalty for being distracted from the Rhine to the Nile, and when, on July 11, the British fleet under Admiral Seymour bombarded the shore batteries and seized Alexandria, the French squadron weighed anchor and steamed out to sea in reproachful silence. The British were now stuck. Gladstone's government, protesting vigorously its good intentions, felt absolutely forced to send an expedition to Egypt to restore order. Twenty-five thousand troops under General Wolseley landed and secured the Suez Canal in August. They then marched overland, and after a daring night approach, they stormed the Egyptian positions at Tel el Kebir. The Egyptians fled in panic, and before anyone knew what was really happening, British cavalrymen were in

Cairo, and the British had another territory to govern. They immediately assured the powers of their intention to evacuate Egypt the minute public order was restored—the French were rather skeptical of this—and the British set about putting the Egyptian house in order. In the event, the last British troops did not leave Egyptian soil until June 1956. Four months later they returned, temporarily, as invaders.

The takeover of Egypt showed how a country might acquire an empire by default, even if it did not really want more territory. Stuck with it, the British determined to do a decent job; they sent out the usual corps of public servants, financial experts, civil engineers, and medical specialists. They began controlling the floods, organizing the educational system, building roads and railroads, balancing budgets, and not incidentally paying interest on Egyptian bonds. They carefully supervised the departments of the indigenous Egyptian government and tried to preserve the fiction that they were only advisers. But what did they do when their colony had an empire of its own?

That problem soon became pressing, for Egypt did have an empire. Back in the days of Mehemet Ali, Egypt had claimed and occasionally garrisoned the Sudan, vast, empty, poor, and hostile. In 1883 a prophet arose in the South, calling himself the Mahdi, and he soon raised thousands of warlike followers named Dervishes. The Egyptian government went to its British masters and asked what to do. The British refused to give advice, whereupon the Egyptians ordered their army in the Sudan to put down the rising. The Egyptian forces, ten thousand strong, led by an ex-Indian Army officer named Hicks Pasha, marched out into the desert and got annihilated at a place called El Obeid. The Mahdi's stock soared, and the Sudan burst aflame from one end to the other. A distraught Egyptian ministry begged the British for some assistance, or at least guidance, and at last Gladstone moved. He decided that the Sudan must be evacuated of Europeans and Egyptians, and to do the job, he sent out Charles Gordon.

Gordon was one of those legendary nineteenth-century Englishmen who, like mad dogs, went out in the noonday sun. A military engineer, he had spent most of his career on leave of absence and had been and fought everywhere; his nickname was "Chinese," because in the 1860s he had commanded the imperial Army putting down the Taiping Rebellion; he won thirty battles, never himself carrying anything but a walking stick. He had once been Governor of the Sudan for the Egyptians, where he had firmly attacked the slave trade. He was deeply religious and more than a little eccentric; he certainly had a martyr fixation, and he was the worst possible choice for a mission involving, in effect, capitulation.

By the time he got to Cairo he had changed his view of his task from evacuation to becoming Governor of the Sudan once again; ignoring Gladstone's original instructions, he sold the Egyptian ministry on his own revised version. He then went up the Nile to Khartoum, and in that fly-specked hole he dallied for months and managed, at last, to get himself besieged.

The daily press in Britain set up a great cry: Gordon must be saved. A furious Gladstone cabinet dragged its feet, but eventually, five months after the siege began, it organized the inevitable relief expedition with the inevitable commander, General Wolseley. Wolseley's trip up the Nile was as leisurely as Gordon's had been. Preparations seemed interminable, including the building of special boats—out of green timber—and the recruiting of a corps of Canadian *voyageurs* to man them; Wolseley had used these men in the Canadian West, and as far as he was concerned, water was water and rapids were rapids, whether on the Nile or the Red River. Wolseley spent the trip up the river giving up smoking, which may explain his mental state, while the troops had bitterly hard work fighting the heat and the rushing waters. Finally, as the relief expedition neared Khartoum, the Dervishes casually swept over Gordon's pitiful defenses, stormed his palace, and placed his severed head before the feet of the Mahdi. After that the British did evacuate the Sudan. Not for thirteen years did they return; then Sir Herbert Kitchener built a railroad into the country and wiped out the Dervishes with Maxim guns and high explosives at Omdurman. So finally the Sudan too became British.

As Egypt and the Sudan went, so did almost all of Africa. At the end of the 1870s, Europeans claimed but a few small toeholds along the coasts of the great continent. By 1914 only Abyssinia—Ethiopia—and Liberia were free from European control. The majority of the "partition" was carried out in the 1880s.

That was not to say that much preliminary work had not already been done. For close to a century Europeans had pushed inland along the great African rivers, often dying in the process but gradually filling in the outlines of the map. The great Scottish explorer Mungo Park had traveled along the Niger before the turn of the nineteenth century, and in the 1820s an intrepid Frenchman, René Caillé, had traversed the Sahara, going from the Guinea coast to Timbuktu to Fez, in Morocco. By then British officers on leave had found Lake Chad. Germans of a scientific bent had done the same in the 1850s, and it was in that decade that David Livingstone crossed the center of the continent and discovered Victoria Falls. By the 1860s it almost seemed that everyone who was anyone was poking around in the Dark Continent. Richard Burton, the man who had visited Mecca in disguise, went out with John Speke and discovered Lake Tanganyika. He and Speke quarreled over which of them had done what. Speke later traced the course of the Upper Nile. Going downstream, he met Sir Samuel Baker coming upstream. Baker was another of those cosmopolitan Englishmen; he was accompanied by his wife, a Hungarian countess he had acquired while building a railway in the Dobrudja. They were also a literary bunch; as Burton had translated *The Arabian Nights,* so Baker was the once-famous author of *The Rifle and the Hound in Ceylon.* Henry Stanley traveled through the continent as a reporter and journalist; it was he who found Livingstone—who was not lost—in 1871, and Stanley presumed on it ever after. By the 1870s, therefore, the country was known to Europeans in broad outline, thanks to the advent of modern tropical medicine and the insatiable curiosity of men who delighted in describing their profession as "traveler." Given the impulses dominating European society at the time, once the country was known, control could not be far behind.

There was at least some awareness that collision might result as British, French, Germans, Portuguese, Italians, and even Belgians vied for choice bits of territory, especially since everyone's line of desirable development crossed someone else's. When the British and the Portuguese made a private deal over south-central Africa, the other powers protested, and Bismarck called a conference, which met at Berlin in 1884 to lay down ground rules for the race to partition. The fact that such a conference was held at Berlin rather than London might apear suggestive, but as the British had recently acquired Egypt, they felt constrained to court German opinion, so they were willing to go along with it.

The biggest decision was about the Congo. None of the great powers wanted any other one to have the heart of the continent; they finally agreed that it should be set up as a free state under the personal sovereignty of King Leopold of the Belgians. This was a mildly shady deal engineered partly by Leopold himself and partly by his factotum, Henry Stanley. Leopold's administration governed the Congo with such "firmness"—a euphemism for cutting off the hands of Congolese who failed to meet production quotas—that international pressure forced him to cede his private empire to Belgium in 1908.

Aside from that, the powers simply decided what would constitute occupation or effective claims and agreed to arbitrate in cases of dispute. Then the scramble was on in earnest. The French actually got the largest territory, but most of it was desert, in the hump of West Africa. The British, spurred by such visionaries as Cecil Rhodes of South Africa, hoped for an all-British strip the entire length of the continent. Moving north, they got Bechuanaland as a protectorate in 1885, and the Central Africa Protectorate in 1891, carrying them as far as Lake Tanganyika. From the north, they had Egypt and then the Sudan. Moving in from the eastern coast, they established a protectorate over Zanzibar in 1890, then took the hinterland of Kenya and Uganda. In West Africa a chartered company—shades of the seventeenth century—took over Nigeria. The Central Africa Protectorate thwarted the hopes of the Portuguese to get a belt across south-central Africa, but the German claim for modern Tanzania, German East Africa, also blocked Rhodes' dream of "an all-red Cape to Cairo route." He had to settle for having a country named after him. It took World War I to clear the German blockage.

There were other trouble spots and frustrations. The Germans got the Cameroons, next door to Nigeria, and they got also Southwest Africa; though there was not much there, the South Africans had tended to think of it as potentially theirs, should they ever care to bother with it. The French, however, appeared initially the most obnoxious and seemed willing to go to enormous lengths to annoy the British. In 1896 a French officer, Major Marchand, set off from the coast of the French Congo with a detachment of Senegalese soldiers, several hundred porters, and a knocked-down iron riverboat. Twenty-four months and twenty-eight hundred miles later he and his expedition arrived at Fashoda on the Upper Nile, put their boat together, hoisted the French flag, and sat down to congratulate themselves. That was in July 1898, a month before Kitchener wiped out the Dervishes at Omdurman. Kitchener, hearing that there were white men with a strange flag upstream, hastened upriver by steamer, to arrive at Fashoda only two weeks after his victory.

Marchand was at a considerable disadvantage. His communications were three thousand miles of desert, Kitchener's a few hundred miles of river; Marchand was a major, Kitchener a general; Marchand had a company of soldiers, Kitchener a battalion. On the other hand,

Marchand was in possession, and it was his flag over the fort. While the two soldiers circled around each other like wary dogs on a dusty road, lights burned late in Foreign Ministry offices, diplomats calculated their chances, and French and British newspapers urged, "Fight! Fight!" But the French could not stand the pressure. Their new Foreign Secretary, Théophile Delcassé, wisely assessed that it was the height of stupidity to alienate Britain when Germany was his real enemy. The French graciously backed off, and ruffled British feelings were soothed. The lion had roared, and the lesser breeds had listened. Fashoda was the last real Anglo-French crisis; from then on the French so diligently courted the British that eventually they seduced them right into an alliance, without their ever realizing it.

By the time of Fashoda, almost all of Africa that was worth taking, and a lot that was not, was gone. The British had gotten the best of it. They had had the best starting points, from the south, from Egypt, and along the Guinea coast. And they had always held the trump card, unplayed but there nonetheless: Their Navy and their domination of the world's shipping lanes, and cable communications, meant that everyone else's empire existed and expanded on British sufferance. They did not say so; they did not have to.

Imperialism was exciting. It sold newspapers. For the late nineteenth century, when life seemed to have assumed the humdrum evenness of civilization, it was the equivalent of an earlier age's blood sport. The latest news from "our correspondent with the expedition" was eagerly awaited. One could thrill vicariously over Custer at the Little Big Horn, or "the last eleven" at Maiwand; for occasionally white troops did get caught, as at those battles, or at Isandlwhana, when the Zulus wiped out the South Wales Borderers, or Adowa, when the Ethiopians massacred the Italians. Reading about Fuzzy Wuzzy breaking the British square was only somewhat less interesting, and far less fatal, than being in the British square that Fuzzy Wuzzy broke. The public appetite remained unsated. Africa was not the only place ripe for partition. Asia awaited as well.

The penetration of Asia necessarily proceeded along different lines from the partition of Africa. In the latter, land was there for the taking, and however great some of the African kingdoms had once been, the continent generally remained in a tribal state to which European organization and technology were irresistibly superior. In Asia, however, there existed old and secure societies, which persisted in regarding the Europeans as barbarian interlopers. In fact, the Europeans were superior to these, as well as to the Africans, but in a more limited sense; here their powers depended upon their military and political organization, manifestations of their outward-looking dynamism, and especially on their technology.

In Asia even more than in Africa the British had the advantage in an imperial contest. By the 1870s, they held a stranglehold on the routes to the East; India was theirs, as well as lower Burma, Singapore, the northern coast of Borneo, and Hong Kong. Australia and New Zealand were not Asian at all but were still British. The Dutch had the great majority of the East Indies under their control but had no ambitions to gain more than that. Spain, also a sated power, ruled the Philippines, and the Portuguese retained eastern Timor, and the island of Macao, off the China coast. The French had controlled Cochin China (part of present-day Vietnam) and Cambodia since the 1860s, a by-product of missionary effort. The Americans and Germans had no holdings at all; there were, of course, Russians far to the north, and the Japanese still had only their own islands.

The great prize was China. By now the Manchu dynasty was palpably collapsing. The Taiping Rebellion, lasting for more than a decade in the 1850s and 1860s, tore the country apart. There were floods and other natural disasters to add to the devastation of armies and warlords, and slowly the prerequisites of power slipped away from the Heavenly Kingdom. Following the British lead of the Treaty of Nanking, all of the foreign powers imposed unequal treaties on China, foreign nationals gained extraterritorial rights, and Europeans soon were stationing their own garrisons in the treaty ports. In 1854 the Manchus inaugurated a foreign inspectorate of customs so that the Chinese Customs Service came to be manned by Europeans, mostly British, a declaration of national spiritual bankruptcy if ever there was one. In 1857, after covert hostilities, the British and French seized Canton, and China was forced to open more treaty ports and allow Christian missionaries into the interior of the country. The missionaries preached peace, but the Chinese knew it was the sword that enabled them to do so. By 1860 the Manchus were still rejecting envoys, and that year the British and French stormed the Taku forts before Tientsin, marched upriver, and entered Peking itself. When the Chinese seized envoys under a flag of truce, the Europeans responded by burning and sacking the Summer Palace, a great desecration that convinced the Chinese they really were dealing with barbarians, as they had thought all along.

They signed another treaty, and they finally did set up a foreign ministry, which they called the Barbarian Affairs Bureau.

For another thirty years the barbarians nibbled away at China; more concessions were granted, and the outlying dependencies fell quietly away. The French pushed up into Laos, Annam, and Tonking, always fractious satellites of China anyway, and began serious economic penetration of southern China itself, using the classic highway of the Red River from Hanoi into Yunnan. The Russians now had the maritime provinces of the North; the Japanese meddled in Korea and advanced claims to Taiwan. And the British, followed a distant second by the Americans, brought their business and their religion into the heart of China itself, moving up the great rivers, the Yellow and the Yangtze. There began to be heard occasional suggestions that perhaps it was time to divide up the country after all.

It was the Japanese who finally stripped bare the façade of Chinese integrity. The two countries went to war in August 1894 over control of Korea, and in a series of hard-fought battles the Japanese destroyed the young Chinese Navy and drove the Chinese Army out of both Korea and Manchuria. An exhausted China sued for peace in April of the next year, and the conditions proposed by Japan brought the other powers forward to claim a share of the spoils. China was to recognize Korean independence, which meant the peninsula would fall completely into the Japanese orbit; to pay a huge indemnity; and to cede Taiwan, the Pescadores Islands, and the Liaotung Peninsula outright to Japan. This Treaty of Shimonoseki would have made Japan the dominant power in China from Hong Kong north, and the other aspirants to China were not willing to put up with it.

Russia, France, and Germany all put pressure on the Japanese, and their claims were substantially watered down. The unholy trinity, having "helped" China, then presented a bill. Russia got the Liaotung Peninsula and railroad rights in Manchuria and Mongolia, Germany got a naval base at Kiaochow, and the French got further concessions in the South. The British, having stood aloof, posed as friends of both sides. For a reward, they got Kowloon, across from Hong Kong, and Weihaiwei, "for as long as Germany should occupy Kiaochow." Therefore they both got something from China and looked as if they were friendly toward the Japanese. The Americans were late to this particular feast, and having received nothing, proposed the famous "open door" policy, in which they offered to share their nonexistent holdings if the other powers would share their real ones.

Humiliated in this way, the Chinese made a short-lived effort to put their house in order. This led to a great deal of internal dissension, and that, in turn, burst out in a rebellion in 1900, the famous Boxer Rebellion. Initially antigovernment, it was channeled by Dowager Empress Tzu Hsi against the foreigners. The international settlement in Peking was besieged, missionaries and traders unfortunate enough to be caught out in the countryside were mobbed and murdered, and China dissolved into anarchy and near-chaos. This caught the British at a bad time, for they were in the midst of the very embarrassing Boer War, but fortunately that was mostly a matter of the Army; China presented the sort of problem the Navy was used to dealing with.

Admiral E. H. Seymour, the senior naval officer of the powers in Far Eastern waters, used his marines to reinforce Peking, and he gathered in ships from stations all over the Far East. This was a gathering of marked men: John Jellicoe was the flag captain in H.M.S. *Centurion,* and Commander David Beatty from *Barfleur* led the British contingent in the relief of Peking. Young Roger Keyes commanded one of the British destroyers, and Commander Christopher Craddock was there from H.M.S. *Alacrity.* So was the German Commander Pohl, who would one day meet these people under different circumstances.

The powers eventually sent about sixty thousand troops to China, the largest single contingent being Germans. World opinion was shocked at the Kaiser's exhortation to his departing troops to strike fear into the Chinese by emulating the Huns of old, and the term "Hun" eventually came to haunt the Germans. But the Kaiser was given to purple passages at the best of times, and he had a peculiar fixation about the "Yellow Peril" anyway. Most of the soldiers arrived after the crisis ended; it was sailors and marines who stormed the Taku forts and who held Tientsin as a foothold against the rebels. The sailors and marines kept the railroad up to Peking intact, and by the time the reinforcements arrived, the rising had largely spent itself. Western power had once more manifested itself through the versatility and mobility of naval forces. And once more China paid indemnities and granted concessions.

By the turn of the century, the available real estate was being taken up at an alarming rate. Africa was allotted now, and the powers had set up their spheres of influence in Asia. And even the Pacific islands were rapidly coming under European control. For years the British had resisted any temptation to annex island groups, seeing relatively little profit and considerable nuisance in it. Australia and New Zealand both developed modest imperial aspirations of their own as they grew up and federated, but the British were able to resist their respectful suggestions. What the British were not able to resist was the thought that others might preempt them. When the French and Germans showed an active interest in Pacific empire, the British moved. In 1874 they annexed Fiji, and a mini-imperial race was on in the Pacific.

It lasted for a generation, until the islands were all gone. France made Tahiti a colony in 1880, providing subsequent inspiration for the painter Gauguin. Four years later, Germany moved in and claimed the Bismarck Islands, and the northeastern quarter of New Guinea, which she named Kaiser Wilhelmsland. She would have taken the eastern half, but that would have put German troops a mere hundred miles from Australia; so the British took the southern part, to provide a buffer. The next year there was a German protectorate over the Marshalls and the Solomons. So it went. Britain took the Cooks and Gilberts; Germany bought the Marianas and Palaus from a defeated Spain after the Spanish-American War. The Americans got Guam.

How silly, or how important, all this was was demonstrated in the case of Samoa. Here the Germans, Americans, and British all had claims, and while the British were not too concerned with it, both the Germans and the Americans were very forceful. The Germans landed troops in 1887, and in early 1889 there were one British, three American, and three German warships in Apia Harbor, all eyeing each other suspiciously. On March 15 a typhoon swept over the harbor; the American ships were driven ashore, as were the Germans; the lone Britisher clawed her way out to sea and safety, cheered by the swamped Yankees as she went; the Germans went aground in sullen silence. In the British penny papers this was variously interpreted as God being on the right side, or true British pluck winning through as always. In any case, it sobered the more excitable, and the three countries reached an agreement on joint administration.

In the Pacific, then, as elsewhere, the British got most of what they wanted. Islands previously left alone now had an administrator, and perhaps a cable station, and a small trading company, and always a growing mountain of coal as the colliers, those modest corpuscles of empire, carried British coal out to form dumps that might someday be needed for something. The Union Jack and a pile of coal were almost inseparable marks of empire at the turn of the century.

Few of the people who became British subjects during the revival of imperialism wanted to do so; almost none of them were given any choice in the matter, and those who resisted generally got short shrift.

For the most part they were aboriginal peoples, and their spears, assegais, or ancient trade muskets were no match for the Martini-Henry or the Maxim gun. It was during this period that one British writer hailed the invention of the machine gun as a great step forward, for it would enable Europeans to civilize natives more quickly. There was an almost unceasing series of frontier wars anywhere in the Empire that the British butted up against native tribes, whether in India, South Africa, or even in Canada. Hundreds of young Englishmen ended their short careers in some unknown gully on the northwestern frontier of India, a school for soldiers for nearly a century.

But the most tortuous frontier of all was that in South Africa, because there the British adjoined not only assorted tribes but also the two Boer republics that had developed out of the Great Trek. There was hostility and mismanagement right from the beginning.

The Boers had left Cape Colony to get away from the encroachments of British life. Neither side made much attempt to understand the other, and distant colonial secretaries and parliamentarians, looking for some rational solution to the colony's problems, seldom considered the effect on individual human affairs, which tend to be anything but rational. If it had just been a question of British and Boer, there might have been mutual understanding, but there were the black race, and all the shades of color, to put into the equation as well. In their dealing with the blacks, the British slowly extended their borders through one war or treaty after another. But the only consistent aspect of their relations with the Boers was inconsistency: In 1848 they claimed sovereignty over the area of the Orange Free State; in 1852, at the Sand River Convention, they recognized the independence of the Transvaal Republic; in 1854 they withdrew from the Orange Free State, and on and on. Acknowledging Boer independence, the British kept annexing native territory claimed by the Boers. The entire situation was then transformed, and further complicated, by the discovery of diamonds in the Orange Free State, and British miners and financial interests flooded in, threatening to swamp the Boers. Slowly the British were surrounding the two huge but sparsely populated states. Then in 1877, in a flagrantly shady deal, a Britisher named Sir Theophilus Shepstone annexed the Transvaal. Boer resentment stood this for three years; then they rose up, slaughtered a British force at Majuba Hill, and the British recognized their independence once again.

That was in 1881. Life still did not go on smoothly; by now the British were in the full flush of imperial enthusiasm, and their control kept creeping up around the Boers, like an advancing tide around a child's sand castle. Five years after Majuba Hill, gold was discovered in the southern Transvaal, and a vast wave of miners and speculators rushed to make a killing. By the turn of the decade there were as many foreigners as Boers in the area, the foreigners' income far exceeded that of the Boer farmers, and the foreigners confidently expected that the republics would become British by the simple passage of time.

The Boers regarded the gold capital, Johannesburg, as a modern Sodom. They hated everything about it, and in a desperate effort to retain their own identity, they passed all sorts of laws inhibiting the *uitlanders* (outlanders) from enhancing their position. By 1895 Cecil Rhodes, the big money man of the wide imperial vision, lost patience. He backed one of his subordinates in a filibustering raid to take over the Transvaal. At the turn of the year Dr. Leander Starr Jameson led a force of some six hundred men on a dash for Johannesburg, timed to coincide with a general rising against the Boers.

The Jameson Raid failed miserably, embarrassingly, publicly. Jameson's men were no match for the hardy Boers, trained from childhood to the life of the open veld, and the Boers rounded them up with humiliating ease. Rhodes was nearly ruined, so was the British Colonial Secretary, Joseph Chamberlain, who got out of it only by being careful not to know officially what he knew full well. From then on, both sides talked, simmered, and slowly began making military preparations. The Boers bought arms in Germany, the British built up their garrisons in the Cape. When President Paul Kruger, an intransigent, wily old fighter, was as ready as he could be, he issued an ultimatum to Britain, and in mid-October 1899 the Transvaal Republic and the Orange Free State declared war on the British Empire and invaded British territory.

In Britain they hardly knew whether to laugh or cry. They started by doing the one and were soon doing the other. On the face of it, the matter was ludicrous. There were possibly eighty thousand male Boers in the two republics, if one counted every male from ten to seventy. The only professional force was a small body of State Artillery. Except for a tenuous line through Portuguese Mozambique, the Boers were completely isolated from outside help. Ranged against them was the entire might of the greatest empire in the history of the world. And it was not just Britons who wanted to fight. In Australia, young men trekked in from the outback to join up; the war issue of the *Canadian Pictorial* showed a cavalry trooper holding a Union Jack aloft over Majuba Hill, the whole entitled "The Call of the Blood Again." The volunteers desperately hoped the war would not end before they could get there—say, by Christmas.

Christmas came and went, in 1899, in 1900, in 1901, and still the Boers fought on. The British had laughingly spoken of "males from ten to seventy," not realizing that among the Boers, young boys and old men fought. These were the finest irregular soldiers in the world. They actually lost the war in the first few weeks, sacrificing their best quality, their mobility, to besiege British garrisons along the frontier. It took the British several months to force the Boer positions and relieve Ladysmith, Kimberley, and finally Mafeking in the North. Then they marched on the Boer capitals, first Bloemfontein in the Orange Free State, and then Pretoria in the Transvaal. In September 1900 the British commander, Lord Roberts, annexed the Transvaal, announced the war was over, and went home. Roberts was wrong; the war was just beginning.

For there was now no specific Boer territory to defend, and they were free to do what they did best—mount up, ride, raid, and destroy. Instead of a mopping-up operation, Roberts' successor, Lord Kitchener, found himself with fifty thousand angry Boers ranging over an area almost as big as Europe. They overran his isolated garrisons, they ambushed his patrols, they blew up his trains, they lived off his supplies. They were a people obsessed with freedom, freedom of such a totality that they would never submit; they would have to be hunted down, almost individually. It was like trying to catch the wind.

The world outside the British Empire watched in delight as the British chased back and forth across the veld. Almost everyone outside the Empire was sympathetic to the Boers, and assorted volunteers got in to help. But there was no foreign recognition of the Boers, and no real aid to them. That was the British Navy again. In Germany the Kaiser considered it; he was incredibly jealous of the British and markedly unstable. At the time of the Jameson Raid he had effusively congratulated Kruger on defeating his enemy "without calling on friendly powers," a statement bitterly resented in Britain. In the early weeks of the war, when the Boers looked as if they were winning, the Kaiser wondered if it were not time to go in on their side. But his generals and admirals showed him German naval figures compared with British naval figures and murmured soothingly, "Not yet, not yet . . ." So the Boer republics died alone.

But they died hard. Kitchener's solution to his problem still staggers the imagination. Along the rail lines he divided up the country. Within rifle range of each other he built corrugated iron blockhouses, and he tied them together with barbed wire and manned them each with a corporal and a squad. Then within these enormous enclosures he put on drives with his cavalry and his mounted infantry, and he kept after the Boers, day after day, week after week, month after month. They outsmarted him, they lost him, they broke through his cordons, they wheeled back and attacked, but gradually they were whittled down. He discovered they were getting supplies from their isolated farms, so he then adopted a policy that estranged Boer from Briton ever after. He burned their farms, and he gathered up their women and children and put them in concentration camps—the phrase is originally British, not German—and in this way he denied the Boers rest and sustenance. He also killed their next generation, for in the squalid camps the women and children sickened and died. Kitchener did not care; it was war, and if the Boers wanted to wage it, they must pay the price. Some Englishmen, and even more some women, such as Emily Hobhouse, did care, and attempted to redeem their country by shaming it with its own actions. But the women and children still died. And finally the war did too. In May 1902 the Boers gave up; faced with the total destruction of their families, they finally surrendered.

The British celebrated their victory, but it was a hollow one. A handful of farmers had stood off a half million men for more than two years. The peace settlement was so lenient that within a decade the Boers dominated a federated Union of South Africa and have done so ever since. For the British won only in a qualified sense; they won if victory consists of turning your opponents' country into a desert. If victory means destroying the enemy's will to resist you, as Clausewitz said it does, then the Boers won, for they emerged from the war more determined than ever: They were a people, and no peace imposed by British guns was going to change that.

The war showed Britain that she needed a new look at her military forces. Though winning in the end—the old bulldog spirit at work—they had had some hard lessons forced on them. And in a wider sense, too, the war had been disquieting. The imperial response was gratifying, but the rest of the world outside the Empire had been too patently delighted to see Great Britain taken down a peg. The new century was going to see some big changes, not all of them for the better for Britain. There were clouds on the horizon, splendid isolation looked something less than splendid, and Britain quietly began shopping for allies.

13

"The Cancer of a Long
Peace . . ."

> *Place in the hands of the King of Prussia the strongest
> possible military power, then he will be able to carry out
> the policy you wish. . . .*
>
> —Otto von Bismarck, 1886

In the year 1887, Queen Victoria celebrated her Golden Jubilee; it was
fifty years since, as a young girl of eighteen, she had ascended the
throne of the United Kingdom. Now she was a widow, mother of nine
children, Empress of India, and the Great White Queen to much of the
world. She would reign for many years yet, and her Diamond Jubilee,
still a decade off, would be the most famous of her celebrations. But
the Golden one, of 1887, was in some ways the more significant. London was full of princes and Indian potentates, and visitors came from
all over to pay homage or just to see the fun.

There were three great reviews of the imperial forces. First the
volunteers marched past Buckingham Palace in a splendor of rather
bizarre uniforms and titles in which the words "royal" and "loyal"
seemed to predominate. Then there was a review of the regular Army
at Aldershot. Khaki had now begun to come in for foreign service, but
at home it was still scarlet tunics for the infantry, topped by the "universal pattern" helmet, a concession to the Prussian *Pickelhaube* in that
it carried a little spike on the top but was of a more shapely design.
Bands blared and banners fluttered and ladies sighed, and on such an
occasion, who would not be a soldier? Yet the most notable of the three
reviews was the last one, when the Queen Empress boarded her yacht

and inspected the great fleet gathered at Spithead. Here even more than at Aldershot was the embodiment of the Empire, the ships of the Channel Fleet in their "Victorian livery" of black hulls, white upper works, and buff funnels, with twinkling brass and signal flags to provide the highlights. It was fortunate they were so colorful, for aesthetically they had little to recommend them. Designers were still trying to work out what a ship ought to be, and the result was some of the ugliest vessels ever designed. The masts and sails had gone at last, so that the impression left behind was of brute power disguised by pleasant colors. For the review the Navy had mustered thirty-five major fighting vessels, and then a host of humbler craft, reaching down to troopships, training brigs, fast little torpedo boats, and a last vestigial paddle frigate or two. It was a brilliant spectacle all in all, and it certainly made an impression on royal visitors.

Among Victoria's guests were her son-in-law, Crown Prince Frederick of Germany, and her grandson, Prince Wilhelm, who came over for the festivities. On their trip across from Germany they had been escorted by a German torpedo flotilla commanded by Alfred von Tirpitz. Frederick was already dying, of cancer of the throat; he reigned as Emperor of Germany for just over three months, in the spring of 1888. The young prince, his son, was passionately interested in navies—they seemed to be such fun—and he had long and interesting conversations with Tirpitz, who was pleased to plant some seeds in the fertile mind of his future sovereign and Supreme War Lord.

Navies were the coming fashion. It now appeared that one of the prime requisites of great power status was the possession of an overseas empire, and those who wanted empires obviously needed navies. The rapid technological change of the period was matched by growing public interest in, and debate about, navies and the roles they ought to play in the new world order. In England after about 1884 there was a growing vogue for naval history and theory, and a brilliant series of thinkers, including the Colomb brothers and Sir John Laughton, added to public awareness of what navies were all about. In the United States Alfred Thayer Mahan was President of the Naval War College; in 1886 Admiral Aube, probably the most important French sailor since the age of sail, became Minister of Marine. Two years later Germany laid down the four battleships of the Brandenburg class, and shortly after that, Mahan published *The Influence of Sea Power upon History;* the Kaiser ordered a copy placed in every wardroom in the

German Navy. Navies were the perfect expression of Europe's sense of itself, for they had not only the organization and precision of armies, but they also added to that the most complicated technological developments of the day in propulsion, signaling, metallurgy, fire control, and gunnery. It was revealing of society's values that the battleship should be the most advanced example of its creative genius and should even be seen as such with pride.

Part of the interest was sparked by the exciting things taking place in naval design. For example, the torpedo had now reached a point where it became a major factor in warfare. The earliest "torpedoes" had been floating mines, no more than that. Inventors had tried to give them mobility by towing them behind small boats, or even riskier, attaching them to a long spar that projected from the bow of the boat. An English naval officer, Robert Whitehead, began the story of the self-propelled torpedo in the 1860s by powering them with compressed air. His efforts were unappreciated at home but picked up by the Austrians, demonstrating once again that the minor powers tended to be more fertile innovators than the greater states, with their interest in preserving the status quo. By the late 1870s the Whitehead torpedo attained battle effectiveness, and the Russians used torpedoes launched by fast torpedo boats against the Turks in 1878. From then on everyone had torpedo boats, and they in turn generated a fast gun-carrying boat, naturally named a "torpedo boat destroyer." This type of ship proved so useful that destroyers soon were one of the main naval classifications, faster and handier than the traditional gunboat, far less expensive to build and operate than the larger major classes of warship.

The necessities of imperial policing led to the development of the cruiser as well. These were the steam era's equivalent of the sailing sloop and frigate. By the end of the century hull design and propulsion had made sufficient progress that these ships could patrol the whole world, steaming thousands of miles at reasonable speeds and, as long as they could get coal, remaining in fighting condition for months at a time. The cruisers H.M.S. *Iris* and *Mercury* in 1879 were the first all-steel ships of the Royal Navy, as the cruisers *Sapphire* and *Diamond,* in 1874, were the last wooden ones. By 1900 there were both armored cruisers, having side armor, and the smaller "protected" cruisers, designed mostly for scouting. Soon after the turn of the century the necessity for faster ships able to work as destroyer leaders led to the development of the "light" or "scout" cruiser as well.

The world's real interest, however, was concentrated on the battleship, the lineal descendant of the sailing ship of the line. The gun-armor spiral continued throughout the later part of the century, and virtually every aspect of battleship design was a matter of impassioned controversy. This led to some notable disasters. In the 1870s H.M.S. *Captain,* built as a low-freeboard monitor type but complete with masts and sails, capsized and sank in a Bay of Biscay squall, taking her entire crew down with her. For some years the Admiralty stayed with muzzle-loading guns because of problems with breechloaders, but in 1879 one of the guns of H.M.S. *Thunderer* exploded after it was dou-ble-charged by mistake, and from then on, more progress was made with breechloaders. New engines and boilers were constantly being tried, and hardly any two ships were exactly alike.

The first real British battleships, incorporating all of the newest features of design, were the Admiral class battleships of 1887–89. H.M.S. *Benbow* had the heaviest guns of the century; they weighed 110 tons and fired a shell 16.25 inches in diameter that weighed 1,800 pounds and could penetrate 37 inches of wrought iron armor. From then on improvements in both armor and gunnery made guns lighter and smaller, and armor thinner, without any loss of strength or power. *Benbow's* guns were so heavy and bulky she could carry only two of them, in barbettes. By the turn of the century the British had stand-ardized on the 12-inch gun in twin turrets.

If the rapid development of technology made it difficult to keep up with comparative naval strengths, the advent of new naval powers introduced yet another complication. The British gradually realized they were being challenged in areas they had hitherto considered their own.

Britannia's rule over the waves for the past three quarters of a century had been deceptive. It derived more from the fact that no one else had cared to challenge her than from any conscious policy deliber-ately pursued. To the British this had come to seem the natural order of affairs, and surprisingly little thought was given to comparative naval strengths or to Britain's real relations with other powers and what the basis of those relations might be. The British had generally favored the process of unification in central Europe. They thought Ital-ian unity all for the good; they were a little less complacent about Ger-man unification, especially as that looked to be aggrandizement of Prussia more than a true uniting of the German states; they were upset by the Danish War in 1864 but failed to do much about it, to some of-

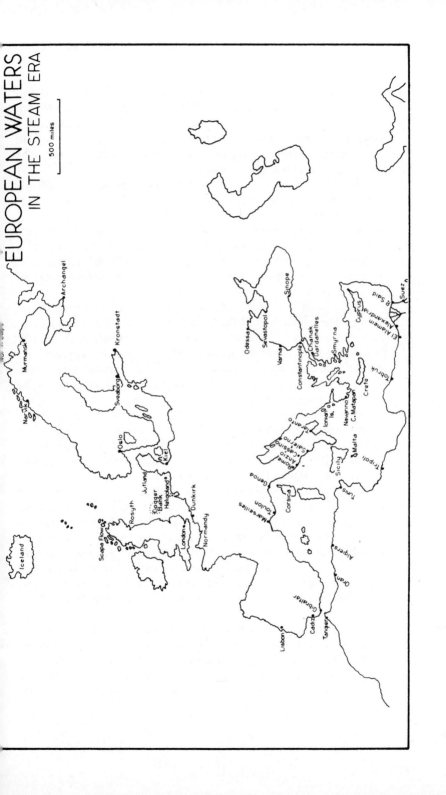

EUROPEAN WATERS
IN THE STEAM ERA

500 miles

Iceland

Narvik
Murmansk
Archangel

Oslo
Svalbard
Kronstadt

Jutland
Kiel
Rosyth
Dogger Bank
Heligoland
Scapa Flow
London
Dunkirk
Normandy

Odessa
Sevastopol
Sinope
Varna
Constantinople
Chanak
Dardanelles
Smyrna
Cyprus
El Alamein
Alexandria
Port Said
Suez
Tobruk

Genoa
Marseilles
Toulon
Corsica
Rome
Anzio
Cassino
Salerno
Taranto
Ionian Is.
Navarino
C. Matapan
Crete
Malta
Tripoli
Tunis
Sicily
Sardinia

Algiers
Oran
Gibraltar
Cadiz
Tangier
Lisbon

ficial dismay. They were quite surprised by the sudden German defeat of France in the Franco-Prussian War, but they distrusted the French anyway and did not readily appreciate the logical consequences of a newly powerful Germany. So there was little public recognition that in the 1870s the entire European political balance had been altered, to the considerable disadvantage of Britain.

By the time of Victoria's Golden Jubilee, Britain was still the major power on the sea, but in the late 1880s the European states generally began building up their navies, and the cumulative effect of this was to erode the position of supremacy that Britain had so far enjoyed. Other states now had the money and the incentive to build, and with the rapid evolution of naval technology, they could build ships as good as anyone else's. Change had wiped out Britain's enormous lead in naval strength.

The world was thus suddenly full of lesser or greater naval powers. There were four of the former and three of the latter. Russia, Italy, Austria, and France all began building relatively small but still respectable navies. For the Russians, the problems of geography remained well-nigh insurmountable. Where other countries might need one or even two fleets, the Russians needed three—a squadron in the Baltic, one in the Black Sea, and one in the Far East. And in each case, egress to wider waters was virtually blocked by a real or potential enemy. Nonetheless, the Russians began new construction; their small Navy had acquitted itself well in the Russo-Turkish War of 1877–78, and in the 1880s and 1890s they constructed the ships that were ultimately to be sunk by the Japanese at Tsushima.

Austria-Hungary began building at about the same time. Their Imperial and Royal Navy never appeared as much of a factor in world naval power, but it was Austrians, with Italians, who had fought the world's first fleet ironclad battle, at Lissa in 1866. Austria was a rival of Russia in the Danubian Basin-Black Sea area and was also vitally interested in the Adriatic Sea. The same impulses that set off the Russians also inspired the Austrians, and eventually they built a quite respectable fleet which, though small, was still a factor in the naval balance.

The Italians were allied with Austria, since the Triple Alliance of 1882. The Italians were, however, in direct rivalry with France over the central Mediterranean and access to the North African shore. They also had their own Adriatic aspirations, so they too began to produce new and powerful ships. Indeed, the Italians, though possessing limited facilities, were always among the forerunners in naval design. And their building caused the French to start, too.

It would be too simplistic to see this as a straightforward domino effect: France building because Italy built because Austria built because Russia built. Each state was responding to its own internal pressures and perceptions, as well as to external ones. In France, for example, Admiral Aube had developed a school of naval thought known as the *jeune école*. He had discovered that what France had always failed at before could now succeed: He reinvented commerce warfare. In his view, Great Britain, which could not be defeated by attacks on her commerce in an age when she had been largely self-sufficient, could now be defeated in an age when she lived by her imports and exports. In the last quarter of the century, Britain no longer fed herself; she was, Aube maintained, vulnerable as never before. The French began building long-range commerce raiders. There were naval scares in Britain in 1884 and again at the end of the decade.

These minor powers put some strain on British resources, but ultimately they were far less significant than the rise of three major powers: Japan; the United States; and above all, Germany. The first two were somewhat distant variables on the world and naval scene; the last became an obsession.

Geographically, Japan was in the same position in the Far East as Great Britain was in Europe: If Japan were to prosper, it must be by sea. Her real expansion began with the Sino-Japanese War of 1894–95, and in the naval Battle of the Yalu River, when Admiral Ito defeated Chinese Admiral Ting's squadron, the Japanese gained an initiative they held for the rest of the conflict. The only other major naval engagement was five months later, at Weihaiwei, a matter of blockade and bombardment, so the Yalu battle, the first real fleet action since Lissa, caused considerable comment and discussion.

By the next round of Japanese expansion, a decade later, Japan and Britain were allies. They signed the Anglo-Japanese Naval Treaty in 1902, and two years later, Japan and Russia fought for control of the Yellow Sea. Once again, seapower was decisive; the Japanese could reinforce and supply far more rapidly by sea than the Russians could across Siberia. When in desperation the Russians sent their Baltic Sea fleet all the way around Africa and Asia, the Japanese met them in the Strait of Tsushima and virtually annihilated them. The war ended soon after that, with both sides practically exhausted but the Japanese holding their major objectives.

All this meant there was a new star rising in the East, or a rising sun, as the Japanese traditionally thought of it, and the British readily acknowledged this. The waters of East Asia, the Sea of Japan, the Yellow Sea, and the East China Sea were of interest to Great Britain as a trading state, but they were absolutely vital to an expansive Japan. By the 1902 alliance and by her financial and political support in the Russo-Japanese War, Great Britain conceded command of those waters to her emergent ally.

More or less the same thing happened in the United States. In the 1870s the United States Navy consisted of old tubs that were more appropriate to a museum than to active service, for at the end of the Civil War the admirals had scrapped their ugly, functional fleet and happily returned to the tall, ocean-going ships that sailors loved. Americans were subject to occasional humiliations at sea by naval powers stronger than themselves, such as Spain and Chile—when the former seized and shot American filibusterers in international waters, or when Chileans mobbed a naval shore party, the U.S. Navy was impotent—but in the 1880s there occurred the same awakening of naval interest as was spreading through Europe. In 1883 the Americans embarked on building the first ships of their modern Navy, protected cruisers with both steam and sail power, the *Atlanta, Boston, Chicago,* and the dispatch vessel *Dolphin,* a group known to the Navy as the "ABCD's." After that there was general progress; a series of "coastal defense battleships" was launched, and in the 1890s Captain Mahan's ideas spread rapidly and gained influential adherents. One of the things Mahan preached was that the United States ought to control the waters in a great arc from Norfolk, Virginia, through Panama to Hawaii. There were American business interests in the islands, talk of a Panama Canal was now general, and there was trouble in the Caribbean, where for years the Cubans had been carrying on a low-level revolt against Spain. In 1895 there was also a dispute with Britain over the boundary of Venezuela, but that was largely for domestic political consumption. Mahan realized that the United States was not going to take on the Royal Navy, which he fervently admired, anyway; hence his arc of control stopped at Norfolk and did not extend, as it logically might have done, to Halifax or Iceland. That would take another fifty years.

As the Sino-Japanese War had marked the emergence of Japanese naval power, so the Spanish-American War was the commencement exercise of the United States Navy. When war broke out over Cuba in 1898—appropriately the blowing up of the battleship *Maine* in Havana Harbor was the proximate cause of the war—Europeans were sure the

Spanish would win handily. No one really thought the Americans could fight. As it happened, they never lost a battle in the war. In May Commodore George Dewey wiped out an inferior Spanish squadron in Manila Bay, and in July Admiral Sampson did the same to the Spanish ships at Santiago Bay in Cuba. In the two battles the Spanish lost seven cruisers, three gunboats, some destroyers, and several other pathetic relics. The entire American casualties were one man killed and nine wounded. Cuba became independent under American tutelage, and the Philippines were taken as a dependency, very much against their wishes.

The Americans then set about fulfilling Mahan's desiderata. In 1901 they succeeded in getting a treaty with Great Britain that left them the exclusive builders and controllers of a canal across the isthmus of Central America. When the area of Panama revolted and declared its independence of Colombia, it was American ships that saw to it the new state was recognized, a small-scale replay of the role of Britain with Brazil and Portugal eighty years earlier. When Roosevelt sent the Great White Fleet around the world in an ebullient publicity ploy in 1908, it coaled at British stations and in effect steamed both on British substance and sufferance. Yet Mahan's arc of control was realized, and once more the British conceded command of some of earth's major seas to another power. The western Atlantic, the eastern Pacific, and the Caribbean were tacitly agreed to be under American domination. This was getting closer to home, but by that time, most of British energies were absorbed by the one overriding concern—the rise of German naval power.

The German Empire was proclaimed in the Hall of Mirrors at Versailles on January 18, 1872. At that time the German Navy was a negligible factor in European affairs; it was only recently a separate service, having been an adjunct of the coast artillery branch of the Army. With a shore that ran from East Friesland to East Prussia, broken by the Danish Peninsula, Germany had little use for naval power. There were no threats to her in the Baltic; the last invader to land on her coast had been Gustavus Adolphus, in 1630. In 1872 Germany had neither a substantial merchant marine nor any overseas interests.

Thirty years later the Imperial German Navy was one of the most important factors in the European balance of power, and from St. Petersburg to London foreign secretaries and naval chiefs were trying to figure out what the Germans intended to do and how to stop them from doing it. The major character in this drama was Alfred von Tirpitz, the dynamic officer who had escorted Crown Prince Wilhelm to Queen Victoria's Golden Jubilee. Tirpitz had joined the Prussian naval service in 1865, and as the Navy expanded after the Franco-Prussian War, his career and his ambitions expanded with it. In 1877 the first Chief of the Admiralty, Admiral von Stosch, made him head of torpedo development. Tirpitz held various administrative posts until 1895, when he took over Germany's small Eastern Asiatic Cruiser Division. The fact that Germany by 1895 even *had* such a formation indicates the extent to which her interests had grown, and it was largely Tirpitz' spadework that got her the base at Tsingtao after the Sino-Japanese War.

Tirpitz was in the Far East only a year, for in 1896 he was back in Germany, as Secretary of State for the Imperial Naval Office. He returned to the center of power just in time to catch the crest of the wave, for shortly he took over command of that office and began diligently to support and to cultivate the Kaiser's view that Germany ought to have a great new navy. Not only did Tirpitz heartily share that view, he also believed that such a navy could only be modeled on—and directed against—Great Britain.

In this he and the Kaiser were in agreement. Both admired the British; Wilhelm was, of course, half British himself. At the same time they envied Britain and aspired to her place in the world. If the Kaiser was entranced by the fleet review in 1887, with its 35 battleships, he turned green with envy at the stridencies of the Diamond Jubilee review, when 173 ships, including more than 50 battleships, were drawn up in lines 7 miles long for the delectation of the old Queen and her public. None of those battleships was more than 8 years old, so fast had the naval progression come on, nor had any been withdrawn from foreign service for the occasion. As a demonstration of British might and determination, it was very impressive. It was also counterproductive, for Wilhelm returned home more certain than ever that Germany too must have a great navy. Tirpitz was just the man to produce it for him, and he immediately began a process of selling the idea of a navy to his countrymen. The Pan-German League and the Colonial Union gave him support right from the start, but most important, he made the all-powerful German heavy industry firms see that a big navy was to their advantage; battleships, after all, meant contracts. The money to found the German Naval League was provided by Krupp. In March 1898 the Reichstag voted 400 million marks for new construction, and the Naval Law called for a fleet of 19 battleships, 8 coastal battleships, 42 cruisers, and numbers of destroyers, torpedo boats, and support craft. With one stroke Germany announced her entry into the naval supremacy sweepstakes. Nineteen German battleships were not going to take on the Royal Navy, but two years later, in the 1900 Naval Law, Tirpitz upped the ante: Germany was now to have 38 battleships and 52 cruisers. That would make her the second naval power of the world, and as she was already the first military power, this was cause for serious alarm in Britain. The Chancellor, in presenting the first naval bill, announced that such an accession of power demonstrated Germany's peaceful intentions.

To explain what he was doing, Tirpitz made public his idea of the "risk theory." His view, or so he said, was that Germany had no desire to challenge Great Britain directly. However, if Germany had a navy of sufficient strength, the British could not take any risk of antagonizing her. If they did, and fought, then the inferior German Navy would so seriously damage the Royal Navy that it would subsequently fall prey to some lesser power. That being the case, the British could not risk war with Germany. What Tirpitz wanted, of course, was respect; what he was using to get it was blackmail. Neither he nor the Kaiser had the perception to realize that what they could get for the asking— British friendship (what they already had, to a great extent)—they could not enhance by bullying. There were other fallacies in his view as well. He assumed that he and the British were operating in a vacuum, and it apparently never occurred to him that instead of being fearful of the third or fourth powers, Britain might simply ally with them and upset his entire calculation, even though Britain publicly did that, with Japan, as early as 1902. Also, he completely underestimated British determination to stay on top. When pounds came to marks, the islanders could afford a naval race more than the Germans could. The German Navy was only an expensive toy to the great continental power with its already huge and expensive Army; the Royal Navy was the be-all of existence for the British Empire. Tirpitz' views, and the mistakes they were rooted in, did much to set the stage for World War I. The British decided they would match Germany ship for ship; if necessary they would build two to her one. As grabbing colonies was the great game of the 1880s and 1890s, building war fleets was the excitement of the new century. Between 1900 and 1906 Great Britain completed 29 battleships.

The race not only meant newer ships, it also inevitably meant bigger and better ones as well. There was an enormous spur to naval design and technology, so that ships, once good for fifty or more years—*Victory* was forty years old at Trafalgar—were now obsolete the minute their design was completed, and in many ways ineffective by the time they were in service. The Admiral class of battleship, of 1884, between her gunnery and her protection, probably could have sunk every ship before her, and the Magnificent class battleships of the mid-1890s could have done the same to the Admiral class ships. There was thus a whirlwind of change sweeping through the world's navies.

This destabilizing influence was epitomized by Britain's most famous sailor of the time, Admiral Sir John Fisher, the First Sea Lord from 1904 to 1910 and again in the early years of World War I. Fisher was a true stormy petrel, a visionary, a radical innovator, a bitter fighter, and an unforgiving hater. Under his domination the leisurely ways of the old Navy were given up. Supported by an enthusiastic band of young reformers, he dragged the Royal Navy kicking and screaming into the twentieth century. His most famous project was the all-big-gun ship, the dreadnought.

Up to this time all battleships had had mixed armaments, to deal with opponents at varying ranges. The *Mikasa,* for example, Admiral Togo's flagship at Tsushima, had four 12-inch guns in her main battery, fourteen 6-inch in a secondary, and twenty 3-inch guns as well, so she could fight at close, intermediate, and long range. Soon after the turn of the century, however, as better methods of directing and controlling gunfire became available, the idea began to dawn that if a ship had all big guns, she would not need the smaller ones. One battleship mounting, say, twelve 12-inch guns would be mathematically the equivalent of three *Mikasas.* With central gunnery control and presenting less of a target, she might even be the equivalent of four or five of them.

On the face of it, it was not in Britain's interest to introduce the all-big-gun ship and in this way throw aside the advantages of her vast existing fleet. But what choice had she? The great Italian naval designer Vittorio Cuniberti was known to be working on such a ship, and in 1905 the United States authorized the building of two examples, *South Carolina* and *Michigan.* Fisher decided to leap in; one of his favorite expressions was *totus porcus* (whole hog), and now he went at building the new ship furiously. Her design called for a ship of about 18,000 tons with 5,000 tons of armor and ten 12-inch guns mounted in five twin turrets. Her speed was to be 21 knots. Fisher had all the material collected in advance; H.M.S. *Dreadnought* was launched a mere

130 days after the keel was laid and completed in 14 months, an incredibly short time. The American ships, by contrast, were not finished until 1910, so they were 5 years from conception to completion. But Fisher not only wanted to show the world a new type of ship, he also wanted to show the world how fast Britain could build when she chose to. So let Admiral Tirpitz—and anyone else who happened to be interested—take note.

With that the building race was really on with a vengeance. Britain and Germany were like poker players each convinced he held a winning hand. Each power turned out more and more dreadnought-type ships, the older battleships now being downgraded as "pre-dreadnoughts." By 1912 the British had gone up to the "super-dreadnought," with 13.5-inch guns. Fisher also introduced the battle cruiser, heavy guns on speed and light armor, on the theory that "anything she couldn't outfight, she could outrun; anything she couldn't outrun, she could outfight." In August 1914, when the Grand Fleet went to war, the Royal Navy possessed twenty-two modern dreadnought-type battleships as well as ten battle cruisers. Germany had seventeen battleships and five battle cruisers.

Outbuilding the Germans was but one aspect of the new competition. The other was the alteration of the existing diplomatic order. By the end of the first decade of this century, the world was divided into armed camps. Great Britain moved in this direction much more hesitantly than she did with respect to the naval race, but the end result was the same: to place her in confrontation with Germany.

As isolation began to look less splendid, there were several possibilities for the British. They might seek alliance with any of the other naval powers, or any of the major continental powers. They might also strengthen the ties of Empire, and they would have preferred to do that. Unfortunately for them, the other parts of the Empire did not wish to surrender their growing independence to some larger form of imperial union.

In the later nineteenth century, federation of the various overseas dominions was the order of the day. British North America once again led the way, and in 1867 their various colonies—Nova Scotia, New Brunswick, Quebec, and Ontario—joined together to form the Dominion of Canada. In many respects this was a cast of desperation, for the middling compromises of the 1840s had broken down, Quebec and Ontario were at loggerheads, and it looked as if British North America might simply succumb to an expansive United States. The movement for federal union that began in the Maritime Provinces soon spread to the St. Lawrence area, and in March 1867 the Parliament at Westminster passed the British North America Act, Canada's constitution for the next 115 years. Shortly thereafter the new federal government bought out the territorial holdings of the old Hudson's Bay Company, vast tracts from which were eventually organized the provinces of Manitoba, Alberta, Saskatchewan, and the Northwest Territories. British Columbia joined the union in 1871; little Prince Edward Island held out until 1873, and Newfoundland, always looking eastward, refused to have anything to do with the new creation. Gradually Canada assumed more and more control of its own affairs, as well as the character of a halfway house, no longer quite British, but certainly not American. The special status of the French in Quebec was guaranteed by law, and if they could not be digested as a people, it looked as if they would be absorbed in the larger English federation. The early verdict on the new dominion was that federation was likely to be a success.

It thus became more or less a norm for contiguous white-dominated colonies. New Zealand was federated in practice, by a slow evolution, in 1875. In Australia, the movement toward federation had the same impulses as in Canada. Whereas the United States appeared a potential threat to the latter, so the German annexation of part of New Guinea upset the former. From the mid-1880s there was a growing federation movement, and on January 1, 1901, the Commonwealth of Australia came officially into existence. On that date there was still bitter war in South Africa, but in 1910 the various colonies of that area joined together, in a closer union than the other federations, and the Union of South Africa was born. The Boers, who now preferred to call themselves Afrikaners, took to politics as readily as they took to war. They managed to get equal status with English for their own language, and to keep everyone happy, the capital of the union was spread around, with the legislature at Capetown, the executive government at Pretoria, and the high court at Bloemfontein.

Federation and constitutionalism were also applied, as much as local conditions would permit, to the nonwhite dependencies of the Empire. India and Burma were under a common administration, and the provinces of Malaya were united in the Federated Malay States in 1896. Though it was difficult for Englishmen to foresee a day when nonwhites would approach the degree of self-government possessed by Canadians or New Zealanders, there was nevertheless a general sense that this was the way the Empire was going to develop. In some distant future the Empire would consist of a series of greater or lesser dominions, possessing a common language, law, and set of traditions. The whole concept remained necessarily ill-defined, but the British were convinced, with considerable justification, of the value of their ideas and the rectitude of their intentions. They knew what was best for the world, and in the fullness of time, the world would benefit from their wisdom.

To many it seemed a shame that the dominions should grow more distant as they grew up, and there were attempts among the supporters of the Empire to find some method by which the emergent states might be kept within the fold. In 1884 the Imperial Federation League was founded in London, its president the liberal Quaker W. E. Forster, whose name was meant to ensure that this was not simply another jingoist organization. Unfortunately for the cause, the members of the league could not even agree among themselves on just what they meant by federation; it was obviously one of those things better left ill defined. About all the league could decide was that there ought to be closer ties among the units of the Empire. Even that was very nearly too much, for such closer ties could be worked out only in a way that meant greater control by the mother country of the children. Like all adolescents, the children were extremely reluctant to surrender their increasing independence. The plain fact was, the colonies were growing up, and no platitudes in London were able to disguise the matter. The Imperial Federation League did not last a decade.

Its high point was the Colonial Conference of 1887, when representatives from all the colonies gathered in London. There was much banqueting, a great many exotic costumes, and a plethora of speeches extolling the virtues of harmony and closer cooperation, but there was little of substance to come out of it. Lord Salisbury, the Prime Minister, made the opening address and alluded to the desirability of a customs union, but this was, after all, a free-trade empire; he also made noises about a defensive union, but no one wanted to spend much money for defense at the time. Royal Naval officers diligently pointed out the desirability of a unified imperial Navy, but the Canadians were cool to that. The Australians and New Zealanders did express some willingness to contribute—this was soon after the German scare over New Guinea—but when they finally did give money for a squadron, they insisted it be stationed in their part of the world, which was not at all what the British had in mind.

In 1894 a conference was held at Ottawa, hosted by the Canadian government. The premier of New Zealand wanted the Empire to embark on a program of blanket annexation of every possible island in the Pacific, but the British were not willing to go that far. These more ebullient ideas gave way to practical ones of an imperial penny post, "all-red" cable routes around the world, and steamship connections among the dominions. Three years later, for the Diamond Jubilee, they tried again. The Colonial Secretary, Joseph Chamberlain, the swashbuckling "Brummagen Joe," brought imperial federation out of the back closet. And once again the dominions demurred; only Tasmania and New Zealand expressed interest. The Canadian Prime Minister, Sir Wilfrid Laurier, did not see Canada as a subordinate of Great Britain, no matter how federation might be phrased. As the Americans had become a distinct nation a century before, so the Canadians were becoming now. The ties that bound were not going to be expressed in red tape.

But they might well be expressed in red blood. However independent the dominions thought themselves to be, when the South African War broke out, they hastened to respond. More than twenty-two thousand colonial soldiers fought the Boers for Britain; some thousands of them died in South Africa, and in general they established a highly enviable reputation as brave and self-reliant campaigners. It was the contrast between the colonials' ability and the helplessness in the open of the average metropolitan Briton that led Lord Baden-Powell to found the Boy Scouts. By the 1900s the British thought they could probably count on the dominions if and when a crisis came. But they knew too that if they wanted formal allies, they were going to have to look elsewhere.

Part of their problem, of course, was that they were not entirely certain they *did* want allies. Classically, it went against the British grain to tie themselves to any other power, and to that extent, to lessen their freedom of action. This was not as good a time for Britain as post-World War I nostalgia made it seem. There was considerable social distress, there was perpetual trouble over Ireland, the old Queen passed away, and there was something of a breakdown in Parliament itself as the House of Lords fought against the progressive diminution of its power. With domestic events preoccupying Britons, their foreign policy was offhanded and vacillating.

Britain did not at first realize that the advent of the German Empire had radically altered the European scene, and for many years the

British persisted in regarding France as the principal enemy. This was, of course, reinforced by the French themselves, talking theoretically of commerce warfare, setting off invasion scares, meddling at Fashoda. It finally took Delcassé at the Foreign Ministry to realize that France and Britain must now be allies. He was the first man in a position of authority who both understood the new order and acted upon it. To the British, France had always been the enemy, at least since 1688, and that was as far back as anyone cared to go. Had they gone back even farther, they would have seen that no one country was the "traditional" foe but rather that whoever was the dominant land power of the Continent was the enemy. In other words, for two centuries Britain had opposed France not because of something inherently wrong with Frenchmen, but because France was the greatest power in Europe. After all that time, Britons were as slow as Frenchmen to perceive that this was no longer the case. By the end of the nineteenth century, Germany was the strongest power on the Continent, and the logic of Britain's opposing her had to fight against the age-old habit of disliking the French. Ironically, Britain would have preferred almost any other ally to France. Germany, Austria-Hungary, and Italy were together in the Triple Alliance after 1882, and the islanders flirted with that. But in the end, she sided not with these traditional friends but rather with her ancient enemies, France and Russia. One might say that logic won over habit, but that, while correct, would be inaccurate, for Britain's entry into the alliance system turned out to be anything but logical.

The process began after the Franco-Prussian War. The great German Chancellor, Otto von Bismarck, having unified Germany and proclaimed her empire, then set out to make his world secure. For a while he managed to keep France isolated and to ally Germany with both Austria-Hungary and Russia. These latter two, however, were enemies in the Balkans. Bismarck realized he could not juggle them indefinitely, and in 1879 he chose Austria; she and Germany formed the Dual Alliance. Italy's adherence to it in 1882 transformed it into a Triple Alliance. Meanwhile, though this was the primary orientation of his policy, he did manage to keep the Russians friendly by a series of subsidiary treaties. Germany married Austria but kept Russia as a mistress. In 1890 Kaiser Wilhelm II dismissed Bismarck and took over direction of Germany's policy himself. As the Kaiser was not nearly as clever as Bismarck was, he rapidly and thoroughly alienated Russia. The cast-off mistress was therefore available on the market, and she was soon courted by France.

For twenty years the French had been isolated in Europe, all their potential allies tied to Germany; now, with Russia free, the French moved adroitly. Both countries were developing a well-founded paranoia about Germany, and when a French naval squadron visited Cronstadt in 1891, the two discovered they had a great deal in common. Correspondents might chuckle at the Autocrat of All the Russians standing at attention for "The Marseillaise" or at determinedly republican French musicians puffing through "God Save the Tsar," but within little more than a year of the Kaiser's stupidity, France and Russia had agreed to be friends, and by 1893 they had an effective military alliance. At this point, then, the five great powers had drawn their prospective battle lines. From then on the question was twofold: one of refining their commitments, which they successively did, and the other of what was to become of Great Britain.

The accession of Britain to either system would result in that side's being substantially stronger. Of the two possibilities, the British definitely favored the German side, but they were gradually moved toward the French both by the stupidity of the former and the calculation of the latter. In 1891, when the Kaiser visited London in state, there was talk of Britain joining the Triple Alliance, but nothing came of it. Lord Salisbury and the Kaiser had long and intimate conversations during the yacht race week at Cowes in 1895. But neither man cared for the other—Wilhelm later even wrote to his grandmother telling her how nasty her Prime Minister was—and the talks only accentuated the misperceptions each country had of the other. From there, things got worse; there was the Kaiser's telegram to President Kruger after the Jameson Raid. After that and above all, there was the naval race, which increasingly soured and embittered relations between the two countries.

By contrast, the French were sweetness itself. Delcassé became Foreign Minister in June 1898; he thus inherited the Fashoda Crisis, which broke just three months after he took office. But he got out of that by a gracious yielding. Of all the European powers, the French were the most restrained in their reaction to the Boer War. In 1902 Britain allied with Japan; the Anglo-Japanese Alliance historically marked the abandonment of British isolation, but at the time it looked like a mere local affair, less significant than it has subsequently appeared. The French again soft-pedaled the matter.

The great breakthrough came in 1903. King Edward VII made a state visit to Paris. As he had been Prince of Wales virtually forever and had been denied by his mother any real voice in public affairs, he had often visited France as more or less a private citizen during all those years when he was "the first gentleman of Europe." In fact, in some quarters he was known as "Edward the Caresser." Now, appearing in an official capacity, he charmed a French citizenry and press that had been prepared to be more than hostile to him, and he departed having created an aura of good feeling. A few months later, President Loubet, accompanied by Delcassé, returned the visit, and within a year these contacts had borne fruit in the Anglo-French Entente. Outstanding differences were settled over the British in Egypt and the French in Morocco. The French gave up their ancient claims on the shore of Newfoundland in return for fishing rights there, and the negotiators made deals over African claims, Madagascar, Southeast Asia, and islands in the Pacific. With their long-standing disagreements resolved, the French next turned their efforts to bringing their allies the Russians together with the British. This was to be a tall order, for of recent years Anglo-Russian antagonisms had been even more bothersome than Anglo-French ones. By 1907, however, they had turned the trick, and the British and Russians agreed to settle their differences over Persia, Afghanistan, and Tibet, and to help each other with regard to various limiting naval conventions. The lion had not quite laid down with the lamb, but it had gone to bed with the sheep and the goat.

In all this the French were immeasurably helped by Kaiser Wilhelm. He was no more certain than anyone else exactly what an entente was, and in his clumsy efforts to find out, he inevitably drove his potential enemies closer together. In fact, it was largely German ineptitude that transformed the entente into a de facto alliance.

The first German effort to put Anglo-French relations to a test resulted in a full-grown crisis that mixed together all the tangled skeins of imperialism, navalism, and the tortuous European diplomacy of the period. One of the areas over which Britain and France had reached agreement was Morocco; the French had for many years aspired to incorporate this unattractive but strategically located sultanate in their growing North African Empire. With British agreement, they moved early in 1905 to do so. A negotiator visited the Sultan and presented him with suggestions for reform that would, if accepted, have turned his country into a French protectorate. Delcassé had cleared this already with Britain, Spain, and Italy. Since the Germans had announced they were not particularly interested in the area, he did not bother to inform them of what he was up to. Such neglect on his part could be taken as a violation of the gentlemen's agreement on the partition of Africa, and the Germans chose to see it in that light. Chancellor von Bulow and Foreign Minister von Holstein decided to take umbrage over this slight and not at all incidentally to try to break up the entente by showing Britain she had backed the wrong horse.

Accordingly, the Kaiser was induced to interrupt a Mediterranean cruise on his yacht and make a sudden descent on Tangier. Mounted on a white charger he had difficulty controlling—the Kaiser had a crippled arm and did not like spirited horses—he paraded through the city, showered the Sultan with profuse expressions of undying friendship, and pointedly insulted the French consul. The resulting crisis ran along merrily for a year. Delcassé was sure the Germans were bluffing and wanted to develop British offers of support, prompted by their fear of a possible German naval base close to Gibraltar. But the French government failed to share Delcassé's view, there was something of a panic in Paris, and he was forced out of office. The upshot of the whole imbroglio was a conference held at Algeciras in Spain, in which all the powers except Austria sided with the French. Baron von Holstein lost his job, so between him and Delcassé, one could conclude that Germany conceded the game after an exchange of rooks. During the conference the British launched the *Dreadnought,* and a month later, Germany decided to increase the tonnage of its new battleships and widen the Kiel Canal to accommodate them.

This First Moroccan Crisis—there was a second in 1911—began a series of upheavals that lasted until the outbreak of World War I. The details and the locations varied, but the results of all of them were substantially the same. The major powers were more and more firmly embedded in their alliance systems; they increased their armaments at an accelerated rate, and they gradually ran out of maneuvering room. In 1907 Russia and Britain reached an accord, and Britain and France began military conversations. In 1908 the Bosnian-Herzegovinian crisis blew up, and the Russians were humiliated by Austria, backed by the Kaiser flourishing his "mailed first." In 1909 the British increased their naval appropriations, to the tune of crowds in Trafalgar Square chanting, "We want eight, and we won't wait!" The people got their wish, and eight dreadnoughts were laid down that year; but in 1910 the Germans completed four and authorized three more. The next year saw the Second Moroccan Crisis, and war clouds were palpably gathering.

It was in response to this crisis that David Lloyd George, hitherto one of the most ardent antimilitarist politicians, stood up in the Mansion House and declaimed, ". . . if a situation were to be forced upon us, in which peace could only be preserved by the surrender of the great and beneficent position Britain has won by centuries of heroism and achievement, by allowing Britain to be treated, where her interests were vitally affected, as if she were of no account in the Cabinet of Nations, then I say emphatically that peace at that price would be a humiliation intolerable for a great country like ours to endure."

So it went. All over Europe there were stirring invocations of national honor and greatness; few could doubt that sooner or later there would be a war, and this time a big one, not one of these silly little things such as broke out in the Balkans in 1912 and flared up again in 1913. Against this backdrop the soldiers and sailors made their plans. Britain still did not have a formal alliance with France and Russia, only an understanding, but for the military people that understanding was very far-reaching. The army agreed to transport a British Expeditionary Force across to France and come in on the French left flank. The French General Ferdinand Foch, asked what was the minimal acceptable British contribution, replied, "One British grenadier, and we'll make sure he gets killed!" The Royal Navy agreed that the British would guard the eastern Mediterranean, the French the western part of it, and the British Grand Fleet would hold the North Sea and the Channel.

The summer of 1914 came, day after day of glorious, sunny weather. It was an exciting time. In March Paris, and all Europe, were rocked by scandal when Madame Joseph Caillaux, divorced wife of the Finance Minister, marched into the offices of *Le Figaro* and shot the editor for publishing her love letters. In London in May the House of Lords rejected a bill to give the vote to women, and Commons passed Irish Home Rule, so that for the next several weeks Britons were excited over the possibility of civil war in Ireland. U.S. Marines had occupied the Mexican port of Veracruz. Charlie Chaplin starred in *Making a Living,* and James Joyce published *Dubliners;* the Socialists were holding a European Congress in Paris. On June 28 a Bosnian student assassinated Archduke Francis Ferdinand of Austria and his wife as they toured the provincial town of Serajevo; most people were too busy enjoying their own affairs to pay much attention to this.

Slowly it dawned on ordinary men and women that this was it, the big crisis had come at last. The Austrians decided that they had had enough of Balkan harassment, and they were going to clean up Servia once and for all. The Russians, humiliated by the events of 1908, were determined to back their clients the Servs; "Serv" carried the connotation of "servile," so Western newspapers began calling the place "Serbia" instead. If the Russians backed the Servs/Serbs, the Germans decided to back the Austrians. Therefore the French had to back the Russians. All of a sudden, so quickly that no one could really pause for thought, the alliance system went into a spin and sucked practically everyone into its vortex. Right to the end the British thought, mistakenly, that they had some residual freedom of action, but they were wrong. On August 3 Germany declared war on France and invaded Belgium; Britain, declaring herself bound by her guarantee of Belgian neutrality, but in fact tied to France, declared war on Germany the next afternoon.

The British Empire responded with an enthusiasm not seen since the last war, in South Africa. Australia and New Zealand both offered to send troops even before war was declared. In Canada Sir Wilfrid Laurier, no longer Prime Minister, gave his party's unconditional support for the war to Robert Borden's government. Talk of civil war suddenly died in Ireland, and the Indian princes offered their money and their men unreservedly. There was not even much discussion, for as the Canadians phrased it, "When Britain is at war, the Empire is at war." Britain was pleased at the response but thought it largely academic; the war would probably be over by Christmas. The Grand Fleet was already at sea. No one recognized that on August 4 the old world had ended.

PART FOUR

THE TWILIGHT OF EMPIRE

When all the experts were proven wrong, as of course they shortly were, when most of those first eager young men were lying face down in Galicia, or along the heights of the Aisne, or blind or legless in hospitals, then the war became serious. Unfortunately, citizens and subjects did not at that point rise up and repudiate the politicians and generals who had led them cheering over a cliff; instead they lined up at banks to buy war bonds, and at recruiting stations to enlist for King and country. If the Great Adventure were not to be over by Christmas after all, then everyone would be able to do his bit. With the pathetic confidence that only a century of peace and security can engender, Europeans rushed to war. Seldom in human history has a society advanced to its own destruction with a more hopeful mien.

It was because the war did not end in the predicted eight to twelve weeks that seapower and empires became important. The essence of navies is that they give a country staying power. Had the war gone as it was supposed to, the Royal Navy would have had relatively little to do with the outcome, and the rest of the British Empire would never have had time to become involved at all. The Germans intended to win the war by a vast single-wing envelopment of the French and a rapid redeployment and crushing of the supposedly inferior Russians. The French and Russians, without giving the matter all the thought it deserved, intended to win more or less by crashing straight through the Germans and meeting somewhere around Berlin. None of these ideas worked; both the French and Russians were defeated along their respective frontiers, and the Germans, after overrunning most of Belgium and northern France, were stopped, exhausted and stretched too thin, along the Marne River east of Paris. By October, when the war should have been ending, both sides were digging in and the struggle was turning into a contest between troglodytes; it was less a vast battle than a vast siege, though very few of the generals who directed it actually realized that. For the next three years they went on vainly throwing men against prepared positions, hoping each time that they would break through into open country, reestablish a war of mobility, and bring the fighting to a successful conclusion. They failed dismally; flesh and blood were not stronger than barbed wire and machine guns. But their failure was not due to lack of trying or of willingness to accept losses. Month after month, year after year, they battered away, and they virtually wiped out a generation in the process, a wanton waste whose only redeeming factor was the sublimity with which the wasted accepted their fate. Not for four terrible years did a break come, until new ideas and mutual exhaustion created conditions that allowed the war to be won and lost.

Given this immense deadlock, the silent, unrelenting pressure of seapower did its slow but deadly work. Navies by themselves seldom win wars; what they do is create the conditions in which wars can be won. That was the role of the Royal Navy, with some help from its Allies, in World War I. It was not a war winner—though it might at two or three points have been a war loser—but its distant presence created conditions that eventually allowed those millions in khaki and horizon blue to win their war on land and bring the Central Powers, defeated at last, to the surrender table.

In spite of all the technological changes, the advent of the dreadnought battleship, the torpedo, mine, and submarine, it was surprising that the Royal Navy had to do the same old thing. The sea had to be kept clear for British uses and denied for German uses. That was all there was to it. It was all there had ever been to it. As Napoleon said, the art of war is very simple; everything lies in the practice. The Royal Navy's tasks therefore were to contain and blockade the main German fleet, to hunt down and destroy minor units that were at large from time to time, and to keep the sea lanes open to the Empire and the rest of the world. Only once during the entire war was the Navy's ability to do this seriously called into question, by a new and dangerous weapon that came close to winning the war for Germany.

As the Germans expected to win the war on land before seapower could be a factor, it was initially of little import to them that their strategic naval position was markedly inferior. The British both outnumbered them in all categories of warships and held immense advantages of position. The German North Sea coast was ringed in by British bases, from the traditional Channel ports in the South of England, up along the eastern coast of Scotland to far northerly positions, where the Grand Fleet took up its battle stations at the barren anchorage of Scapa Flow in the Orkneys. German warships made no attempt to interfere with the passage of the British Expeditionary Force over the Channel to France. The German leaders did not see the B.E.F. as any threat to their plans. In fact, when the Germans advancing through the Low Countries made first contact with the British, they did not know who they were; they were still ignorant of the fact that the British had crossed the Channel. The German High Seas Fleet was the Kaiser's toy, and he was not going to risk losing it for nothing; after all, it took far longer to build a battleship than the Germans expected to take to win this war. To their formidable handicaps of geography the Germans added yet another one: the fact that the Kaiser insisted on playing admiral.

Yet the British problems were almost as great as the Germans'. In July and August, as war loomed, the Royal Navy had staged a practice mobilization for summer maneuvers, so the Fleet was manned and ready. Admiral Sir John Jellicoe assumed command the day war was declared, being ordered to replace the elderly admiral who had competently run the Fleet until that moment. But Jellicoe could not produce the sort of instantaneous victory the public had come to expect of the Navy; indeed, he said that he had no intention of trying to do so. The margin of strength was not so wide that he could afford great risks. He could not take his fleet steaming boldly into German waters, over mines and submarine traps, looking for trouble. He must wait for the Germans to come out, then catch them at sea. When they refused to sally forth, a frustrated Royal Navy could only sit and wait. The Grand Fleet was Britain's shield, but it looked like a shield against which no one was striking any blows.

As the Germans declined to play their allotted role, it was up to the British to trap them. Under modern conditions that proved extremely difficult. In late August, the British tried. They had returned the island of Heligoland to Germany in 1890, after holding it since the Napoleonic wars. It now functioned as a guard for the North Sea entrance to the Kiel Canal; British submarines scouting the area noticed that the Germans relieved their patrol ships on a regular basis. Commodore Roger Keyes, commanding the subs, suggested the German forces might be lured off and then mousetrapped by a surface sweep. The Admiralty agreed and sent out a cruiser force under Commodore Reginald Tyrwhitt, supported by battle cruisers. Then at the last moment they altered the plan, without telling the participants, and sent out a second battle cruiser force, led by Admiral David Beatty. Meanwhile, the Germans, suspecting that this might be in the wind—both sides consistently listened to each other's radio traffic, and decoded just enough of it to confuse the issue—planned a trap of their own, with cruisers to back up their destroyer patrols.

The result was that several dozen ships, from submarines to battle cruisers, barged into each other in the early morning of August 28. There was a wild melee, and several times the British nearly fired on each other, ignorant as individual units were of their total strength. Yet they did have the superior numbers and firepower, and they came off the winners, sinking three German light cruisers and a destroyer, inflicting more than a thousand casualties for losses of but thirty-five British sailors. The Navy kept to itself the deficiencies revealed by the battle; to the public at large, watching the German juggernaut roll inexorably across northern France, the skirmish appeared a reassuring reminder that the Royal Navy was still master of all it surveyed.

The Germans seemed to agree, for they did not come out again in any numbers for five months. By then the Western Front was in a stalemate, with trenches extending from the Channel coast to the Swiss border; on land there was a hiatus between the frantic battles of 1914 and the even more frantic ones of 1915. The German naval staff ordered Admiral Hipper, commanding their battle cruisers, to scout the Dogger Bank in the hope of trapping British ships there, essentially a reversal of the Heligoland action. By now, however, the British knew the German codes; the Russians had recovered their code system from the hulk of a sunken cruiser in the Baltic and turned it over to the Admiralty. For the rest of the war, British naval intelligence deciphered German signals. Therefore, when Hipper appeared off the Dogger Bank with three battle cruisers and an older armored cruiser, Beatty showed up with five battle cruisers. The biter was bitten.

Hipper sighted the British at about twelve miles' distance and wisely discovered pressing business at home; he turned his ships around and ran for his base. Beatty took up the pursuit, and his huge ships—the three leaders, *Lion, Tiger,* and *Princess Royal,* known to the Navy as the "splendid cats"—worked up to full speed, plowing along, thirty thousand tons of steel at thirty knots, great gouts of spray and smoke flying from them, battle ensigns whipping at the mastheads, the very picture of British seapower. They began to overhaul the Germans, especially the older, slower *Blucher,* and *Lion* opened fire, ranging on the last of the German line. It was only nine in the morning, and Hipper was in for a very long day unless something happened to rescue him. Soon the action was general, with British and German ships firing at long distance; the British, however, made a mistake in their fire distribution, so that for some time the second German ship, *Moltke,* was unhit. She was thus able to concentrate her fire on Beatty's flagship, *Lion,* and by midmorning *Lion* was slowing and losing power. The Germans too had been badly battered, but only *Blucher,* at the rear, was in serious trouble. About eleven she swung out of line, battered and on fire, and limped away from the battle. At the same time, *Lion*

was hard hit, and she too was forced to drop out of the action. Beatty
hoisted a flag signal, "Course northeast; engage the enemy rear."
In the smoke of battle, with the flags hard to see and the enemy indistinct, the following battle cruisers misconstrued Beatty's intent; magnificently they swept on by the wounded *Lion*, turned northeast, and
pounded the already sinking *Blucher* under the waves while Hipper
and his three battered battle cruisers got away to fight another day.
The famous photo of *Blucher* rolling over while her crew scrambled
over her sides was little compensation for the fact that the British
should have had all four and had to settle for a weak one. Beatty was
furious. So was the Kaiser; he replaced his fleet commander and ordered his new admiral to be more cautious in the future. It was more
than a year before the Germans came out in force once again.

On the broad seas, the details were different, but the results were
the same. German ships and squadrons at sea when the war began
were accounted for, though often with much pain and many errors.
There were two in the Mediterranean, the battle cruiser *Goeben* and
the light cruiser *Breslau;* in what looked like a comedy of errors but
was actually a failure of diplomatic Intelligence, the British missed
these, and they got safely to Turkey, where they entered the Dardanelles and anchored at Constantinople. British relations with Turkey at
that moment were touchy. On the outbreak of the war the British had
seized a Turkish battleship building at Armstrong's in Newcastle, renamed her *Agincourt,* and commissioned her for the Royal Navy. The
battleship, paid for in part by Turkish schoolchildren's pennies, was an
expression of Turkey's new national pride, which was thus mortally
affronted. The Germans capitalized on this error by handing over their
two ships officially to the Turks; *Goeben* eventually became the long-
est-living of the World War I-vintage ships, for the Turks kept her
until the 1960s. When Turkey entered the war on Germany's side, it
was attributed to these naval matters, though in fact the pro-German
ministry had agreed to a German alliance even before the war began.

If the loss of Turkey to the Allied side was a diplomatic failure,
the sequence of events around South America could be laid squarely
on the Admiralty's doorstep. In August 1914, Admiral Graf von Spee
had the German Pacific Squadron on a training cruise in the Caroline
Islands. Spee detached the cruiser *Emden* to raid in the western Pacific
and Indian oceans, and himself headed for the coast of South America,
hoping to find rich pickings among the many British ships on that

route. Magnified hundreds of times by gunpower, armor, and speed, his squadron was a modern equivalent of those frigates and privateers the French or Americans used to send out against British shipping. During the War of 1812 the American frigate *Essex* had wiped out the British whaling industry in the same waters Spee was now heading for.

Meanwhile, the Admiralty sent a small mixed squadron under Admiral Sir Christopher Craddock down to the Falkland Islands. The political First Lord of the Admiralty, Winston Churchill, was an amateur strategist and kept bombarding Craddock at long range with confusing and often contradictory signals, orders, and suggestions. Craddock's biggest ship was an old slow pre-dreadnought, the *Canopus,* and when he left the Falklands to seek out Spee he simply left her behind. On the afternoon of November 1 the two squadrons met off Coronel, on the coast of Chile. Spee had five cruisers—two armored, one protected, and two light; Craddock had two armored, a light cruiser, and an armed merchantman. The Germans here had the best-trained ships in the Imperial Navy; they had superior gunpower and speed and modern, centralized direction control. As if they needed anything more, they were indistinct against the haze of the Chilean coast, while the British were clearly silhouetted against the evening sky. Soon after six, Craddock sent his last radio signal: "I am going to attack the enemy now."

The next hour and a half was less a battle than a ritual execution. The cruiser *Good Hope,* Craddock's flagship, was blown up after taking some thirty hits. The other armored cruiser, *Monmouth,* was reduced to a battered hulk; with no guns and little power left, she refused German summonses to surrender, turned her bows to them, and vainly tried to ram before she was sunk. The light cruiser *Glasgow* and the armed merchant cruiser *Otranto* slipped off in the darkness. At the cost of two men wounded, Spee had wiped out two cruisers and seventeen hundred men.

He had also used up half his ammunition, however, and while he went off to Valparaiso to celebrate his victory, the British got themselves straightened out. Churchill, who insisted he had nothing to do with the disaster, was determined to make amends for it. He sent a major squadron under Vice Admiral Sir Doveton Sturdee careering south all the way to the Falklands. Sturdee arrived at Port Stanley to coal ship late on December 7; he had two battle, three armored, and two light cruisers, and he was there the next morning when Spee arrived to destroy the radio station.

Had the Germans borne right in, they might have caught the British at a disadvantage, for they were in the midst of coaling; instead, Spee ran for it. The British were soon at sea, and their battle cruisers, with an eight-knot advantage, rapidly overhauled even the fastest Germans. In this case, the battle cruiser could both outrun *and* outfight its adversary, and one after another the Germans were caught. *Scharnhorst* and *Gneisenau,* the two armored cruisers, were sunk by Sturdee's big ships while the other cruisers took their opposite numbers. The *Kent,* the black sheep of her class, steamed after the German *Nurenberg; Kent* had never done more than twenty-one knots, but now her stokers performed wonders; they even tore the woodwork out of the old tub to feed her fires, and she inched up to twenty-four knots, overhauled the German ship, and sank her in a private battle. By the end of a long day, Spee's squadron no longer existed. One collier was interned in Argentina, and the *Dresden,* hunted off the seas, was blown up at Juan Fernandez, off the Chilean coast, three months later.

The Germans did not have another squadron at sea, but they did have various independent ships, which functioned as raiders and which required an inordinate effort to track down. The most famous of these was probably the *Emden,* which Spee had detached as he sailed eastward. Captain von Muller entered the Indian Ocean in September and at one point was such a ubiquitous threat that the Australian and New Zealand governments held up the sailing of their troopships to Europe for fear of him. He captured several merchantmen, and he bombarded an oil tank farm at Madras, setting off spectacular fires in an attempt to show the Indians the British were not as good as they thought. He scraped his hull at the lonely island of Diego Garcia, where he was careful not to tell the isolated British inhabitants that the war had started; he sank a French destroyer and a Russian cruiser in Penang Harbor; and he then decided to destroy the cable station at the Cocos (Keeling) Islands, south of Sumatra.

He showed up there on November 9 and sent a landing party ashore. However, the radio operators had time to signal that a strange ship was approaching, and by German bad luck, there was an Australian convoy only fifty miles to the south. The Australian cruiser *Sydney* steamed up to investigate and caught the *Emden.* A brand-new cruiser with six-inch guns, *Sydney* simply stood off out of the German ship's range and pounded her to bits.

So it went; the half-dozen raiders the Germans had at sea did a great deal of damage and caused considerable inconvenience, but they lacked the numbers, and above all the support facilities, to have more than nuisance value. The British might have to send out twenty searchers to find one ship, but they could do it, and they did. One by one the raiders disappeared—interned, blown up, trapped, or sunk. By the end of 1914, as the dominions were ready to send their sons to Europe, the Royal Navy had cleared the seas for their passage.

During four years of war, Great Britain and the rest of the British Empire mobilized 8,904,000 men. Of those, 908,000 were killed or died of sickness, 2,090,000 were wounded, and 191,000 were taken prisoner or reported missing, or 35.8 percent casualties. This compared, of the major Allies, with a high of 76 percent for Russia, 73 percent for France, and a low of 8 percent for the United States. Among the European parts of the Empire—that is, Britain itself and the white-dominated dominions—there were no striking disproportions. Of every person in Britain—men, women, children—one in nine went abroad to war, and of those who went, one in seven did not come home. Of the six who returned, two had been wounded. Canada and Australia both sent to Europe one in fifteen of their populations, almost 500,000 Canadians and more than 300,000 Australians. New Zealand and South Africa both sent one in ten—a little less and a little more than 125,000, respectively. Of all these young men who went overseas to fight, one in twenty South Africans was killed, one in eight Canadians, one in six New Zealanders, and one in five Australians. The Canadians fought exclusively on the Western Front; the Australians and New Zealanders, or Anzacs, in the Middle East and in France; the South Africans in Africa and France; and Indians in the Middle East, East Africa, and France as well. It was an outpouring that would have astonished those who, a generation earlier, had watched the Imperial Federation League founder for lack of interest, and the statistics did not even begin to tell the story.

Canada had steadfastly refused to take part in prewar schemes for a larger imperial defense. She had founded her own Navy, ostensibly independent, in 1911, but had not gone very far with it. The dominion government had accepted the principle of compulsory military service for home defense but had done nothing to implement the idea. There had been some interest in the militia movement at the turn of the century and after, but the government was extremely reluctant to spend any money on it, Prime Minister Laurier blandly remarking that Canada was protected by the Monroe Doctrine. By 1908 the Canadian

Army—the Permanent Force, as it was called—numbered a grand total of 2,730 men. But by 1914, there existed on paper organizational schemes to turn the militia into six divisions, and there were close to fifty thousand part-time soldiers, many of whom had trained at their own expense and bought their own equipment. It was these amateur soldiers who became Canada's contribution to the war. This, of course, was true for all the Empire, for Britain alone among the great powers had rejected the idea of conscription. The professional British Army itself was virtually wiped out in the opening months of the war, and most of the vast struggle was fought by temporary soldiers.

Canadian mobilization proceeded through immense confusion. It started in total chaos and never got much beyond controlled anarchy, thanks to an energetic Minister of Militia, Colonel Sam Hughes, who started the process by scrapping all the carefully laid-out plans and doing everything in his own inimitable way. Nonetheless, on October 3, 1914, two months after the declaration of war, the first Canadian division set sail for England, thirty-three thousand men in thirty-two transports, with a Royal Navy escort. Princess Patricia's Canadian Light Infantry entered the line on January 4, 1915. Eventually there was a full corps of four divisions, and by the end of the war it had a Canadian commander, Sir Arthur Currie, one of the best workaday soldiers of the war.

The colonial and imperial troops soon established reputations as elite units, jealously maintained and bitterly won. Each of the dominions had its own epics—Second Ypres and Vimy Ridge for the Canadians, Delville Wood for the South Africans, Beaumont Hamel for Newfoundland, and Gallipoli for the Anzacs. It was at Second Ypres, in April 1915, that the Germans first employed gas in an attack on the Allied positions. No one was prepared for it; French Intelligence had picked up something, but as they did not know what to do about it, the field commanders simply left their troops in ignorance. When the gas rolled over them, the French territorial unit on the Canadian left gave way and left a huge gap in the Allied line. The Canadians, choking, vomiting, trying to breathe through urine-soaked handkerchiefs, desperately held on, often surrounded and fighting blind, until finally a line was stabilized behind them.

But their true mettle was shown not in defensive battles but in attacking. The most spectacular Canadian triumph came in April 1917, when the Corps, operating as an autonomous national unit, attacked and overran the German line on Vimy Ridge, clearing the way for the Battle of Arras. Vimy had been fought over several times before this and was thoroughly entrenched by the Germans. The attack was a small set piece, carefully constructed and meticulously planned, though such words hardly seem applicable to the confusion, noise, and pain of battle. After the war the Canadians put their war monument, the most beautiful of all those sad memorials, on the crest of Vimy, and when, in later years, Charles de Gaulle demanded the removal of Canadian and other NATO troops from French soil, he was asked pointedly if that included all those Canadians who had died to keep France free.

Vimy Ridge at least was a victory. The young men of Newfoundland were virtually wiped out in the first day of the Battle of the Somme. The Newfoundland Regiment was one of two nonmetropolitan units involved in that terrible day. Slated as a follow-up battalion in the push toward Beaumont Hamel, the Newfoundlanders attacked at midmorning over open ground with no supporting fire. In 40 minutes they lost 658 men and every officer out of a total strength of 752. They never even got to the German wire. July 1, 1916, was the worst day British arms had ever suffered, with 57,000 of the Empire's best young men, the volunteers of "Kitchener's Army" casualties at the end of it.

Yet the Somme battle went on for four and a half months. It came nearest to success, if any such butchery could be considered a success, in mid-September, when the South Africans took Delville Wood. The Germans were at their last gasp, and for a few moments, British horse-cavalry threatened to break through to open ground between Delville and High Woods. But the supports were too slow, the Germans put down artillery and launched a desperate counterattack against the South Africans, and for hours the South Africans fought frantically to hold open the path to that elusive victory. All in vain; when the fight died down for lack of human fuel, the German line was there again, and the South Africans were as shattered as the wood, youth and pride and manhood gone with the splintered trees and blasted topsoil. The course of the trench line in France contains some of the richest soil in human history, fertilized with blood and bone, but little grows on it even now.

Calvary for the Anzacs was far distant, along the rocky ridges and dusty slopes of Gallipoli. When Turkey entered the war on the side of the Central Powers, it put pressure on the Suez Canal and denied the Allies one route to get supplies to Russia. Prompted largely by Winston Churchill at the Admiralty, the British decided to force the strait of the Dardanelles, thinking by this to knock Turkey out of the war.

The Navy tried early in 1915, but it failed by a narrow margin. Churchill then talked the Army into a landing on the Gallipoli Peninsula, to take the Turkish gun positions in the rear and open the way for the ships. The assault was made on April 25, with British troops landing at the tip of the peninsula, and the Australians and New Zealanders up the coast a few miles at a place subsequently called Anzac Cove. Fighting was desperate and confused, and by the end of the first day the Turks had managed to contain the landings. The Gallipoli Peninsula became a miniature Western Front, a stalemate in which neither side could move.

It stayed that way for the rest of the year, with both sides occasionally making sallies and launching attacks. Around Anzac Cove the Turkish and Anzac trenches were so close that troops had to roof them over to be safe from hand grenades; in some spots, one side of the parapet would be Australian and the other side Turkish. In August the British made a last futile attempt, but it went as sour as all the previous ones had done, and soon after the new year the peninsula was abandoned, the troops leaving behind much of their materials and their dead comrades in the one successful move of the entire campaign.

The Dardanelles was a peculiarly galling affair, because the British had long considered that they knew all there was to know about amphibious warfare and that it was their particular forte. For years they had told themselves they needed only a small army because of the mobility conferred upon it by seapower. Now they found that their earlier successes had resulted from lack of opposition rather than from their own abilities. Their Indian Army already knew that. In November 1914, their troops had attempted an opposed landing at Tanga in German East Africa and been slaughtered by German machine guns as they came ashore. They did better in the Persian Gulf, where Indian forces were a major component of the drive toward Baghdad and indeed throughout the British Middle Eastern campaign, right up until Allenby's dusty soldiers marched into Jerusalem in December 1917.

The civilian populations that had so cheerfully sent their men off to war found it almost harder to bear the endless strain than the soldiers did. By the middle of the war there was hardly a family in Britain or the rest of the Empire that had not had some tragedy connected with it because of the war. The manpower pools began to dry up, and the various governments, spurning the occasional murmurs for a negotiated peace, began facing up to conscription. The war had become Leviathan, consuming those who nurtured it, and the greater the sacrifices already made, the more it demanded. Leaders claiming to speak for the dead demanded that those millions of deaths not be in vain; somehow victory must be wrenched out of all the waste and sorrow, and so the war went on.

The conscription problem threatened a crisis in every part of the Empire where it arose. In Britain itself Prime Minister Asquith's government backed into it, losing much of its credibility in the process, and produced such a muddled scheme that its success was highly arguable. By stating certain occupations to be absolutely essential, the conscription legislation may have kept more men out of the Army than it brought in. Officially all men from eighteen to forty-one were liable to call-up, though the government promised not to send anyone under nineteen overseas—a promise it broke in 1918. There was enormous dissatisfaction that the law did not apply to Ireland, and the whole issue became closely tied with the fact that on Easter Sunday in 1916, a handful of Irish nationalist extremists rose up and seized the Dublin post office, thinking in that way to start the great rebellion. The British easily put this down—the post office was not, after all, the center of power in Ireland—but they then fumbled whatever chance they had of a statesmanlike solution to Irish problems. Asquith was a gentleman, but no one ever accused him of being a statesman, and his government was doomed anyway. He was soon to be replaced by David Lloyd George, a politician of harder metal.

Overseas, the conscription issue was even more serious. No one had any objection to being drafted for home service; it was thought only appropriate. But to be drafted overseas raised fundamental questions about the nature of one's state, its independence, and its relation with the mother country. New Zealand made little fuss; the people there were the most British in the Empire outside Britain anyway. In Australia, however, there was a great deal of argument. The Australian Labor Party was in power; its leader, William Hughes, was a noisy, radical imperialist. Hughes visited France in the summer of 1916 and came home advocating overseas conscription. Yet the party was split; a vast number of its members were Irish Catholics with no love for Mother England, and though they were intensely proud of Australian military prowess, they were reluctant to send men to Europe who did not wish to go. When the government held a referendum on the issue late in 1916, Hughes was defeated. Though he remained premier after reshuffling his cabinet, he never could get overseas conscription through, and Australia had to rely on volunteers for the entire war.

The problem similarly dogged Canadian politics. The early effort there had been voluntary but unequal. By 1916 nearly four hundred thousand Canadians had already gone overseas, but official estimates were that about half of them were Canadians who had been born in Britain, and of the other half, fewer than thirty thousand were French-Canadian. Quebec had never had the influx of Europeans the rest of Canada had, and Francophone Canadians had almost universally descended from the old settlers dating before the English conquest of 1759. Europe was very distant to them; they felt little tie with France and less with Britain. If English Canadians wanted to go home to fight for their Mother Country, that was their business. English Canadians, however, insisted that the war was Canada's, not just Britain's and not just theirs, and they insisted that French Canadians bear a hand. The government had badly bungled the matter from the start. In 1914, for example, it appointed an Anglican bishop to control recruiting in Quebec; English was the Army's language, and it took the personal intervention of Sir Wilfrid Laurier to get the Army to set up a French-speaking unit, the Royal 22nd Regiment, popularly famous as the "Van-Doos." Prime Minister Borden, like Hughes of Australia, came home from a visit to the front in 1916 convinced that conscription must come in. He introduced a bill for it in the summer of 1917. Quebec was solidly opposed, so were the farmers and the labor unions, but the Liberal opposition split, and the bill carried handily. It did more harm than good. By the spring of 1918 there were anticonscription riots in Quebec, and farmers demonstrated angrily in the streets of Ottawa when the government dropped their exemption. Of all Canada's war effort, a mere sixty thousand men were conscripts, and few of them went overseas, a meager gain for the bitterness the act engendered at home and the split in the always-fragile unity of the confederation.

The war caused even more trouble in South Africa, for here the union was but a few years old, and memories of the Boer War were still fresh and bitter. The government, headed by a former Boer general, Louis Botha, agreed to support Great Britain but only at the expense of alienating the more intransigent Afrikaner nationalists. South African forces soon moved into German Southwest Africa but had to be called back when some of the old diehards rose up, thinking this was their last best chance to get rid of the British. They found instead that times had changed. The most famous of the pro-British Boers, Jan Christiaan Smuts, destined to be one of the postwar imperial statesmen, handily put down the rising. The horse commando was an anachronism now, when faced with armored cars and machine guns, and all the Boers got out of it was a few more martyrs to add to the Afrikaner saga. South African soldiers went on to do much of Britain's colonial fighting in Africa, taking over former German colonies, with the aid of thousands upon thousands of black Africans serving as carriers and workers during the little campaigns.

One of the reasons that conscription became such an issue was that the war brought full employment and prosperity to much of the Empire. War is the greatest consumer of goods, money, and services, as well as of men, yet devised. Canadian farmers and lumbermen and Australian ranchers were all at full stretch, for modern war demands everything—iron, steel, barbed wire, cans, hospital dressings, pit props for trenches and mines, canned corn beef, tea, boots, and on and on. The infant manufacturing industries of the Empire outside Britain got an enormous shot in the arm from the demands of the war, and the basic extractive industries got even more. Day after day the ships loaded in Montreal and Halifax, in Sydney and Auckland, in Madras and Bombay and started their voyages toward the all-devouring heart of the war. Here the value of the great seaborne Empire was truly revealed. By itself Britain was an important but geographically small part of the world. Supported by the rest of its Empire and all the resources of plains, jungles, mountains, and seas, it was the most formidable of the world powers. As long as those resources remained available, the titanic struggle in France could continue. The task of the Royal Navy was to keep those vital arteries open. The Germans, with their surface raiders, had significantly failed to cut them off. As the war progressed, however, they found another weapon. In the submarine, Germany discovered the commerce raider par excellence, and with it she very nearly won the war.

The idea of the submarine had been around for centuries, but more of the early ones went down than came up again. In the late 1800s designers began developing submarines that worked. The first one commissioned was the *Gymnote,* in France in 1888, and Italians and Russians were also experimenting with possibilities. But major credit for the first submersible usually goes to an American, John P. Holland. In 1895 the U.S. Navy gave him a contract to produce a boat called *Plunger.* Holland was obviously a better designer than he was a businessman, for he learned so much with this boat that he gave the Navy its money back and built instead the *Holland,* commissioned in 1900. By the start of the war all the major navies had submarine forces, though no one was sure exactly what to do with them. Their introduction had been prompted by concurrent naval development; by 1905 or so it seemed that the only way a torpedo craft could survive to deliver its weapon at effective range was if it were underwater. The submarine was therefore seen more as an adjunct to the battle fleet than as a weapons system in its own right. No one, for example, considered that it would be used against merchant shipping. Civilized states simply did not sneak up on noncombatants and sink them without warning. Commerce raiders of the period were expected to abide by what were known as the "cruiser rules," in which a raider must warn her prey, board her to make sure the cargo was a legitimate contraband, and then sink her only after making satisfactory provision for the safety of crew and passengers. Such rules would be impossible for submarines, but no one expected submarines to function in that fashion anyway.

Certainly the Germans did not. In 1914 they had but forty-five U-boats, fewer than half the British had, and less than France or Russia or even the United States had. The role the Germans projected for their submarine force was as scouts for the battleships, or as an outlying force to weaken the British before a major engagement. On September 22, 1914, the submarine *U-9* caught three old British cruisers—*Aboukir, Hogue,* and *Cressy*—patrolling on the Broad Fourteens off the Dutch coast. When the *Aboukir* was hit, the other two thought it had been an internal explosion and immediately stopped to rescue survivors, whereupon the German sub sank them as well. The effect of this was something of a U-boat panic in the Royal Navy; every floating log became a periscope, and the entire Grand Fleet withdrew from the North Sea and took up temporary quarters in Northern Ireland. Panicky though it was, this action was not as silly as it might look; at the time there was absolutely no defense against submarines, no detection devices, no depth charges, nothing. The only way to destroy a sub was to catch her on the surface and ram her, and this in part explains why Admiral Jellicoe was so determined to fight a cautious surface campaign and preserve his marginal numerical superiority over the High Seas Fleet.

The belligerents' failure to win the war as rapidly as they had expected led inescapably to its widening. In November the British declared the entire North Sea a war zone, and the Germans soon countered by declaring all the waters around the British Isles a war zone. With no surface vessels capable of getting out for independent action, however, the Germans could do little to make good their new policy. In February 1915, after very heated discussion among military and naval leaders, they announced a "submarine blockade." Admiral von Tirpitz himself was against this escalation; for one thing, he did not think the Germans had enough submarines to make it work. He was also worried about the possibility of American intervention. As the greatest neutral, the Americans immediately protested that such a blockade was illegal, and the Germans hinted they would call it off if the Americans could induce the British to modify *their* blockade. This, of course, the British refused to do, as the blockade was their most effective weapon. The German campaign began in late February.

It was not very successful, for they really did not have enough ships to make it work. In addition to that, the British tightened their own blockade, using German actions as an excuse. The war at sea escalated in a two-tracked way, each side developing new and more terrible weapons, each justifying their introduction by reference to what the other was already claimed to be doing. As the Germans struck without warning, the British produced listening devices, depth charges, decoy ships, and aircraft patrols. The British expanded the contraband list, and the Germans extended the war zone, and so it went.

The greatest shock in the process came on May 7, 1915, when *U-20* sank the Cunard liner *Lusitania* off the Old Head of Kinsale, south of Queenstown. Her loss was shrouded in charge, countercharge, and controversy that has only recently been cleared up by British researchers. The German embassy in New York had warned passengers not to sail in her; the Admiralty failed to provide escorts as she entered the war zone, and Churchill, the First Lord, had speculated publicly on the propaganda value for Britain if a large liner carrying neutrals should be sunk with major loss of life. When the Germans obliged, there was a huge storm of protest. The Germans responded with the technical defense that the *Lusitania* was in fact a merchant cruiser and that she was carrying substantial amounts of ammunition. The British heatedly denied the charges, which were true. Of the almost 1,200 lives lost, 128 were American, and the United States took a very hard line with Germany. President Woodrow Wilson sent a strong note of protest, though it was notable that his Secretary of State, William Jennings Bryan, resigned rather than be what he considered a British catspaw.

The submarine campaign continued until August. Then when *U-77* sank the *Arabic* with the loss of three more American lives, the United States threatened to go to war. The Germans backed off; though Tirpitz had by now become converted to the idea of submarine warfare of this type, the submarines were not really making sufficient headway to offset the outrage of neutrals. Britain had launched more tonnage than she had lost in the six months' campaign, while Germany had lost more U-boats than she had commissioned since the war began. At this stage, therefore, the best policy appeared one of conciliation. The Germans promised to behave, and they turned their undersea attention to the Mediterranean, where there were both rich pickings and fewer American vessels. At this stage, the Germans still believed they could afford a choice of options, so by the end of 1915, the submarine effort was downgraded. There was a short-lived resurgence in early 1916, while the Kaiser and his advisers vacillated. In March *U-29* sank the French Channel steamer *Sussex;* there were Americans aboard, and the government in Washington again protested. This time the Germans promised exemplary behavior, issuing what came to be known as the *"Sussex* pledge." Admiral von Tirpitz resigned as naval minister, the commander of the High Seas Fleet was also replaced, and the Kaiser and his merry men decided to try conventional surface war again.

By the spring of 1916 the blockade was really hurting Germany. The British had closed off most third-party access, they controlled all the major sea routes to the Continent, they had their tentacles deep in all the neutral countries. American firms trading with the Germans, for example, were politely told that if they continued to do so, they and their suppliers would be blacklisted. As American prosperity was by then intimately tied up to the war effort, and especially to the Allied war effort, this sort of threat was fairly effective. At sea the British licensed, inspected, and often impounded cargoes, and did to Germany much the same as they had done to Napoleon. The Americans protested all this, too, but their protests to the British over seizures were definitely and naturally less forceful than their protests to the Germans over sinkings. The war on land had apparently degenerated into a wretched, brutal stalemate, while the British were slowly winning the war at sea.

At this time the chief of the German General Staff was General Eric von Falkenhayn. He had been in office since the failure of Germany's original war plans, and though history usually does not give him the highest military marks, he was one of the few soldiers in the war to perceive clearly the directions it was taking. He recognized that Germany was besieged and that the war was a contest of staying power, a war of attrition. He was on the verge of trying his greatest effort to break France, in the Battle of Verdun. But he was frustrated by the Kaiser's reluctance to employ his great battle fleet. Here, after all, was the force that had done so much to antagonize Britain and bring her into the war, and what had it done since 1914? Precious little, except sit in harbors while the enemy's blockade slowly grew more and more strangling.

This frustration was fully shared by the Navy's leaders; it was not their fault they were kept in port, as they continually pointed out to anyone who would listen. In January 1916, when Admiral Reinhard Scheer took over command of the High Seas Fleet, he immediately began pressing the Kaiser for permission to act, and in early February, the Kaiser reluctantly assented. The Battle of Verdun was in full swing; the *Sussex* sinking was a month off; if Scheer could somehow trap and destroy, or even heavily damage, the Grand Fleet, if he could get control of the North Sea the entire complexion of the war would change. If he could not, he was no worse off than he had been before. Along this line of reasoning, the Germans began moving toward the greatest dreadnought battle in history.

Nothing could have pleased the Grand Fleet more. Admiral Jellicoe had worked his ships and squadrons up to a fine pitch of readiness; if anything, they were overtrained. They had longed for the appearance at sea of the German main units and an end to the constant alerts and fruitless sweeps in the rough waters of the North Sea. The Royal Navy was perfectly conscious that it was doing the job it was supposed to do, but it was equally aware that its effort did not seem particularly effective when the British Expeditionary Force was suffering the long agony of war in the trenches. Seapower had taken a quarter century to defeat revolutionary and Napoleonic France; if it took that long to strangle Germany, there would be few British left by the time it was over. Jellicoe had several times tried unsuccessfully to lure the Germans out to battle. By the spring of 1916 both fleets had blood in their eyes.

Action picked up in April, when German battle cruisers threw some shells into Lowestoft. In late May the British planned a seaplane attack against the German coast, but it was spoiled by bad weather. Then at the end of the month the High Seas Fleet came out, intending to spring a full-scale trap on the British. Their radio traffic gave away part of their intentions, and late on the afternoon of May 30 Jellicoe ordered the Grand Fleet to sea.

The battle fleet left Scapa Flow and was joined later by Admiral Jerram's battleships stationed in Cromarty Firth. Meanwhile, Admiral David Beatty took the battle cruiser force out of its base at Rosyth. Jellicoe had ordered a rendezvous of the two bodies for the late afternoon of May 31, fifty miles southwest of the southern tip of Norway, fifty miles off the coast of Jutland on the Danish Peninsula. Taken together, the Grand Fleet was the mightiest armament ever to sail the seas. The British had one seaplane tender, seventy-nine destroyers, twenty-six light cruisers, eight armored cruisers, nine battle cruisers, and twenty-eight battleships. None of the latter was a pre-dreadnought; they had guns from twelve inches up to the fifteen-inchers of the new Queen Elizabeth class, and any one of the twenty-eight battleships could have wiped out the Spanish Armada or the entire fleets of both sides at Trafalgar without suffering a scratch. The names they bore rolled down the centuries—the first *Vanguard* had been commissioned in 1586, the first *Temeraire* in 1694—and reeked of the Empire and past glory: *Agincourt, Emperor of India, Canada, Revenge, Invincible.* Ships bearing these names had ruled the oceans of the world when Berlin was a mud-streeted village and Prussians were still chasing each other around the Baltic swamps.

Admiral Scheer's High Seas Fleet was more than a David facing this Goliath, however. When his Scouting Force under Admiral Hipper was combined with his main battle force, he too had a formidable array, sixty-one destroyers, eleven light cruisers, six pre-dreadnoughts, five battle cruisers, and sixteen dreadnoughts. His fleet has been assessed by experts as being numerically about a five to an eight for the British, but it was well equipped, in some respects better designed than its enemies', and it was as proud of its young traditions as the Royal Navy was of its old ones. Through spotty weather the two fleets, neither sure the other was out, approached their great meeting.

The battle on May 31, which the British call Jutland and the Germans Skagerrak, has produced endless argument as to who won and who lost, who made mistakes and who achieved what. Naval experts and historians playing detective have reconstructed as closely as is humanly possible the movements of each unit and even each separate ship and have agonized over the signals sent by captains and flag officers. In essence, the battle consisted of five distinct phases, like a perfectly constructed five-act play. There was the approach and contact, the run south, the run north, the main action, and the denouement.

At midafternoon of May 31, Jellicoe was seventy-five miles west-southwest of the Norwegian coast; Beatty, seventy miles southeast of him, was about to turn north for their assigned meeting. Scheer with his main body was a hundred miles north of his base at the mouth of the Weser, and Hipper was fifty miles ahead of him. That put Hipper forty-five miles east of Beatty. The British had preserved radio silence, so the Germans did not know they were out. The Germans had handed over their radio traffic to the guard ship back at base, so the British, though they suspected the Germans were out, were not certain of it.

Beatty's scout cruisers were seven miles ahead of him and five miles apart in a line twenty-five miles long—in other words, just within visual signaling distance. This formation used up fifteen of the forty-five miles between him and Hipper, and the latter's scouts were in an eight-mile arc in front of him, using up that much more space. Contact came when German destroyers from Hipper's left flank stopped and investigated a Danish merchantman and were thus spotted by H.M.S. *Galatea,* the scout cruiser on Beatty's left flank. She signaled "Enemy in sight," and Beatty's force took off after the German ship. As soon as they spotted Hipper, and he them, they raced on to engage; Hipper in turn reversed his course and led them down toward Scheer. The first act was over, the run south now began.

During this, which lasted roughly two and a half hours, from soon after two to nearly five, both sides pounded each other furiously. Visibility was not too bad; the British formation was awkward, as Beatty had been about to turn north when contact was made. It was unfortunate that his most powerful ships, the super-dreadnoughts of the 5th Battle Squadron, came into action last, for their fifteen-inch guns were badly needed. Both sides raced south wreathed in blowing smoke, with red tongues of flame lashing out at each other. *Lion,* Beatty's flagship, took a hit on her midships turret and was saved from blowing up only by the sacrificial flooding of the magazine by the men trapped inside it. The battle cruiser *Indefatigable* was less fortunate. At 4:05 P.M. she took two hits from *Von der Tann,* each on a turret. There was an immediate flashback from the turret down the ammunition hoists into the magazines, and two huge explosions literally blew her apart. Still going at full speed, she rolled over and sank, taking all but 3 of her 850 men with her. Twenty minutes later another salvo straddled the battle cruiser *Queen Mary;* an enormous fireball climbed up into the sky, and beneath it the great ship, thirty thousand tons, simply disappeared. Beatty turned to his flag captain, Chatfield, and produced a classic understatement: "There seems to be something wrong with our bloody ships today. . . ."

But the Germans were suffering as well, their fire falling off and increasingly erratic. When the 5th Battle Squadron came into action, its fifteen-inch guns did incredible damage, and though none of the Germans was sunk, all were fiercely punished. Hipper was relieved to see Scheer's main fleet breaking the southern horizon. The run south ended at about 4:45 P.M. as Hipper swung around and took up position leading the entire German fleet north.

During the run back north, the Germans were already counting their victory, for they did not know that now it was their turn to be trapped. Beatty played the role Hipper had just given up as he turned his ships around and headed for Jellicoe. The latter was steaming at speed toward the battle; no one was exactly sure of his position relative to anyone else, and it called for precise timing on the part of the British to get their main body deployed exactly right. Jellicoe handled it nicely. For over an hour, as Beatty led the chase north, British cruisers scampered off Scheer's bows, sending position reports and telling their admiral just what he needed to know. At six o'clock Jellicoe spotted Beatty off to his right front. Beatty swung his line around through north to easterly, while Jellicoe deployed his six columns of battleships, and Beatty fell in on his left. Between six-fifteen and six-thirty, a total of 140 ships passed "Windy Corner" as all the hitherto separate squadrons met.

Scheer, now steering northeast, herded around by Beatty, came out of the gathering fog and mist to find himself heading toward a semicircle of British steel. Jellicoe had achieved the classic "crossing the T," where all his guns could fire on the Germans, but few of the Germans could reply. The fifteen minutes between six-twenty, when the Germans appeared out of the fog, and six thirty-five, when they turned back into it, could be said to represent the culmination of surface naval warfare to that time. Scheer was fairly trapped, but the Germans remained formidable. Yet another British battle cruiser, *Invincible*, suffered one of those fatal turret hits. She broke in half and sank immediately, bow and stern rearing above the waves, shattered midsection resting on the shallow bottom, and the six survivors of her eight-hundred-man crew cheered crazily as the Grand Fleet swept majestically by her grave, pouring fire on the dimly seen Germans in the center of their arc.

Scheer could not stand this, no ships on earth could, and he ordered a sudden reversal of course, a simultaneous maneuver called a "battle turn away together." His rear became his van, and as suddenly as they had appeared, the German ships vanished into the smoke, mist, and fog. While light units covered their withdrawal, British range-finders searched the gloom for their targets. Adjusting his course, Jellicoe kept on.

If Scheer was now heading away from immediate destruction, he was also heading away from ultimate safety, away from his bases, so after twenty minutes he turned back once again, and a second time he blundered out of the mist into that deadly British line. Had it been a clear day with a westering sun, the High Seas Fleet would have been doomed right then and there. The British guns lashed out again; Scheer's leading battle cruisers were so badly battered they could hardly reply. Sending them and some destroyers on a death-or-glory attack to buy time, he turned away a second time. The Germans were swallowed up in the dusk, and the main action was over.

Jellicoe now took up a southerly course, intending to avoid a night action but to be between the High Seas Fleet and its bases early next morning. He put his heavy units in front and his lighter ones in the rear and settled down for the night. Scheer knew that the British were be-tween his fleet and safety, so he could do nothing more than order his ships to make for home, crossing through the British line as best they could. The night action thus took the form of an elongated "X," with the British sailing down one arm and the Germans down the other. Where they met at the middle, there was bitter night fighting, little flare-ups in which friend blundered into foe, ships rammed, and shots were made at shadowy forms in the darkness. The British heavy units displayed an amazing lack of curiosity about the distant noises and flashes to their rear; intercepted signals that would have tipped Jellicoe off to German intentions were not passed on to him by the Admiralty, and by an early dawn, the Germans were safe behind their minefields, and the Royal Navy steamed serenely along, master of an empty sea.

That was not the end of it, for the Germans claimed a victory. Outnumbered eight to five, they had inflicted casualties on the British in exactly that proportion, eight British for five Germans. As with the French of old, they seemed to think it was a victory just to have been able to sail on the same ocean with the Royal Navy. The Admiralty is-sued a somber communiqué, citing only heavy fighting and heavy losses, which seemed to confirm the German claim, and there was im-mense dissatisfaction in Britain, where the public since 1914 had been anticipating a total victory. Jellicoe had won nothing near that, but he remained, as Churchill called him, "The only man who could lose the war in an afternoon," and he had not done that either. On June 1, 1916, not quite a "glorious first of June," the Grand Fleet was still at sea and ready to fight; the High Seas Fleet was safe in port and lucky to be there. German sailors might still want to fight, but the next time these two fleets met would be November 1918, when the defeated Germans sailed into Scapa Flow to be interned.

With the one major German surface challenge met and matched, life went on as before. The great Battle of Verdun, Falkenhayn's attempt to "bleed France white," bled Germany nearly as badly as it did France. A month after Jutland, the British launched their offensive on the Somme, and well into the winter Germans and Allies ground away at each other. The Russians that summer made their greatest gains of the war, in General Brusilov's offensive in Galicia, but there again the battle died out before any real victory was attained. By the end of the year, with nothing to show but a couple million more killed and maimed, the war still rolled along.

There were changes, though. In most of the governments harder men, even more committed to a fight to the finish than their predecessors had been, had come to power: Lloyd George in England, soon Clemenceau in France, the generals themselves in Germany. Europe was exhausted, but there was little sign of flagging; governments demanded more rather than less effort, and their subjects obliged, resignedly if no longer enthusiastically. Things were especially hard in the civilian sectors of the Central Powers; the British blockade was now biting deep into the supply of goods from the rest of the world, and in spite of impressive "requisitioning" in conquered territories, things were still bad in Germany and worse in Austria-Hungary. The 1916–17 winter went down in common parlance as "the turnip winter." Servants disappeared into war industry as young men disappeared into the trenches; faces were pinched and clothes threadbare, and talk everywhere was of the war, the war, always the war.

No one could find a way out other than in some distant victory. New theaters had not worked; Gallipoli was long gone now; gas had not worked, the first tanks had done little. The Allies had bought Italian support in 1915, with no appreciable effect; they had talked Romania into the war in 1916, and the Germans had handily overrun the country and added its resources to their own. Peace proposals put forth by either side made such ludicrous claims that there was no common ground for discussion, and the more losses the powers suffered, the more inflated their claims grew. In France they tightened their belts and mourned their dead; in Britain they tightened the blockade and hoped for American help; in Germany they set up a Supreme War Council and looked for ways to break the stalemate.

There appeared to be only one remaining weapon, only one idea not yet fully utilized. In the early months of the war the Germans had sunk one British ship for every three submarines lost. Between improved techniques and progressive disregard for the prewar niceties, they had reversed that ratio to fifteen to one by late 1916. On the strength of such figures, the naval leaders predicted that they could win the war by starving Britain if they were allowed a completely free hand—if, in other words, they launched another campaign of unrestricted submarine warfare. The Army commanders, despairing of reaching a firm decision on land, gradually came around to the Navy's view. The civilian members of government, most notably Chancellor Bethmann-Hollweg, feared that such a move would bring the United States in, but they were shunted aside by the soldiers and faced revolt in their own ranks if they did not accede. At the end of 1916, the Germans decided to go all-out.

The naval reasoning behind this was predicated on several assumptions. Britain at the time had available almost eleven million tons of merchant shipping, but four million tons of it were under neutral flags. The German Admiralty estimated that ignoring training, maintenance, and rest for its crews, it could put enough U-boats at sea to sink six hundred thousand tons a month, or three million tons in five months. At that rate, Britain's economy would collapse at the end of the period. Neutral shipping would be driven from the seas, the British-flag tonnage remaining would not be sufficient to supply the island's needs, and England would be starved into surrender. Here were Admiral Aube's theories, put into practice by the submarine.

The fly in this ointment, or the flaw in the theory, was what such a campaign would do to the United States. Foreign Office objection had been based on the reasonable idea that if the Germans could not beat Britain, France, and Russia, they could not beat them plus the United States. The sailors had an answer for that, too. First of all, the Americans might not enter the war; so far they seemed eager only to stay out of it. Second, even if they did enter, they had but a minuscule Army, worth about two days' good fighting on the Western Front, so that was not worth considering; it would take them at least six months to build a respectable fighting force, and the Germans planned to win the war in a month less than that. Finally, even if somehow the war were prolonged until the Americans were ready to fight, the German U-boats would keep them from getting to Europe anyway. This particular line of reasoning, had anyone stopped to examine it, was suspiciously parallel to the line that Tirpitz had used in constructing his fallacious "risk theory," but the Germans were desperate. At the new year, they played what Bethmann-Hollweg called "the last card." With about eighty submarines around the British Isles, they announced the commencement of unrestricted submarine warfare for February 1.

For a while it looked as if it might work. Sinkings skyrocketed. Britain in 1916 had lost close to a million and a half tons of merchant shipping, slightly more than a hundred thousand tons a month. In the first three months of 1917 she lost nearly three times that rate, and in the second quarter of the year, with the German campaign gathering momentum, she lost more than four hundred thousand tons a month. One ship in four that left the British Isles did not return; Britain in fact was losing the war, and by June, when the crisis was reached, she was six weeks away from starvation. If the Germans could keep up the pressure, and if nothing else happened, Germany would win.

Something else happened, and the Germans could not keep up the pressure. In April the United States declared war on Germany. Though their initial military contribution was small and slow in coming, there were soon American ships operating with the Royal Navy; even more immediate and more important—for Britain was actually closer to bankruptcy than she was to starvation—American loans gave the Allies the financial resources they needed to keep going. Most important of all, however, the Royal Navy met and mastered the challenge of the U-boat. It now had new weapons, the hydrophone for detection underwater and the depth charge for destruction, and at last, in the convoy system, it found the saving grace to protect the merchant ships and offer them a fair chance for survival.

Convoys, some of several hundred vessels, had been a routine feature of sea life in the age of sail. For several reasons the Royal Navy had decided they were impractical in the steam era. Bunched arrivals and departures would clog ports and unloading facilities, targets would be gathered en masse for enemy surface raiders, the Admiralty could not afford to weaken its main fleet to provide escorts, merchant officers were thought incapable of station keeping, there were initially no anti-submarine weapons anyway, and on and on. Nothing is more vigorously defended by its supporters than a policy that has cost lives, so once having decided convoys would not work, the Admiralty steadfastly refused to budge. In spite of the plain fact that almost all of the imperial troops had reached the war zone in large escorted convoys, and done so safely, the Admiralty still insisted the thing could not be done.

Finally, however, faced with the stark fact that they were going to lose the war, officialdom gave in. A small band of devotees got political support from Lloyd George and help too from the newly arriving Americans, especially Admiral Sims, and the Admiralty reluctantly agreed to a trial convoy. The first one came safely through from Gibraltar in May 1917. Within four months the convoy system was in general operation, and German U-boat captains, instead of finding lone victims scattered over the ocean and waiting to be picked off, now found the merchantmen herded along behind a ring of little escort vessels. The crisis was past by fall, the Royal Navy still ruled the seas, vast numbers of Americans were arriving, and the German Navy had lost yet another gamble.

Bethmann-Hollweg had called the submarine campaign Germany's last card, but she now found she had yet one more. Not the least irony of the war was that in February 1917 Germany initiated a policy that brought the United States into the war; a month later, for practical purposes, Russia dropped out. Revolution began there in March, and by midsummer the Russian armies were in utter disarray. Now the Germans transferred their troops westward and hoped by a series of great offensives in France to win the war early in 1918, before massive American armies stifled their chance forever. On March 21, the Germans began their great spring offensive.

Once more, the German plan almost worked. Under the overall direction of General Erich Ludendorf, with his senior colleague Field Marshal von Hindenburg now the de facto ruler of Germany, the revitalized armies struck with hammer force. They were employing new tactics first used by Brusilov in 1916 and refined by the Germans against the Russians and then on the Italian front. With surprise, deception, shock troops, and short bombardments, they blasted a forty-mile dent in the British line. It looked like 1914 all over again, and it was only after desperate fighting by the exhausted B.E.F. that the Germans were finally halted. From March until August the Germans battered unceasingly at the Allies as Ludendorf mounted five offensives, each designed to support the last and pave the way for the next. But he could not quite find the formula for final, strategic success. The weary French and British held on, the Americans entered the line in increasing numbers, and by mid-July the newly appointed Allied supreme commander, Marshal Ferdinand Foch, was planning his war-winning counteroffensive.

Ironically, the very success of the Germans contributed to their defeat. The winter had been incredibly hard for them; half the babies born in 1916 died before the end of the war; in Acting-Corporal Adolf Hitler's regiment the troops ate cats during the 1917–18 winter. The only thing that carried them into those first great drives was the thought that the Allies were also reeling, and ready to collapse. They were amazed and appalled when they broke into the British rear areas only to find mountains of Australian mutton and Argentine beef and luxuries that had long disappeared from all but memory in Germany. German morale plummeted in the midst of their success, and the effect of those captured supply dumps was not the least of the Royal Navy's contributions to final victory.

On August 8 the Allies answered Ludendorf with a British attack at Amiens. Led by 450 tanks, they broke the German line and advanced eight miles on the first day. Some German formations crumbled with hardly a shot fired, and troops marching up as reinforcements were jeered by retreating infantry. This, as Ludendorf said, was "the black day for the German Army." Foch's overall idea was that he should mount a vast pincer movement, French and Americans attacking north from around Verdun, and British attacking east from their line up in Flanders. The Allies had three months' hard fighting ahead, but the issue was no longer in doubt.

For Great Britain, the tide barely turned in time. Marshal Foch had 220 divisions to work with; of those, 102 were French, 42 American, 12 Belgian, 2 Italian, 2 Portuguese, and 60 British. All but the Americans were old and battle-weary, and among the B.E.F., there had been a reorganization at the start of the year to keep the numbers up. Well over 100 British infantry battalions had been broken up and their men sent to strengthen other formations. Divisional numbers were maintained by reducing the troops, usually infantry, in each of them. Even so, of the 60 British divisions, 10 were from the dominions. The Canadians, Australians, and New Zealanders had refused to shuffle their units around—wisely so, for theirs remained the strongest among the British troops, and the imperial divisions were employed throughout the final offensives as shock assault troops. Australian General Sir John Monash, one of the greatest commanders of the war, had his corps fought out by September. They were thought to be the most reliable troops on the British front, and when they were finally reinforced, it was not by British, but by two new American divisions.

If there was one Empire formation in better shape than the Australians, it was the Canadians, for even during the spring crisis their government had resisted British pleas to separate the corps and use it to shore up British breaks. The Canadians had been throughout the war critical of British command and techniques. As far back as 1915, the Canadian Minister of Militia had answered a request for more troops with the remark that the way the British fought, he might as well send over steers as men. Later, the Canadians had flatly refused to fight under one army commander in whom they had no confidence and had been transferred to another army. By 1918, the four divisions of the Canadian Corps represented the best striking force in the B.E.F. When the great attack was delivered at Amiens, it was made by British on the left, Australians in the center, and Canadians on the right, and it was the latter two who made the deepest penetrations of the day.

From then on the hammer blows came thick and fast as the Germans wilted away. They still fought hard, but it was a despairing fight, and the prisoner count mounted increasingly. Allied supplies kept pouring in; the convoy system had long mastered the U-boat threat, and the dark days of early 1917, when Britain was losing the war at sea, were gone now. Thousands upon thousands of fresh American troops were entering the battle lines, and the Allies ground steadily ahead. The Central Powers collapsed all along the line. Turkey, Bulgaria, Austria-Hungary, and finally Germany begged for peace. There were riots at home; when the German Admiralty ordered the High Seas Fleet out on a last glorious sortie, the sailors mutinied and raised the red flag. With their armies literally falling apart, the Kaiser and his generals gave up; the Supreme War Lord took a train to neutral Holland and exile, and his military men asked for an armistice. Their defeated troops streamed back to the frontier, while Allied armies followed hot on their heels. On the morning of November 11, bagpipers played the Canadians into Mons, where the old B.E.F. had first met the Germans light-years ago, in 1914.

So it ended, but the victory had a hollow sound to it. The war had gone on too long and had cost too much. The frantic rejoicing, with an air of hysteria about it, was not so much for victory as for survival. Europe was war-torn and disrupted, families everywhere were broken and grief-stricken. Starvation and influenza raged, governments collapsed. Only war itself had won.

15

Weary Britain

This was one of those awful periods which recur in our history, when the noble British nation seems to fall from its high estate, loses all trace of sense or purpose, and appears to cower from the menace of foreign peril, frothing pious platitudes while foemen forge their arms.
—Winston Churchill

It was in January 1919 that the representatives of the powers met in Paris to make the peace. They faced awesome problems, not just from men, who had laid Europe in waste, but from nature as well, for the worldwide influenza epidemic was killing further millions, as if to demonstrate it was not to be outdone by the most destructive of its species. There were delegations there from twenty-seven different states, though some were conspicuously absent. The Germans were not invited, nor the Austrians nor the Turks. The Russians, who had given so much to Allied victory, were now busy fighting each other, and no one wanted to give credibility to the Bolsheviks by inviting them to a respectable gathering. The gaps among the states were made up by little groups of hopefuls who stood around the edges with their hands out—Czechs, Poles, Armenians, various Orientals, and sundry gentlemen from the Middle East. During the war almost all of these had been promised something by someone, and now, like shy but determined tradesmen in the presence of their social superiors, they sought to present their bills. Most of them were going to be told to wait their turn.

Notable in the second rank of powers were the delegations from the dominions—Canada, Australia, New Zealand, South Africa, and from the Indian Empire. At first Great Britain had thought she would

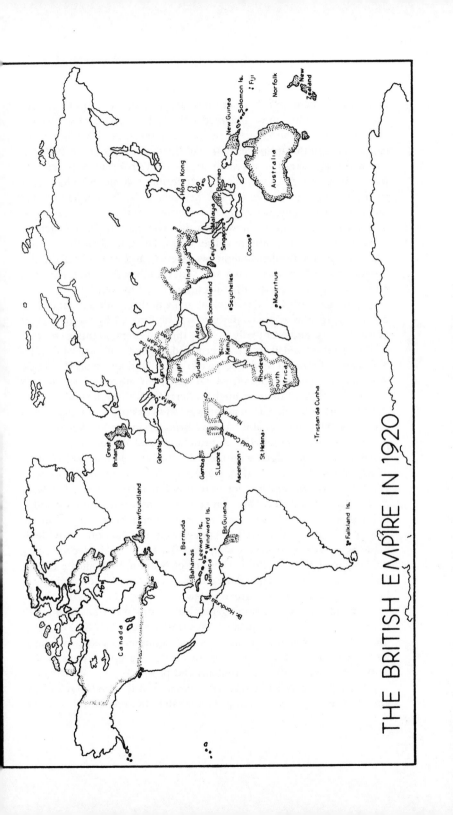

THE BRITISH EMPIRE IN 1920

take care of them and that her voice alone adequately spoke for the Empire. The other units disagreed politely but vehemently. Canada had too often seen her interests sacrificed on the altar of Anglo-American amity, and the antipodes both had their own aspirations. If Portugal, which had sent two divisions to the Western Front, was going to have a place at the peace table, so were former colonies who had functioned as major military powers in their own right. Britain had needed the dominions enough to create an Imperial War Cabinet at the height of the war; she could not now, with the crisis passed, expect them to revert to the colonial status of earlier times. The Canadian Prime Minister, Sir Robert Borden, fought his case so successfully that the dominions had it both ways: They sat as independent delegates, and they put representatives on the British Empire panel as well.

In terms of the broad settlement, none of this made a great deal of difference, for the whole conference was dominated by the four great power leaders, and eventually by only three of them. Premier Orlando of Italy soon subsided into a disgruntled minority of one, while Clemenceau of France, Lloyd George of Britain, and above all Woodrow Wilson of the United States tried to create their brave new world. Unfortunately, each of them wanted a different world, so the end product did not work too well. Clemenceau wanted to destroy Germany; Lloyd George wanted her rehabilitated as Britain's major market but had publicly committed himself to her ruination; and Wilson, a former political scientist, was filled with noble but regrettably impractical ideas of national self-determination, leagues of nations, and no more war. His lofty pronouncements not only infuriated his partners but were eventually repudiated by his own countrymen, leaving him a prophet not without honor, but what was worse, without a bargaining position. Wilson thought if he agreed to enough compromises on shady deals made by the Allies during the war, that all these would be redeemed by the League of Nations. But the League of Nations, without the United States in it, was a cripple, and the compromises proved more important in the long run than their greater object.

One of the most pressing general questions was what to do with the territories of the vanquished. Austria-Hungary had broken up at the end of the war into its more or less component parts, and these were all recognized as new states in central Europe. Germany and Turkey presented different problems and prospects.

Once Germany had conceded command of the sea to Great Britain, all of her overseas holdings immediately became hostages to for-

tune. Through the war the Allies had gathered in her colonies one by
one. Japan had attacked and taken her naval station in China, at
Tsingtao; the Australians and New Zealanders had immediately
moved to occupy Kaiser Wilhelmsland and the German islands of the
South Pacific. South Africa had overrun German Southwest Africa,
and British and other imperial troops had spent the entire war chasing
Colonel von Lettow-Vorbeck back and forth across East Africa. An
Anglo-French force had taken over Togoland and the Cameroons, on
the West African coast.

The Ottoman Empire, as it broke up, presented even better pickings. Though most of the effective fighting against Turkey had been
done by British and other imperial troops, this area was so crucial that
the French had to be given a cut. During the war the British had also
broadcast promises to everyone they thought might be useful to them,
the Italians and the Greeks, and the Jews and several conflicting sets of
anti-Turkish Arabs. These people not only hated the Turks, but they
also hated each other, so the Middle East provided the peacemakers
with a real witches' brew to divide up.

President Wilson had an answer for this; in Point Five of his famous Fourteen Points, which were supposed—by him—to be the basis
for a genuine peace, he had called for an impartial adjustment of all
colonial claims, with regard both for the colonial peoples and for the
governments that were then ruling them. On a broad construction, that
might be said to apply both to the victorious British and French empires as well as to the conquered German and Turkish ones. That was
certainly the construction the Germans had chosen to put on it, but of
course they were not around in Paris to press their point of view. The
other Allies insisted to Wilson that he was talking only of enemy territory, and the actual occupiers of that territory simply took the line
that they had taken it, and it was theirs, and they were going to keep
it, and what had the war been for, anyway, if not to get a bit of reward
out of it?

The deadlock on this—and it threatened to ruin the peace conference—was neatly sidestepped by Jan Christiaan Smuts. Smuts was
thought by his fellow Afrikaners to be a bit Jesuitical, a little too clever
by half, which may be why he became one of the leading men of the
Empire. He produced a solution to the colonial question that allowed
the conquering states to have the game while permitting the League of
Nations to have the name. Though the League might retain official
title to these conquered territories, they would be "mandated" out to

nearby states, who would administer and supervise them. The idea was certainly not new with Smuts; in fact, it had been kicked around at one international conference after another ever since Berlin in 1885, when the ground rules for the partition of Africa had first been drawn up, but Smuts is usually associated with its adoption by the Paris Peace Conference and its incorporation in the Covenant of the League of Nations.

The mandated territories were divided into three categories. The first, or "A," included the French mandates of Syria and Lebanon, and the British of Trans-Jordan, Palestine, and Iraq, and these were to be prepared for independence in the very near future. That took care of most of the former Ottoman Empire, allowing full independence for Saudi Arabia. Category B mandates were most of the former German African possessions, and these were to be treated as normal colonies— that is, kept under tutelage for the foreseeable future. Togoland and the Cameroons were divided between British and French; German East Africa went to Britain as Tanganyika, and the western part of that, as Ruanda and Urundi, was passed on to Belgium. Finally, there were Category C mandates; these in fact were the thorniest bits of territory; they were thought unlikely ever to achieve independence. In this class the Australians and New Zealanders got the German holdings of the South Pacific, the Japanese those in the North Pacific, and the Union of South Africa got German Southwest Africa. Given the tenacity with which the claimants pressed their case, it was painfully obvious that the imperialistic attitudes that had done so much to create the prewar crises were still as vigorous after the war as before it.

One thing absent from this imperial spoils system was any thought that the peoples concerned should be consulted on whether they wished to be ruled by Britain, or France, or anyone else. Wilson's original point was that due regard should be paid to the wishes of the colonial peoples, but even Wilson had not suggested how their wishes might actually be determined. The men of Versailles vigorously resisted Japanese claims, and Japan had been a more or less major ally. They were highly suspicious of the Chinese delegation, especially when it intimated that it wanted to raise questions about colonialism. And no one had any intention at all of listening to Ho Chi Minh, a Vietnamese pastry chef working in Paris, who produced a plan for the end of French colonialism in Indochina. In spite of everything they had just gone through, European leaders remained confident that they, and they alone, knew what was best for the remainder of the world.

But the remainder of the world was no longer so certain of that. Over the years Europe had done its work too well. In all of the non-white colonies or dependents there were arising young, Western-educated classes who had absorbed Europe's ideas and now believed that the time had come for them to go their own ways. Over the next generation, most of these men were going to complete their political education in British or French jails. The most important of them all was a homely little Indian named Mohandas Karamchand Gandhi.

India had made steady but very slow political progress in the half century since the Mutiny. There had been administrative reform and massive public works projects. In the forty years between the opening of the Suez Canal and the Great War, India's manufactured exports trebled. In 1885 a retired Indian civil servant named A. O. Hume founded the Indian National Congress, the first and for a time the only Indian political party. This was greeted with some enthusiasm by the Viceroy, Lord Dufferin, on the old ground that imitation is the sincerest form of flattery, but Dufferin soon cooled as the Congress became nationalistic in tone and demanded a greater share for Indians in their own governance. Almost from the beginning there was trouble between the Hindu majority and the Muslim minority, though it was not until 1906 that the rival All-India Muslim League was set up. From that time on, the Congress, containing the Hindus, claimed to speak for all of India, and the Muslim League, which was solely Muslim, ran a constant counterchorus of "What about us?" This was a dichotomy the British were never able to solve, and in the end their efforts to create a united India foundered on it.

Meanwhile, the British were proceeding on the old method of letting the locals into government at the bottom and having them slowly work their way up. There were elections to local legislative councils in the 1890s, but the Indians believed the British were content to move an inch a century, and the British believed the Indians would make progress eventually—but not quite yet. These conflicting views were vitally important, for the pattern they formed was to be repeated time and again as the colonies moved toward self-government. Small, educated, sophisticated local elites invariably equated their entire people with themselves and were anxious for power. The ruling British equally invariably regarded these elites as agitators and possible criminals and looked instead at the vast masses of docile peasantry or tribesmen and convinced themselves they must stay a long time yet.

In 1906 the Congress demanded that India be given dominion status; the Muslim League countered with the demand that there should be separate representation for them. So it went; in 1909 the British brought in the Indian Councils Act, popularly known as the Morley-Minto reforms, because Minto was Viceroy and John Morley was Secretary of State for India. The legislative councils were enlarged and given increased powers, and separate electorates were introduced for Hindus and Muslims. Congress leaders, secure in the knowledge that the Hindus were the vast majority, condemned the latter provisions as divisive. Their party had now split into moderate and extremist factions, and after some bomb-throwing, the government imprisoned the extremists. When the Great War came, most of India responded loyally; money was voted, and more than a million Indians served either as soldiers or as lines-of-communication laborers. The Muslim leaders protested against war with the Ottoman Empire, on the grounds that it was their spiritual home, and they went off to jail, too. By late in the war there was increasing unrest over high prices and taxes and over the military losses incurred by British bungling in Mesopotamia. The British response was the old familiar carrot and stick, a definite commitment to work for self-government, and two acts for the imprisonment without trial of anyone the government declared an agitator. At least both Congress and the Muslim League could agree on opposing that. At this point enter Gandhi.

Gandhi was born in 1869, in the port city of Porbandar, on the Arabian Sea. He came from an orthodox background but defied its prohibitions to study law in London, where he was inspired by Dadabhai Naoraji, the first Indian to be elected to the British Parliament. By 1893 Gandhi was making five thousand pounds a year as a brilliant lawyer in Bombay when he suddenly gave it up to go to South Africa, where thousands of imported Indian laborers were living and working in primitive conditions. Arnold Toynbee, projecting a pattern of behavior for great spiritual leaders, said they must all go through a process of "withdrawal and return," as with Christ in the wilderness. Gandhi's withdrawal lasted for twenty-one years, which he spent in South Africa opposing discriminatory legislation and arguing for the rights of Indians. He maddened the authorities, but he also served as a stretcher-bearer in the Boer War. Few people can be more infuriating than a principled politician whose principles do not agree with one's own. In 1914 Gandhi returned to India, where he supported the war effort and further developed his own maturing ideas of nonviolence, *satyagraha,* or "soul force," and ultimately of civil disobedience. By

1918, when some of the earlier Congress leaders had spent their force, Gandhi was coming to the fore, a man who combined a British education and background with a deeper current of Indian consciousness and who now believed that Europeans had lost their title to rule, that India must be independent. He was to prove a potent force indeed.

In response to the antisedition acts, Gandhi called for a one-day national strike and fast; his announced aim was to achieve *swaraj*, or home rule, within a year, and he believed that if the British were faced with unanimous noncooperation by Indians, they would have no choice but to pack up and go home. Gandhi himself was surprised at the numbers in which Indians answered his call, but the effect was not what he hoped. He preached pacifism, but many of his followers were anything but pacifist. Rioting broke out in many places and threatened to get out of hand. Up in the Punjab, in the city of Amritsar, on April 10, 1919, mobs killed five Englishmen and beat an English woman.

The local military commander in the city was General Reginald Dyer, and Dyer firmly believed that he was faced with a new version of the great Indian Mutiny. He was determined to stop the matter in its infancy, so three days later he marched his Gurkha troops into the city, surrounded a crowd in a marketplace, and sealed off all the approaches and exits. He then ordered the Gurkhas to open fire into the mass of Indians, which they did until they ran out of ammunition. Trapped in the square under withering fire, the Indians surged to and fro but could find no escape. When the Gurkhas finally ceased firing, the square was a sodden mass of blood and pain. Twelve hundred people were wounded and nearly four hundred were dead. Dyer believed he had done his duty, and many Englishmen, especially those in India, agreed with him. But the government was appalled, and the "Amritsar Massacre" became part of the legend of the Empire and reinforced the Indian conviction that it was time for the British to go. Dyer was rapped over the knuckles; and Gandhi, shocked by his compatriots' inability to handle nonviolence, called off his campaign for the moment. The events in India footnoted what the Great War had proclaimed in shouting terms: European rule was based on technology. As a young Chinese then studying Marx at the University of Peking was later to say, power comes from the mouth of a gun.

However unpalatable that idea might be to Gandhi, it was already well known in other parts of the Empire, and especially in Britain's oldest colonial failure, the unhappy island just across the Irish Sea.

Just before the start of World War I the British Parliament had at last passed a home rule bill, which caused open drilling and talk of civil war in the Protestant North; the Great War had shelved all such questions for the duration, as far as the British were concerned. The Irish believed differently, however, and it was that that set off the abortive Easter Rebellion in 1916. The truth was that history had created a situation in which there could be no clear winner; if the British continued the status quo, they would be hated by the majority of Catholic Irish; if they granted home rule—or worse, independence—they would be hated by the Anglo-Irish Protestants. The latter, though a significant minority in the whole of Ireland, were a substantial majority in the six northern counties. Their ancestors had owned plantations and manned military settlements there since the seventeenth century, and the Protestants had for generations adopted a garrison mentality. Their leaders preserved their privileges and their economic advantages, draped themselves in the Union Jack, beat the Protestant drum—"Home rule is Rome rule!"—and carefully played off one faction against another. Through all the years the Catholic Irish majority in all of Ireland had never been sufficiently clever, or articulate, or united among themselves to resolve this historical conundrum.

One of Britain's leading historians, A.J.P. Taylor, points out how ironic it was that of all the great states involved in World War I, it was only in Britain, consistently vocal in her insistence that she was fighting for freedom and democracy, that there was a domestic rebellion, the Easter Rising. The British government itself was conscious of its problem, and in little more than a year, most of the rebels had been granted an amnesty. In 1918, when the government moved to impose conscription on Ireland, it could not do so and had to rescind the act. At the end of the war, when Lloyd George held his "khaki election" and won a landslide victory, the Irish elected practically a full slate of independence candidates, pledged not to a British party, but to their own, Sinn Fein, "We Ourselves," a political movement founded in 1905. Meeting separately, they voted not to attend at Westminster and instead simply organized their own parliament, the Dail Eireann, and declared that Ireland was an independent state.

This was early in 1919, and Lloyd George's government did not get around to doing much about it for some months. The British were busy with the peace conference, and Ireland was an embarrassment better left alone. But in September the government forces suppressed the Dail and raided Sinn Fein party headquarters; two months later it outlawed the party, and a low-level civil war began. Constabulary posts were attacked, and British troops were ambushed along the country roads. It was a war of terrorism, betrayal, and reprisal; in the new year the British brought in reinforcements, recruited largely from Army veterans; known as the Black and Tans from their uniforms, they matched the Irish in their ferocity and were soon hated throughout the land. The Irish attracted great sympathy across the Atlantic, and of course with their Celtic mythic gifts were much more successful in telling their story than the British were in presenting their case.

The government forces won by a partial concession, which succeeded in splitting the Sinn Fein down the middle. It offered home rule and the establishment of dominion status for the Irish Free State. The man who was probably the most attractive of all the nationalist leaders, Michael Collins, negotiated with Lloyd George and accepted the deal. The more intransigent nationalists, led by the half-Irish, New York-born Eamon de Valera, rejected any connection with Britain at all and determined to go on fighting. From 1922 on, most of the fighting was among the Irish themselves as the British slowly pulled out from the imbroglio of the southern counties. By then most Irish were heartily sick of killing and rick-burning, and the compromise was eagerly supported by the vast majority. Yet Collins was gunned down, De Valera was imprisoned, and for another five years the Irish Free State was torn by internecine strife before some semblance of order was established. Even then, the problems of the northern counties, of the relation to Britain, and of the ultimate form of government were shelved rather than resolved. Extremists vowing never to give up until Ireland was fully united were only driven underground, not stamped out, and undercurrents of violence periodically came to the surface. North and South, Protestant and Catholic, the Irish continued to export their sons and their daughters and their music and to nurse their grievances and their ancient hatred of their neighbors and of each other.

David Lloyd George was a politician of Byzantine complexity, of serpentine turns and convolutions, a radical pacifist who had become the most rabid of wartime leaders; it was fitting that his fall should be occasioned by events in the Middle East, where he was finally trapped by the inconsistencies of his own policies. When the Ottoman Empire collapsed at the end of the Great War, Britain and France had divided up its outlying dependencies. They had assigned to both Greece and

Italy parts of Asia Minor itself—that is, of the heartland of Turkey. Italy was given Rhodes and the Dodecanese Islands as well as an enclave in southwestern Anatolia; the Greeks, for whose Premier, Eleutherios Venizelos, Lloyd George felt an inordinate affinity, got the rest of the Turkish islands in the Aegean, the province of Thrace, and temporary occupation of the important city of Smyrna. These and other concessions were forced on the tottering Ottoman government in the Treaty of Sèvres at the end of the war.

The Sublime Porte, however, no longer had much claim to power. The land was in the throes of revolution, and modern Turkey was arising from the ashes of the old Ottoman Empire, led by a genuine war hero and military leader, Mustapha Kemal, later named Ataturk or Father of Turkey. Kemal was building his base and mustering his support in the interior of Asia Minor as the Greeks and Italians were landing troops on the coast to take over their spoils. Kemal's movement, however nasty it might prove at the sharp end, was fully in accord with all those Wilsonian principles of national self-determination, and as he took over more and more of old Turkey, he gained increasing international recognition. The French soon came to an agreement with him, and the Italians did shortly thereafter. But the Greeks were determined to get their pound of flesh—there had been major Greek settlements in western Asia Minor, after all—and Lloyd George was equally determined to back them. In March 1920 British troops had landed at Constantinople, seized the city, garrisoned the strait, and sent many of the leading nationalists into exile. In a move that looked suspiciously like their occupation of Egypt back in 1882, they protested to the world that they were doing this solely for the Turks' own good. While Kemal continued putting his house in order, Lloyd George arranged conferences here and there and secretly encouraged the Greeks to keep advancing into the interior of Asia Minor. This charade went on into the middle of 1921, but then in six weeks of desperate fighting at Sakarya the Turkish forces finally battled the Greeks to a standstill. Both sides were now exhausted, and after a year of rebuilding and posturing, Kemal launched an offensive in August 1922. Within a month the Greek armies had fallen utterly apart and were fleeing back to Smyrna. The city fell in mid-September amid scenes of rape and carnage. As British cruisers rescued hundreds of Greek refugees, thousands of others died in fires or before the furious advance of the Turks.

Lloyd George saw opportunity knocking in the midst of all this tragedy. He landed a British force under General Sir Charles Harrington at Chanak and ordered him to shoot if the Turks came up to his lines. He called on France and Italy for support, invoking the spirit of the wartime alliance, and he also cabled all the dominions and asked for their unconditional support as well. Having sounded the trumpets, he then decided that he would fight and win an election on the issue: Lloyd George at Thermopylae, preserving Western civilization against the onslaught of the villainous Turks.

At Chanak, Lloyd George, not for the first but certainly for the last time, had thoroughly misjudged the general mood; he assumed that because he was excited, everyone else was too, and he was quite mistaken. France and Italy both turned him down; his response from the dominions was even more chilling: New Zealand and Newfoundland agreed they might help out; everyone else returned a firm refusal, the more galling in that it was public, for Winston Churchill, Lloyd George's chief supporter in the government, made the mistake of releasing the British appeal to the newspapers before it was answered by the dominions. Even General Harrington, down at Chanak, played his own hand. Desperate to force the crisis and regain his political control, the Prime Minister instructed Harrington to deliver an ultimatum to the Turks and start fighting. Harrington instead simply sat on his orders, and as the Turks had no intention of shooting British soldiers—they knew they were winning already—the crisis rapidly ran out of fuel. When Lloyd George wanted to call the election, his own ministers repudiated him, and he fell from power in the same way he had arisen, by a backroom maneuver. Alone of all the important ministers, Winston Churchill followed his master into the wilderness. Lloyd George never held office again, and Churchill wandered in the cold for eighteen years.

Judged solely by events in India, Ireland, or Turkey, the times appeared truly out of joint. Yet the Empire had been enlarged by the war. With the accession of German East Africa, there was now a realization of Cecil Rhodes' old dream of an all-red Cape to Cairo route. A whole new sphere of British influence had been created in the Middle East, with the mandates of Iraq, Jordan, and Palestine. Indeed, it was in this post-World War I period that the Empire reached the greatest extent of its territory. In spite of the losses of war, almost nineteen million tons of merchant shipping flew the red ensign, and the British Empire was still the greatest power on earth, or that ever had been on earth. The King-Emperor reigned over a quarter of the world's people, and, of course, Britannia still ruled the waves.

At least she still ruled most of the waves. For she had no sooner disposed of the German challenge than a new potential threat arose, just as Admiral von Tirpitz had predicted it would. In that sense Tirpitz was correct, and having destroyed the immediate threat, Britain was in a position where she might fall prey to a hitherto secondary competitor. The United States now seemed to be taking Germany's place.

At the end of the war the Royal Navy possessed a main battle fleet of forty-two capital ships and was unquestionably the most powerful naval force in the world. She might have added to this the major German units, interned at Scapa Flow, but these, in a spectacular gesture, were scuttled by their skeleton crews in June 1919, when the sailors learned the ships were to be handed over to the Allies to do with as they wished. That still left the British at the top of the heap, for France and Italy were exhausted, Austria was dismembered, Russia had collapsed. Only the United States and Japan remained as serious naval powers. The Japanese, though they had built several units during the war and had also expanded their naval construction facilities, were firmly allied to Britain and were not perceived as any threat. The United States was different, however.

As the Great War had taken its course, it impinged on Americans mostly in a maritime way, between British blockade and German submarines. Ever since its rebirth near the end of the nineteenth century, Americans regarded their Navy as "the first line of defense." Americans had joined in the dreadnought race at an early stage, and in 1914, though fairly small, their Navy was eminently respectable. As what President Wilson considered America's neutral rights were flouted by the belligerents, the Americans moved to strengthen their military posture. On land there was a fashion for "preparedness" and a great deal of rather amateurish summer training of volunteer units. The sea change came in 1916; that year Congress authorized a major capital ship construction program and proposed to lay down sixteen battleships and battle cruisers. Had they been completed, these new classes would have provided the United States Navy with thirty-five ships against the British forty-two at the end of the war, the largest of the U.S. ships with sixteen-inch guns, most of them newer and all of them qualitatively superior to their British opposite numbers.

As it happened, only four of these ships had actually been laid down when the United States entered the war, and the immediate need then was for small escort vessels rather than capital ships. The Americans agreeably suspended their program, pushed through a massive building effort for destroyers and submarine chasers, and fought the war otherwise with the already existing major units. The American dreadnoughts that served with the Grand Fleet in 1918 were thus an important addition but never a numerical challenge to it.

That was the way the British thought matters should remain, but President Wilson went home from the Paris Peace Conference a sadder, wiser, and if anything more determined man than he had been when he arrived. He had for the first time experienced Old World politicians at their best and worst, and he had not enjoyed the lesson. They rejected his ideas about colonies, they rejected his ideas about freedom of the seas, they owed the United States money, but they acted as if they still owned the world. In 1919, when the Navy came forward with its request for appropriations from Congress, Wilson not only supported its desire to dust off the 1916 program, he also readily agreed to the idea that it should be doubled. The United States Navy would be the greatest in the world; *then* it would be time to talk about freedom of the seas.

When the news of these proposals reached London, the British were utterly shocked. What on earth could the Americans be thinking of? How could they suggest that the rule of the Royal Navy was not sufficiently benign for the entire world? Lloyd George, still in power then, was furious. As far as he was concerned, it was, "Lay on, Mac-Duff, and cursed be he who first cries, 'Hold, enough!' " If the Americans wanted a naval race, they would have it!

It was one thing to react in that way, and another to make good the reaction. The treasury was empty; the war had transformed Britain into a debtor country, and a nation that lost thirty-five million working days to strikes in 1919 was not going to welcome an increase in taxes for a new naval race. Perhaps, Lloyd George thought, Britain and the Japanese together might match the Americans. But when he consulted the dominions, they returned chilling answers: Canada was not about to antagonize its southern neighbor, and the Australians and New Zealanders were far more wary of the Japanese than they were of the Americans. Cold comfort there.

When in doubt, talk, is the great motto of politicians. The British suggested a conference, and it was duly held at Washington from November 1921 to February 1922. As the Berlin conferences of 1878 and 1885 had marked Germany's emergence on the international scene, so the Washington one of 1921–22 celebrated America's arrival, though by then the Americans were already retreating from the scene rather than assuming their place in it. They had rejected the Treaty of Versailles, they had refused to honor a defense pact with France, they had limited immigration, and they had raised their tariffs against foreign imports. When President Harding, the invalid Wilson's successor, issued his call for a conference on naval and Far Eastern affairs, he was actually inviting delegates to Fortress America.

All the major naval and colonial states attended, with the exception of the Russians, who were not invited. The United States had not yet recognized the Bolshevik regime so could not have any official dealings with them. But the British, French, Italians, Japanese, Chinese, Portuguese, Belgians, Dutch were there. In the course of three months they settled several matters of outstanding interest. Britain, France, the United States, and Japan all agreed to preserve the status quo in the Far East, and in return for this guarantee, the Anglo-Japanese alliance of 1902 was abandoned. There were assorted deals about China, and then there was the famous naval agreement, which could be seen either as the cornerstone, or the hamstringing, of naval policy for the next fifteen years.

The powers agreed on a capital-ship building holiday for ten years; some ships still on the ways would be completed, but others would be scrapped, and the world's capital ships were to be stabilized at a ratio of 5:5:3:1.67:1.67 for Great Britain, the United States, Japan, France, and Italy, respectively. The first two were to be allowed 525,000 tons, the Japanese 315,000, and the latter two 175,000. They also agreed on a maximum size for ships in various categories. To effect this tonnage figure, both the British and the Americans had to scrap ships, especially the ones in the initial stages of the new American program. The Japanese were thoroughly disgusted at their lesser figure, though in fact they had to continue building to reach it; even though they were actually better off than previously, they were resentful of being regarded as inferiors in the figures. This seemed to them a small compensation for loss of their British alliance and a further aggravation of the recent American immigration attitudes. The Anglo-Americans therefore agreed to sweeten the pill: The Americans pledged not to fortify any bases in the western Pacific, and the British similarly allowed that they would not fortify anything east of Singapore. Essentially they said that the North Pacific area from Hawaii to Malaya could be regarded as a Japanese preserve. That seemed a better idea in 1922 than it did in 1942.

The Royal Navy thus emerged from Washington soundly defeated. The government was pleased; the naval race was avoided, the drain on resources averted. Canada was elated, Australia and New Zealand rather less so. A longer look would have shown that this was the first time since the early eighteenth century that Britain had conceded parity on the seas to another power. She had successively mastered challenges from Spain, Holland, France, and Germany, and now with a stroke of the pen she had accepted American equality. Admiral von Tirpitz, sitting in his study in Germany, smiled, and behind that must have been the equally smiling ghosts of Villeneuve, Tourville, De Ruyter, and a host of others.

The Admiralty took the unusual step of protesting publicly against the strictures of the Washington treaty, but it did them little good. Those great ships the Germans had been unable to sink now went to the breakers' yards, to disappear under the cutting torches. There was never going to be another war, after all, so why keep up a lot of expensive dinosaurs? The drive to dismantle the fleet was encouraged by the fact that in 1922, the short-lived postwar boom came to an end, and Britain lurched into financial crisis.

The most important naval effect of this was the infamous "Geddes ax." Sir Eric Geddes was a brilliant businessman who had made his name in railroads. During the war Lloyd George had recruited him into the government, made him a general so that he might resolve the chaotic British rail transport system in Flanders, and then made him an admiral to reorganize the naval supply system. He had been First Lord of the Admiralty in 1917 and 1918, the hatchet man to force the Navy into convoys. In 1922, he was appointed chairman of a committee on public expenditure. By this time sick of being a government troubleshooter, Geddes struck out with a heavy hand. He recommended deep cuts in education and public health, the abolition of several civil service departments, and slashes in the Army and Navy budgets. The military forces were about the only popular target for Geddes' committee; the national debt had to be carried, and the amounts of money voted for social services could be reduced only at the political peril of the government. The public mood, naturally enough, was one of revulsion against war and all its handmaidens, so the services suffered badly. Seamen were discharged, more ships were scrapped, and the officer corps was embittered by the arbitrary retirement and dismissal of several thousand career members. It was almost a reversion to the old bad days of eighteenth-century administration, when officers had to keep one eye over their shoulders, with more enemies at home than abroad.

The Geddes ax came to be coupled with a second policy that the Navy in later years recalled with shudders. The customary procedure during the palmy prewar days of the Empire had been for the Navy to go to the government and say, "These are our commitments, this is what we need to fulfill them, and this is what it will cost," and the government would then, usually without too much fuss, meet the bill. That was when navies were fashionable and when all the world loved a sailor. That was also when Britain was at the peak of her prosperity and when government had not yet entered the social services scene in a big way. In the prewar decade, for example, the Navy had received about 25 percent of Britain's annual budget. In 1919, however, when the Admiralty went to Lloyd George, prepared, now that the upsetting confusion of war was over, to revert to the good old days, Lloyd George had replied, "Nonsense! There is not going to be a major war for another ten years. Cut your estimates accordingly." Not until 1925 did the admirals ask again, and then they were told the same thing. In fact, the Geddes committee had recommended that the entire process be reversed and that instead of the forces telling the government what they needed, the government should first tell the forces what they could have. The Great War had demonstrated all too clearly, as Clemenceau said, that war was too serious a matter to be left to generals. The age of the accountant had arrived. Though Lloyd George was gone by 1922, his idea of no war for ten years was so attractive that it was elevated into a dogma by his successors. In 1926, 1927, 1928, and finally in 1932 the forces were still held under the "ten-year rule." The politicians officially abandoned the rule in that year, but by then the Great Depression was at its peak, and Neville Chamberlain, the new Chancellor of the Exchequer, introduced the lowest military and naval budget of the interwar period. Chamberlain's hopeless misdirection of the national service or conscription issue in 1917 had given him an abiding dislike of things military. From 1931, when he took over the Exchequer, until 1940, when he gave up the Prime Minister's office, he and the services were practically the bane of each other's existence, and much of Britain's weakness in the face of the dictators can be laid at Chamberlain's door. Lloyd George had called him a "pinhead," so there were some things that even Lloyd George and the forces agreed on.

The condition of the military services was by no means unique.

The simple fact was that Great Britain no longer occupied the position of unchallenged eminence she had once done. She was now a debtor nation. Though she had loaned others among the Allies more than eight and a half billion dollars, the United States had loaned her four and a half billion. Directly or indirectly, the war had cost her about fifty billion dollars, and her own national debt had risen to stratospheric proportions, ten times its prewar level. If these sums do not seem alarming in days of hundred-billion-dollar annual deficits, it must be remembered that the figures are in 1920 dollars, when the world was still on a gold standard, and when citizens and states still thought they ought to pay their debts and balance their budgets.

Nor was Britain likely to recover her former position. Her manufacturing plant was outmoded, her ships were old, her people were weary of war and strain. Political power was shifting with the emergence of the masses, and the first Labor government took office in 1924. Men asked why a country that ruled a quarter of the world could not pay its workers a decent wage and educate their children. In the "khaki election" in 1918, the government had promised to make Britain a "land fit for heroes," and now Britons wanted at least some share of that promise fulfilled, rather than unemployment and the dole. In 1926 the coal miners went on strike when the government proposed to stop subsidizing their industry. For a week in May the labor unions managed a general strike, with two and a half million workers off the job and on the streets, but they could not bring the government to terms.

The arrival of the Depression at the end of the 1920s made it all worse. By the turn of the decade its effects were hitting Britain hard. The Labor government, which had had the misfortune to be elected in August 1929, set up the May committee of financial experts to tell them what to do. At the time two million workers were unemployed, and the committee, none of whom was unemployed themselves, recommended a cut in welfare and the dole as well as a rollback of civil and military salaries. The report caused a split in the cabinet, the resignation of Prime Minister Ramsay MacDonald, and the eventual formation of a coalition government. And when the government finally moved to implement some of the new policies, it also caused a mutiny in the Navy.

The budget proposals of the new coalition were that there should be an across-the-board cut of 10 percent in all government salaries. There were some exceptions; teachers were to be cut 15 percent, and police only 5 percent, which is some indication of priorities. The Admiralty intended to apply its cuts with a fine, impartial hand; an admiral making several thousand pounds a year would be cut 10 percent; so would an able seaman making a few pounds a year. There were also to be cuts in supplementary allowances, such as sea pay, but what could be fairer than that?

The sailors of the Atlantic fleet at Invergordon thought a lot could be fairer. Many of them, especially those married and with families, would lose homes because of the cuts, for of course payments still had to be made, even if the sailor had no money to make them. A wave of dull bitterness swept over the fleet, and on September 15 the men went on strike. Scheduled to go to sea, many ships could not sail when the hands refused to clear the lower deck and man stations for leaving harbor. The Admiralty tried to assign the blame to Communists and underhanded union agitators, the establishment's universal villains of the period, but the facts were too plain for that, and the sailors' grievances were too genuine. Within a few days the Admiralty and the government had both backed down; the cuts were modified so that no one lost more than the stated 10 percent, and the Navy got back to work. The country did not; there was already a run on the pound, and the Invergordon riots definitively killed public confidence in Britain's money. Four days after the strike began, the Bank of England suspended payments, and two days after that, Britain officially abandoned the gold standard. It seemed as if the world must come crashing down.

The world did not crash down, but in the 1930s it was obviously a different world from what it had been. The phrase "as solid as the Bank of England" no longer applied, and Britain got out of the thorny war debt question by simply defaulting, for that was what all the verbiage about moratoriums amounted to. No one else paid Britain back the war loans she had advanced them; the Germans adroitly slid out from under reparations. The British managed to discover that the loans they had gotten were tied to the loans they had given, and they simply passed the losses on to the United States. The whole question was artificial anyway, in that there was not enough money in the world to pass it around that way in reality, but it dogged Anglo-American relations for the entire interwar period.

Like everything else in the Depression world, the Empire also appeared to be coming apart at the seams. The white-dominated dominions had now advanced so far on the road to independence that some public acknowledgment of existing fact became necessary. An imperial conference in 1921 had significantly failed to reach agreement on any definition of status at all and had broken up with the time-honored conclusion that some things are better left alone. Two years later, another conference recognized that the dominions had the right to make separate treaties with foreign powers. In 1926, when the Governor General of Canada, Viscount Byng, the former British general who had commanded the Canadian Corps at Vimy Ridge, refused to dissolve Parliament and call an election at the request of the Prime Minister, Mackenzie King, there was another great constitutional wrangle. It ended with the imperial conference of that year declaring that the governors general were representatives of the sovereign and not of the British Parliament. The power of the old Colonial Office was whittled away, and the conference produced a statement that was passed into law in 1931, in the Statute of Westminster. This said that "Great Britain and the Dominions ... are autonomous communities within the British Empire, equal in status, in no way subordinate to one another in any aspect of their domestic or external affairs, though united by a common allegiance to the Crown, and freely associated as members of the British Commonwealth of Nations." In this way, after a century and a half of building the second British Empire and failing to define what exactly it was, the British demonstrated their political genius by producing a negative formula: They explained what the British Empire was not. They now had the Commonwealth, a usefully ambiguous term that the next half century would equally fail to define. The Dominions appointed high commissioners, a euphemism for ambassadors, in London, and the Colonial Office spawned the Dominions Office.

Constitutional wordmongering was all very well for politicians, but more practical matters were discussed the following year at the Ottawa Economic Conference, whose main result was the abandonment of the historic policy of free trade. Legal formulas invariably lag behind reality. For forty years after she had become the dominant economic power in the world, Britain had clung to the traditional mercantilist Empire; now, half a century after she had ceased to enjoy that position of supremacy, she finally gave up free trade, which had become as outdated a shibboleth as mercantilism had been in its day. Most of the Empire was protectionist already, the various dominions having long adopted tariffs designed to shelter their own domestic manufactures. The establishment of an official imperial preference ironically had the effect in some cases of lowering duties rather than raising them. Britain agreed to give tariff protection to imports, mainly agricultural, from the Dominions, and in turn they adjusted their rates for British products. The simple fact was that the world of the early 1930s was not a very nice place. Economic forces were apparently out of control, soon to be joined, unfortunately, by political forces as well. The Ottawa agreements represented a natural tendency in time of troubles to repair the castle walls and flood the moat. For the entire decade Britain was ruled by a coalition government and party lines were crossed, a reliable sign that democracy was in retreat. Neomercantilism was in. There was a wrenching monarchical crisis in 1936 when the new King, Edward VIII, abdicated to "be with the woman I love"; many people approved of this as a sign that love conquered all, but many more regarded Edward as regrettably typical of a time that seemed willing to sacrifice duty to pleasure. As Britain floundered through a succession of weak cabinets and the Dominions went their own way, and India was racked by riots and violence, the mutter of drums could be heard offstage.

If Britain did not react very positively to the turmoils of the 1920s and 1930s, neither did other states. In France there was ministry after ministry, scandal after scandal, crisis after crisis; in the United States there was President Hoover after President Coolidge after President Harding. And these were countries with a strong democratic tradition. Most of the states of Europe actually failed to weather the storms besetting them. Benito Mussolini seized power in Italy in 1922, and the President of Poland was assassinated that year. Military officers staged a coup in Bulgaria the next year, and Primo de Rivera became dictator of Spain. In 1925 there was a military coup in Greece; the next year Salazar was dictator of Portugal, Pilsudski seized power in Poland, and there was another coup in Lithuania. In 1929 King Alexander made himself a dictator in Hungary; he was assassinated at Marseilles in 1934; in 1930 King Carol of Romania set up a personal rule. Adolf Hitler came to power in Germany in early 1933, and there were coups in Austria, Latvia, and Estonia in 1934. The Russians were under a dictatorship all along. That left the Scandinavian states, Czechoslovakia, the Low Countries, Switzerland, France, and Britain with parliamentary governments still more or less intact in Europe. There was little to be done about this totalitarian drift; in the early 1920s France showed some inclination to intervene in other states' affairs, especially those of Germany, whom she was determined to keep down. But the French were even weaker after the Great War than the British, and the

French too became absorbed with their own internal difficulties. Even in the democratic countries there were strong reactionary movements, and Britain and France had their own extremist parties, on the left and the right, welcoming the advent of dictators if they mouthed the appropriate slogans.

The British government certainly did not shun the totalitarian states on ideological grounds. The first-ever Labor cabinet took office on January 22, 1924, and it recognized Soviet Russia on February 1. The British objected neither to the advent of Mussolini—after all, "he made the trains run on time"—nor, at first, to Hitler. Britain hoped only for peace and wished to get along with the world. She was the main prop of the truncated League of Nations, and she subscribed to various general and regional agreements, such as the Locarno Treaty. When Adolf Hitler unilaterally set aside the Versailles limitations on Germany's military forces, the British returned only polite nothings. Concerts with France mouthed platitudes, but in 1935 the British signed an Anglo-German naval agreement. Hitler agreed not to build his Navy beyond 35 percent of existing British strength. Stanley Baldwin's coalition government thought this was a good deal and neglected the fact that the French, unconsulted, were outraged at such a blatant disregard of Versailles. Japan was already on the march in Manchuria, the disarmament movement had collapsed ignominiously, Germany was unveiling its Air Force, and the shadows were darkening. In London, Winston Churchill began to sound warnings but was discredited as a warmonger; Baldwin drifted indecisively; and Neville Chamberlain, clutching the purse strings, still pooh-poohed the British military forces' increasingly desperate requests for more men and new equipment. Such was the situation when Italy invaded Ethiopia in the fall of 1935.

In 1935 Ethiopia and Liberia were the only remaining independent African states. Liberia, on the western coast, had been set up as a refuge for Africans returning from the United States. Ethiopia (Abyssinia) had preserved a somewhat precarious independence through the period of the partitions. The British had invaded it with a punitive expedition in 1867; the Italians had tried to conquer it in 1896 and been massacred at the Battle of Adowa. It remained a little-known enclave, with Italian Eritrea to the north of it along the Red Sea, and Italian Somaliland to the east and south, along the Indian Ocean and the Horn of Africa. The country was now ruled by Emperor Haile Selassie, who was doing his best to westernize and modernize a poor and backward people. For half a century Ethiopia had been an area of Italian economic interest and exploitation, and in 1935, encouraged by the example of Hitler in Germany and his success in disregarding treaties, Mussolini decided to transform this into outright political control.

Mussolini's rise to power had in itself been an expression of Italian frustration. The country was always the weakest of the great powers, and unification had not brought about the benefits that Italians had expected from it. In the Great War Italy had literally sold her services to the highest bidder, but at Versailles the Allies had reneged on several of their promises to her. When Mussolini seized power in 1922, he immediately carried Italy into the camp of the revisionists, and for more than a decade he had made loud noises and thrown his weight around, especially in the Balkans and eastern Mediterranean. Britain and France, not wanting to alienate the country but not wanting to give in too overtly to Mussolini's bullying, had walked a tightrope with him. Now, when he moved on Ethiopia, it was but a logical extension of what he had been talking about all along; it was also a failure to realize that the world had moved on and that the colonial game of half a century ago was no longer in vogue.

He might at first have been forgiven for making such an error, for the French Foreign Minister, Pierre Laval, agreed to what he was up to and sold the idea to the British Foreign Secretary, Sir Samuel Hoare. The infamous Hoare-Laval agreement would have given Italy a good two thirds of Ethiopia without blinking an eye. When news of that old-fashioned deal hit the press, however, there was such a storm of public protest that Hoare was forced to resign; the French like to consider themselves more cynically realistic, so Laval went on to become Premier of France. On October 3 Italian forces invaded Ethiopia.

The crisis lasted eight months. The Ethiopian forces proved hardy fighters but essentially no match for modern Italian equipment. Against them the Italians employed tanks, machine guns, heavy artillery, and especially airpower, which they used for bombing, strafing, and dropping poison gas. Italian newspapers featured lyric descriptions by pilots of the beauty of bombs bursting among horsed cavalry and the aesthetic effects of flowers of blood, horse guts, dust, and high explosives, an example of Fascist manliness that most of the rest of the world found disgusting.

But the rest of the world was strangely reluctant to do anything to stop it. Within four days of the invasion, the Council of the League of Nations declared Italy an aggressor and begged members to assist Ethiopia. Italy was, in fact, highly vulnerable; all her supplies had to pass through the Suez Canal, right under the noses, or guns, of the British Mediterranean Fleet. The British refused to close the canal. Eventually the League voted to apply sanctions against Italy. The idea of this was that by the cutting off of her supplies, an aggressor would be made to desist, without recourse to war. This could have worked in Italy's case, for her entire war effort was absolutely dependent upon imported oil. Britain and France refused to extend the sanctions list to oil. When the Canadian delegate suggested the idea, he was hastily repudiated by his own government.

Nonetheless, in spite of the pusillanimous posture of the two great democracies, tensions ran high. The Royal Navy reinforced the fleet anchored at Alexandria and at one point put it on war alert. Both sides were really bluffing. Mussolini had ordered his Navy not to fight if the British offered battle. But the British took counsel of their own weaknesses and overlooked the Italians'. The British knew only that they had little aircraft protection, no anti-aircraft ammunition, and that they had heavy shells for only fifteen minutes' general action. At Alexandria the sailors thought fifteen minutes ought to be enough to sink the Italian Navy, but the government thought differently. They backed down, and the Italian conquest went on unhindered by outside intervention. In May 1936 Italian soldiers triumphantly, if a trifle belatedly, entered the capital of Addis Ababa, on May 9 King Victor Emmanuel was formally proclaimed Emperor of Ethiopia, Mussolini standing on his balcony and orating to wildly cheering crowds, and two months later the Council of the League of Nations voted to suspend sanctions, for what good is a sanction after it has failed to work? Haile Selassie appeared before the League and proclaimed its funeral oration, after which he went into dignified exile.

Italian ships in the Suez Canal were not precisely equivalent to De Ruyter sailing up the Channel with a broom at his masthead, but the affair was humiliating enough. And the next imbroglio was even worse.

In Spain, after several years of dictatorship, disorganization, and fragile republicanism, the country burst into war in 1936. The Spanish Civil War became the great ideological watershed of the 1930s. The Nationalist side, with the majority of the Army, the Church, and the landowners, received immediate help from Italy and from Germany, and the vast majority of its supplies and resources came from the European dictatorships.

The Republican side appealed for help to the rest of the world, but once again the democracies held back. Russia supplied money and arms and advisers but did so with a careful calculation that supported the Communists, and aside from them, did the Republican cause as much harm as good. France agreed to help but progressively watered down its commitments. In Britain the government backed and filled. Popular opinion was divided, though generally pro-Republican. A small host of genuine volunteers went off to fight for the Republic, joining other "international brigades" from France, Czechoslovakia, and North America, as well as antifascists from the dictatorships themselves. But the British government's chief concern was to remain aloof. When Germany and Italy recognized Generalissimo Francisco Franco's Nationalist government as legitimate, Britain and France called a conference to try to isolate the conflict. They succeeded in setting up a nonintervention committee but accepted Germany and Italy as members of it. So the Italians, with upward of fifty thousand "volunteers" fighting in Spain, sat and discussed methods of supervising nonintervention. This exercise in hypocrisy became even more difficult to sustain when the war was extended to the sea. Ships bringing supplies to the Republicans were sunk by "pirate" submarines, generally acknowledged to be Italian, and finally Britain got the other states to agree to participate in a neutrality patrol. When Republican planes attacked the pocket battleship *Deutschland,* being hard put to distinguish between Germans as neutrals and Germans on Franco's side, German warships responded with a shore bombardment of Almeria, which was not quite what the nonintervention scheme was designed for. Germany and Italy both withdrew from the patrol over this outrage, and for a while it looked as if ships from the four countries might start shooting at each other. The French, in one of their more belligerent moods, wanted to open the frontier and send large amounts of supplies to the Republic, but the British government, newly under Neville Chamberlain, talked them out of it. The two did reorganize the naval patrols by themselves and announced they were no longer fooling; the pirate sinkings stopped forthwith.

That was late in 1937; it took Franco nearly a year and a half more to win his war. Britain and France recognized his government in February 1939, Madrid surrendered in March, and the last sad remnants of the Republic filtered over the passes and into France, while the German and Italian volunteers staged a great victory parade in the capital and then went home. As in Ethiopia, Fascist might had again displayed its prowess, but by now, the whole world was aware of it anyway. The democracies were making frantic efforts to rearm and to find allies, for by early 1939, almost anyone could see that a major war was not far off.

Of the several failures during the interwar years, one of the most complete was that of the disarmament movement. No one had been able to reconcile the demands of the separate states for security with the demands of their neighbors for equality. There had been several naval conferences after the one held in Washington, and some minor successes in extending ratios and tonnage limitations to lesser classes of ships, but essentially by 1930 these had reached the end of the road. The great League of Nations Disarmament Conference in 1932 achieved nothing more than an agreement to meet again the following year. When it did, it broke down in the face of German demands for immediate equality—equality as counted by Germany—and in October Germany withdrew from the conference and the League both.

Counsels continued to be divided in Britain. Though the ten-year rule was officially abandoned in 1932, it was not until 1936 that a serious attempt to rearm began. The intervening four years had been lost in wranglings among the service chiefs on the direction British defense should take, a wrangling of which a government indisposed to spend any money took full advantage. In 1935 the government took the unprecedented step of producing a "white paper" that spelled out the official view of world events, and announced, in effect, the demise of collective security and the official beginning of rearmament. The effect was ironic: a vast public yawn in Britain, the announcement by Adolf Hitler that in view of Britain's hostility he was introducing full-scale military conscription.

The difficulty within the British military services was whether the money ought to be spent on ships or aircraft, for now, in the mid-1930s, it looked as if perhaps the Navy was no longer the first line of national defense. As the German threat grew, so did the cries that the Royal Air Force must be kept up to meet the challenge. These were the days when airpower visionaries were at their most vocal, shouting, "The bomber will always get through!" and creating visions of London in total ruin. The battleship admirals, of course, dismissed this as airy nonsense and demanded that the available money be used to strengthen the Navy. In fact, British airpower proved stronger than the admirals said it would and weaker than its champions said it would, but the argument, and the pictures painted to support it, were enough to paralyze defense policy. In these middle years the Navy got slightly more money than the Royal Air Force, and neither got as much as they had during the 1920s, before the Depression. As for the Army, it was all but lost in the shuffle; it got a mere 20 percent of what the Navy got and was reduced to the role of a colonial police force. When Britons talked of their land forces the operative sentence was, "Thank God for the French Army." It was the eighteenth century all over again, when Britain willfully destroyed her own armed forces between every war in the name of economy.

The man who played Robert Walpole in this modern scenario was Neville Chamberlain. As Chancellor of the Exchequer in the early 1930s, he insisted that there was no money for the military services. Service ministers were reduced to political impotence, and military officers were virtually muzzled. Cabinets employed the time-honored political trick of the circular argument, telling the services they must trim their demands to meet preconceived budget figures, and when they did so, using their own statements to show that they had not needed more money in the first place. When Chamberlain became Prime Minister in 1937, he entered the office with the already firm belief that Germany had legitimate grievances and aspirations, and that if these could be satisfied, there need be no war. Acting on this belief, which assumed the status of dogma with him, he initiated a policy he called "appeasement." Such a policy did not make him receptive to the plaintive cries of the soldiers, sailors, and airmen who were going to pay for Britain's weakness if he were somehow proven wrong. Throughout the later 1930s, even when Britain had officially accepted the idea of rearmament, he dragged his feet; while in Germany they marched shoulder to shoulder, resolutely facing forward for the glory of the Reich and the Fuehrer, in Britain few people marched at all. The Army was kept discreetly out of sight, the Royal Air Force was called "the best private flying club in the world," and the Navy limped along hoping for better days.

Eventually, of course, and just barely in time, things began to move. The big-ship building vacation finally came to an end; during it Britain had completed only two battleships, hybrids allowed her under the terms of the Washington treaty, the *Rodney* and the *Nelson*. Now at last, in 1936, a new class was laid down, the King George V class of five battleships. None was ready at the declaration of war. In September 1939, Britain had fifteen battleships and battle cruisers in service. Only four had been rebuilt to modern standards; two more were undergoing rebuilding, and the five new ones were still in various stages of construction. This failure to modernize was going to cost Britain dearly, the price paid for keeping old ships constantly in service around the routes of the Empire.

There was also a new type of capital ship, the aircraft carrier. The British, even the battleship admirals, had acknowledged the utility of aircraft for scouting and reconnaissance and local air cover, and in the immediate postwar years had actually led the world in the employment of naval aircraft and carrier development. However, they had slowly fallen behind. When war began, they had seven aircraft carriers in service, compared to five for the United States and six for Japan. Only one of these seven was modern, however, and both the Japanese and the Americans, even with fewer carriers, could carry more planes than the British. Even worse was the state of British naval aircraft themselves. From 1918 until the mid-1930s the Fleet Air Arm had been an adjunct of the Royal Air Force, with the result that it had been on the short end for development funds and new aircraft. In 1939 it did not possess one naval aircraft that was equivalent to similar American and Japanese types; it was still flying biplanes—in one famous case, that of the Swordfish, until the end of the war. Setting aside all these technological shortcomings and political quarrels, rearmament finally began. In April 1936 the government announced plans to build thirty-eight new warships, the biggest move since the Washington treaty, and out of this program came the ships that provided a narrow margin of sea supremacy over the Axis in the darkest days of World War II, the King George V class of battleships, the Illustrious class of carriers, the famous Tribal and J and K classes of destroyers. The first modern British fighter plane, the Hawker Hurricane, entered squadron service with the Royal Air Force in December 1937, followed by the Spitfire in the fall of 1938. That was the fall of Munich, and slowly a sense of urgency began to permeate the British political establishment.

Before Munich one could think that Chamberlain might be right and that there would not really be a war again. After Munich only Chamberlain might think that, and even he was soon to be disabused. Ever since Hitler had come to power in Germany, in January 1933, he had progressively increased his strength and his demands, and it should not really have required preternatural foresight to see where he was going. He had already told the world where he was going, in his turgid autobiography and political statement, *Mein Kampf,* but most people could be forgiven for not having waded through that. Within a year and a half of his accession, Hitler had remade Germany in his own image. He rapidly rid himself of all sources of opposition, and then he was ready to move externally. In early 1936 he denounced the Locarno treaties and sent his troops marching into the demilitarized Rhineland; the Western democracies were already in disarray over the Ethiopian war, which was then at its height. The French military leaders realized that the loss of the Rhenish buffer was an absolute body blow to their foreign and defense posture—"We have just lost the next war," one of them said—but they were too conscious of their own fears to do anything about it, especially when the British made it absolutely clear that they would not resort to force. Through the year Hitler and Mussolini gradually drifted together, natural allies as the two bullies of Europe, and in October they set up the "Rome-Berlin Axis," so the British truckling to Mussolini to keep him out of Hitler's clutches had gone for nothing. During 1937 the Spanish Civil War raged, and Japan began her march of conquest in China. By the next year German rearmament was progressing steadily and Hitler was ready to move again, in spite of the hesitations of his own military advisers. In March he invaded and annexed Austria, again a clear violation of treaties; he gained six million new subjects and a clear route into the Balkans. There was no opposition in Austria itself; the German Army found "it was roses all the way" to Vienna. The British government had already resigned itself to the event, and once more a German aggression passed without much notice from Whitehall.

The real crunch came that fall, when Hitler turned his sights on his next target, Czechoslovakia. The only viable democracy in central Europe, Czechoslovakia had a good Army and a firm alliance with the French. When Hitler demanded territory in the western borderlands, the Sudetenland, the Czechs refused, and it looked as though they would fight. They asked their allies for help. Instead of standing firm, the French passed the buck; Premier Daladier consulted with Chamberlain, making it clear that France's actions would be governed by Britain's. Chamberlain was delighted at the chance to leave his personal mark on international affairs, and he visited Hitler first at Berchtesgaden and then at Godesberg. This was the first time the Prime Minister of Britain had flown. He meant this as a mark of his sincerity and his desire to find a fair solution to the crisis; Hitler took it as a sign of weakness. By the time a third meeting was arranged, at Munich late in September, the clever German had maneuvered France and Britain into doing his dirty work for him. It was they who gave up the Czechoslovak position and then bullied the Czechs into accepting it. The French seemed not to care that their entire alliance system was in ruins; they were pleased only that someone else could be blamed for it. Chamberlain, genuinely wanting peace, believed he had achieved it; Hitler, he said, was a man of his word, and he waved his umbrella at the cheering crowds, showed his little scrap of paper, and said he had gained "peace for our time . . . peace with honor."

It was neither, and it gradually dawned on the British public that they had suffered a crushing defeat. Even Chamberlain was constrained to acknowledge it, when in March of the new year the Germans suddenly moved and annexed the rump of Czechoslovakia that had been left independent after Munich. This was Hitler's first move to incorporate peoples historically non-German, and it negated everything he had promised in the past. The scales fell from Chamberlain's eyes, and now, at the eleventh hour, with a position far weaker than it had formerly been, his government and France gave Poland a broad guarantee that they would protect her from Germany if yet another crisis arose. How they would do that was problematical, and in fact they hoped to get Russia to do it for them. As a Polish crisis developed through the summer of 1939, Russia instead allied with Germany. The British and French were left with a guarantee they must honor, and little way to do it.

The Dominions of the Empire were all passionately interested in these events, and argument about British policy and what it ought to be raged throughout the English-speaking world. But the Australians and New Zealanders were, as always, far more concerned with the Japanese question than the German, and the Canadians were evolving into a much more American than European nation, while India had its own internal troubles to worry about. The Dominions were thus content to leave any initiatives to Britain, reserving their right to criticize freely what Britain did. They could not have had too much influence on international affairs, and they chose not to exercise the little they could. One Canadian senator had summed up his country's situation back in the 1920s, when collective security was in vogue. He said that Canadians lived in a fireproof house far from any flammable materials; they were therefore a first-class insurance risk and should not have to pay heavy premiums. In international affairs, the spirit of "It can't happen here," and "I'm all right, Jack" dominated the Dominions. Canada, for example, had no armaments industry, and during the 1930s it concentrated what few defense efforts it made on the Pacific coast, being more worried about the Japanese than the Germans and not very worried about either. The Royal Australian Navy had six cruisers, one dating from before World War I, and five destroyers, only one of which was less than ten years old. The biggest ships in the Royal Indian Navy were two escort sloops, and in the Canadian seven destroyers. When toting up his balances, Hitler was quite free to discount the British Empire outside Britain.

Through the summer of 1939 the European situation thus moved toward its tragic conclusion, undisturbed by those millions of Americans, Canadians, Africans, and Asians whose lives would be forever altered by it. Chamberlain had characterized Czechoslovakia as "a faraway country, of which we know nothing"; Hitler, his sights set on Poland, now scornfully asked if anyone wanted to "die for Danzig" and was sure no one did. For months agitation and alarms continued, and then with stunning suddenness the crisis burst. Germany and Soviet Russia signed their nonaggression pact on August 23. Two days later Hitler demanded of the British and French a free hand in "solving the Polish problem"; the British pleaded for more time and called their merchant ships out of the Baltic and Mediterranean. The Poles stood fast and declared a partial mobilization on August 30. On the morning of September 1 Hitler unleashed his forces in the world's first example of blitzkrieg. The British and French still hung back, hoping for some last-minute reprieve, but there was none, and on September 3 a tired Chamberlain rose in the House of Commons to announce that Great Britain and Germany were at war. The French immediately followed suit. And so did the rest of the Empire; within a week, and with remarkably little discussion, the Dominions joined the mother country. There was not the enthusiasm of 1914, for people had learned their lesson in the Great War, but the Empire still retained its coherence, its ties of blood, language, and custom. The children had pretty well grown up, but they remained part of the same family.

16

The Lion at Bay

And Crispin Crispian shall ne'er go by,
From this day to the ending of the world,
But we in it shall be remembered—
                                      —Shakespeare, King Henry V

World War II completed the work begun by the Great War. In 1945 much of Europe, from the Atlantic shores to the Urals, lay in ruins and devastation; the era of Western European dominance of the world was over. The great powers of Britain, France, Germany, and Italy, and Japan in the East, and their empires, were exhausted, to be replaced upon the world scene by two new "superpowers," the United States and Soviet Russia. The war and its side effects—disease, starvation, and genocide—killed between thirty million and forty million people and caused the greatest shifting of populations certainly since the Industrial Revolution and possibly since the Black Death. It brought the most advanced technology in existence to the most backward peoples in the world; Stone Age natives in New Guinea looked on American and Australian soldiers with the same awe that transfixed the Aztecs when they first saw Spanish conquistadors in armor mounted on horses. Highways were built through the Alaskan wilderness and air bases hacked out of the jungles of Brazil. The Great Depression ended in a burst of war-inspired prosperity, and men once more discovered the sad but ancient truth that their energies could be most fully employed in killing their fellows.

Not the least irony of war is that it almost invariably has results different from those intended by the men who start it. Academic historians, who find war a messy process distressingly resistant to logical classification, prefer to study its causes and its results rather than its course and do their best to ignore the fact that it is the course of a war that determines what those results will be, and all too often therefrom, what the causes of the next war will be. Certainly Adolf Hitler when he began his war did not expect to commit suicide in a bunker under ruined Berlin some five and a half years later; Mussolini when he joyously joined in the triumphant summer of 1940 did not realize he would end hanging upside down from a lamppost in Milan.

Perhaps Chamberlain did not expect to gain much at all from the war; his whole recent career had been devoted to the concept of appeasement, so the fact of war itself was the ruination of his political ambitions. This did not mean he would resign, of course, for politicians who have maneuvered their country into a mess invariably think that they are then the only ones capable of maneuvering back out of it. The first duty of a politician, after all, is to remain in office. On the outbreak of war, Chamberlain reconstructed his cabinet—he brought that fire-eater Churchill back to run the Admiralty again—and settled down to what he planned as a comfortable war. Determinedly uninspiring, he announced Britain's slogan for the war effort—"Business as usual," an unconsciously revealing tag not only on how Chamberlain looked at war, but also on how he viewed Britain and the rest of the Empire. The war was a nuisance, and Hitler a tiresome fellow who had already demonstrated he was no gentleman. Since they now had the experience of the Great War to guide them, the British put into effect immediately all those mechanisms that had taken years to develop in 1914–18: convoys, movement control, rationing, government allocation of resources, price and wage controls. All this was done resignedly, routinely, and without any real enthusiasm. No one should be disturbed unduly.

If they knew what to do to manage a wartime economy, they had also learned what not to do on the battlefield. The new model British Expeditionary Force, Mark II, went to France as its fathers had done a quarter of a century ago, but it was small and intended to remain so. No one in this war was going to be sucked into a vast, endless slaughter, throwing away a generation of young men. That lesson had been absorbed the last time. The French had the biggest and presumably best Army in the world; let them do it.

But then the French did not want to do it, either. Their casualty ratio had been twice as high as Britain's in World War I; they thought they had found a new answer to modern war, and indeed they had: They were perfectly prepared to fight World War I over again. They had learned that defense was the master, and they had built a great series of prepared fortifications. They would just sit in them and let the Germans commit suicide attacking them.

None of this did any good for Poland, the country on whose behalf Britain and France had entered the war. During the course of September, while Poland writhed in its death agonies, the French sat in the Maginot Line and the B.E.F. got over to northern France, where it sat, too. Fire and death and massacre in Warsaw, business as usual in London and Paris. Poland disappeared, gulped down whole by Germany and her partner in crime, Russia, and Hitler offered peace. What was there to fight about?

The Western Allies would not wage war, but neither would they make peace. Hitler's stock as a conqueror might be high; his credibility as a diplomat had sunk to invisibility. He ordered his generals to do a rapid redeployment and attack France late in the fall, even as Poland was still being digested, but his generals, as fearful of the French as the French were of them, dragged their feet. The fall rains came on; French troops sat in the line watching their uniforms mildew and their morale rot. Neutral American journalists wrote about the "sitzkrieg" and the "phony war." Everyone expected a deal somewhere along the line, and only at sea was the war real.

In the last days of peace, Allied and German shipping had scurried home. One British submarine commander, with a big German liner split by the crosshairs of his periscope, had radioed, "Request permission to start the war." A few days later one no longer needed such permission, and a scant four hours after the British ultimatum to Germany expired, the British cargo liner *Athenia,* outward bound from England to the United States with a load of tourists returning home, was torpedoed and sunk by *U-30.* Of the 112 people killed, 28 were American. The Germans announced that it was a mistake and reprimanded their submarine captain. They first tried to claim that Churchill had had a bomb planted aboard the ship to discredit them. Though the U-boats were temporarily held in check after that, the war at sea this time escalated far more rapidly than it had done in the First World War. The Germans were soon using their submarines to full advantage, and the British adopted the time-honored techniques of blockade. There were in 1939 about thirty million tons of merchant shipping available to the Allies, two thirds of it British, and strict measures were brought in almost at once for its control. The neutrals as always protested against the restrictions of the blockading system. American ships officially bound for Germany were directed instead into British- or French-controlled ports; goods addressed to Germany were seized off neutral ships, and the British even claimed the right to open mail to or from Germany to see if it contained contraband—or, of course, any useful information. It was no good being gray when black and white were at war.

As in 1914, the British immediately moved against German warships at sea. The most spectacular event in this campaign came in December, when three cruisers—*Exeter, Ajax,* and the New Zealand ship *Achilles*—caught the pocket battleship *Graf Spee* in the South Atlantic. The *Graf Spee* was one of the new ships of the German Navy, a modern version of the battle-cruiser type, with large eleven-inch guns on what was basically a cruiser hull. Of the British ships *Exeter* was a heavy cruiser, and *Ajax* and *Achilles* were light. The German Captain Langsdorff, whose guns outranged the British by five miles, could have stood off and destroyed them with immunity, as *Sydney* had done to *Emden* in 1915. Instead he misidentified the British as a light cruiser and two destroyers, got into range, and took a severe pounding. So did they, but in the end he broke off the action and fled for neutral Montevideo, in the mouth of the Plate River, and there he took refuge while the battered British steamed impudently back and forth at the edge of international waters. Instead of coming out to fight when his neutral grace period was up, Langsdorff, short of ammunition, took his ship into the middle of the Plate estuary and scuttled her. Returning to his hotel room, he committed suicide, thinking thereby to redeem the honor of his Navy.

This was the first real British success in the war. In October a U-boat had penetrated the fleet anchorage at Scapa Flow and sunk the battleship *Royal Oak.* In November the Germans had gotten out two new battleships, *Scharnhorst* and *Gneisenau.* Breaking through the line from Scotland to Iceland, they had encountered the armed merchant cruiser H.M.S. *Rawalpindi.* The latter, suffering no illusions about the ability of her unarmored sides and her four old six-inch guns to take on the eighteen eleven-inchers of the two battleships, nonetheless engaged. It took the Germans but a few moments to finish her off, but discovered, they decided to head for home and aborted their cruise.

In February of the new year British destroyers violated Norwegian neutrality to rescue merchant ship prisoners being held aboard the German supply vessel *Altmark.* The latter had served as a tender for *Graf Spee* and was now sneaking home through the neutral, coastal Norwegian Leads. The Norwegians protested this violation of their territorial waters. The British, impatient with neutrality and seeking to profit from the Russo-Finnish War in the North, decided to mine the Leads. The Germans at the same time, inspired by the same impulses, decided to invade Norway. As April approached, the war gathered momentum.

After the winter of discontent, the spring of disaster. On April 9 German forces occupied Denmark; the Danes wisely capitulated with but token resistance. The same day the German Navy landed soldiers at most of the major points of Norway—Oslo, Bergen, Trondheim, and other ports. The minuscule Norwegian Army and Navy fought, in a few cases successfully. The British and French stumbled. Misinterpreting the German move as a sortie into the Atlantic, the Royal Navy sailed off on an intercept course to the northwest, taking it out of the action. By the time Anglo-French units were landed in the middle of the country, the Germans had achieved local air control. British shipping losses were heavy, and by early May the waist of the country had to be given up. Only up in the North, around the ore port of Narvik, could the soldiers and sailors fight in the time-honored way, without the intervention of tactical airpower, and here the British scored heavily, sinking major enemy naval units and landing a sizable force of their own. It was all too little and too late. The Allied response had been a series of half measures, mostly insisted upon by Winston Churchill, and their patent inadequacies finally brought down the Chamberlain government. He retired, to die later in the year, and was replaced by the aged, growling warrior. Churchill's time in the wilderness was at last over; his policy, he said, was "to wage war."

It was nearly past time for that. Five days before the invasion of Norway and Denmark, Chamberlain had complacently announced to the world that Hitler had "missed the bus." The man who fought a war with "business as usual" and whose enemy "missed the bus" remained determinedly prosaic to the end. Churchill became Prime Minister on May 10. That same day German armies crashed into the Netherlands, Belgium, and northern France, and the war turned real with sudden and terrifying brutality. The Netherlands collapsed within four days, and as the British and French armies along the frontier raced to the rescue of the Dutch and Belgians, the Germans cut in behind them, sending their tanks with ease through the supposedly impassable Ardennes Forest. Hit hard in front and flank, the northern Allied armies retreated, first south, and then toward the sea. Within eleven days there were German tanks on the Channel coast, at Abbeville, the mobile Allied forces were cut off, and it was suddenly apparent that this was not to be World War I after all. French generals thought at the pace of a marching man; German generals moved at the speed of a fast tank.

By the last week of that terrible month, British and French troops were enclosed in a perimeter around the little coastal town of Dunkirk, once a nest for privateers. The French, true to a tradition of military wall-building, talked vaguely of organizing a fortress; the British moved toward evacuation. The Royal Navy entered the narrow waters of the Channel in force, and a flood of small craft, government and private, from ancient paddle wheel ferries to trim motorboats and yachts, crossed to bring the soldiers home. The Germans left the destruction of the perimeter to the Luftwaffe, but strafe, bomb, and sink as it might, it could not prevent the British from carrying off 200,000 of their own troops and about 140,000 French. With the peculiar British penchant for celebrating their defeats, they turned a military defeat into a human triumph.

That obscured but did not alter the fact that there was still a disaster of immense proportions. The B.E.F. came home with no armor and no equipment, a skeleton force that had to start all over again. And across the Channel, on that still-embattled shore, what had been known as the greatest army in the world was in its death agonies, bombed from the sky, encircled by the ubiquitous tank columns, wasted by the outdated ideas and resolute stupidity of its officers, and ultimately betrayed by its political masters. Not even in 1871, not since the defeat of Prussia by Napoleon at Jena and Auerstadt, had there been such ignominious and utter national collapse in Europe. In despair the French threw the reins of government to the hero of Verdun, the great father figure of twentieth-century France, Marshal Pétain, and his response to crisis was to surrender to it completely. On June 25, fighting in France ceased, and Britain and her Empire stood alone against an engorged Hitlerian Europe.

Alone and virtually unarmed. The Army was pathetically re-equipped with relics hauled out of museums from the previous war, the Royal Air Force had dangerously whittled away its fighter strength during the Dunkirk fighting, and the Navy had taken severe losses in light units. The Italians had now entered the war, and the British government assessed that if the French fleet were joined to the German and Italian, that could well be the end. It was too risky to rely on

French promises. In the first days of July the Royal Navy seized French ships in British ports, and at Oran, after negotiations broke down, the British shelled and sank French battleships and battle-cruisers. It was a brutal, heartbreaking action for the men involved, but these were the dark days, when Britain had little more for her own defense than the sonorous phrases of Churchill's speeches, rallying his own countrymen and their Empire to their finest hour.

The great question of that summer was would the Germans, could the Germans, invade England? It took them until late July to get their Air Force redeployed and organized, and in August and early September the issue was fought out. Day after day the Germans sent their air fleets over the Channel to the southeastern counties, to hit the ports, the air bases, the radar network, the factories, and eventually London. They came close to victory several times, but never close enough; day after day the Hurricanes and Spitfires of the Royal Air Force Fighter Command rose up to challenge them, David against Goliath. British schoolchildren were evacuated to the countryside, then to Canada; American movie audiences later watched Greer Garson in *Mrs. Miniver*. British pilot strength dipped closer and closer to catastrophe, but there remained just enough young men—only a few hundred altogether—to tip the balance. Without command of the air, there could not be command of the sea, and for all the power of his vaunted Wehrmacht, Hitler stood rooted on the Continent, as impotent against the islanders as Napoleon or Philip of Spain. General de Gaulle, that most aggravating of Frenchmen, summed it up. "Ah, yes, the Channel," he remarked, "the greatest antitank ditch in the world . . ."

The war was not lost in 1940, but it was still a long way from won. But at least now the British knew that it was a war, and they were in it to win. And to lead them they no longer had a modern Robert Walpole, with his economies and his umbrella and his refusal to acknowledge that the world could not be run on a balance sheet alone; they had instead a reincarnation of the Elder Pitt, with a quicksilver mind not always correct but always eager, an orator who could move the heart as well as the mind. Winston Churchill thought the British Empire was the greatest edifice the mind of God and the hand of man had ever created, and he led it willingly into the lists against the gangsters across the Channel.

The imperial response was on the whole gratifyingly positive. Dunkirk and the Battle of Britain galvanized the Empire as Pearl Harbor was to do to the United States eighteen months later. The war had

seemed distant and unreal a year before, but now it was all too immediate, and young men rode in from the Australian outback or the lumber camps of New Brunswick and British Columbia to put their names
on the line, in much the same way as their fathers had done a generation earlier. The Dominions might not be quite in the front line as the
British were, but their men soon were, and it was a source of real pride
that from June 1940, when France collapsed, until June 1941, when
Hitler invaded Russia, and while the Americans still argued about
whose war it was, the Empire alone held the pass for the free world.

It was not smooth sailing at home, for if the war brought a surge
of prosperity that carried the Dominions finally out of the lingering
end of Depression, it also brought grave problems of politics and of the
nature of their contribution to the general war effort. In the antipodes,
Australia and New Zealand raised what were universally regarded as
some of the finest fighting troops in the world, and they were soon on
their way to the Middle East, to support the British position there. But
both Australia and New Zealand were worried about Japan—wisely,
as the issue showed—and remained leery of weakness in the Far East.
South Africa fought the war under a coalition government led by Jan
Christiaan Smuts, still the leading advocate among the Afrikaners of
cooperation with the British. He had begun to fade by the time of the
war, but the British made him a field marshal in 1941; the South Africans, like their cousins from the other end of the Indian Ocean, fought
throughout the Mediterranean with immense credit.

The Canadians were divided on how the war should be fought.
Prime Minister Mackenzie King wanted Canada to make its contribution more in manufactures than in men. He thought the war should
make Canada a great industrial power, and he hoped to avoid a major
manpower commitment. King, who was Prime Minister three different
times for a total of twenty-one years, the longest in all of Commonwealth history, was a strange man who appeared the most lackluster of
politicians. Only after his death did his diaries reveal that he sought
political advice both from his dog, and through séances from his de-
ceased mother. His general approach, and his longevity, reflected the
Canadian passion for the middle of the road. And as always, he had
problems; the Premier of Quebec, Maurice Duplessis, thought Canada's part in Britain's war should be absolutely minimal, while the
Premier of Ontario, Mitchell Hepburn, thought Canada should make
much more effort than she did. Public pressure was such that King
could not stick to his nonmilitary war effort; the first Canadian troops

arrived in Great Britain late in 1939, and after Dunkirk they were practically the only trained and equipped units in the country. The Royal Canadian Navy was rapidly expanded, especially its escort forces, and eventually it was doing most of the convoy work in the western Atlantic. Canada trained airmen from all over the Commonwealth and from most of the conquered Allied nations, such as Norway. Her bomber and fighter squadrons operated as integral parts of the Royal Air Force.

Their separate geographical locations gave each of the white-dominated dominions a peculiar role to play in the war. South Africa was the least important in this respect, perhaps, because of its distance from the enemy, but especially during the middle years of the war, when the Mediterranean lifeline was virtually cut, South Africa enjoyed its old, pre-Suez Canal importance as the vital way station to and from the East. Canada was the indispensable entrepôt for materials going from North America to the battle fronts in Europe, and her East Coast ports were busy as they had seldom been before and have not been since the war, with huge convoys lying in Bedford Basin, waiting to make the perilous trip from Halifax to Britain. Once Japan attacked the Western powers, and especially after Singapore fell, Australia and New Zealand were the vital bases for the Allied reconquest of the western Pacific and East Asia.

The smaller outposts of the Empire were equally important. If in some cases, such as that of Hong Kong and Singapore, they proved indefensible hostages to fortune, in others they proved vital to the entire fabric of the war. Suez and Egypt the British held with a death grip. At the other end of the Mediterranean, Gibraltar guarded the strait there as always. Hitler sent officers down to look it over and tried to entice Franco into attacking it, but the Spanish dictator proved to be the one man who ever outtalked Adolf Hitler, and he preserved his neutrality, even if he bent it in the process.

Above all, in the center of the maelstrom lay Malta, right at the crossroads of the Mediterranean. Any British convoys from Gibraltar to Suez went past it; more important, so did any Axis convoys from Italy to North Africa. For three years it was a bone in the throat of the inland sea, attacked first by Mussolini's Regia Aeronautica, then by Hitler's Luftwaffe. At one point supplies could be brought in only by submarine, and Malta became the single most bombed place of the entire war. But the past is always present in Europe, and the Maltese lived surrounded by the ancient battlements of the Knights of St. John of the Hospital. The stones that had withstood the Turks in 1565 now sheltered the islanders from German bombs, and a spirit not cowed by the Ottomans could not be broken by the modern Hun. King George VI eventually awarded the entire island the George Cross for gallantry.

But not everyone accepted the British view of what they were fighting for or what the Empire represented. Egypt was for some time the focal point of the war, yet the country remained what it had been for centuries, an occupied territory with a garrison in control. The British had taken over Egypt officially during World War I, replacing Turkey as the sovereign power. They had recognized Egyptian independence in 1922, though remaining in control to protect what they considered their vital interests. In 1936, a few months after young King Farouk acceded to the throne, they had signed a twenty-year treaty that called for progressive withdrawal of British troops to the immediate area of the canal and increasing Egyptianization of the country. Unfortunately, neither side entirely understood the other's point of view. The leading Egyptian politician of the 1920s, Zaghlul, was shrewd but unprincipled and basically cowardly; he incited riots and at one point came very close to complicity in the murder of the British head or Sirdar of the Egyptian Army. The British always thought the Egyptians unappreciative of the generosity shown them; the Egyptians never thought that in their own country they should have to be the recipients of generosity from their occupiers. During the war, they were encouraged only to keep out of the way while their land became a huge British base. A specious wartime prosperity did little to assuage their feelings, especially as it was usually seasoned with the contempt of the thousands of soldiers passing through. Had the Axis forces gotten past El Alamein, they would have found the Egyptians perfectly willing to exchange one set of occupiers for another.

In India this feeling was less intense, but it was still there. Throughout the interwar period, efforts to find a solution to the question of governing the country had foundered on the Hindu-Muslim antagonism, and on the demand of the Congress Party for full independence, the sooner the better. These political problems were really but the tip of the iceberg, for India remained a vast, overpopulated, and poverty-ridden land. There was some industrial development during the 1930s as local entrepreneurs moved in to take the place of disappearing foreign investment. But the population increased by leaps and bounds; by 1940 there were nearly four hundred million

Indians, of whom 85 percent were poor rural peasants and 90 percent were illiterate. These problems did not interest the relatively small educated and politically articulate classes, who were busily blaming everything on the British and demanding that they leave as soon as possible. Gandhi continued to be the great Indian leader and to bounce into and out of British jails. To break the British salt tax, he marched to the sea and panned salt illegally. One month he was in jail, the next in London negotiating with British officials, the next living in poverty among the lowest castes, and the next back in jail for fostering civil disobedience. Hindus continued to denounce any measure that was short of full independence, and Muslims to reject any such measure that would leave them at the mercy of the Hindus.

In the late 1930s, with the British still unable to square the circle, the knowledge of Japanese expansion on the Asian mainland began to temper Indian attitudes, for they recognized clearly that however bad they found the British, they would find the Japanese far worse. When the war finally came, the Indians were generally supportive of Britain's efforts, though looking, like MacKenzie King in Canada, to their own advantage first, and their leaders tended to ask how Britain could claim to be fighting for the freedom of Poles and Czechs while denying that freedom to Indians. Asking that question did not prevent the dispatch of Indian units to the Middle East, to Italian East Africa, to the Western Desert, and ultimately to Italy, where the troops of the Indian Army, always the most professional of soldiers, upheld their long traditions as fighting men. It was readily acknowledged that only the best British formations could be brigaded with Indians, because only they could match them in their military qualities.

But at home there continued to be division. In the fall of 1940 Britain promised India a new constitution after the war; in 1942 a British emissary, Sir Stafford Cripps, met with the nationalist leaders. Cripps was a cold fish, of whom Churchill once remarked, "There, but for the grace of God, goes God"; he was not the ideal man to negotiate with the Indians. When he offered independence after the war in return for cooperation during it, Gandhi sarcastically replied that that was "a postdated check on a crashing bank." The Indian leaders demanded immediate independence, and back they went to jail. The deadlock continued to the end of the war.

The Japanese invasion of Burma, however, made the British presence far more acceptable than it had been for many years. Loss of Burma's rice meant near-starvation for many Indians, and it was British rationing, and distribution by the British Army of rice hoarded by Indian entrepreneurs, that averted famine. Under these circumstances, the constitutional question was held in abeyance while the war was fought and won.

There were problems nearer home than India, also. Throughout the 1930s, under the prodding of Eamon de Valera, Ireland had moved closer and closer to full independence. Given the intransigence of the Protestants in the North and the republicans in the South, there could be no definitive solution to where the Irish Free State fit in the imperial or Commonwealth scheme of things. The Irish answered the question by ignoring it, and a series of laws progressively neglected definition of the whole relationship. In the 1930s the Irish waged a tariff war with Britain and lost; Ireland continued to export her sons and daughters to work in English factories and to send home enough money to keep her economy afloat. In 1939 the Irish government could hardly see the war as Britain saw it; in England's difficulty they glimpsed further opportunity and they immediately announced their neutrality. This seriously compromised the British naval effort in the western approaches and led to a great deal of bitterness. Many individual Irishmen disagreed with their government, however, and thousands of them stepped across the border to the North and joined the British forces. Irish opinion therefore remained as divided as always, as divided as the country itself.

In the year from mid-1940 to mid-1941 the war changed direction. Stalemated in the West, Hitler turned east, first to the Balkans and then to Russia. And while he made up his mind, the focus of the immediate fighting centered on the Mediterranean. Mussolini had entered the war in the dying days of the French campaign, not so much to get at the British as to take over the French North African territories. He was denied these by the rapid signing of the armistice and therefore turned to the East, to British-held Egypt rather than French Tunisia, and he confidently sent his Fascist legions across the frontier from Libya, marching triumphantly for Alexandria and the Suez Canal.

They came out a good deal faster than they went in. In eight weeks over the turn of the year the British, outnumbered five to one, took 130,000 prisoners and threatened to overrun all of Libya. The Royal Navy had already taken the measure of the Italian Navy, and as early as July, Admiral Cunningham's battleships steamed impudently into the Strait of Messina, caught an Italian task force, and chased it into Calabria in ignominious haste. On November 11 the aged Sword-fish biplanes of the Fleet Air Arm launched a daring torpedo attack against the Italian naval base at Taranto. They sank three battleships and heavily damaged four other ships, for a loss of two of their twenty-one museum pieces. The Britons' equipment might be old, but they introduced techniques that the Japanese were glad to adopt a little over a year later. In February Cunningham bombarded Genoa and other northern Italian ports, and in March, off Cape Matapan, he caught their fleet again, damaging a battleship and sinking three cruis-ers in a near-perfect night action.

The Italian fleet seldom ventured out in force after that, and be-tween its humiliation and the crushing defeats in North Africa it looked as if Mussolini were all but finished. Unfortunately, the Ger-mans then took a hand, and the British threw away most of their ad-vantage by an ill-considered intervention in the Balkans.

It should almost be a motto of great power politics to avoid the Balkan Peninsula. Hitler, with his eyes on Russia, decided to secure his southern flank. Hungary and Romania were already his satellites, and the Italians had taken over Albania and were carrying on a desultory campaign against the Greeks on the latter's northwestern frontier. Hitler thought it would be a good idea to control Yugoslavia, and he ordered his generals to work up a quick plan for taking over the coun-try. The British had a mutual defense treaty with the Greeks, and as the German moves became apparent, the British government, sure that Greece was their ultimate Balkan target, invoked the treaty and sent units, first of the R.A.F., into southern Greece. This ensured the inter-vention it was designed to prevent, for Hitler could not tolerate British bombers within striking distance of his Romanian oil fields. The Ger-mans rapidly overran Yugoslavia in ten days, in early April 1941, and then kept right on coming down the Vardar Valley and into Greece. The British ground forces hurrying into the country were hustled out before they could get dug in and had to be evacuated from the south-ern ports under intense aerial bombardment. They fell back to Crete, and the Germans, this time not impressed by blue water, launched a major airborne invasion, landed their troops by parachute and cargo plane, and drove the British handily out of Crete as well. It cost Hitler most of his airborne troops, but it cost the British heavily in destroyers and cruisers lost during the evacuation, and it made the Germans look like supermen.

They had not only taken a hand in Greece, but they had also

joined first in the central Mediterranean and then in North Africa. Initially small German units, the genesis of the Deutsches Afrika Korps, under General Erwin Rommel, crossed over to support the Italians. Rommel launched a rapid offensive, and met no opposition at all; the greatest part of the British forces were off in Greece, being beaten there. British General Sir Archibald Wavell, one of the great soldiers of the war, threw a garrison of Australians into the little port of Tobruk, where they were besieged for the next several months. Rommel rolled on into Egypt but could not go all the way without more supplies and ports to stage through. By midsummer the campaign stalled, with the Axis well ahead on points, and Wavell was relieved of command, essentially for not being able to juggle the Italians, Germans, the whole Middle East, and the amateurish meddling of his own government. From that time on, for more than another year, the desert war seesawed back and forth, first one side and then the other having a momentary supply advantage and taking the offensive. Not until late in 1942 did the British definitively regain the initiative.

Britain's ability to do that, or anything else, depended as always upon the sea. With only the resources of the home islands, the British were not strong enough to defeat a Germany that could call on the entire Continent for supplies. Britain must have raw materials for her own industries, aluminum for aircraft, iron for tanks and ships, oil for fuel, food to keep everyone going, rubber for tires, manganese and phosphate, beef and cotton. Even in the old days of the mercantile Empire, when her population fed itself and when technology was far less complex, Britain had to import and export to live. Now, with a worldwide interdependent economy and advanced technology, it was even more imperative that her access to the outside world be maintained. Hitler and his geopoliticians might talk of autorky, of making the Continent self-sustaining; the British knew there was no substitute for seapower and the things it could bring. The longest and ultimately most important battle of the war was therefore the Battle of the Atlantic.

There were few secrets to it this time; they had been unlocked in the Great War. But to know how to do it was one thing, to be able to do it another. At the start of the war the British were short of escorts. Having mastered the submarine before, they underrated it in the 1930s; when they signed the naval agreement with Germany in 1935, they even agreed to submarine parity, yet another example of their shortsighted defense policies of that era. As war approached, they began to develop their escort forces. For a while they thought that oceangoing convoys could be protected by converted fishing trawlers, forgetting what the North Atlantic does to men in small vessels. The answer they finally hit on was a conversion from a whale catcher, two hundred feet long, a thousand tons, the corvette. The only thing racy about it was its name, and the Flower class bore the brunt of the early years of the war.

The convoy and escort system was fully developed as the war progressed. In the North Atlantic it remained largely a British and imperial affair, for the Americans, even after they were fully committed, concentrated elsewhere. Canadians in the western Atlantic and British in the eastern, they gathered up the huge gaggles of merchant ships, rusty, battered, weatherbeaten, to face both the cunning of the Germans and the impersonal fury of the North Atlantic, the worst ocean in the world. The Allies developed better ships as the war went on, the Castle class and River class frigates, and better techniques, hunter-killer groups, and air cover, both over the convoys and long-range maritime patrols. But the Germans got better as well, with wolf packs, improved torpedoes, and larger, more efficient submarines. The war was fought both at sea and in the laboratory, a peculiar combination of fine technical skill, brute strength, and above all, endurance. Only those who have suffered through it know how wearing it is to stand week after week of watch on, watch off, always cold and wet, living on tea and corned beef sandwiches, in a little ship that never stops rolling.

The statistics were astounding. The Battle of the Atlantic lasted five years and eight months, the entire length of the war in Europe. The Germans sank 23,351,000 tons of Allied shipping, yet during the war the Allies built 42,485,000 tons, a net gain of nearly 20 million tons. The Germans lost 785 U-boats; of 41,000 men who served in them, 5,000 were taken prisoner and 28,000 killed, the highest casualty ratio of any German services. The British alone had 2,177 merchant ships sunk, 30,000 merchant sailors killed, and at times, as in 1942, the crisis year, it looked as if they were losing the war.

Against this grim and unrelenting battle of the small ships and their convoys, there was an occasional flare of a larger surface action. With nothing like the fleet of 1914–18, the Germans were forced to use their few heavy units as expensive commerce raiders. On May 24, 1941, Empire Day, the *Bismarck* sank the *Hood,* the great battle cruiser that had long been the pride of the Royal Navy. It seemed as if the stars had altered in their courses; in reality, it was another price paid for stretching ships too thin between the wars and not providing upkeep and modernization. *Bismarck* herself was caught and pounded to death three days later. The *Scharnhorst* was sunk in the Battle of the North Cape, at Christmas 1943. Her sister ship *Gneisenau* was bombed in Kiel by the Royal Air Force, and the most formidable of them all, the *Tirpitz*, attacked from air and underwater, ended her days ignominiously as a floating anti-aircraft battery at Tromsø. Bombed again and again by the British, she finally capsized.

As in 1914–18, and as in 1793–1815, the Royal Navy fought all over the world to keep the sea lanes open. Any mere summary is inadequate to that effort, but consider, for example, the fate of the Tribal class of destroyers, sixteen beautiful ships built in the late 1930s, just in time for the war: *Maori*, sunk in an air raid on Malta, 1942; *Cossack*, torpedoed off Gibraltar, 1941; *Mashona*, sunk by bombs in the North Atlantic, 1941; *Mohawk*, sunk in destroyer torpedo action off Tunisia, 1941; *Sikh*, sunk by gunfire off Tobruk, 1942; *Zulu*, sunk by aircraft in the eastern Mediterranean, 1942; *Matabele*, sunk by a U-boat in the Barents Sea, 1942; *Punjabi*, sunk by collision in the North Atlantic, 1942; *Bedouin*, sunk by aerial torpedo in the central Mediterranean, 1942; *Somali*, sunk by torpedo off Iceland, 1942; *Afridi*, sunk by aircraft off Norway, 1940; *Gurkha*, sunk by aircraft off Norway, 1940. *Matabele*'s motto was a tribal saying, "Hamba gahle" (Go in peace). She was torpedoed in a northern Russian convoy in mid-January; she sank immediately; two of her two hundred men were picked out of the Arctic water. Four ships of the sixteen survived the war. That was a microcosm of the Royal Navy's battle and what it cost to win it.

Stupendous as it was, Britain's effort was dwarfed in June 1941, when Hitler invaded Russia; suddenly millions of men and thousands of tanks, aircraft, and guns were locked in a battle that raged from the Pripet marshes to Moscow, from Leningrad to the Black Sea. Hitler was making the same mistake Napoleon had made, attacking the Russians while leaving an enemy on his western flank. Hitler thought he knew better than his predecessors; so had Napoleon. Churchill, the great anti-Communist who in 1939 had wanted to go to war with Russia as well as Germany, immediately offered British aid: "If Hitler were to invade Hell, I should make favorable reference to the Devil," he said, and there were soon British tanks wearing the red star, and Hawker Hurricane aircraft in Russian squadrons. To their enormous convoy burden the British added the worst of them all, the routes to northern Russia, to Archangel and Murmansk. Attacked by aircraft, submarines, and surface vessels from Norway, braving bad weather and ice in the winter, perpetual daylight in the summer, the convoys doggedly fought through, to be met at the end by sullen stares and complaints that Britain was not doing enough. To Russians locked in a life-and-death struggle, the British effort in the Mediterranean seemed pretty peripheral, and the Allied bombing effort, taking an inordinately long time to bear fruit, was not the equivalent of a second front. By December 1941, the Germans were closing in on Moscow, trying, in the first snows of winter, to end the massive campaign.

It was at that point that the entire complexion of the war was transformed. Churchill knew that the British Empire alone was simply not strong enough to defeat a Nazi Germany that dominated the whole Continent. Even allied with Russia, Britain might not be strong enough for that, for in 1941 Russia looked more like a liability than an asset. Ultimate victory lay only with the United States; the Americans must eventually realize that this was their war as well as Europe's and must take an active role in it. But most Americans did not see it that way; a relatively small percentage of them were for intervention, but the vast majority wanted to stay out of it. No one yet knew about the slave labor and the death camps, the gassings and the mass executions. What little suspicion of these trickled through was dismissed as anti-German propaganda; no human beings in the twentieth century would do what a few fanatics said the Germans were doing. Americans had a large residual suspicion of continental Europe and of Britain, dating from the aftermath of World War I. They did not want to be used a second time.

Given this national mood, President Franklin D. Roosevelt did not move very fast; he sold things to the British, and when they began to run out of money, he set up a lend-lease arrangement. While American soldiers drilled with wooden guns, he got the Army to release rifles and ammunition to Britain, and the Navy declared fifty old destroyers as surplus. They went to Britain too, but the Americans took basing rights in the Caribbean in return for them. Large numbers of American-built aircraft were transferred to Canada and Britain, but the average American held resolutely aloof from the war. A draft passed in 1940 by a narrow margin and was continued in 1941 by a mere one-vote majority in Congress. Roosevelt and Churchill met in Newfoundland in 1941, the American ships still resplendent in peacetime colors, the British looking dirty and battleworn. The two leaders got along well, and agreed on a basic approach to the war. By fall of 1941 American ships were escorting British convoys around the fringes of the western Atlantic; one of the U.S. ships was even sunk by a U-boat, but Roosevelt held back. He simply did not have popular support for the war.

That problem was resolved by Japan. Britain's onetime ally, over-populated, overproductive, hemmed in on its small islands, was on the march of empire. From the time of their opening to the modern world, the Japanese had rapidly become expansive, and the Sino-Japanese War, the Russo-Japanese War, and World War I had all seen them grab new territory. The policy continued; in 1931 Japan seized Manchuria and set up a puppet state there, and through the early 1930s she intervened in the affairs of China. In 1937 Japan openly invaded China and began the conquest of that war-torn land. The outbreak of war in Europe, and the concentration of most of the imperial powers on events there, gave her more or less a free field, and her tentacles wrapped ever more tightly around China. By 1940 China was virtually cut off from the outside world, able to receive help only through British Burma.

But the Japanese could not win the war; they were wearing themselves out killing Chinese, but not finishing them off. In frustration, Japan began to look elsewhere. French, Dutch, and British imperial holdings looked ripe for the picking and would give them the resources they so badly needed. Their Navy was unemployed, and the only potential opposition to a sweep over the entire western Pacific was the United States Pacific Fleet, based in Hawaii. Hegemony was there to be grabbed, and the Japanese decided to grab it. Through 1941, relations between them and the Western powers rapidly deteriorated; the former's demands became more aggressive, and the latter's economic and diplomatic pressure grew increasingly restrictive. By early December, things were so tense that the American government sent out a war alert through the Pacific.

Nevertheless, when the Japanese struck at Pearl Harbor on the morning of December 7, they caught the Pacific Fleet asleep at its moorings. In one of the most devastating blows of modern warfare, they reduced that fleet to a shambles. Of eight battleships, four were sunk, and all were seriously damaged; over two hundred planes were destroyed, and the U.S. armed forces suffered forty-five hundred casualties. By this one bold stroke the Pacific Fleet seemingly was removed from the board for the foreseeable future, and as the Japanese pilots flew triumphantly back to their carriers, the conquest of Asia opened up enthrallingly before them. Few realized that out of the chaos and smoke behind them would arise the nemesis. The sleeping giant awoke at last, and young men who had spent Saturday night drinking beer and arguing lazily about "Europe's war" were standing in long lines before the recruiting stations on Monday morning. Churchill's first thought on hearing the news was, "Now, thank God, we have won the war!"

Concurrently with their Pearl Harbor strike, the Japanese hit American bases in the Philippines, and British establishments along the Asian rim. The British had never realistically expected to hold Hong Kong; it was gone by Christmas, its garrison of British and Canadian soldiers sacrificed to the small expediencies of war. A far more shocking failure was that in Malaya, for the Japanese overran Singapore, the great bastion of Britain in Asia, with humiliating speed.

The very name of Singapore conjured up visions of the white man in the Far East, Lord Jim on his way to redemption, pink gin at the bar of the Raffles Hotel, stories by Somerset Maugham. In the years between the wars Singapore was supposed to be the Gibraltar of the East, the farthest fortified British base, according to the Washington treaties. Unfortunately, the British never really got around to fortifying it. The services argued; it was agreed that the Navy needed Singapore as a firm base, but it could not be agreed how to make it firm. The R.A.F. insisted that only airpower could protect a naval base, but then maintained that only ground forces could protect the airfields. The Army accepted this responsibility, but having done so, said only air control could guarantee their ability to operate. This circular argument went around and around several times, to the delight particularly of successive Labor governments who did not want to spend money on Singapore anyway. In the end the British set up guns to prevent a seaward attack that never came, decided the Malayan jungles were probably impassable—any reports that said they were not were quickly pigeonholed—and did their very successful best to forget the whole thing. There were, after all, problems nearer home than Singapore.

As war threatened in the Far East, the Navy did its part. The new battleship *Prince of Wales* and the old battle cruiser *Repulse* were sent East. An aircraft carrier was to have accompanied them, but she ran

aground on trials and had to be docked for repairs. Admiral Phillips
did not care; he was a battleship admiral, and when he got to Singapore, he made little effort to utilize the minimal air support the R.A.F.
made available to him.

Japanese forces were landing in northern Malaya while their colleagues were approaching Pearl Harbor, though because of the international date line, it was the morning of December 8 in Singapore.
They were soon consolidated and moving south through the jungle,
outflanking the scanty British forces along the roads and tracks, setting
up blocks and ambushes, and proving themselves vastly superior to the
poorly organized and hastily deployed imperial forces who tried to
stop them. In an attempt to intercept Japanese troop convoys at sea,
Admiral Phillips took the *Repulse* and the *Prince of Wales* out into the
Gulf of Siam. He went without air cover, though the R.A.F. tried to
provide a squadron of fighters, but he thought he might make a quick
strike in the darkness and then get away again after doing significant
damage.

He failed to find the Japanese, but they found him. The two great
ships were sighted by a patrol aircraft at 0630 hours on the morning of
December 10. Before noon the skies were filled with bombers and torpedo planes, and in a couple of hours of fierce attacks at midday, the
two ships were sunk. *Repulse* went down at 1233 hours, *Prince of Wales*
almost an hour later. Several hundred men were lost with them, and
the death of the two ships sent shock waves across the world. Winston
Churchill was stunned and later remarked that that was the only night
of the war he did not sleep soundly but tossed and turned in anguish.
The long argument of battleship versus aircraft was finally ended; here
for the first time were battleships in full fighting array, manned and
ready and at sea, and still sunk helplessly by a flock of buzzing airplanes. December 10, 1941, was the definitive end of the battleship era.

It was also the beginning of the end of Singapore. Unimpeded in
their supply lines, the Japanese marched south, stolid little men in
khaki green, with rifles and bayonets almost as tall as they were. The
British had considered them poor fighters, but these were well-trained
troops, hardy in the field and seasoned in China. At every turn they
outmaneuvered and outfought the dismayed British, Australians, and
Indians. By January 31, the last of the weary defenders marched across
the causeway from Johore to the island of Singapore itself, hoping to
make a lengthy stand. It did not work. The Strait of Johore was shallow and narrow, and the Japanese were quickly across. Fighting was
confused—in some cases desperate, in others desultory. With the Japa-

nese in control of the reservoirs, the city with its large Malay and Chinese population under artillery fire, and the garrison running out of ammunition, the British opened negotiations. On February 15 General A. E. Perceval surrendered unconditionally. It was the greatest single reverse ever suffered by British arms; 138,000 men went into prisoner-of-war camps, and the Japanese swept on—toward the islands and Australia in one direction, toward Burma in the other. By March 7 they occupied Rangoon and flooded north from there. By May they had overrun the Dutch East Indies and the Philippines and were in New Guinea, hanging like a cliff over northern Australia. The European colonial empires had been exposed as rotten husks, and it looked as if the day of the white man in Asia was over for good.

The white man, of course, had other problems at the moment, and while emaciated Australians hung on to New Guinea and the thin line of American naval remnants fought to hold the waters of the mid-Pacific, the major Allies turned their first attention to stopping the Germans. In early 1942, as the disaster in the Pacific reached high tide, the Germans were still holding the initiative in Europe. Their spring offensive in Russia, in the South, looked just as formidable as the previous year's drives. Rommel in North Africa was poised for a final push to Alexandria and the Suez Canal. The Russians were crumbling, the British stretched thin everywhere, the U-boats winning the Battle of the Atlantic.

Yet the German tide too was slackening, even if it did not look like it. In southern Russia they were capturing mostly empty space. In the Mediterranean Malta hung on grimly, taking its toll of Axis supplies. In Egypt the British were at last winning the buildup battle; day after day the salt-grimed convoys sailed through the Canal following their long, wasting journey around Africa. A reformed and revitalized British Eighth Army, under new commanders and now equipped with heavy American-built tanks, put the Germans and Italians under a severe time penalty: If they could not win their war in a few months, they could not win it at all. Rommel, aware he was losing the race, launched his last drives and fell short. The British lines held, and as the fall neared, they began to gird themselves for the great offensive. In Russia the Germans were trapped in a bottomless pit named Stalingrad, and in the Western Desert, General Montgomery and the Eighth Army opened the great Battle of El Alamein. Two weeks later British and American troops swarmed ashore in French North Africa.

The decision to invade the French territories was the result of prolonged military and political argument. The Americans did not want to be sidetracked into the Mediterranean, which they saw as a British sphere of activity, a war fought essentially to preserve imperial interests. Their preference was for a direct cross-Channel invasion and a toe-to-toe fight to the finish right in the heart of the enemy's territory. Given the state of American—or, indeed, of Western Allied—power at that time, the view was extremely naïve, and the British finally convinced the Americans they simply were not up to such a strategy. But at the same time it was politically imperative, both to satisfy Russia and to placate domestic American opinion, that United States ground forces should come into contact with the Germans as soon as possible. By a process of compromise and elimination, the Anglo-Americans thus settled on French North Africa as the only reasonable solution. The invasion achieved the desired ends both of coming to grips with the Germans, who rapidly moved major forces into the French colonies, and of bringing the French Empire back into the war, but it did also delay a Channel crossing. Whether the Mediterranean strategy ultimately shortened or prolonged the war is still a matter of argument among specialists.

Caught on two fronts, the Axis could not continue the struggle across the Mediterranean. It might be possible to take Crete across blue water, but it was not possible to sustain a full-scale campaign in the face of British dominance of the narrow seas. The Eighth Army swept inexorably across the Western Desert and Libya and soon joined with the other British, American, and French units in the hills of Tunisia. On May 13, 1943, the last Axis forces surrendered, a quarter of a million men, a fitting match for the huge losses in the Russian winter at Stalingrad. An exultant Churchill told his people that it was not the end, nor the beginning of the end—but it was the end of the beginning.

The question then arose as to where to go next. The Americans still wanted a cross-Channel invasion, and the British still contended that Allied forces were too weak for that at this stage. Early in 1943, when the leaders met at Casablanca, the British remained the senior partners in the alliance, not just in terms of time invested, but also in armed forces in the field. The Americans were building and equipping a mighty armed force; their bombers were now joining the R.A.F. in its campaign against German industry; their Navy, growing by leaps and bounds, had already turned the scales at Midway in the Pacific, and their ground forces, Army and Marines, were fighting the Japanese in the Solomon Islands and the Germans in Tunisia. But it was still British and Commonwealth soldiers who must bear the brunt of a land campaign in continental Europe and who would do so well into the closing stages of the war. Yet the British resources were severely limited; they had already dipped far deeper into their human and material capital than the Americans, and they knew they were going to get only one chance to defeat Germany. If they took it prematurely and lost, they were finished. They had to delay, to weaken the enemy around the periphery of Europe until they were certain of victory in the final, climactic struggle. This view prevailed, and the Americans agreed that the war in the Mediterranean should be continued, the winning streak there exploited to the fullest. On this basis, the Allies decided to ease their shipping problems by clearing the central Mediterranean routes so they could avoid the long haul around Africa. They invaded Sicily in July.

The island was rapidly overrun, with British, Canadian, and American forces working successfully, in spite of some low-level Allied rivalry. The Italian garrisons faded into the hills, and the Germans evacuated the island after delaying actions. But the campaign caused the overthrow of Mussolini's government and led the Allies on into mainland Italy, which was not part of the original plan. In the first week of September, British and Canadian troops made an assault crossing of the Strait of Messina and landed on Fortress Europe four years to the day from the declaration of war.

The Allies hoped to grab southern Italy without fighting, to gain political capital by knocking out one of the Axis partners, and to get a base for air operations across the Adriatic in the Balkans. But the Germans, perceiving the Allied thrust as weak, decided to fight, and southern Italy became one of the worst battlefields of the war. The Germans held along successive river lines halfway up the peninsula to Rome, and it took nearly a year of hard fighting to lever them out. The Italian front became the most truly international of all the campaigns of the war. At its high point—the May 1944 offensive that broke the Cassino position and led to the taking of Rome—the Allied order of battle read like a dress rehearsal for the United Nations. There was the American Fifth Army, made up of American, British, and Free French Expeditionary Corps. The British Eighth Army had three British, a Canadian, and a Polish corps. There were three Indian divisions, a New Zealand infantry division, and a South African armored division. Men had gathered literally from the ends of the earth to free the Eternal City, and all of Europe, and all too many of them died before the work was finished. Rome was liberated on June 4, 1944.

But the Italian campaign remained a frustrating distraction, destined never to pay the dividends promised by its supporters, chief of whom was Churchill himself. There was hard fighting there right through to the end of the war, both Allies and Germans justifying it by claiming they were tying down enemy forces that could have been better employed elsewhere. From June 6, 1944, on, that elsewhere was in France.

On that day, in what was probably the single greatest event of the war, the Allies invaded Fortress Europe on the Normandy coast. By air and by sea, several hundred thousand men—American, British, Canadian, and French—stormed ashore and crashed through the vaunted Atlantic Wall that Hitler hoped was impregnable. They landed by parachute, by glider, in swimming tanks and wave-tossed landing craft, and they fought their way past pillboxes and minefields, through barbed-wire entanglements and up sheer cliffs. Helping them were thousands of aircraft and hundreds of those gray ships that had kept the sea lanes open to make it all possible. Heavy gunfire support was provided by three American and three British battleships, among them the grand old lady of the seas, H.M.S. *Warspite,* whose fourteen World War II battle honors read like a capsule history of the entire war. If Tunisia was the end of the beginning for the Allies, Normandy was the beginning of the end for Hitler's Germany.

That end took another terrible year as the Russians stormed out of the East to overrun central Europe and as the Western Allies fought their way across northern France and the Low Countries. On the left flank as the invasion wheeled around from Normandy to move east, the British and Commonwealth troops had very heavy fighting, for they provided the hinge of the Allied move, and the Germans hit them with everything they could muster. The city of Caen, only ten miles from the Normandy coast, was a D-Day objective, but it was not taken until late July. The breakout to the Seine and the exploitation toward the Low Countries went fairly rapidly, but by the approach of fall, the Allies had outrun their supplies, and the Germans were stiffening. Through fall and winter there was desperate fighting in Belgium and Holland, and terrible losses. The Americans were forced to comb their rear areas for infantry replacements; the British had just about reached the bottom of their manpower pool, and in Canada the necessity of conscription for overseas service caused another political crisis, just as it had done in the First World War. The Allies were not strong enough to finish the war in Europe in 1944, as some of them had fondly hoped they would do.

Yet by early 1945 the Germans were palpably weakening. The Allied bomber offensive had risen to a crescendo and laid waste much of German industry. American and British fighter-bombers ranged at will over the West German countryside, shooting up trucks, locomotives, and anything else that looked like a target. The Luftwaffe was finished, its planes outclassed, its pilots untrained youths, and its operations crippled by an all-encompassing fuel shortage. The Germans' last gasp was a winter offensive in the Ardennes, which succeeded only in using up the remnant of their strategic reserves. As spring came in, with the Russians in the suburbs of Berlin, a tidal wave of Western armies broke across the Rhine and surged through the ruins of the Fatherland. Adolf Hitler committed suicide in Berlin, the last of the U-boats came sullenly to the surface and raised black flags of surrender, and the Continent of Europe and the seas around it were freed at last. Seapower and the coalitions it made possible had once more proved superior in the long run to the ambitions of a land-bound conqueror.

Seapower was the issue in the war against Japan even more, if possible, than in the war against Germany, for Japan's was almost purely a seaborne empire. Like the British, the Japanese then had to go by ship virtually everywhere they went; unlike them, the Japanese lacked the merchant shipping capacity to sustain their effort. Their entire war was run on a shoestring, and eventually that string broke.

But the breaking of it was not easy, for the Japanese had a first-class Navy, and an Army that was well trained, inured to privation, and above all, willing and even eager to die for its Emperor. It took three and a half bitter years to push the sons of Nippon back to their home islands, and the process altered the shape of the East Asian world for the foreseeable future.

After the fall of Singapore and the Philippines and the overrunning of the Dutch East Indies, the Japanese had pretty much what they had started out to get. Their initial idea was to conquer these territories, which they dubbed the Southern Resources Area, then to consolidate and build up a defensive perimeter. With a strong Navy, interior lines, and a firm defense position, they figured they should have eighteen months before the Allies recovered sufficiently to attack them. By that time, they should be secure. When the enemy, chiefly the

Americans, did attack, they would defeat them at sea, somewhere on their perimeter, and from then on, they believed the Allies would accept the status quo and make peace. In this, of course, they completely misjudged the character of their opponents, but such misjudgments are why wars are fought.

Their initial success was so great as to be delusive. By April 1942 they had all but secured their perimeter, they were making good progress in Burma, were soon to close off British access to China, and they were raiding far afield—into the Indian Ocean in one direction and down past Australia to the Solomons in the other. These easy victories, plus a daring U.S. air raid on Tokyo in mid-April, caused them to overreach themselves, and they moved out beyond their originally planned perimeter. In early May they were fought to a draw by U.S. carrier forces in the Battle of the Coral Sea, and a month later, at the great Battle of Midway, the Americans sank four Japanese aircraft carriers for the loss of one of their own. In the vast Pacific distances, aircraft carriers were the queens of the battle, and with these losses the Japanese were forced to fall back within their planned perimeter and let the Americans come to them. They remained confident of their ability to hold their line.

In mid-1942 the Allies thus began a series of converging drives against the Japanese Empire. There were a number of these, depending on how one chose to count them. Taking them clockwise around the perimeter, the Americans attacked up in the Aleutians, in a short campaign that was fought as much against the weather as the enemy. In the central Pacific the U.S. Navy fought its way westward past the different island groups, bypassing bases and leapfrogging from one group to another. In the Southwest Pacific the Americans, with the Australians, came up the island chain from the Solomons, to the Bismarcks, along the coast of New Guinea, and into the East Indies and the Philippines, where they joined with the central Pacific thrust. Meanwhile, the British held on in Burma, fighting for two years an essentially defensive campaign before they were able to move definitively to the offense in 1944. They also secured their hold on the Indian Ocean. Finally, in China, in spite of American aid and advice, the war had largely stalemated, though millions died in seesaw battles and as a result of war-induced starvation. Later, the Americans undertook a long-distance bombing campaign of the Japanese home islands from Chinese bases.

The startling Japanese successes at the beginning of the war had caused the patchwork Allied command system to collapse. When their forces reorganized in the spring of 1942, they agreed that the Pacific, and China, should be under American strategic direction, while the Indian Ocean, Burma, Malaya, and Sumatra should be under British. This was a logical division at the time; its long-term ramification was to bring Australia and New Zealand under the American umbrella. The New Zealanders always remained more British than the British, but Australia had since the turn of the century been responsive to American ideas; the Americans were going to end up not only dominating the Pacific, but even dominating British nations in the Pacific.

While Australian sailors, soldiers, and airmen fought alongside their American allies in the South Pacific, the British and Indians battled desperately to hold Burma from the Japanese. The country is extraordinarily difficult, with different climate zones varying from intense jungle to near-desert. Overland communications from India were practically nonexistent, as all the prewar traffic had gone by seaborne coastal routes. By May 1942 most of the country had been lost. The remnants of British and Indian forces had been chased north to the Indian frontier; Burmese local forces, poorly equipped and ill trained, had fallen apart; and Chinese troops sent across the mountains to help out had been badly battered by the Japanese. British counteroffensives were ill prepared and unsuccessful. Burma was the farthest corner of the Empire, and little could be spared for it when the Germans were knocking at the gates of Alexandria. It was not until late 1943 that the Allies began to make some progress in the northern part of the country. But the Japanese held hard; there was bitter fighting around places like Imphal and Kohima, on the frontier, and it was the end of 1944 before any significant progress was made.

After that, things went much better. By the last year of the war, the Japanese were beginning to collapse. The Americans had fought their way through to the Philippines and were closing in on enemy home territory. The Japanese merchant marine was all but gone, wiped out by Allied submarines, and the Imperial Japanese Navy was a ghost of its former formidable self, its carriers sunk, its battleships bombed, the whole force starved for fuel. In 1945 the British made steady progress in central Burma, and units of the British fleet were able to strike effectively at Japanese holdings, especially oil refineries, in Sumatra.

Yet in the final victory, the British and Commonwealth forces were more or less squeezed out. In part this was due simply to the massive strength of American arms. By 1944 and even more by 1945, the United States simply did not need British or Australian help to defeat Japan—though, ironically, it courted Russian. As the Americans swept north along the Pacific island chains, the Australians were left behind to clear Japanese forces in the East Indies. Though the Australian government protested the use of its men in secondary operations, its murmurs were simply disregarded by the Americans. The British formed a Pacific Fleet in November 1944, but it did not join in operations until March 1945. The Americans did not entirely welcome an interloper and dragged their feet on joint operations until the British had built up their own support system and were able and prepared to move on lines the Americans had developed in the previous three or four years.

Though the British Pacific Fleet consisted of 2 battleships, 4 carriers, 5 cruisers, and 11 destroyers—22 ships, a formidable array in other times—it was but a small force compared with the American armada. Designated Task Force 57, it was about the size of one task group of U.S. Task Force 58, which consisted of 318 combat vessels. The British took part in the covering operation for the invasion of Okinawa and came under heavy attack by the Japanese suicide planes, the kamikazes. Here the British showed their worth, for though their carriers could handle only half as many planes as American flattops, the British had armored flight decks, which the Americans lacked. British carriers after hits were back in service within hours, where American ships suffering similar hits were out for days. Small though their force was, the Royal Navy rapidly made a place for itself.

The problem, however, was not simply one of logistics or of different operating techniques. It went deeper than that. Right from the start of American participation in the war effort, there had been subtly divergent views of what the war was all about and what kind of world the victors wanted at the end of it. When Roosevelt and Churchill first met, at Argentia in August 1941, they drafted a statement of principles that came to be known as the Atlantic Charter. It was in fact a press release rather than a formal document, but it was gradually enshrined as a general pronouncement. The third point of it said that Britain and the United States "respect the right of all peoples to choose the form of government under which they will live; and they wish to see sovereign rights and self-government restored to those who have been forcibly deprived of them." The first clause stated the general point; the second was designed, unsuccessfully, to limit its applicability. The British wanted a stronger, more overtly anti-Axis second clause, while the Americans wanted one with a wider interpretation. The phrase "sovereign rights" was inserted at British insistence, for it meant that only those who had previously enjoyed such rights could hope to have them in the future. They were thinking of places such as Poland and Denmark, overrun by the Germans. The Americans, however, came to see the charter as applying to the entire world. After all, had not Ceylon also been deprived of its sovereign rights? The British soon recognized that they had opened up a Pandora's box of troubles here, and some government leaders were diligent in pointing out that you could not equate the British Empire with Nazi hegemony. Others were not so sure; for example, Clement Attlee, Deputy Prime Minister in the coalition government and leader of the Labor Party, traditionally anti-imperialist, explicitly stated that Britain was fighting for the "freedom" of the whole world, black as well as white, colonial peoples as well as conquered. Obviously this part of the charter had not had the thought it needed; it was therefore going to get public definition after the fact, which is not usually satisfactory to those who originally propose such statements. The Governor of Burma, for example, reported that the Atlantic Charter was received there with rejoicing and that its impact would be very difficult to overcome. When he was told by the Colonial Office that the Charter had nothing to do with Burma, he responded, in effect, "Try telling the Burmese that," and Burma was one of the areas where there was significant collaboration with the Japanese when they invaded the country. They were even able to form a small Burmese army to fight on their side.

Through the war the British carefully backed away from any wider commitment about the end of empire and the colonial era. The Americans, on the other hand, became more convinced than ever that this was a war for the freedom of all subject peoples, British Africans as well as East European Jews. In spite of dollar diplomacy in Latin America or the possession of the Philippines—to which they had already promised independence—the Americans saw themselves as free of the taint of colonialism. There were a few among their leaders, some of them in the Navy, who did not want to dismantle imperialism as much as they wanted to replace the British brand with the American brand, especially in the Pacific. But for the most part, official American opinion moved in the direction of an end to all colonial empires. It was such ideas as these, in addition to purely mundane military ones of supply and communications, that made the Americans uninterested in

17

Recessional

Here was a people whom after their works thou shalt see
wept over for their lost dominion. . . .
—*The Arabian Nights*

In 1897, the year of Victoria's Diamond Jubilee, when England was at the height of her imperial glories and equally at the height of her self-satisfaction with them, Rudyard Kipling wrote his famous poem "Recessional," in which he compared "all our pomp of yesterday . . . with Nineveh and Tyre." There was a storm of outraged public protest; how could the archpoet of imperialism betray his readers? How could he dare suggest that the British Empire might one day pass from the scene as its ancient predecessors had done? The thought, in 1897, was not to be borne. Seventy-five years later, the repetitive last line of his poem— "Lest we forget"—had been adopted as a motto by the veterans' associations of the Empire, and the entire piece was a hymn regularly sung on Remembrance Day. The holiday itself, November 11, the date of the Armistice of the Great War, had become one of the few remaining imperial occasions, when Union Jacks, faded medal ribbons, and thinning ranks of aging warriors were momentarily honored for what they had been and done in an increasingly dim past.

In 1897 Britannia still ruled the waves as well as a quarter of the world. Fifty years and two world wars took care of that. By 1945 the world scene had immeasurably changed. Naval power was counted in a kind of ship that had not even existed at the Jubilee, the aircraft carrier. At the start of World War II Great Britain had fourteen of them built or building; the United States had ten. In 1945 Britain had eleven fleet carriers; the United States Navy had twenty-nine. Britain had thirty-seven lighter escort carriers; the United States had ninety-five. Even more significant, perhaps, was the fact that all of the British escort units had been built in American yards and transferred to the Royal Navy by the United States. There could be few more practical examples than that of the falling of the mighty. The Royal Navy and the British Empire were more powerful at the end of World War II than they had ever been before, but even stronger were the armed forces of the United States and the Union of Soviet Socialist Republics. Power, after all, is a relative thing.

So is will. One of the basic questions of World War II was that of empire. In large part the war had been fought for it, to establish or enlarge the Italian, German, and Japanese empires, or to preserve the British, French, and even Dutch and American empires. The Axis had had their try, and they had lost. The French and Dutch had lost but were about to attempt a comeback. The Americans and Russians had indisputably won; both were now immensely greater powers than they had been in 1939, the former at relatively little cost, the latter at the price of untold suffering and destruction. Whether Great Britain won or not was problematical; she had paid heavily in blood and treasure and also in future promises to her friends and dependents. She was still a great power, one of three. The question now was whether she could hold on against the winds of change. Did she wish to hold on? Did Britons individually and collectively still have the buccaneer spirit, to face down Indians and dominate Africans, or were they weary of the burdens of empire? Was it time to let the children go, to put up the sword and lay to rest the urgings of imperial memories?

Winston Churchill, tired after five years of war but still ready to fight on, answered with a resounding no: "I have not become the King's First Minister in order to preside over the liquidation of the British Empire!" What, Churchill thought, had the war been all about if not for the preservation of the Empire, and the values he equated with it? He was an unrepentant imperialist to the end. But others were not. With Germany in ashes, and before the war against Japan was over, Churchill called an election. He met triumphantly with Stalin and the new American leader, President Truman, at Potsdam on July 17. When the second session met on July 28, he was not there. The Labor Party had won a sweeping victory, 393 seats to 213 for the Conservatives, and Winston Churchill was suddenly a politician out of office in a procedure that must have startled Joseph Stalin.

The Conservatives had campaigned in the good old way—Churchill's leadership, the King, the Empire, Britannia still ruling the waves. The Laborites offered new housing, full employment, social welfare programs. Churchill had given Britain "her finest hour," but that by definition is unique. People cannot live at fever pitch forever. So while the country embarked on a period of severe economic dislocation, the result of the grinding down of the wartime economy, the Labor government moved at last to implement all its dearly held theories. The armed forces were largely disbanded, the coal industry nationalized; health services and communications were brought under the government's wing, and the right to strike was extended. In February 1946 the holy of holies of free enterprise disappeared when the Bank of England was nationalized.

All this was done in the face of extreme privation, bread rationing, coal shortages, and misery for the masses. The Americans had immediately canceled lend-lease at the end of the war, quite unconscious of how near Britain was to collapse by 1945. At the end of that year they had to advance her a loan of nearly four billion dollars, and soon even the Canadian government was chiming in with a loan of another billion and a quarter, like an affluent child acknowledging a needy parent.

A government that was hard put to feed its own people was not likely to be overly interested in empire, and Labor was traditionally opposed to the concept anyway. Attlee and his ministers were willing to see the Empire outside Britain go if it chose to do so. He said in the House that the Empire "is not bound together by chains of external compulsion," and later, "We do not desire to retain within the Commonwealth and Empire any unwilling peoples." India must choose for herself what she would do; so must Burma. Churchill growled in opposition that the Empire was running out as fast as the American loans and wondered why Britain had fought so hard to retain her Empire if she were going to abandon it as soon as the war was won. But that indeed was what she was going to do; the will to hang on was no longer there.

The white-dominated dominions were already gone, of course. For them the Empire had imperceptibly merged into the Commonwealth. Canada passed its own citizenship act in 1946, and over the next quarter century ceased being a British colony and became, militarily and economically, an American one. A nationalist party was elected in South Africa, and the old Afrikaner spirit of the *laager* (fortress) reemerged; immigration for nonwhites was severely restricted, and racial inequality, apartheid, became the ever-festering law of the land. In Australia and New Zealand the first colonials were appointed as governors general, the representatives of the Crown, and governments followed their own courses toward regional associations and closer ties not with Britain but with the new paramount power in the Pacific, the United States. In 1951 they signed a joint defense treaty with the Americans, to dismay in Britain.

Such developments were natural continuations of trends begun before the war and enhanced by it. Even with the potential for racial tragedy in South Africa, the white-ruled Dominions were little trouble simply because Great Britain exercised little dominion over them anyway. It was different in the nonwhite parts of the Empire. If Attlee and his government truly meant what they said, and only willing members of the club were wanted, then a lot of people who had once been under the Union Jack were not going to be there very much longer.

India was the first to go. That vast, teeming land, the brightest jewel in the Crown of Empire, had almost as many problems as it had people. Hundreds of languages, hundreds of religions, dozens of separate states great and small, all had been given a veneer of unity by British rule and British railroads. But it was no more than a veneer; the Indians could not even agree that they wanted the British to go, though they came closer on that subject than on anything else. When the British offered to discuss the autonomy proposal made back in 1942, the Indians refused; all they wanted, they said, was for the British to get out. Yet by early 1946, when Attlee's government offered full autonomy, the Hindus and the Muslims were already at each other's throats, British authority breaking down in the face of riot and massacre, with scenes as bad as anything during the recent war. The Muslims, led by Mohammed Ali Jinnah, demanded a separate state, Pakistan, denying the fragile unity the British had imposed; while the Hindus, confident of their vast majority status, continued to argue against partition.

Faced with this irreconcilability, the British decided to cut the Gordian knot. In February 1947 they announced that they would get out of India by mid-1948, and to help hasten the process, they appointed Lord Louis Mountbatten as Viceroy. Mountbatten was one of the last great names of the Empire; his nephew was married to the future Queen Elizabeth, and Mountbatten had had a distinguished if somewhat stormy and well-publicized military career. He was perhaps an odd choice for a Labor government, but he had the sort of panache the job needed. Six months after he arrived, India and Pakistan became independent, to the accompaniment of splendid ceremonies and brutal massacre. Pandit Nehru became the first Indian Prime Minister and asked Mountbatten to stay on as Governor General. The Hindu Indians immediately started fighting with the Muslim Pakistanis, and Nehru, who had learned his politics at Gandhi's knee, began a long career of irritating the rest of the world by preaching peace and neutralism while invading Kashmir and arbitrarily taking over the residual rights of the various princely Indian states. India got its first indigenous Governor General in 1948 and became a republic in 1950. Gandhi himself did not live to see it; the great apostle of civil disobedience and nonviolence was assassinated by a Hindu who blamed him for the partitions. Pakistan became a republic in 1953, and Ceylon, in 1948, chose to become a self-governing dominion within the Commonwealth, the first nonwhite colony to decide to do so.

India at least remained within the Commonwealth, feeling such an organization sufficiently vague that it could be lived with. But Burma decided on full separation. Churchill might fret and fume over its abandonment, but by the end of 1946 the government began talks on the transition to independence. Burmese political leaders wanted nothing less, and a constituent assembly called for an "independent sovereign republic." The transition was not easy, and several leaders of the provisional government were assassinated, but early in 1948 Burma was fully independent, with no residual ties with Britain. For the next decade, the Burmese fought with their neighbors and among themselves until finally a military government seized power.

India and Burma both had ancient civilizations whose traditions and ideas long anteceded the rule of the British. Yet even with their own resources to fall back on, both suffered periods of war, terrorism, and massacre before reaching some degree of stability. If these societies had difficulty making the transition to full independence, how much more of a problem was an awaking Africa likely to present? For the freedom conceded to Indians could not indefinitely be kept from the peoples of Africa. Anti-colonialism was in full cry, and every newly independent state added to the United Nations joined its voice to the rising chorus. Liberal Western opinion applied a curious double standard to the process of empire; in 1948 there was the Russian takeover of Czechoslovakia to set against the independence of Burma, yet it was still the British who were castigated as the great imperialist villains. The Russians had learned you could get away with anything as long as you called it "people's democratic liberation."

In the quarter century between the end of the war and 1970, virtually all of colonial Africa gained its independence, though it happened in different ways. The French tended to haul down one flag, haul up another, and continue as before; the Belgians, when finally pressured out of the Congo, simply packed up and left, and let the country collapse into bloody anarchy behind them. The British tide receded from black Africa, too slowly for some opinion, too rapidly for other. In some cases the transition was made quietly and without a great deal of fuss, though African leaders showed a considerable tendency to promote themselves suddenly from sergeant to president and to use modern weapons to wipe out old tribal enemies. The places that caused the greatest difficulty were those where there were substantial white ruling minorities. These farmers, miners, and businessmen were the second- or in some cases third-generation descendants of the whites who had carved out their territories back in the late nineteenth century. They enjoyed a peculiarly parental relationship with the black Africans, in which they were conveniently dominant, and they fervently believed that the country was theirs as much as it was the Africans'. They had a totally different concept of land ownership and use than the Africans did, and whatever the historical rights or wrongs of either side, they were as ready to fight for their patrimony as some Africans were to regain theirs. It was an inevitably explosive situation, and it involved both the people on the spot and the British at home in agonies of division.

Nigeria was one of the first African colonies to get a measure of autonomy and had become fully independent by 1960. The British were safely out of there before the country exploded into bloody, genocidal war in the late 1960s. Kenya was still British, however, when a terrorist movement known as Mau Mau broke out there in 1952. Local defense forces and regular troops sent in by the British government spent four years and millions of pounds putting down the insurgency, which featured attacks on isolated farmhouses, roadblocks, and ambushes, and peculiarly revolting atrocities, most of them, of course, committed by the terrorists against the vulnerable African peasantry themselves. Eventually, late in 1963, Kenya became independent within the Commonwealth, with Jomo Kenyatta, another leader who had learned his lessons in British jails, as President. The country made a rapid transition to a one-party state. By the end of the decade, in a sad footnote to imperialism, the native Kenyans drove out the small-business class, consisting largely of Indians and Pakistanis who had moved in after World War I. Unwelcome in a home country most of them could not remember or never knew, these refugees tended to go not back to Asia, but rather to Britain itself, where their presence was to generate considerable ongoing racial tension, leaving them among the truly unfortunate flotsam of the Empire.

African leaders who insisted the British stay out of their country were adamant that the British should intervene in other countries, and as South Africa followed its own determined path, its hinterland was gradually whittled away. Northern Rhodesia, Southern Rhodesia, and Nyasaland, the great fruits of the last rush of Empire-building at the turn of the century, were combined into a federation in 1953. When the northern state gained black majority rule, it dropped out and became Zambia in 1964. Nyasaland went in the same year, emerging from the cocoon as Malawi. That left Southern Rhodesia alone, with its population of a quarter of a million whites dominating four and a half million Africans and determined to keep on doing so. During the late 1960s and 1970s the white Rhodesians, led by Prime Minister Ian Smith, defied all Britain's efforts, as well as those of the rest of the world, to make them learn their arithmetic. They unilaterally declared their independence, and Britain imposed economic sanctions on them. Of course, South Africa supported them, the Afrikaners seeing the black tide edging closer, but eventually black majority rule had to come and did, accompanied by the usual exodus of embittered white settlers. Eventually only South Africa was left, with its prosperous economy and its black laborers eagerly seeking employment from all over sub-Saharan Africa in spite of the restrictions placed on them by an intransigent government. The Boers were left free to circle the wagons and fight off the children of Ham, like their grandfathers before them, with a gun in one hand and the Old Testament in the other.

The imperial recession in Asia and Africa was concurrent with, but not caused by, the decline of British naval strength. It had been the Royal Navy's dominance of the oceans that had enabled Britain to gain the greatest share of empire in the first place. Naval power continued to be a vital component of the world balance, but it was not as immediately crucial to the end of the Empire as it was to the founding

of it. New technology, air transport, and perhaps above all instantaneous global communication probably had more direct impact on the
end of the Empire than the absence of naval force. In fact, the loss of
the Empire had more effect on naval decline than the reverse, for
without the Empire, there was little need for a large Navy. The abandonment of the overseas possessions completed the work begun by the
Germans. It had always been British naval policy to concentrate
against the more persistent threat, back to the days when Blake held
the Channel against the Dutch, or Nelson against the French. The
growth of Germany had brought the great ships of the Royal Navy
home once again, to hold the narrow seas in two world wars. Once
those wars were over and the Empire loosed as a consequence of them,
the Navy never regained its worldwide position. What use was it to
guard the road to India if India were no longer British?

This was neither immediately recognized nor acknowledged. The
decline of the Navy was more a matter of budgets and piecemeal developments than it was the result of any clear-cut vision. The Empire
and the Navy had, like Topsy, "just growed" together; now, in the
same fashion, they just shrunk together. In the Cold War era and
under the Russian threat Britain committed herself to a continental
defense posture, and her overseas obligations were given up, one by
one, gradually to be assumed by the United States. Britain had
thought, for example, to hold on to her position as arbiter of the Balkans, but eventually it was Americans who had to assume that burden,
in Greece, with the Truman Doctrine. By the 1950s it was an American
fleet, rather than a British, that was the chief naval presence in the
Mediterranean. In the late 1960s the British announced their impend-
ing withdrawal from the Persian Gulf, as from the Far East, and another area of the world's water was passed over to the Americans to
guard—or to the Russians, if they could gain entrée to it. All over the
world first Cold War tensions and then regional systems replaced the
power that had once been wielded by Great Britain and the Royal
Navy.

The change appeared a gradual one while it was taking place.
Only in a longer perspective, after it was completed, could it be noted
how sudden it had actually been. A power that had been building for
very close to four hundred years was gone in the space of a short generation. It was not a smooth process, of course; there were attempts to
reverse the flood, and the most notable of them, and the saddest, came
in that old hotbed, that crossroads of world empire, Egypt, in 1956.

The Suez crisis was almost—not entirely, but almost—the last gasp of nineteenth-century gunboat diplomacy.

The year 1956 was a bad one; the Cold War was at its height, and world tensions were acute. In the United States Secretary of State John Foster Dulles had recently pronounced that neutralism was immoral and was practicing his policy of "brinkmanship," taking the Russians to the edge of war in the expectation that when faced with it, they would back off. Unrecognized at the time, the Russians were trying to do just that, unsuccessfully. When they loosened their grip on their satellite system in central Europe, it threatened to blow up in their faces, and the result was a renewed clampdown of their power, leading to armed insurrection and military suppression in Hungary. In the midst of all this, the Middle East exploded.

British and French power had receded from the Levant as elsewhere. French and British forces got out of Lebanon and Syria, which they had held during World War II. The thorniest problem of all, however, was what to do about Palestine. The British had held this as a mandated territory ever since World War I; they had never been able to resolve the conflicting demands of the resident Arabs and the Jews for an independent state. Jewish, or Zionist, immigration to Palestine, especially in the aftermath of Hitler's genocidal policies, upset the precarious balance the British had maintained, and world opinion, strongly in favor of some form of recompense for Jewish suffering, was against the Palestinian Arabs. There were riots and terrorist activities, especially those of the Jewish "Stern Gang." In 1946 the Jewish underground blew up the King David Hotel in Jerusalem, British headquarters, killing nearly a hundred people. Various British proposals for federal solutions were rejected by both sides, and in May 1948, the day after the British mandate over Palestine officially ceased, the Jews declared themselves to be the sovereign State of Israel; the United States and Russia accorded them immediate recognition, and the surrounding Arab states equally immediately went to war with them. The Arabs had the numbers, but the Israelis had a determination to survive forged in the ghettos and the death camps of Germany. They also had American money and sympathy. In a year they had fought off their enemies and established a precarious place for themselves. The British, traditionally attuned to the Arabs, observed with a somewhat jaundiced eye.

At the same time, the British were being pressured out of Egypt.

The minute World War II ended, the Egyptians demanded the British evacuate their forces from the country and restore the Sudan to Egypt as well. The British agreed to negotiate but announced they would prepare the Sudan for independence and would keep their troops in the immediate zone of the Suez Canal. These issues hung fire for five years while each side drew up series of proposals that were unacceptable to the other. In the early 1950s the King of Egypt, Farouk, was overthrown by a military coup, and in April 1954 Colonel Gamal Abdel Nasser emerged as the ruler of the land. Late in the year he signed a treaty with Britain in which the latter agreed to evacuate the Suez Canal Zone within twenty months, turning over military control of the vital waterway to the Egyptians. The canal would continue to be operated, of course, by the Suez Canal Company.

Through the next two years, as Nasser attempted to modernize his country, he gradually drifted into the Communist orbit. When the United States and Britain hemmed and hawed on their foreign aid for Egypt, the Russians moved in with far-reaching promises. Once more the British government watched disapprovingly. It was at the time Conservative, in power since 1951 and led since 1955 by Anthony Eden. Eden had for many years been Winston Churchill's understudy, and when ill health forced Churchill to retire at last, Eden naturally succeeded him. Many observers thought Eden too old for the job, that his time had passed, and when the Egyptian crisis began to mature, he was ill and short-tempered, lacking the command of diplomacy that had made him the white hope of the Tories twenty years earlier. Nevertheless, he held to his bargain, and on June 23, 1956, the British flag came down and the Egyptian flag went up; seventy-four years after Gladstone had announced his temporary occupation of Egypt, British troops left the country. Two weeks later, Nasser, still desperate for funds, announced the nationalization of the Suez Canal Company.

Eden was livid. He professed to see in Nasser an Arab Hitler, and he was determined not to repeat Neville Chamberlain's mistakes of Munich. The French joined in this view, as they were in the midst of a war to hold on to their colony of Algeria, and they believed, mistakenly, that Nasser was the chief source of supplies for the Algerians. Frantic and intemperate conferences failed to achieve an agreeable solution. Finally, in a rage, the British, French, and Israelis concocted a scheme. Pleading Arab plots, the Israelis would launch a preemptive invasion of the Sinai Peninsula. As they neared the Canal, the British and French would intervene to stop the fighting and protect the waterway, and they would then be back in the Canal Zone, and this time they would stay there. By a series of too-subtle hints, half disclosures, and misinterpretations, Eden deluded himself into thinking he had American support for this imbroglio, and he carried along with him the reluctant members of his cabinet. The fuse nearly fizzled—ignominy of ignominies—over the time it took Britain to get together a naval strike force, but on October 29 the Israelis drove across the frontier into the wastes of Sinai. That was the same day that rioting Hungarians were driving the Russian occupation forces out of Budapest. Two days later, British and French forces appeared off the Suez Canal and began an air and naval bombardment of Egyptian positions. On November 5 French and British paratroops dropped on Port Said, and the next day their ground troops stormed ashore. The Egyptians immediately blew up several ships, blocking the Canal, the Russians threatened war, and President Eisenhower issued a war alert to American armed forces around the world. The commander of the U.S. fleet in the Mediterranean is reputed to have replied, "We're ready to fight. Who's the enemy?"

Faster than it had blown up, the crisis collapsed. Faced with Russian saber-rattling and utter repudiation by the United States, the British and French were caught in the untenability of their position. They insisted to the end that they had intervened only to keep the Canal open, even though their action had precisely the opposite effect. Fighting lasted only a day; the United Nations mustered an emergency force, and by December the last British and French had left Egypt once more. Eden retired early in the new year. He lived until 1977, but he never once admitted he might have been wrong on Suez, and he never admitted to collusion with Israel. The *Times* of London in his obituary called him "the last prime minister to believe Britain was a great power and the first to confront a crisis which proved she was not."

So the retreat from the Empire continued. The ongoing confrontation between the superpowers drew the British increasingly into the American orbit, both in technology and in her defense posture. American submarines were based in Holy Loch in Scotland, American bombers on British airfields. It was not merely a re-creation of the situation of World War II, it was a re-creation of the fifteenth century, when the Dutch and the Hanse merchants dominated British trade and claimed rights and powers that infringed on national sovereignty. The

British mounted a nuclear submarine strike force—but they did so with American Polaris missiles. The overseas bases were given up, the defense percentages of the national budget shrank and shrank, famous regiments were disbanded or amalgamated, ships were sold to foreign states, and in the ultimate act of imperial gunboat diplomacy, Britain was not the aggressor but rather the victim. In the spring of 1982, Argentina decided to take over the Falkland Islands.

The Falklands group has only rarely figured on the pages of history, but there has been a crisis whenever it has done so. At one time or another, the British, French, Spanish, and then Argentines have all claimed the cluster of barren islands, four hundred miles off the southern tip of South America. There was a flare-up in 1770, when France and Spain almost went to war with Britain over them. In 1833 the British evicted an Argentine garrison that it said had occupied them illegally, and in 1914 Admiral Sturdee sallied forth from the Port Stanley to sink Graf von Spee's squadron and revenge Coronel. Since that time little had been heard of the islands, and their two thousand inhabitants, sheepherders and their families, lived in a not unpleasant isolation that over the years had made them more British than the British.

Argentina had never relinquished the claims she had inherited with her independence from Spain, however, and periodically made diplomatic noises or military moves that kept her memories alive. To her the Falklands were the Islas Malvinas, stolen by the British; as President Franklin D. Roosevelt once remarked, the British would take any rock or sandspit anywhere in the world at any time. In 1977 the British had had to send a nuclear submarine to the South Atlantic to keep the Argentines aware of their presence, but by 1981 they had seriously downgraded even the token forces stationed there. The South Atlantic station ship was recalled, and the government had considered various schemes for getting out of its commitment to the Falklands, all of them failing on the absolute insistence of the islanders on remaining British.

Britain was hardly prepared for a campaign waged over a distance of eight thousand miles. In the twenty-five years since Suez her defense policy had been radically reoriented. Nuclear deterrence, then continental defense, had come first; next was maintenance of the sea lanes around the home islands, and defense of overseas territory had fallen to a poor fourth and last place in national priorities. The Navy had been allowed to run down to the point where one cabinet minister had resigned over its parlous state. Its biggest ships were a twenty-three-year old aircraft carrier, scheduled for the breaker's yard, and a smaller light carrier, already sold to Australia. When Argentine military forces invaded the islands on April 2 and quickly overran the small Royal Marine garrison, the British government could hardly believe what was happening.

Nonetheless, the response was determined and rapid. A few partisan political shots were fired, but in general, the country was united as seldom in recent years. The House of Commons met on a Saturday, for the first time since Suez, and argument was not on whether there should be a reply or not, but on how soon and how fierce it ought to be. Three days after the invasion, with what was really remarkable speed, the first elements of the British fleet set sail for the South Atlantic.

There was a vast air of unreality about the crisis. World communication is now virtually instantaneous, but the Atlantic is a big ocean, and ships still steam at a relatively leisurely pace. It would take the ships a month to reach the Falklands. The governments in both Britain and Argentina, and ordinary people everywhere, reacted during that month as if this were some sort of international soccer game, with pep rallies and jaunty airs played on the background for the news broadcasts. The Argentine military junta, a shaky right-wing triumvirate of armed forces officers, was gratified by a burst of popular support at home. The first female Prime Minister of Britain, a traditional Conservative named Margaret Thatcher, expressed outrage and determination sufficient to disguise the fact that her government had been caught asleep at the switch. American magazines commented bemusedly on the whole matter, obviously enjoying the idea that someone else was in the heat for a moment, and when Mrs. Thatcher spoke of honor and commitments, suggested that these were rather quaint and outmoded guides for national policy.

The fun suddenly went out of the whole affair. No one expected the Argentine fleet to do much. Its aircraft carrier was thirty-nine years old, and had been British, Dutch, and finally Argentine by turns. Otherwise its largest ship was a cruiser, the *General Belgrano,* a pre-World War II American vessel, once the U.S.S. *Phoenix.* This the Argentines sent out, and on May 2 she was torpedoed by a British submarine, and three hundred men went down with her. From then on it was a real war, and the spectators were suddenly jolted out of their complacency. As the British ships reached the end of their lengthy voyage, they were repeatedly attacked by Argentine jet aircraft, which they were hard put to contain with their limited fleet air cover. Before they were firmly ashore, the British had lost two destroyers and two frigates and a cargo ship; the Argentines took heavy losses in their Skyhawk aircraft before conceding local command to the enemy. Once ashore in isolated spots, the British consolidated their position and then began to advance on the Falklands' capital, the little town of Port Stanley. Gradually they penned in the ill-equipped and poorly trained Argentine conscripts, completely outclassed by Royal Marines and paratroops who had learned their trade in brushfire conflicts in Aden, Borneo, and above all the back streets and lanes of Northern Ireland. An intense artillery bombardment, a night storming of the town, and it was over. The Argentines surrendered, the Union Jack went up once more, and the force commander ended his victory report with the traditional, "God save the Queen." Except for the modern hardware, it might have been the eighteenth century all over again.

So the circle came full around. In the 1580s Great Britain had been an island on the fringe of world affairs, with Spain and Portugal the mighty powers of the time. Four hundred years later, she was again on the fringe of things, while the United States and Soviet Russia had emerged as the two superpowers of the world. Those four centuries had seen the first tentative steps toward world empire and dominion. John Hawkins had sailed to the south, and Francis Drake around the world. Raleigh and Hakluyt had dreamed their dreams of overseas colonies, and the Pilgrims and the East India Company had established them, the one for religion and the other for profit. A nameless flood followed them, evicted Scots crofters, starving Irish, the penniless from London slums, solid Yorkshiremen and sturdy Welsh miners, Catholics to Maryland, Anglicans to New Zealand. Generation after generation they poured out, to the rich plains of the Canadian West and the dust and heat of India, and they built their families and their fortunes and their nations and left their bones far from the land of their birth. Through it all the oceans tied them together, ruled by the British flag, whether red duster for the thousands of humble merchant ships, or white ensign for the Royal Navy. British ships and British sailors from Blake to Nelson to Jellicoe made the seas safe for those who pursued "their lawful occasions" upon the waters.

There are few final judgments in history. One age's hero is another's villain, one generation's dearest beliefs are another's hypocrisies. Every great historical movement is a mixture of good and bad; the critic or cynic will point out that if the British stamped out the slave trade, they had earlier been the greatest profiters from it; if they handled Chinese Customs fairly, they had been the ones to push for the introduction of opium. But on the whole, in the admittedly short perspective allowed by the recent demise of the Empire, the Pax Britannica appeared to have been one of the better periods. Edward Gibbon, writing fondly of the best days of the Roman Empire, thought that the Age of the Antonines, in the second century of the Christian era, would have been the happiest time to have lived. From the vantage point of a century later, one might well say the same for the nineteenth century, the period of British dominance of the world. No society ever fully achieves the ideas it professes, but the British Empire's shortcomings were those of particular people in particular circumstances at particular times. The ideas themselves, of justice, of freedom, of prosperity—John Locke's Enlightenment trinity of inalienable rights, life, liberty, and property—were and are universal.

Suggestions for Further Reading

The subject covered by *Navy and Empire* is so diffuse that it would be possible to amass a bibliography as long as the book itself; scholars and writers have been working on the Royal Navy, and the British Empire, almost as long as either have been in existence, and there is a vast number of both general and specialist studies available; episodes dismissed with a few general remarks have often provided a life's work for serious scholars. Most of the titles that follow contain bibliographies of their own, and the student should be aware that these suggestions cover not even the visible part, but rather the very tip, of the iceberg.

GENERAL STUDIES

Any number of general histories of modern Europe is available. The standard multivolume one is the *New Cambridge Modern History* (Cambridge: Cambridge University Press, fourteen volumes, various dates). Rather more interpretive, and less detailed is the series edited by William L. Langer *The Rise of Modern Europe* (New York: Harper & Row, 1936–71) in twenty volumes. *The Oxford History of England* is a comparable set for Britain itself; the last eight volumes cover the period since Elizabeth. For single-volume treatments L. S. Stavrianos, *The World Since 1500* (Englewood Cliffs, N.J.: Prentice-Hall, 1966) takes a designedly global perspective; Keith

Feiling's *History of England* (London: Macmillan, 1952) is a standard account, and Albert Tucker's *History of English Civilization* (New York: Harper & Row, 1972) is a more recent wide-ranging coverage.

The *Cambridge History of the British Empire,* appearing at various dates, is an exhaustive multivolume treatment. Single volumes are James A. Williamson's *Short History of British Expansion* (London: Macmillan, 1955) and C. E. Carrington, *The British Overseas* (Cambridge: Cambridge University Press, 1950); both are good for the periods they cover, even if they must now be qualified both by more recent scholarship and by what has happened to the Empire since they appeared. D. K. Fieldhouse's *The Colonial Empires: A Comparative Survey from the Eighteenth Century* (New York: Dell, 1967) is useful on later periods and looks at the other colonial empires as well, but as the title implies, it has only the most general treatment of the earlier colonial period. Lord Strang's *Britain in World Affairs* (New York: Praeger, 1961) is a wide-ranging survey of "the fluctuation in power and influence."

Surveys of seapower must deal extensively with the Royal Navy. One of the best is E. B. Potter, *Sea Power* (Englewood Cliffs: Prentice-Hall, 1960); though this concentrates heavily on the period of the two world wars, it has fine coverage of the age of sail as well. More recent is Clark G. Reynolds, *Command of the Sea* (New York: Morrow, 1974). Jacques Mordal's *Twenty-five Centuries of Sea Warfare* (English edition, London: Abbey Library, 1973) is widely available; originally written in French, it provides useful insights from what has often been "the other side of the hill." The drawback to that is that some "glorious affairs" seen from this direction become virtually unrecognizable. Admiral Sir Herbert Richmond took a wide-ranging, if episodic, view of the Navy's role in British history in *Statesmen and Sea Power* (Oxford: Oxford University Press, 1946). A useful short history is Oliver Warner's *The British Navy* (London: Thames and Hudson, 1975). All sorts of odd information is contained in W. L. Clowes' seven-volume *The Royal Navy: A History from the Earliest Times to the Present* (London, 1897, reprinted New York: AMS Press, 1966). For serious work on the Royal Navy, the indispensable collection is the *Navy Records Society Publications* series; launched in 1894, this has now gone to more than 120 volumes, ranging from Tudor times to the present and covering everything from "Nelson's Letters to His Wife" (Volume 100) to "The Russian Fleet Under Peter the Great" (Volume 15). The equivalent series on voyages of discovery and exploration is that published by the Hakluyt Society.

THE DAWN OF EMPIRE

General coverage for the Tudor and Stuart periods is in J. B. Black, *The Reign of Elizabeth, 1558-1603* (Oxford: Oxford University Press, 1959);

G. Davies, *The Early Stuarts, 1603-1660* (Oxford: Oxford University Press, 1959), and Sir George Clark, *The Later Stuarts, 1660-1714* (Oxford: Oxford University Press, 1956), all volumes of the Oxford History of England. Royal biographers are plentiful; a standard life, *Queen Elizabeth I*, is by J. E. Neale (New York: Harcourt Brace, 1934); David Matthew wrote *James I* (London: Eyre and Spottiswoode, 1967). Antonia Fraser has made a career of lives of kings, queens, and assorted others with *King James* (London: Weidenfeld and Nicholson, 1974); *Royal Charles* (New York: Knopf, 1980), on Charles II; and *Cromwell: The Lord Protector* (New York: Knopf, 1973). John Bowle wrote *Charles I* (Boston: Little, Brown, 1975), and one of C. V. Wedgewood's early studies was on Charles's adviser, *Strafford* (London: Cape, 1935). Peter Earle wrote *The Life and Times of James II* (London: Weidenfeld and Nicholson, 1972), and John Miller, *James II* (Hove, Eng.: Wayland, 1977). Most of the prominent figures of the era have had biographies, though some not for a long time. John Winton wrote a popular *Sir Walter Raleigh* (New York: Coward, McCann and Geoghegan, 1975), and Willard Wallace a scholarly *Sir Walter Raleigh* (Princeton: Princeton University Press, 1959). James A. Williamson covered *Hawkins of Plymouth* (London: Black, 1949), as well as *The Age of Drake* (London: Black, 1952); there is also G. M. Thompson, *Sir Francis Drake* (London: Secker and Warburg, 1972), and Ernle Bradford, *Drake* (London: Hodder and Stoughton, 1965); on significant episodes of these lives there is Rayner Unwin, *The Defeat of John Hawkins: A Biography of His Third Slaving Voyage* (London: Allen and Unwin, 1960). For the fascinating career of a perpetual Stuart, there is Bernard Fergusson's *Rupert of the Rhine* (London: Collins, 1952); older studies are available for *Monk* (London: Macmillan, 1889), by Julian Corbett, and for *Blake* (New York: Appleton, 1886) by David Hannay, as well as Roger Beadon's *Robert Blake* (London: Arnold, 1935), and Blake's papers are in the Navy Records Society publications. The great Admiralty clerk is covered in Arthur Bryant's *Pepys* (Cambridge: Cambridge University Press, two volumes, 1933, 1938), the second volume of which is especially concerned with the Navy.

Various events and themes of this period have had separate coverage, as in A. L. Rowse's *Expansion of Elizabethan England* (London: Macmillan, 1955), or A. D. Innis, *The Maritime and Colonial Expansion of England Under the Stuarts* (London: Low, Marston, 1931). The American colonies have all had individual studies; two general treatments are Max Savelle, *A History of Colonial America* (New York: Holt, Rinehart & Winston, 1964), and E. P. Chitwood, *A History of Colonial America* (New York: Harper & Row, 1961). The first great imperial struggle came in the 1580s, and the classic study is Garrett Mattingly's *The Armada* (Boston: Houghton Mifflin, 1959); more technical is Michael Lewis, *Armada Guns* (London: Allen and Unwin, 1961); a new look is David Howarth's *The Voyage of the Armada:*

The Spanish Story (New York: Viking, 1981). If one wishes to speculate on what might have happened had the Spanish gotten ashore, there is C. G. Cruickshank's *Elizabeth's Army* (Oxford: Oxford University Press, 1966). The best naval history of this earlier period is G. J. Marcus, *A Naval History of England: The Formative Centuries* (Boston: Little, Brown, 1961). The classic treatment of the English Civil War is C. V. Wedgewood, *The King's Peace, 1637–1641*, and *The King's War, 1641–1647* (London: Collins, 1955 and 1956). After *Elizabeth's Army* there is C. H. Firth's *Cromwell's Army* (London: Methuen, third edition, 1921), and for the maritime side, John R. Powell, *The Navy in the English Civil War* (Hamden, Conn.: Archon, 1962). For the Anglo-Dutch wars one can still read Mahan's classic, *The Influence of Sea Power on History, 1660–1783* (Boston: Little, Brown, various editions); general studies of England's fiercest rival are C. R. Boxer, *The Dutch Seaborne Empire, 1600–1800* (New York: Knopf, 1965) and Charles Wilson's *Profit and Power: A Study of England and the Dutch Wars* (London: Longmans, Green, 1957). A. P. Newton's *European Nations in the West Indies* (London: A. and C. Black, 1933) covers colonial rivalry in the cockpit of empire; F. B. Eldridge, *The Background of Eastern Sea Power* (Melbourne: Georgian House, 1948) has material on that area, while James P. Lawford, *Britain's Army in India* (London: Allen and Unwin, 1978), covers land campaigns on the subcontinent until the conquest of Bengal. On *The Glorious Revolution* there is Maurice Ashley's book (London: Hodder and Stoughton, 1966); William of Orange's role is explored by Lucille Pinkham in *William III and the Respectable Revolution* (Hamden, Conn.: Archon, 1969). An older, more specialized study is E. B. Powley, *The English Navy in the Revolution of 1688* (Cambridge: Cambridge University Press, 1928).

TOWARD THE ZENITH

English history in the eighteenth century is covered in two volumes in the Oxford History, Basil Williams' *The Whig Supremacy, 1714–1760* (Oxford: Oxford University Press, second edition, 1962) and Steven Watson's *The Reign of George III* (Oxford: Oxford University Press, 1960). R. K. Webb in *Modern England* (New York: Harper & Row, 1980) and K. B. Smellie in *Great Britain Since 1688* (Ann Arbor: University of Michigan Press, 1962) both start with this period, and there is also Dorothy Marshall's *Eighteenth Century England* (London: Longmans, Green, 1962). For specific periods two beautifully written sets, both to be treated with caution, are G. M. Trevelyan, *England Under Queen Anne* (London: Longmans, Green, three volumes, 1930–34), and Arthur Bryant's trilogy about the Revolutionary and Napoleonic wars, *Years of Endurance, Years of Victory,* and *The Age of Elegance* (all London: Collins, 1943–50). Almost every significant political figure of the century has had his papers published—this was also an exceptionally rich era for diarists—and has had one and often several biographies. On the sovereigns there is G. M. Trevelyan's old but classic *England Under Queen Anne* (London: Longmans, Green, three volumes, 1930–1934); J. H. Plumb, *The First Four Georges* (London: Batsford, 1956); Stanley Ayling's *George III* (London: Collins, 1972); and John Clarke's *The Life and Times of George III* (London: Weidenfeld and Nicholson, 1972).

Historically and imperially the century staggered from war to war. General studies of colonial warfare to the American Revolution are Howard Peckham's excellent survey *The Colonial Wars* (Chicago: University of Chicago Press, 1964) and Douglas Leach's *Arms for Empire, 1607-1763* (New York: Macmillan, 1973). Specifically on the War of the League of Augsburg there is John Ehrman's *The Navy in the War of William III* (Cambridge: Cambridge University Press, 1953) and E. B. Powley, *The Naval Side of King William's War* (London: John Baker, 1972). All of Louis XIV's wars are covered in J. B. Wolf's great biography *Louis XIV* (New York: Norton, 1968); for the last and worst of them, the War of the Spanish Succession, there are John Owen's *War at Sea Under Queen Anne, 1702-1708* (Cambridge: Cambridge University Press, 1938), and more general works by John Cresswell, *British Admirals of the Eighteenth Century: Tactics in Battle* (Hamden, Conn.: Archon, 1972), and J. H. Parry, *Trade and Dominion: The European Overseas Empires in the Eighteenth Century* (New York: Praeger, 1971). For the period to the Austrian succession there is J. H. Plumb's *Sir Robert Walpole: The Making of a Statesman* (Boston: Houghton Mifflin, 1956) and *The King's Minister* (London: Cresset, 1960). Sir Herbert Richmond wrote an exhaustive *The Navy in the War of 1739-1748* (Cambridge: Cambridge University Press, three volumes, 1920).

Many works are available for the Seven Years' War, the first climax of the Anglo-French struggle. William Pitt the Elder has a host of biographers, including O. A. Sherrard, *Lord Chatham* (London: Bodley Head, three volumes, 1952-58), and P. D. Brown, *William Pitt, Earl of Chatham* (London: Allen and Unwin, 1978). The struggle for North America reaches its culmination in L. H. Gipson's massive *The British Empire Before the American Revolution* (Caldwell, Ida.: Caxton Printers, and New York: Knopf, fifteen volumes, 1936-70). C. P. Stacey's *Quebec, 1759* (New York: St. Martin's, 1959) is an acerbic bicentennial look at Wolfe's campaign, while Francis Parkman's much older *Montcalm and Wolfe* (Boston: Little, Brown, two volumes, 1884) can still be read with great enjoyment and no little profit. More general material on Canada is in Edgar McInnis' slow-moving survey, *Canada: A Political and Social History* (New York: Rinehart, 1947) and G.F.G. Stanley's *Canada's Soldiers, 1604-1954: The Military History of an Unmilitary People* (Toronto: Macmillan of Canada, 1954). On the naval side there are the classic by Sir Julian Corbett, *England in the Seven Years' War* (London: Longmans, Green, two volumes, 1918), W.C.B. Tunstall's *Admiral Byng and the Loss of Minorca* (London: Allan, 1928), and R. F. MacKay's

Admiral Hawke (Oxford: Clarendon Press, 1965). Anglo-French rivalry in India also peaked at this time; general histories are T.G.P. Spear, *India: A Modern History* (Ann Arbor: University of Michigan Press, 1961), Stanley Wolpert, *A New History of India* (New York: Oxford University Press, 1977), and Alfred Lyall, *The Rise and Expansion of British Dominion in India* (New York: Fertig, 1968). Philip Woodruff's *The Men Who Ruled India* (London: J. Cape, two volumes, 1953–54) is an excellent study. Starting just after this period are Michael Edwardes, *British India, 1772–1947* (London: Sidgwick and Jackson, 1967), and Sir Herbert Richmond, *The Navy in India, 1763–1783* (London: Ernest Benn, 1931).

The American Revolution has been most recently and brilliantly surveyed in Robert Middlekauf's *The Glorious Cause* (New York: Oxford University Press, 1982); this is Volume II of the projected eleven-volume Oxford History of the United States. A standard operational military survey is Christopher Ward, *The War of the Revolution* (New York: Macmillan, two volumes, 1952), while a shorter one is Howard Peckham, *The War for Independence* (Chicago: University of Chicago Press, 1958). More modern than either in the questions it deals with is Don Higginbotham's *The War of American Independence* (New York: Macmillan, 1971). David Hannay's old biography *Rodney* has been reprinted (Boston: Gregg, 1972), and the French contribution is assessed in C. L. Lewis, *Admiral de Grasse and American Independence* (Annapolis: Naval Institute Press, 1945). Specific episodes have been covered all the way from Thomas Fleming's *Now We Are Enemies: The Story of Bunker Hill* (New York: St. Martin's, 1960) to Harold Larrabee's *Decision at the Chesapeake* (London: Kimber, 1965), on the Yorktown campaign.

For Australia and its development, R. M. Crawford's *Australia* (London: Hutchinson, 1970) and C.M.H. Clark's *A History of Australia* (London: Cambridge University Press, 1962) give general coverage. Colonial affairs in the next years were subsumed in the great struggle with Revolutionary France and Napoleon. The most comprehensive current coverage is G. J. Marcus, *The Age of Nelson: The Royal Navy, 1793–1815* (New York: Viking, 1971). A. T. Mahan's earlier *Influence of Sea Power Upon the French Revolution and Empire, 1793–1812* (Boston: Little, Brown, two volumes, 1892) remains a classic. Somewhat more specific titles are Piers Mackesy's *The War in the Mediterranean, 1803–1810* (Cambridge, Mass.: Harvard University Press, 1957) and C. N. Parkinson's *War in the Eastern Seas, 1793–1815* (London: Allen and Unwin, 1954), while A. B. Rodger's *War of the Second Coalition* (Oxford: Clarendon Press, 1964) makes sense of the French expedition to Egypt. On particular men or episodes there are Oliver Warner's *Glorious First of June* (London: Batsford, 1961), James Dugan's *The Great Mutiny* (New York: Putnam, 1965), Sir William James's *Old Oak: The Life of John Jervis* (London: Longmans, Green, 1950), and David

Howarth's *Trafalgar: The Nelson Touch* (New York: Atheneum, 1969). That inevitably brings up Britain's greatest sailor, and there are almost countless lives of Nelson. The best on the sailor is still Mahan's (Boston: Little, Brown, two volumes, 1897), and the best on the man is Carola Oman's (London: Hodder and Stoughton, 1947). For a charming period piece, one might still read Robert Southey's *Life of Nelson* (London: John Murray, 1813).

THE SUN NEVER SETTING

It could almost be said that in the nineteenth century world history was British history. Sir Llewellyn Woodward's *The Age of Reform, 1815–1870* (Oxford: Oxford University Press, 1962) and R.C.K. Ensor's *England, 1870–1914* (Oxford: Oxford University Press, 1960) cover the period for the Oxford History, while Asa Briggs' *The Age of Improvement, 1784–1874* (London: Longmans, Green, 1959) is a good general treatment; a more recent one is J. B. Conacher, *Waterloo to the Common Market* (New York: Knopf, 1975), the last volume in the Borzoi History of England. Elizabeth Longford's *Queen Victoria: Born to Succeed* (London: Weidenfeld and Nicholson, 1964) is one of the more recent of many biographies of the Great White Queen. From about this time on, prime ministers became more important than sovereigns, and almost every notable minister has had his biographer: for example, John W. Derry, *Castlereagh* (New York: St. Martin's, 1976); Jasper Ridley, *Lord Palmerston* (London: Constable, 1971); Philip Magnus, *Gladstone* (New York: Dutton, 1954); and Robert Blake, in his classic *Disraeli* (New York: St. Martin's, 1967).

A variety of naval studies is available, both general and specific. C. J. Bartlett's *Great Britain and Sea Power, 1815–1853* (Oxford: Clarendon Press, 1963) covers the end of the sailing era, while Bernard Brodie's *Sea Power in the Machine Age* (Princeton: Princeton University Press, 1941) is a wider treatment of new navies. Gerald Graham wrote *Great Britain in the Indian Ocean . . . 1810–1850* (Oxford: Clarendon Press, 1967); W.E.F. Ward, *The Royal Navy and the Slavers* (New York: Pantheon, 1969); John Selby, *The Paper Dragon: An Account of the China Wars, 1840–1900* (New York: Praeger, 1968); Barry Gough, *The Royal Navy and the Northwest Coast of America, 1810–1914* (Vancouver: University of British Columbia Press, 1971); and Anthony Preston and John Major, *Send a Gunboat: A Study of the Gunboat and Its Role in British Policy* (London: Longmans, Green, 1967). Technological matters, European affairs, and the rise of rivals occupied the later part of the century, and these are covered in Peter Padfield's *Rule Britannia: The Victorian and Edwardian Navy* (London: Routledge and Keegan Paul, 1981), D. M. Schurman's *The Education of a Navy: The Development of British Naval Strategic Thought, 1867–1914* (London: Casell,

1965), Arthur Marder's classic *Anatomy of British Sea Power* (New York: Knopf, 1940) and his trilogy on Sir John Fisher, *Fear God and Dread Nought* (London: Oxford University Press, three volumes, 1952–59). The potential allies and rivals are discussed in E. L. Woodward's *Great Britain and the German Navy* (Oxford: Clarendon Press, 1935), Jonathan Steinberg's *Yesterday's Deterrent: Tirpitz and the Birth of the German Battle Fleet* (London: Macmillan, 1965), Harold and Margaret Sprout's *The Rise of American Naval Power* (Princeton: Princeton University Press, 1944), Ian H. Nish's *The Anglo-Japanese Alliance* (London: Athlone, 1966), and Samuel R. Williamson, Jr.'s *The Politics of Grand Strategy: Britain and France Prepare for War, 1904–1914* (Cambridge, Mass.: Harvard University Press, 1969).

If the Navy controlled most of the water, the Army did most of the fighting. Most of the period's campaigns are covered in Donald Featherstone, *Colonial Small Wars, 1837–1901* (Newton Abbott, Eng.: David and Charles, 1973), Byron Farwell, *Queen Victoria's Little Wars* (New York: Harper & Row, 1972), and Brian Bond, editor, *Victorian Military Campaigns* (London: Hutchinson, 1967). Christopher Hibbert's *The Destruction of Lord Raglan* (London: Longmans, Green, 1961), on the Crimea, and his more recent *The Great Mutiny: India, 1857* (New York: Viking, 1978) are both excellent. On South Africa there is Rayne Kruger's highly readable *Good-bye Dolly Gray* (London: Cassell, 1959) and Thomas Pakenham's *The Boer War* (New York: Random House, 1979). For some of the imperial characters Warren Tute's *Cochrane* (London: Cassell, 1965) covers a colorful career, as does Anthony Nutting's *Gordon: Martyr and Misfit* (London: Constable, 1966).

Many writers have worked on the transformation of the old British Empire and the new wave of imperialism that struck Africa and the East. Donald Creighton's *Dominion of the North* (Boston: Houghton Mifflin, 1944) is a standard history of Canada; for the other side of the world W. H. Oliver and B. R. Williams edited the *Oxford History of New Zealand* (Oxford: Oxford University Press, 1981), and a general survey is Peter Lowe, *Britain in the Far East* (London: Longmans, Green, 1981). For Africa there are R. Oliver and J. D. Fage's *A Short History of Africa* (Harmondsworth: Penguin, 1962), Eric A. Walker's *A History of Southern Africa* (London: Longmans, Green, 1957), K. Ingham's *History of East Africa* (London: Longmans, Green, 1962), and Lord W. M. Hailey's *African Survey* (London: Oxford University Press, 1957). On Egypt Peter Mansfield's *The British in Egypt* (New York: Holt, Rinehart & Winston, 1971) is an excellent survey, and provocative theories on imperialism in Africa have been advanced by A. P. Thornton, *The Imperial Idea and Its Enemies* (London: Macmillan, 1959), and R. Robinson, J. Gallagher, and A. Denny, *Africa and the Victorians* (London: Macmillan, 1961).

THE TWILIGHT OF EMPIRE

The material available on the twentieth century, and especially on the two world wars, is both exhaustive and exhausting. General surveys are H. Stuart Hughes' *Contemporary Europe* (Englewood Cliffs: Prentice-Hall, 1961), R.A.C. Parker's *Europe, 1919-1945* (New York: Delacorte, 1969), A. F. Havighurst's *Twentieth Century Britain* (New York: Harper & Row, 1966), and the last volume of the Oxford History, A.J.P. Taylor's *English History, 1914-1945* (Oxford: Oxford University Press, 1965). Two very readable royal biographies are Philip Magnus, *King Edward VII* (London: John Murray, 1964) and Harold Nicolson, *King George V* (London: Constable, 1952). Useful general coverages of the 1914–18 war are Cyril Falls, *The Great War* (New York: Putnam, 1959), and my own *A Short History of World War I* (New York: Morrow, 1981). Geoffrey Bennett's *Naval Battles of the First World War* (London: Batsford, 1968) is a general naval history, while Corelli Barnett's *The Swordbearers* (New York: Morrow, 1964) presents an intriguing look at the supreme commanders. For specific episodes, Robert Rhodes James' *Gallipoli* (London: Batsford, 1965) is excellent, as is John Irving's *The Smoke Screen of Jutland* (New York: McKay, 1967); and Colin Simpson's *Lusitania* (London: Longmans, Green, 1972). Martin Middlebrook's *The First Day on the Somme* (New York: Norton, 1972) is a classic, while John Terraine in *To Win a War: 1918, the Year of Victory* (New York: Doubleday, 1981) argues his view that the war on the Western Front was well handled.

Material on the interwar period covers an obviously wider variety of topics than the war histories. C. L. Mowat's *Britain Between the Wars, 1918-1940* (Chicago: University of Chicago Press, 1955) is a fine general survey. Some imperial problems are covered in Ann Williams' *Britain and France in the Middle East and North Africa* (London: Macmillan, 1968) and Elizabeth Monroe's *Britain's Moment in the Middle East, 1914-1956* (London: Chatto and Windus, 1963); and a wider look is in Colin Cross, *The Fall of the British Empire* (New York: Coward, McCann, 1968). Captain S. W. Roskill wrote *Naval Policy Between the Wars* (London: Collins, 1968), and some of the problems of the 1930s are in C. A. MacDonald, *The United States, Britain, and Appeasement, 1936-39* (New York: St. Martin's, 1981), and Telford Taylor's excellent *Munich: The Price of Peace* (New York: Doubleday, 1979). Moving toward the war there is David Reynolds, *The Creation of the Anglo-American Alliance, 1937-1941* (Chapel Hill, N.C.: University of North Carolina Press, 1981).

There are many general surveys of the Second World War, including Louis L. Snyder's *The War: A Concise History* (New York: J. Messner, 1960), Martha Byrd Hoyle's *A World in Flames* (New York: Atheneum,

1970), and my *Short History of World War II* (New York: Morrow, 1980). Surveys of the Royal Navy's activities are Peter Kemp, *Key to Victory* (Boston: Little, Brown, 1957) and S. W. Roskill, *White Ensign* (Annapolis, Md.: Naval Institute Press, 1960). Almost every major and most of the minor actions of World War II have had at least one book written about them, and the many works on, for example, Cassino, Dieppe, or Normandy include the imperial contribution. Some titles of particular relevance to the theme of Navy and Empire are W. R. Louis, *Imperialism at Bay: The United States and the Decolonization of the British Empire, 1941-1945* (New York: Oxford University Press, 1978), and H. P. Willmott, *Empires in the Balance: Japanese and Allied Pacific Strategies to April 1942* (Annapolis, Md.: Naval Institute Press, 1982). More specifically naval are Martin Middlebrook's *Convoy* (Harmondsworth: Penguin, 1978) and his and Patrick Mahoney's *Battleship: The Loss of the Prince of Wales and the Repulse* (Harmondsworth: Penguin, 1979). John Winton's *The Forgotten Fleet* (New York: Coward-McCann, 1969) is on the Royal Navy's comeback in the war against Japan.

Slightly less material is available on the end of the Empire, though much has been done on the various emergent states. Useful treatments are George Woodcock, *Who Killed the British Empire?* (New York: Quadrangle, 1974) and C. E. Carrington, *The Liquidation of the British Empire* (Toronto: Clarke Irwin, 1961). The backdrop of international affairs is in André Fontaine, *History of the Cold War* (New York: Random House, two volumes, 1970), and Victor Rothwell, *Britain and the Cold War, 1941-1947* (London: Jonathan Cape, 1981). R. N. Rosecrance wrote *Defense of the Realm: British Strategy in the Nuclear Epoch* (New York: Columbia University Press, 1968); longer-range is Paul Kennedy's *The Rise and Fall of British Naval Mastery* (London: A. Lane, 1976). Assorted crises and traumas are covered in Larry Collins and Dominique LaPierre's journalistic *Freedom at Midnight* (New York: Simon and Schuster, 1975), on Indian independence, and in Sir Michael Carver's encyclopedic survey *War Since 1945* (New York: Putnam, 1981). Hugh Thomas wrote a good short analysis, *Suez* (New York: Harper & Row, 1967), and Donald Neff a very critical one in *Warriors at Suez* (New York: Linden, 1981). Material on the Falklands is still coming out, and Christopher Dobson, John Miller, and Ronald Payne put together *The Falklands Conflict* (London: Hodder and Stoughton, 1982) while British troops were still marching on Port Stanley. One can conclude this abbreviated list with the thought that most of the Empire and most of the Navy may be things of the past, but historians will be busy with them for a long time yet.

Index